SAFER SKYWAYS:

Federal Control of Aviation, 1926-1966

The Iowa State University Press /

SAFER
SKYWAYS

Federal Control of Aviation, 1926-1966

DONALD R. WHITNAH

Press Building, Ames, Iowa. U.S.A.

ABOUT THE AUTHOR

DONALD R. WHITNAH is Professor of History at the State College of Iowa. He received the B.A., M.A., and Ph.D. degrees at the University of Illinois and has taught at Valley City, N. Dak., State College. He is author of *A History of the United States Weather Bureau,* first published in 1961 with paperback edition issued in 1965.

353. 008777
W616

© 1966 The Iowa State University Press
Ames, Iowa, U.S.A. All rights reserved

Composed and printed by
The Iowa State University Press

First edition, 1966

Library of Congress Catalog Card Number: 66–24402

**TO MY MOTHER, SISTER, AND THE
MEMORY OF MY FATHER**

PREFACE

THE PERSONNEL of the Federal Aviation Agency, Civil Aeronautics Board, and their predecessors have taken part in the development of one of the most exciting and important scientific advancements in history, that of aviation which in the sixties witnesses an even greater dream—the conquering of outer space. This study reflects much of the scientific growth of aviation in the United States. Government employees were not responsible for every successful invention of aeronautical aid, airplane design, or aviation promotion to the public. However, a great degree of help along with several actual inventions involving federal officials will be cited.

This book examines the federal control of civil aviation in the United States since 1926. Licensing of airmen and mechanics, testing and certifying aircraft and parts, and providing and maintaining navigational aids as well as air traffic control are all functions of the present Federal Aviation Agency.

Tracing the technological advancements introduced since 1926 underscores the primary purpose of governmental regulation—making the airways safer for all forms of aircraft and passengers. The precedent for government control of transportation could be found in the establishment of the Interstate Commerce Commission in 1887. Unhappily, in the forty years since the passage of the Air Commerce Act (1926), the safety record, while reflecting a tremendous degree of success, was nonetheless dotted with instances of poor design, pilot error, faulty maintenance, occasional failure in the operation of navigational aids, inappropriate action on the part of airline personnel, and the ill luck involved in cases of inclement weather. The resulting accidents, usually with a large number of fatalities, constitute the one sordid part of this study. Congress and the public directed scathing criticism, often unjustifiable, toward federal officials because of these tragedies.

Another aspect of the FAA-CAB account might be focused on these two examples of the rapid growth of federal agencies in this century along with the resulting personnel problems and administrative headaches so common to Washington, D.C. Part of the history of any agency involves the cooperation and/or rivalry with other units of the government, particularly the military. In the case of the FAA-CAB, cooperation was absolutely imperative with such other units as the Weather Bureau, the Federal Communications Commission, and the Department of State. Special mention should be made of the heroic and effective support given to the United States military forces during World War II. In the war zones several CAA civilian workers gave their lives for the defense of their country, and the CAA supported the war timetable immeasurably abroad and at home through electronic aids and traffic control.

With their functions closely related to the earning potential of the huge aeronautics industry, the activities of the FAA and CAB would at times produce strained relations between industry and the government. Pilots would resent the blame assessed by the CAB to a dead colleague as an alleged cause of an air disaster. A regulation of the FAA and/or the CAB might cost the airlines millions of dollars, for example, installing radar equipment or flight recorders on airplanes. Compulsory retirement of jet pilots at sixty years of age appeared dictatorial to the pilots. Flight engineers resented any reduction in the size of the flight crew which could possibly eliminate their livelihood. In these and other areas of concern, the tremendous power of the federal officials was apparent. All in all, however, the day-to-day activities of the FAA-CAB concerning industry have struck a happy balance in our economic system which features the private ownership of the means of production—with the increasing involvement of the national government in the form of direct aviation subsidies and the other regulatory and promotional functions of the two agencies.

On the present horizon, leaders of the FAA and CAB witness the great international rivalries inherent in the development of supersonic aircraft for commercial adaptation. They cast a wary eye on the gigantic expenses involved at the very time the major airlines have apparently recovered from the financial shock of conversion from piston craft alone to the use of many jets since 1959. And yet, with the public eye fixed on cheering "firsts" in space conquests, nobody is willing to suggest a slower pace for commercial aviation.

International cooperation is another theme of the era, even though arguments over fares and routes have marred the accord sought by officials in the FAA and CAB. Certainly the actions of the International Air Transport Association and the International Civil Aviation Organization illustrate the attempts toward global understanding in aviation.

The search for documentation began with the perusal of the unpublished correspondence of officials in the agencies and the Department of Commerce, which assumed housekeeping control over the entire regulatory activities of the FAA's predecessors with the exception of 1938–1940. The personnel of the Labor and Transportation Branch and the Business and Economics Branch, National Archives, Washington, D.C., were most helpful in providing me with the official correspondence of the Civil Aeronautics Administration and its predecessors. They also allowed me to use the correspondence files of the Department of Commerce. Though the collections of the Library of Congress were examined, nothing from the available material was found to be significant for this book. Additional unpublished correspondence of the White House and the CAA-CAB was found at the Harry S. Truman Library, Independence, Missouri. Here Philip Lagerquist and others provided me excellent service in locating materials. I look forward with great interest to the time when aviation records at the Dwight D. Eisenhower Library will be opened to scholars.

I am also indebted to several employees of the Federal Aviation Agency, Washington, D.C., for the use of unprinted sources on the role of the CAA in World War II in addition to other notes on the history and organization of this agency. Dr. Arnold E. Briddon, agency historian, has been of great value to me in locating materials, including the latest statistical data, and with his expert answers to my questions on aviation provided from his long experience as a pilot in the Air Force. I offer special thanks to Charles E. Planck, formerly with the FAA, for his personal interview and permission to use his taped interview with William MacCracken, first head of the Aeronautics Branch. Howard Bingham and others in the FAA's Office of Public Affairs have been most helpful in providing me useful FAA literature. Karl E. Voelter, recently retired from the FAA, was especially helpful in providing insights about the federal regulation of aviation from the time he was a rookie pilot during the twenties to his joining the CAA in 1946.

In Chicago L. M. Marriner and Mel Fischer of the FAA's Airports Division answered numerous questions about the vital role of this program. At Des Moines, Iowa, long interviews and the observation of the various field operations over a long period of time made me better acquainted with the FAA. My deepest thanks go to the following in air traffic control at the Des Moines airport: Donald Murphy, chief controller; and controllers Loren E. Long, Robert Ford, and Norman D. Spencer, Central Region Terminal Councilor (ATCA), for much additional information about the Air Traffic Control Association. Also at Des Moines, Raymond W. Kruke, chief operator of the FAA's Flight Service Station (formerly the Communications Station) capably explained this facility to me. Interviews at the Des Moines FAA Flight Standards District Office (previously known as the General Aviation District Office) contributed helpful suggestions from J. H. Ostiguy, General Supervisor, and engineers Eugene Anderson and Harold Phillips. I appreciate also the courteous help given me by the FAA controllers at the Kansas City, Missouri, airport. I offer similar thanks to Gordon Atzen, Chief of the Airway Facilities Sector at Waterloo, Iowa.

Oswald Ryan, former member of the CAB and now general counsel for the Air Traffic Control Association, assisted me greatly in answering many questions on the activities of the CAB. For the illustrations used in the book, I am indebted to Irv Ripps of the FAA's Office of Information Services.

The personnel of the reference section of the library at the State College of Iowa were most helpful in securing materials here and for obtaining congressional hearings and other data on interlibrary loan. Thanks go also to the reference library personnel of the main library at the University of Illinois (Urbana).

I deeply appreciate the research grants extended to me by my colleagues at the State College of Iowa and the encouragement of my department head Professor D. F. Howard. The editorial guidance of Merritt E. Bailey, Raymond Fassel, and Mrs. Nancy Schworm, all of the Iowa State University Press, has been most beneficial.

DONALD R. WHITNAH

State College of Iowa
Cedar Falls

CONTENTS

SAFER SKYWAYS:

Federal Control of Aviation, 1926-1966

1

AMERICAN AVIATION'S STRUGGLE TOWARD FEDERAL CONTROL

CIVIL AVIATION is one of America's leading industries of the 1960's. Prior to the advent of federal control under the Air Commerce Act of 1926, however, it had attained only a limited degree of maturity. In the middle twenties, the status of aviation clearly indicated that the average American did not accept flying as the best means of transportation. Nor can it be said that the aircraft of those days had proved capable of overcoming a majority of the known hazards to flight, including that of adverse weather. On the other hand, one might derive these conclusions about the aviation of this period: men and women had, during 1903–1926, demonstrated beyond a doubt that heavier-than-air craft could remain aloft for a number of hours. The airplane had provided man with an instrument of transit whose utility in war and peace had become an established fact, witnessed by the aces who participated in World War I, the brave airmail pilots and the innumerable other examples of daring exploit—the transatlantic skippers, aerial photographers, crop sprayers, and the pioneers in the realm of passenger and freight service.

Soon after the conclusion of World War I, aviation enthusiasts realized that the heartaches and tragedies incidental to the new form of aeronautics had already cast a pall over the goals of capturing public confidence. They realized that continuation of a poor safety record could literally destroy this infant industry. Already, crashes had gained such glaring attention that they detracted from endurance and distance records and the many instances of years of flying without accident or even engine failure.

GROWTH OF RAILROADS

In the setting described above, Americans could learn to fly and share in the thrills of flying, entirely outside the reach of medical examiners, inspectors, civil air regulations of the federal variety (few meaningful state restrictions existed), or the effective control of air traffic at the landing fields. How could such a chaotic situation long endure? The answer rests in the past experience of the country regarding kinds of transportation other than aeronautics. American railroads continued to grow with the tremendous gift of federal subsidy during the middle and late nineteenth century. However, what may be labeled effective control of this mode of travel arrived on the scene long after the turn of our present century, despite the establishment of the Interstate Commerce Commission (ICC) in 1887. Similarly, the automobile and its later refinements became accustomed adornments in America long before elaborate procedures of licensing, regulation of speed, and other incidentals of control emanated from state capitals. Indeed, the United States never did assume the ultimate—uniform control and regulation of automobile transportation. To be sure, the ICC has extended its arm of authority to trucks and buses. But it is readily apparent that, like the early railroaders and goggled motorists, the American aeronaut and aviator could invent his wares and test the same unchecked before the advent of established authority.

Immediately, one must point out a distinction between authority, control, or regulation by the federal government, and the genuine interest, encouragement, and support of federal scientists and politicians—whether in the area of research and development or direct subsidy. Elements within the second category were directed toward aviation in this country long before 1926.

A brief survey of flight in America reflects the deep concern of a host of well-wishers, both in and out of government, toward the progressive stages of invention and the practical application of man's theories that suggested he could soar above the earth and control his direction and destination. Considering all the types of flight, the lighter-than-air craft appeared initially on the American shore, as in Europe, in the 1780's.

BALLOONISTS

The early, trailblazing balloonists endured a similar experience to that encountered by their first successors with the heavier-than-air machine over a century later: "The early pioneers of modern aviation were at first looked upon as lunatics or at best foolhardy visionaries, and even a century of American flying history could not avert this initial prejudice."[1] As a result, many of the experiments undertaken during the eighties and nineties bore the cloak of secrecy to the consternation of newspaper reporters dispatched to record the accomplishments of this era.

Balloonists proved to be the most successful of the early aeronauts, gaining support from the federal government for local experiments, as well as spinning their dreams of conquering the wider vista of the Atlantic.[2] Reconnoitering behind enemy lines, collecting weather data, and attempting to produce rainfall through the use of explosives were just a few of the enterprises undertaken by balloonists who received the support of scientists but often the ridicule of the masses when they became entangled in the rooftops or encountered difficulty in descending at all. The professional balloonist, however, has not seen his vocation accepted as a feasible mode of transport. His contribution to aeronautics has rested more with his ability to stimulate the imagination of the public at fairs and exhibitions to the point of anticipating the achievements of flight.

GLIDING

Ballooning embraced a large gallery of entertainment seekers. Dangerous escapades involving gliding emerged during the 1880's and 1890's. Europeans had initiated the first official tests in this area of aeronautics during the sixties, while John Jacob Montgomery of California allegedly glided some short distance in 1883.[3] Interest in gliding, appearing at the height of manned-balloon ascensions, must necessarily be considered as an important step toward the ultimate facet of man's aim in flight, the heavier-than-air machine. Numerous patents for gliders and power-driven aircraft were issued by the federal authorities during the era of unsuccessful experiment from 1838 to 1903. Nor did nineteenth-century man fail to consider the age-old design of the helicopter. Here, too, Europeans and Americans designed their craft and conducted their tests, but they convinced few onlookers at this early time.

LACK OF GOVERNMENTAL SUPPORT

Considering all the frustrations of the air age in America prior to the twentieth century, one might have predicted a feeling of deep despair among the aeronauts. But this was hardly the case. Even if man could not yet remain aloft in heavier-than-air machines, his detailed plans increased in both quality and quantity. The role of Octave Chanute is unmistakably noteworthy in this connection. Collating all the known information on flying, Chanute encouraged the establishment of a national aeronautical group and became chairman of an 1893 Chicago international conference on aeronautics. Meanwhile, attempts to obtain financial support from Congress failed, thus frustrating the stimulus which might have hastened the success of aviation in the United States.

Accompanying the quickening pulse of the American nation under its tempestuous President Theodore Roosevelt were the successful air travels of Wilbur and Orville Wright and the "hide-and-seek" antics of most aeronauts. False claims or rumors of actual flight, legal challenges in the clamor for patents and government sponsorship of airplane design loomed as threats to aviation, diminishing in the eyes of some contemporaries the tremendous feats of the brothers at Kitty Hawk in 1903. Constructing their machine with their own hands, these wily, astute, skillful epoch-makers could claim the quiet respect and acknowledgement of such an air pioneer as Chanute.[4] However, the uncanny ability of friends and reporters to misrepresent soon perpetrated a rift between the Wrights and their good friend Chanute. By 1910, the year Chanute died, it was apparent the Wrights no longer enjoyed reading about "Chanute, their teacher."[5]

Despite continuing success with their flights in 1904–1905, the Wrights were yet unable to interest the War Department in granting a contract for aircraft designed especially for use in war.[6] Much has been written about this rebuff from the War Department, but apparently this refusal was based on the contention of the Wrights that a contract was in order before any testing of the type of plane involved. Samuel Pierpont Langley, whose contemporary efforts at flying were often misrepresented by the press as a feud with the Wrights, also was refused assistance by the War Department. Langley died in February, 1906. The brothers continued their phenomenal success in flight, Wilbur navigating in France and Orville in the United States. In 1905, Orville was seriously injured in the crash of his plane, inflicting the initial death in a power-driven plane on Lieutenant Thomas E. Selfridge, Orville's enthusiastic passenger and a brave flier. Undoubtedly, the first decade of the twentieth century belongs to the Wrights when one considers the world's total achievements in aviation.

THE AERO CLUB OF AMERICA

Aviation in the United States reached a critical turn at the end of this first decade. The Army finally purchased the Wright plane in 1908. Civil aviation was split into rival camps: the backers of the Wrights and those of Glenn H. Curtiss.[7] Expensive law suits, dragging on for years, had been instigated as a result of jealousy over patents. A semblance of order in civil aviation came to be maintained only through the efforts of the Aero Club of America, official representative of the *Federation Aeronautique Internationale*. The stabilizing influence of the Aero Club, unquestionably not as effective as the later government regulation, nevertheless proved a boon to aviation through its sanctioning of meets and contests and the licensing of promoters. A second generation of fliers now took over as the pupils of the Wrights and Curtiss. New achievements in flight were not to emanate from the Wright brothers because of Wilbur's untimely death from typhoid fever on May 30, 1912.[8]

WOMEN FLIERS

American women excitedly watched the experiments of male aviators and soon became contenders for all the many honors and contests at hand. As was the case with lighter-than-air machines, Europeans became the first female pilots of airplanes beginning with Thèrèse Peltier of France in 1908. Two years later, Bessica Raiche won the distinction of becoming the first woman aviator in America. There soon followed in the annals of the Aero Club the names of several pioneer female aviators, all of whom were accorded proper licenses. Harriet Quimby, colorful dramatic editor of *Leslie's Weekly*, obtained license Number 37 and took to the air in 1911.[9] In less than two years, Miss Quimby gained international acclaim by her solo flight across the English Channel (the first by a woman), but she met sudden death in another flight.

OUTBREAK OF WORLD WAR I

Although the U.S. government had failed to exercise control over aviation, interest in flying had gained a new impetus with the outbreak of war in Europe in the summer of 1914. The United States had been the first nation to possess a military plane, the Wright model of 1909. However, at the outbreak of hostilities in 1914, European aviation was markedly superior to that in the United States.[10] Fortunately, a turning point was close for Americans. In Europe during the early weeks of 1915, a German airman was killed by rifle fire from an Allied craft, aerial bombings were begun, and a Frenchman became the first pilot to shoot down an enemy.

NATIONAL ADVISORY COMMITTEE FOR AERONAUTICS

Meanwhile, on March 3, in Washington, D.C., President Woodrow Wilson signed into law the Naval Appropriations Act with a rider which established the Advisory Committee for Aeronautics, whose purpose would be to direct "the scientific study of the problems of flight, with a view of their practical solution." [11] President Wilson immediately turned to Secretary of Commerce William C. Redfield for suggestions on one appointment to be made from the Bureau of Standards.[12] Soon to be known as the National Advisory Committee for Aeronautics (NACA), this body came to exert a profound influence on the military phase of aeronautics during the remainder of the war. It assumed a position as well in the forward ranks of those promoting the federal control of civil aviation. From its inception, NACA was considered an independent agency even though its initial funds originated in the Department of the Navy. The war naturally commanded the immediate attention of NACA leadership as conferences were called with aircraft manufacturers and the various departments of the government. Promotion of all aspects of research was always present as the major goal. Aside from military plans, NACA also recommended, prior to our entrance into the war: the establishment of airmail service, cross-licensing of aeronautic patents in order to prevent litigation over basic patents, and the preparation of three-year plans for aircraft production as requested by the Secretaries of War and Navy. A vast majority of these recommendations became standard procedure with amazing rapidity.

The United States officially entered the war on April 6, 1917, and NACA swung into action in an effort to improve the nation's inventory of some eighty-three pilots of the Signal Corps, Navy, and Marine Corps, and 109 military aircraft. The Aircraft Production Board was created at the instigation of NACA; mass production of engines was quickly facilitated with a decision to order the 12-cylinder Liberty motor. Simultaneously, the Navy, under Acting Secretary Franklin D. Roosevelt, ordered the development of the "NC" flying boat capable of crossing the Atlantic. No such trip could be completed until after the war ended. Further experimental activities were encouraged at Langley Field, Virginia, on the radiotelephone, and a technician from NACA supervised altitude tests on the first Liberty engines at Detroit, Michigan; and Pikes Peak, Colorado. All the while, the Curtiss JN–4 "Jenny" became the training plane for thousands of American pilots. The important relationship of meteorology to aviation gained considerable attention from NACA, which requested funds for the Weather Bureau to conduct research and issue reports benefiting aviators.[13] Throughout its research activities, the National Bureau of Standards performed invaluable service to NACA, including the construction of an altitude laboratory for the testing of engines. Scientific and technical data on aeronautics were compiled by the Office of Aeronautical Intelligence, also established by NACA. During the final year of World War I, America shipped Liberty motors to France; Americans took part in military balloon ascensions in France; and an American-built craft, a DH–4, was assembled in France. However, when the Armistice was signed, the air power of the United States was yet "on its way" to delivering its might with over 10,500 airplanes owned by the military, not to mention the more than 27,000 officers of the Army Air Service, the Navy, and the Marine Corps.

FEDERAL SUPERVISION AND CONTROL

Coordinating many of the most important decisions made during 1915–1918, NACA set important precedents of federal supervision and interest in aviation, none of which disappeared merely because the war ended. These accomplishments played no small part in alerting the aeronautical experts to the facts of life; the United States possessed the capable and logical leadership to assume control of aviation throughout the country. Unhappily, Congress and the public saw no dire emergency when NACA first recommended, shortly after the Armistice, the enactment of legislation for the control of civil aviation, designating the Department of Commerce as the logical arm of enforcement. Dr. S. W. Stratton, director of the Bureau of Standards, soon followed with similar advice to President Wilson, suggesting the creation of a board consisting of the Secretaries of State, War, Navy, Commerce, and Treasury.[14] Stratton received welcome support for his suggestion from Howard Coffin, representing the Advisory Commission of the Council of National Defense. Coffin advised President Wilson that Great Britain possessed elaborate plans to regulate aviation; at the same time, the United States lacked the aircraft art and stood in fourth or fifth place internationally.[15] In addition to domestic aviation, Coffin also stressed the urgency of international laws governing aviation, hoping that the Allies would accomplish such beginnings at the Paris Peace Conference. Coffin, echoing the sentiment of the leading aeronautical interests, sensed the imminence of a genuine crisis: "The future of aviation in this country will depend very largely on what support Congress gives the Army and Navy for its development work. The civil use of aircraft should also be encouraged."[16]

President Wilson responded by instructing Secretary of War Newton D. Baker to appoint an interdepartmental board to draft a proposed act covering air navigation and civil aviation in the United States and its island possessions.[17] Baker selected J. S. Ames, NACA; J. B. Lennon, Labor; S. W. Stratton, Commerce; Otto Praeger, Post Office; C. F. Marvin, Agriculture; W. C. Carpenter, State; Captain Stanley V. Parker, Treasury; Commander J. L. Callan, Navy; and Colonel John F. Curry, Army. The membership of NACA continued its plea for regulation, considering this item its principal recommendation for 1920.[18] Numerous petitions reached NACA in favor of the proposal.

THE POSTWAR SCENE

These unsuccessful efforts to obtain legislation for control of aviation were continued, rather quietly, immediately after the war. The momentum brought about by the world struggle was now paying aeronautical dividends with individual exploits reflected in the headlines. Indeed, one could well argue that aeronautical achievements in this country during 1919–1926 far surpassed the most optimistic prewar dreams. A majority of the exploits had to do with distance, time, and altitude records; the testing of new and more powerful aircraft; transatlantic crossings; the amazing but dangerous endeavors of pilots flying the airmail; and the several attempts, some successful, to inaugurate both passenger and freight air service. At the same time, the financial status of the aviation industry in this country became extremely unsteady, finding no easy adjustment to the postwar scene. With such a large stock of war planes on hand, nonmilitary uses became imperative. One manufacturer even turned his plant to the production of furniture to avoid ruin until orders were resumed in 1921.[19]

TRANSATLANTIC FLIGHTS

The war legacy proved helpful as military fliers continued their assault on records while testing aircraft. Requiring eighteen days, four Curtiss JN-4's completed the first army transcontinental flight during December, 1918, followed by two similar runs with the DH-4 Liberty in subsequent months.[20] Crossing the Atlantic Ocean, formerly a dream of many bygone generations of balloonists and now a dream of airplane pilots, became a reality in May, 1919, as the navy Curtiss seaplane, the NC-4, commanded by Lieutenant Commander Albert C. Read, flew from Newfoundland to Plymouth, England, via the Azores and Portugal. This flight had many stops, but later the same year, two Englishmen gained credit for the first nonstop, transatlantic airplane crossing, and the British dirigible R-34 successfully mastered the Atlantic in July, 1919. These transatlantic heroics were not to be improved upon for some years, but the transcontinental time came to be lowered drastically on February 21, 1921, when an army DH-4B was flown from San Diego to Jacksonville in 22 hours and 27 minutes. During April 6—September 28, 1924, two army Douglas "World Cruiser" biplanes flew 26,345 miles in 363 hours' flying time to amass the following records: first round-the-world flight, first transpacific flight, and first westbound Atlantic crossing.[21] Meanwhile, attempts to enter the field of dirigibles continued in this country as the famous navy airship *Shenandoah* made its initial flights using helium gas in September, 1923. Unhappily, after numerous successful flights, this ship crashed two years later, killing 14 of 43 persons aboard and halting further work on this type of airship.[22]

INTERNATIONAL CONTROL SOUGHT

Meanwhile, peacetime activities of NACA turned to the effort of keeping the United States abreast of foreign countries in the field of aeronautics. Perennially, this organization submitted detailed recommendations to Congress which was alerted to the need for licensing pilots, inspecting aircraft, and regulating the use of landing fields. NACA also took upon itself the task of co-ordinating the ideas apparent in the various executive departments of our government prior to the signing of the International Convention on Air Navigation in Paris, October, 1919. Though it was not to be carried out at the time, it is interesting to note the appeal at this early date for international control of air navigation at a time when the United States lacked even the laws to regulate domestic air movements. On an optimistic note, the world meeting established a Commission for Aerial Navigation under the League of Nations and affirmed the principle of national sovereignty in airspace. Though international accord had not yet materialized, officials in the United States expressed their government's deep appreciation in 1920 when the Air Board of Canada temporarily allowed the flight of American planes over Canada.[23] During the summer of 1920, NACA was able to inaugurate research, using its own facilities, when the 5-foot wind tunnel was placed in operation at Langley Field. Not that NACA attempted in any way to dominate the field of aeronautical research; continual efforts were directed toward encouraging military and civilian engineers to further research at the Massachusetts Institute of Technology (MIT) and elsewhere.

AIRMAIL SERVICE

Promotion of aviation by NACA, along with the feats of war-trained aviators, would not have enabled aeronautics to reach the heights it did by 1926, had it not been for the amazing innovation by the Post Office Department of its airmail service. Of course, airmail, as such, was hardly new. In fact, letters were carried in a balloon across the English Channel in 1785 by Jean Pierre François Blanchard and an American, Dr. John Jeffries.[24] John Wise, among other Americans, advocated a system of airmail, carrying sacks of letters in his balloon in the middle of the nineteenth century. French and British pilots, in 1911, were the first to carry mail by airplane, although an American, Earle L. Ovington, also carried it later the same year. Instantly, the Post Office Department took notice of this mode of transportation, allowing Ovington—and soon others—to make short flights with the mail. Never accomplishing a regular schedule and long harassed by crashes, these early pilots failed to establish regular airmail service. However, the interest generated by these feats nurtured the hopes of government officials until success became a reality. With the support of NACA, the Post Office Department received an appropriation of $100,000 for the flying of mail. Reluctantly, Secretary of War Baker assented to the request for army pilots to fly the mail, a plan backed by NACA. In May, 1918, army pilots inaugurated the flights for the Post Office Department, commencing with the New York–Washington, D.C. route. Inauspicious, indeed, were the beginnings of this service with spare planes, green pilots, public reluctance to pay the 24 cents postage, not to mention the lack of adequate landing fields.

Unquestionably, postal authorities' dreams of extending the service far transcended any realistic appraisal of the status of aviation in this country when premature attempts were instigated on December 12, 1918, to open service between Chicago and New York.[25] Here, as was the case with other means of earlier transportation, the Alleghenies proved to be a major barrier, the "Graveyard Run," until the Chicago–New York service achieved regular status. Again, limitation of flights to a daytime schedule, plus the nonexistence of many airfields or radio beacons, doomed the service to further chagrin. Then, too, public interest faded even when first-class mail was carried for no extra cost for five years (1919–1924). The only solution lay in a transcontinental schedule, utilizing as much night flying as possible. Issuing this decision early in 1921, it was late 1926 before the lighted transcontinental airway could be finished. In the interim, the "mail did go through" in the amazing saga of flight recorded by the "gypsy" pilot. But the postal leaders remained unhappy; after all, the mail was transferred to the railroad at night. Shortly before the end of the Wilson Administration, the initial night airmail flights were begun, the pilots starting out from New York and San Francisco. Success of the famous Jack Knight and his fellow relay pilots is a story often told, the tale of a harrowing passage from Omaha to Chicago, though Knight had expected to end the run at Omaha, all part of the transcontinental epoch-making trek covering over thirty-three hours. Aviation scholars agree that, although regular San Francisco to New York service was not begun until 1925, Knight and his fellow trailblazers provided the impetus for such a routine.[26]

Not all the gypsy fliers attained glory; a total of twelve accidents occurred in 1921. Confidence in flying remained in jeopardy for several years as 31 of the first 40 pilots hired by the Post Office died in crashes, lowering the longevity for such an enterprise to just four years. Carrying the airmail over unlighted routes was an unusually hazardous undertaking. Unfortunately, other aspects of aviation came to be invaded by inexperienced and reckless pilots, many of whom lost their lives as a result. Lack of government regulation, to be sure, shared the responsibility for such a trend as the huge war stocks of airplanes found their way into the hands of anyone with the price of purchase. Many of these airplanes had by then been judged unsafe for the military. Added to the controversies of 1921 was the beginning of a long struggle within the American military over the true value of aviation, that is, the feud between Brigadier General William Mitchell of the Army, the great promoter of a unified air force, and his critics in the Navy and elsewhere. His court-martial in 1925 silenced this outspoken and sincere believer in the military potential of a strong air service.

TRANSPORT AND PASSENGER SERVICE

In addition to the many gypsy aviators, one must surely mention the advent of another group, the early transport operator, who owned his plane and maintained one base of operations. At least 100 of these promoters were in business by 1923. Forerunners of the major transport companies, these pioneers took their financial risks without federal subsidy, but, likewise, often succumbed to the plight of unregulated airways, in the end asking the government for help.

It is difficult to ascertain which company deserves credit for starting the first passenger service on a regular basis. The St. Petersburg–Tampa Airboat Line functioned between those two cities during the tourist season in 1914.[27] Aero Limited in 1919, was organized to carry passengers between New York City and Atlantic City, while another line, Aeromarine, flew passengers to other nearby resort towns. West Indies Airways began the lucrative project of carrying passengers between Key West and Havana in 1919. Other routes were added; Juan Trippe, later tycoon of Pan American Airways, got his start in 1923, with the Long Island Airways.[28] Incredible as it appears to the observer today, these passenger agents also operated outside the jurisdiction of governmental control in connection with inspection, licensing, schedules, and safety standards of any type. Luckily, the safety record of these lines was commendable even though the financial risks caused a drastic rate of bankruptcy. Airmail and passengers gained attention as fruitful items of transport. In 1925, Henry Ford looked to a third realm of exploit when he started the initial regularly scheduled air-freight line between Detroit and Chicago.[29]

GOVERNMENT REGULATION

Heroic efforts to keep the United States even with Europe in aviation development following World War I are manifest in the foregoing descriptions from several aspects of American pursuits. However, the European counterparts to our aviators, operators, and manufacturers possessed the number one ingredient still missing on this side of the Atlantic—complete governmental regulation of civil aviation with generous subsidies. Because of this difference, European countries held an undisputed advantage in many facets of airline operation.

Americans refused at this time to accept the European principle of direct subsidy to private aeronautical interests. Nevertheless, a long drive for government regulation of civil and commercial aviation came to a successful conclusion in 1926, just in time, indeed, to bring order out of a most chaotic situation. Of course, government funds had been expended for the airmail flights and the developing system of airway radio beacons on the transcontinental system, again for one purpose—an airmail service.

No exact first date exists for the visionary suggestions that government must take over the regulation of civil aviation. Mention has already been given to interest in balloons during the 1890's. A more sustained zeal directed toward similar ends, this time with airplanes involved, emanated early in the second decade of the twentieth century as reflected by the comments and requests brought to bear in Congress. Ostensibly, these proposals envisaged governmental control of aviation and not merely the numerous examples of federal promotion and interest in this pioneer form of locomotion. Pleas for the investigation of aeronautics actually preceded the move for control as witnessed in one instance during February, 1913.[30] Shortly after the outbreak of World War I, congressmen offered statements on the value of aviation in terms of national defense, discussed its uses

for both offense and defense, and suggested that another function
—the carrying of airmail—could be added. Next evolved the
movement for the National Advisory Committee for Aeronautics,
already discussed.[31] By the latter portion of 1916, definite support appeared for some type of department of aeronautics on the
federal level. Spurred on by outside interests, Congressmen Lincoln Dixon and Charles Lieb, both of Indiana, promoted this
suggestion on the House floor.[32] A series of similar attempts,
offered in the form of bills, gained attention in both houses in
1917, though attention was diverted, because of war, to military
aspects of aeronautics. Moreover, interest reached a number of
officials at the same time over the prospects of airmail.[33]

Cessation of hostilities in Europe did not provide the immediate setting for concerted action favoring regulation, but in
the fall of 1919, Congressmen Charles F. Curry of California and
Harry E. Hull of Iowa each submitted bills calling for a department of aeronautics. Curry's bill suggested combining military
and civilian operations under one head.[34] During the early weeks
of the second session of the Sixty-Sixth Congress, additional bills
offered the same approach to the question, together with a strong
appeal from a Conference of State and Local Bar Associations,
which cogently stressed the necessity for federal control. Executive support for a department of aeronautics emanated from
President Wilson early in 1919, as already mentioned, but
certainly aviation did not gain a high priority of concern in the
immediate postwar scene as Wilson's diplomatic frustrations
dominated the stage only to be followed by his untimely physical
collapse at Pueblo.[35] Though President Wilson found his future
successor to be extremely dull, Warren Harding managed to
express his desire for aviation; he, too, wanted a department of
aeronautics.[36] Harding appointees scurried to acquaint themselves with the aviation question, Secretary of State Charles E.
Hughes asking the Postmaster General his views before he "plugs
it."[37] E. H. Shaughnessy, Second Assistant Postmaster General,
favored the Department of Commerce for aeronautic control but
wished to keep NACA out of the whole question.[38] As in the past
(in fact since 1918), NACA continued its support of such proposals, drafting bills for members of Congress.[39]

The American Legion, the neophyte but popular pressure
group with so many recent veterans, lent its voice to the Senate
with a resolution seeking the establishment of a civil department

of aeronautics, which would become an integral facet of national defense though the control of such a group would be vested in the Department of Commerce. Senator James W. Wadsworth, Jr. of New York, a notable supporter of aviation, expressed similar leanings with introduction of his bill on August 22, 1921.[40] Meanwhile, numerous complaints against unregulated flying had led police in New York City to arrest a number of known offenders, offering the term "reckless flying" to the American vocabulary. The colorful congressman from New York City, Fiorello La Guardia, urged not only stringent measures of regulation for his subordinates but also the dire need for nationwide restrictive measures.[41] Despite the absence of legislation, Secretary of Commerce Herbert Hoover (1921–1928) offered the full support of the Bureau of Standards for the Navy's development of aeronautical navigation aids.[42] Though he agreed with those citizens who registered complaints against unregulated aviation, Hoover reminded the dissatisfied that his office could not act without federal statutes.[43]

The battle for control, despite the emergence of such diverse testimonials, faced a rugged trail of further heartache before attaining the ultimate victory. Back in Congress, Representative Frederick C. Hicks of New York, in 1922, joined Senator Wadsworth to push forward another measure for regulation.[44] Hicks correctly observed that federal establishment of airways and airdromes, as well as policies of licensing and inspection, must be inaugurated. Secretary Hoover reported that the aviation industry appeared to be the only private enterprise asking for governmental control. That private and commercial aviation desired government aid is evident from the many inquiries received in Washington. Confined mostly to the question of regulation, requests for subsidy were also included. Stephen Davis, Acting Secretary of Commerce, advised William B. Robertson of St. Louis: "The federal government does not help in the financing of commercial aviators and I know of no plan to put such a system into effect."[45] Numerous comparisons reflected the high degree of regulation in European countries, along with subsidies, in France, Great Britain, Germany, Holland, Rumania, and Belgium. Furthermore, eighteen states, thirteen cities, and Los Angeles County in this country now had some type of law concerning aviation. Interstate supervision would come about as a natural adjunct to the growth of aeronautics. Unhappily,

Wadsworth, Hicks, and a handful of other congressional sympathizers had not reckoned with the suspicions and reluctance on the part of their fellow legislators who found it easy to bury such lofty proposals in committee or on the calendar. Among those unconvinced at the time was Senator William E. Borah of Idaho, who moved earlier to abolish NACA and transfer its property and duties to existing agencies.[46] Charles D. Walcott, Chairman of NACA, quite naturally protested vigorously to President Calvin Coolidge any such transfer or death of this organization.[47]

Typical of the indifference reflected toward such legislative moves was the reaction of Representative Meyer London of New York, who asked, "Have not legislatures done enough mischief on land and sea without extending their activities into the air?"[48] New bills offered the same general proposals before the Sixty-Eighth Congress when Senator Kenneth McKellar of Tennessee questioned whether the bill would grant exclusive air routes to individuals or corporations. Honestly expressing his opinion for that day but certainly not foreseeing later conditions, Senator Wadsworth assured his colleagues that no trouble would arise over exclusive routes or franchises.[49] It was also the intention of the framers to exclude foreigners from owning American machines, but foreign airplanes would not be prevented from entering and leaving the country. In case of disputes, federal district courts would have jurisdiction. The stage of serious debate had been reached; the Senate passed the bill, S. 76; but House action did not materialize, a familiar pattern of delay to be repeated until 1926. Samuel E. Winslow of Massachusetts, in the House, became cosponsor of the drive for regulation with Senator Wadsworth. Again, the majority of aeronautical spokesmen favored legislation. Godfrey L. Cabot, President of the National Aeronautic Association, expressed his views to Secretary Hoover: "We are in hope that the Winslow Bill may become law in the near future."[50] Meanwhile, without governmental controls, additional "flying clowns" performed their stunts over congested areas; some, fortunately, were caught and arrested. Laxity prevailed at times, particularly in the case of a military pilot, who flew at a level below the housetops, only to be acquitted in court.[51] Attempting to placate the public, the War Department placed a ban on such activities.

THE KELLY ACT

Nor did unanimity prevail as to the proper jurisdiction of a possible new department or commission in charge of aviation. Annual efforts were expended to unify civil and military aviation under one head, with the airmail duties of the Post Office Department included. This approach continued up through 1925.[52] Several different problems relating to aeronautical legislation entered the picture at this time. In the first place, energetic attempts to authorize the Post Office Department to let contracts for civilian flights with airmail reached fruition with the passage of the famous Kelly Act, which became law in February, 1925. As one author put it, "The ownership of the air was transferred from the government to private companies."[53] Private industry's bonanza was called the public's loss of the best airline the world had ever known. Beyond a doubt, the Kelly Act set the pace for aviation development to follow, that is, the federal authorities would provide subsidy, either directly or—as in the case of airmail—indirectly, in addition to technical skill and eventually the long-sought regulation. Henry L. Smith correctly assessed the picture: "Subsequent events also proved that there were many more who objected to the term 'subsidy' than to the 'practice' properly sugar-coated."[54]

PRIVATE vs. FEDERAL OWNERSHIP

Private ownership must be maintained in all cases without the competition of governmental aviators, whether in the flying of airmail or other nonmilitary pursuits. One might easily detect from the records a general easing up on the part of the federal government wherever its competition with private enterprise was to be found.[55] The National Aircraft Factory had ceased its active production, serving for over a decade after 1923 as merely a repair station and warehouse. This was soothing to the political and economic philosophy of both President Coolidge and Secretary Hoover, who leaned over backward to please the entrepreneurs of private business. The Post Office Department, indeed, did not further extend its airmail operations at this time, letting the transcontinental line serve as a sufficient endeavor. Aircraft manufacturers often complained bitterly of too much competition from government but ignored their critics when reminded of the helpful developmental activities provided free to private concerns. The essence of the federal government's approach, with many amendments and additional huge subsidies, has persisted as American policy to the present. In a sense, the new Kelly law set off a chain reaction. Specifically, the sudden upsurge of interest in commercial aviation reached the ears of congressmen who heretofore had turned aside the drive for government regulatory measures.

COURT-MARTIAL OF GENERAL MITCHELL

The second item of note during the same year, the court-martial of General Mitchell, again brought to a focus the haphazard manner in which aviation had been allowed to develop (primarily via the "law of the jungle") in this country. Mitchell's drastic criticism probably cannot be cited as the major cause of the Air Commerce Act of 1926, but his trial definitely aroused a sufficient amount of attention to warrant an investigation of the entire status of aviation.[56]

THE MORROW BOARD

A third event of 1925 worthy of attention was the creation by President Coolidge of the President's Aircraft Board, commonly known as the Morrow Board. Here, credit must be extended to Secretary Hoover, who had taken a direct hand in drafting the series of unsuccessful bills advocating federal controls over aviation. Hoover and others persuaded Coolidge to name financier Dwight Morrow as chairman of the group. Originating at the same time as the Mitchell trial, the Morrow Board espoused the principle of federal regulation of commercial aviation but wanted such regulation separate from the federal role in military phases of aeronautics.[57]

Meanwhile, the basic deficiencies confronting aviation in America gained further attention from the mass news media, one reporter declaring that aviation, in 1924, was so bound up in the public mind with armaments that its value as a speedy medium of communication and transportation was overshadowed by its utility as a war machine.[58] Precious little, so far as appropriations were concerned, would be asked of Congress in the only large nation in the world without national air legislation. Of 470 crashes resulting in 221 deaths in the last three years, the editors claimed that 91 per cent had been caused by inexperienced pilots or cheap and unsafe equipment. Loss of the *Shenandoah* and the case of a navy flying boat adrift for nine days on a trip to Hawaii moved Senator Hiram Bingham of Connecticut to comment, "It is no secret that in England and France commercial aviation is safer than in the United States."[59] Bingham foresaw little difficulty in assigning the various tasks of regulation to existing groups within the federal domain. For instance, the Department of Commerce might lay out and maintain the navigable air routes while the Bureau of Lighthouses could authorize lights and beacons. Navigational charts could well be supplied by the Coast and Geodetic Survey, leaving the issuance of meteorological information to the Weather Bureau. Postal authorities would continue to supervise the letting of liberal contracts for the transportation of mail and parcel post by air.

AIR SAFETY

A quick glance at some of the investigations of accidents reveals the wide range of foolhardy actions involving aircraft and their operation. True, the International Convention on Air Navigation, meeting at Versailles, in 1919, had laid down definite rules and regulations for aerial navigation. But the United States, alone among the major world powers, had failed to ratify this convention.[60] Significantly enough, on the eve of the passage of the Air Commerce Act, American aviation sponsors had produced an Aeronautic Safety Code, covering every phase of aircraft operation: structure, power plant, equipment, signals, airdromes and airways, traffic rules, qualifications for airmen, etc. Taking part in the drafting of the regulations were the Society of Automotive Engineers, the Bureau of Standards, and the American Engineering Standards Committee. The code included this advice:

> The control mechanism shall be arranged so that it cannot be jammed by loose objects inside the fuselage, baggage under the seats, the clothing of a pilot or passenger. . . . We can remember one accident where the rudder bar was entangled in a lady's moderately long skirt, with fatal injury to pilot and passenger alike.[61]

Among other items, the code emphasized the necessity of 700 cubic feet of fresh air per hour for every passenger in an airplane. Fire already had proved to be a serious menace to flight. The location of gasoline tanks should be as far from the engine as practicable, if possible on the wings and not in line with the engine. A fire wall, made of sheet steel and asbestos backing, must separate the engine completely from the rest of the fuselage or nacelle. Further difficulty had been encountered with air intakes on the carburetors which should be completely outside the engine cowling so as to eliminate the danger of backfire igniting a collection of gasoline vapor under the cowling. In summary, the experts agreed: "These precautions are simple, but alas, not always followed."[62]

Leading aeronautical authorities in the United States were joined by a prominent British publisher, Sir Robert Donald, in extolling the virtues of German aviation: "Germany today is unrivaled master of the air in commercial flying."[63] The air carrier Lufthansa issued every passenger a $6,000 life insurance policy and offered customers a 99.997 per cent chance of safety, according to one calculation covering 3,013,171 miles flown during the years 1924–1925. American pilots, working without governmental regulation, did not fare as well, although it appears that data for exact comparisons are lacking. A total of seventeen airmail pilots tragically lost their lives in 1921, yet only two each were killed in 1925 and 1926, certainly a major improvement with total miles flown ranging from 1,770,658 in 1921 to 2,501,555 in 1925. One author concluded, "When there is an airplane accident the fault is usually human, not mechanical."[64] He maintained this to be true in 90 per cent of the accidents occurring in the Army Air Service.

PASSAGE OF THE AIR COMMERCE ACT

This critical publicity, the Kelly Act, the trial of Mitchell, and the Morrow Board, together with the long-standing favor of the executive branch of government, helped in no small measure to bring about the final victory for control. In the very next session of Congress, additional proponents lent a hand, including Senator Bingham and Representatives Schuyler Merritt of Connecticut and James S. Parker of New York. Recalcitrant members of the House were reminded by Parker that the automobile, too, in its early days had been considered dangerous but had outgrown this stigma. Aviation already had presented to the public a reduced fatality rate, and this bill (Senate bill 41) provided an additional means toward increased safety just as did the federal government's appropriations to light harbors and channels for safer navigation. Quoting official statistics, Parker noted that the fatality rate for the airmail service had been reduced from one per 64,000 miles in 1918, to one per over 200,000 miles in 1925. Strenuous debate soon followed, ranging from ridiculous chiding to cautious apprehension of theoretical shortcomings in the bill's present form. Illinoisan Edward J. King suggested protection of people who are walking on earth: "It is a very fine plan and I am in favor of it, but some of us might get hit."[65] Parker assured King that such action could be left to the discretion of the Secretary of Commerce, whose department would control civil aviation. Interests of the Post Office would not be encroached upon as that department would continue to control the airmail. Thomas L. Blanton, a Texan, in declaring his opposition to the bill, cited his desire for one agency to control both military and civil aviation and saw no danger to military regulation of the civilian similar to the case of the army engineers' control of our rivers.

FEDERAL SUBSIDY

Federal subsidy, the perennially thorny issue in this country (particularly under President Coolidge), then entered into the debate. Parker recalled that every other civilized country of the world had taken up some form of subsidy. One legislator, J. Mayhew Wainwright of New York, actually hoped for more sweeping forms of subsidy, claiming that the bill regulated but did not foster aviation in a nation of pioneers in the field of aeronautics. Urging liberal support, he reported the following annual appropriations in foreign lands: Germany and France, each $2,500,000; and England, $1,750,000.[66] Parker had suggested, far too modestly it would rapidly prove to be, a figure of $250,000 for the United States during the initial year. Representative Merritt contrasted the trim, 19-page bill with its bulky, 55-page predecessor of the previous year. Hoover confided to those interested that a shorter bill like Bingham's had a better chance.[67] Another benefit of regulation would be the licensing of all airmen and an end to acrobatics at fairs and other crowded scenes. The battle lines tightened when George Huddleston of Alabama rose in opposition directing ". . . my feeble voice against the future evils of the bill." Accusing the proponents of being prophets instead of lawgivers, Huddleston told the small throng of thirty to forty colleagues that it saw visions of ". . . heavens filled with commerce—pilots of the purple twilight dropping down with costly bales." The annoyed Southerner asked if it were possible to fly in your own back field without a license. Engendering partisan politics and the theory of states' rights into the question, Huddleston concluded:

> Mr. Hoover, who has already been made dictator of the radio, now with this bill becomes lord of the air. . . . Perhaps even a disembodied spirit will not be permitted to wing its way upward into a better world without petitioning Mr. Hoover and getting a pilot's license before he starts.[68]

Fortunately for American aviation, Huddleston's remarks brought forth an abundance of laughter but gained him no spirited following. Undaunted, Huddleston asked if the woodpecker would be protected under this bill as an aviator or if Jove must obtain a license to hurl.

INTRASTATE COMMERCE

Interestingly enough, Huddleston did correctly reflect the concern of many legislators about the question of federal jurisdiction in the air over the various states, or intrastate commerce. His amendment to omit national control of intrastate aviation lost in the House, 68 to 16, but found adherents in the Senate.

This and other matters faced crucial scrutiny in the conference committee, bringing progress to a temporary halt by mid-April. House conferees, in addition to Parker and Merritt, were: Sam Rayburn, Texas; Clarence F. Lea, California; and John G. Cooper, Ohio. Senators joining Bingham were: Bert M. Fernald, Maine; Duncan U. Fletcher, Florida; Joseph E. Ramsdell, Louisiana; and Wesley L. Jones, Washington. Outside forces aided skillfully in fostering the compromise. The NACA leadership disagreed strongly with the Bingham bill, which would promote federal establishment and ownership of airports. As a result, this item was amended to allow for governmental emergency fields but not airports.[69] Private enterprise and states' rights won a victory here. The definition of air commerce proved to be the second major issue in the conference. Here, again, caution prevailed in the long run, only to plague federal authorities for some years. In its ultimate form, the original Air Commerce Act omitted federal jurisdiction over purely intrastate commerce. In theory, at least, a state could rule against interstate flight over its borders; happily, this situation did not arise. On the other hand, the President was empowered to restrict air space for the military. In yet another case, the type of penalties to invoke against violators, leniency won out, because the House version calling for use of criminal penalties was rejected for the Senate's request adhering to the utilization of civil penalties. No wonder that Senator Bingham observed that this was the most liberal law of all countries. Much can be said in support of the compromise, however, for by this time most proponents agreed that any law could be amended in the future and, indeed, questions of interpretation might be settled as they arose. Further delay must be avoided at all costs. It has been stated that the Air Commerce Act fostered later confusion between the Post Office Department and the Department of Commerce, not to mention the Interstate Commerce Commission.[70] Subsequent developments have indicated, however, that the entrustment of aeronautical regulatory functions to a particular agency has been a problem attacked several times, with some reservations still held in 1966 by those who gain satisfaction out of tinkering with reorganization schemes. Public Law No. 254, known as the Air Commerce Act, received President Coolidge's approval on May 20, 1926, ten full years after the establishment of NACA, eight years after the first airmail was flown, and nine years after the executive branch had condoned the regulation of air commerce by the federal government.[71]

One compulsory rule included in the act proved to be extremely useful: "It shall be unlawful to navigate any aircraft otherwise than in conformity with air commerce rules."[72] The constitutional basis of the act rests with the famous commerce clause, similar to the approach used by the federal lawmakers in establishing the Interstate Commerce Commission. Other departments or agencies would be called upon to aid in the regulation of aviation through functions already assumed, for example: rules of entry, Treasury; immigration, Labor; meteorology, Agriculture; designation of military airways, War; and research, the Bureau of Standards.[73]

A military reservist, stressing the necessity to regain eminence with European aviation circles, summed up the development this way, "After having invented the airplane, America sidetracked it, and left it in an orphanage hangar. Only when she saw her child on parade, in charge of a foreign nurse within the past year or so, did the mother country grow jealous."[74] The act's importance must be compared with the creation of the Interstate Commerce Commission and the National Good Roads Law.

THE AERONAUTICS BRANCH:
BOON TO BUSINESS

THE FEDERAL VICTORY with the enactment of the Air Commerce Act marked only the initial step in the struggle for control over civil aviation in the United States. Obtaining the goodwill of the public—especially the pilots, mechanics, operators, and manufacturers, all of whom had heretofore represented their vocation unfettered by regulation—loomed as a distinct challenge. Students of history might possibly detect a note of irony when confronted with this extension of federal supervision over a major segment of American industry at this time of general prosperity. Furthermore, President Calvin Coolidge, the rock-ribbed, conservative friend of free enterprise, eschewed to the end of his career in Washington any maneuvers on the part of liberal politicians to enlarge the power and scope of our federal government. Secretary of Commerce Herbert Hoover, holding much the same view of the relationship between business and government, would not be expected to advocate a wide departure from the status quo.[1]

The truth of the matter rests in the simple fact that neither Coolidge nor Hoover expected radical change; the new law was enacted to strengthen and enhance the aviation business more than to hamper, restrict, and dictate policy to this example of private enterprise. Indeed, the Air Commerce Act, not unlike the earlier legislation creating other bureaus within the Department of Commerce, could be envisaged as a "shot in the arm" for industry. After all, private ownership had reigned supreme in all portions of the act; manufacturing airplanes and owning airports would not become federal duties. Moreover, in 1926, rate fixing and the awarding of exclusive operating franchises to airlines, both functions to be assumed later, were hardly conceivable to the majority of the framers of aeronautical regulation. Cautious legislators recoiled from the European example of granting liberal subsidies to the airlines. The American public little realized the existence of a minority of federal officialdom leaning to a more radical approach just prior to the enactment of the Air Commerce Act. Withheld from the public as confidential, the report of a fact-finding body known as the Committee on Civil Aviation in the Department of Commerce, urged widespread governmental support, including cash subsidies.[2] Obviously, the shock from rumors of this proposal helped lead Congress to its conservative legislation, ignoring the advocacy of what became common practice as part of the welfare state in the country as a result of the Great Depression.

THE NEW BATTLE FOR FEDERAL CONTROL

Whatever actual control the federal government would exert over civil aviation lay in two categories. First, the industry must be regulated insofar as standards of safety were concerned, a type of police action provided gratuitously and embracing licensing of aircraft and pilots, lighting of airways, and further periodic inspection. Second, the national authorities would perform a tremendous service to aviation by way of promotional activities which, in general, could nurture the public confidence in aeronautics and, in this manner, raise the status of the industry both financially and in the realm of public service. In reality, the Air Commerce Act simply conformed to the American brand of the economic tradition known as *laissez faire*. In this case, government purported to serve aviation in the role of policeman and promoter; profits, rights of ownership, and other intricacies of the business remained untouched. Survival of the fittest still applied, in 1926, to a scene where hardy operators continued to vie for the airborne traffic, all within the framework of rules intended to aid business and the public.

WILLIAM P. MacCRACKEN, JR.

It would seem only natural to assume that Secretary Hoover and his close associates should turn to friends in aviation circles for help in implementing the intent of the Air Commerce Act. Such was the case in the selection of the leadership for what came to be known as the Aeronautics Branch of the department. William P. MacCracken, Jr., a prime booster of aeronautics since 1917, became the first chief of the new service, officially, as Assistant Secretary of Commerce for Aeronautics. In 1917, MacCracken, though already twenty-eight, had taken his training as a cadet and gained his "wings" within a year at Ellington Field.[3] Immediately after the war, MacCracken returned to his law firm in Chicago, retaining his fervent admiration toward his new avocation (he already had had six years of legal experience prior to America's entry into World War I). Deploring the dearth of interest in aviation among his colleagues, MacCracken finally obtained the enthusiasm of several friends for the theories of George Bogart, Dean of the law school at Cornell University and Chairman of the Conference of Commissioners on State Uniform Law. The latter group held meetings with a new committee of the American Bar Association, MacCracken serving as a member of the committee. Soon MacCracken struck up a friendship with Congressman Samuel E. Winslow and was in the thick of the battle for federal legislation to control civil aviation. In the meantime, MacCracken had performed legal work for a number of private aeronautical firms and for the National Aeronautics Association (NAA), organized during 1922 in Detroit. Three years later, the future assistant secretary was named a cocounselor of the new National Transport Association (NTA) at the instigation of its first president, Howard Coffin of the Hudson Motor Company. The NTA had the responsibility of organizing air traffic over the New York–Chicago leg of the new airways system. Here, MacCracken aided his superiors in obtaining bids and contracts from the Post Office. He also was called to Washington for the numerous hearings conducted by the famous Morrow Board. In 1962, MacCracken reflected on the difficult time confronting the airmail service in those earlier days when the sack often outweighed the letters within it. One registered letter would be carried in a sack with padlock, the sack accounting for approximately 80 per cent of the revenue, which was based on weight of the sack and the mail.[4] The Chicago attorney, then secretary of the American Bar Association, reported that in early August, 1926, he had no inkling of his impending appointment prior to the telephone call from Walter Drake, the Assistant Secretary of Commerce. Modestly asserting that two or three other candidates had been considered previously, MacCracken recalled that he was sworn into office on August 11, and became Acting Secretary on the following day when Hoover, Drake, and Stephan B. Davis all went on vacation. The new appointee felt overwhelmed by the immensity of the task, together with the lack of precedents within the department, but acknowledged the apparent friendliness toward aviation manifested by several colleagues and especially the capable support of Harold Graves, his administrative assistant.

Undoubtedly the choice of MacCracken proved to be an excellent move because of his ensuing cautiousness in inaugurating unprecedented regulations upon an industry which was growing so rapidly.[5] During October, 1926, MacCracken held a series of conferences with representatives of the aviation industry in order to incorporate this group's suggestions into the code of regulations, which was then redrafted and put into effect at the end of the year.

CLARENCE M. YOUNG

Another outstanding personality associated with the department's aviation chores was Clarence M. Young, who was at first Head of Air Regulations and then became Director of Aeronautics officially on July 1, 1927. The relationship between MacCracken and Young proved to be a happy one, hardly that of boss and assistant but more like a team of equals.[6] Young, born in Colfax, Iowa, moved to Des Moines at the age of twelve. He later attended Drake University for two years before completing his legal training at Yale University, whereupon he returned to Des Moines to practice law. Receiving his ground flight training at Urbana, Illinois, the lawyer-aviator reached the war front and participated in bombing raids on Austrian railroads. During one of these raids, his plane was hit by antiaircraft guns, forcing him to crash. He was captured and remained a prisoner of war in Austria for five months. Following World War I, he returned to Des Moines, selling surplus airplanes on the side while encouraging local officials to build an airport. Young had become a good friend of Charles Lindbergh and continued his own interests by taking up passengers and performing as a stunt flier at local fairs. Youthful in appearance, alert, and pleasant, Young avoided giving speeches, while MacCracken loved them. The two lawyers often worked at the office from eight in the morning until late at night. The Iowan, a good friend of Secretary Hoover, shunned politics, though he was extremely popular around Washington, not solely because he was a bachelor and good dancer. Young did not show much excitement over flight for pure glory and was proud of the fact that he had never used a parachute (and did not intend to in the future), despite the thousands of miles he had flown during each year.

Meanwhile, MacCracken planned diligently and methodically the initial regulatory functions of his organization throughout the latter half of 1926. Almost immediately after gaining appointment, he became a natural at the task of promoting aviation, answering all inquiries to his office. MacCracken predicted at the end of August that the new rules would go into effect before the end of the current year, a correct estimate of the actual date, December 31.[7] By mid-September, the Assistant Secretary advised an inquirer that the aircraft inspectors would not be hired until November or December.[8] A military friend in Hawaii was told that the days were not long enough to enable MacCracken and his fellow workers to accomplish their goals.[9] As late as October 11, no airplanes had been authorized for use by employees of the Aeronautics Branch.[10]

EARLY FUNCTIONS

The very first objective in the implementation of the rules rested with the hiring of experienced aviation men as inspectors to work in the field throughout the country. The first of these individuals were already in the field when the regulations went into effect. It remained difficult to obtain enough men who met the qualifications of above-average ability as pilots, suitable personality, and a wide knowledge of the various aircraft and engines. Fifteen experienced inspectors were hired during the initial fiscal year; the goal for the next year was set at an additional thirty-five in order to keep up with the factory output of 100 new airplanes per month, plus the registration and certification of the thousands of airmen and aircraft already in operation before federal regulation.[11] The first official inspection of aircraft was completed on December 7, 1926, by Supervising Inspector R. G. Lockwood within a day after receiving the request to inspect a plane being delivered to Canada. He followed the Canadian schedule of inspection.[12] Lockwood, formerly a pilot in the Royal Air Force, had later served as a civilian test pilot at McCook Field, learning the intricacies of all the army airplanes. A major omission in the appropriations for the initial fiscal year had to do with the lack of traveling expenses for the new inspectors.[13] Furthermore, even after this discrepancy had been eliminated, these key figures in the new regulatory operation often contended with the much slower automobile or train as means of transportation, a source of deep chagrin to the promoters of air travel.[14]

Inspectors began their chores in the field, while another long-sought endeavor was initiated. On December 7, 1926, the first new federal beacon, No. 71, lighted the federal airways 15 miles northeast of Moline, Illinois, on the Chicago–Dallas route. Ten additional beacons soon augmented this advance in the program, and the first night flight along the lighted airway between Chicago and St. Louis, the scene of daring exploits by Charles Lindbergh, took place during the next month.[15]

Acting on the advice of early advocates of federal legislation, MacCracken labored within the restriction of refraining from establishing an entire new bureau within the Department of Commerce. Thus, the total, scattered duties pertaining to civil aviation became known as the Aeronautics Branch. The care of the navigational aids to aviation became the responsibility of the Lighthouse Service. An airway-mapping section worked under the Coast and Geodetic Survey, and scientific research was entrusted to the Aeronautical Research Division of the Bureau of Standards. Only two new divisions were established within the department, those designated to supervise air regulations and air information.[16] This cautious expansion could well be understood when one considers the paltry sum of $550,000 allocated for all functions during this fiscal year. The Air Regulations Division encountered all the complexities involved in the licensing of airmen and aircraft, in addition to the identification of all aircraft through a system of markings. Traffic rules had to be applied on a nationwide scale. Various classes of licenses for both pilots and mechanics were devised, along with the appropriate mental and physical examinations. Leaders of the Aeronautics Branch maintained that aircraft operations in the United States encompassed a wider diversification than in other nations, a trend encouraged by the tremendous war surplus of now rebuilt craft, making the task here even more unprecedented. Immediately, these federal officials recognized also the urgent necessity of advising manufacturers about the airworthiness and suitability of proposed new aircraft before and throughout the actual construction. In the field of inspection, the vital airplanes finally began to arrive at the department late in the fiscal year—only five craft being in operation by June 30, 1927. An unsuccessful effort was made to

adapt these surplus planes of the War and Post Office Departments to use by the Aeronautics Branch.[17] The first plane made
available to the department, a DH, came from the surplus stock
of the Post Office Department. The initial airplane purchased
was a Stinson.[18] New at the time, as was the Cessna, these airplanes could be more easily justified financially than the Ford tri-
motors costing $20,000. A conservative estimate at this moment
indicated that less than one-half the airmen in the nation had
been registered. Only a small portion of the aircraft had been
examined.

FIRST LICENSES

An interesting incident arose over the honor inherent in receiving the first pilot license issued by the department. Secretary
Hoover and Young felt inclined to extend this privilege to Assistant Secretary MacCracken, who, in turn, believed that the
physical examination could be waived in this case in order to issue the license to Orville Wright. Wright graciously declined,
joining Hoover and Young in bestowing the honor on Mac-
Cracken, who took the magic first license while Young earned the
runner-up spot. Several quite prominent aviators took their examinations and obtained low-numbered licenses—Lindbergh,
Phil Love, C. S. Jones, James Doolittle, Amelia Earhart—just to
mention a few.[19] Long before the end of the first year of activity,
certain typical violations became apparent. MacCracken, com-
menting in detail on these discrepancies, mentioned three: equip-
ping the airplane with a type of engine not specified in the certification obtained; remodeling and flying an airplane without having it rerated; and failing to file the proper periodical reports.[20]
The first regulations concerning pilot licenses stipulated an age
minimum of eighteen and United States citizenship for the industrial, limited commercial, and transport categories; the minimum age for the private license was sixteen, with any citizenship
acceptable. Applicants for the transport license needed 100
hours of solo flight, twice the number required for the other classifications. The first flight examinations required a private pilot
to maneuver at 800 feet around two pylons or buoys 1,500 feet
apart, execution of five figure eights, and three satisfactory landings to a full stop. Transport pilots had to land close to a mark,
with and without engine, complete the familiar figure eights, and
demonstrate their ability in sideslips and "emergency stalls,"
among other requirements. Though far from complete by the

summer of 1927, officials of the Air Regulations Division exerted major attention in the following areas of regulation for immediate enforcement: minimum heights, acrobatic flying over congested areas, crossing aircraft, right-of-way, dropping objects from aircraft in flight, weather and distress signals, and lights for night flights.[21] For the purpose of establishing a system to check the physical fitness of pilots, a medical director was appointed, and approximately 200 physicians and surgeons in the nation were designated as medical examiners for the Aeronautics Branch.

A RELUCTANT PUBLIC

Public acceptance of the regulatory and investigatory activities had not materialized. One military official summarized it this way: "There is no popular conception as yet of the scope and potentiality of the Air Commerce Act of 1926."[22] Certainly verification of this observation could be found in a number of instances. Many pilots paid little heed to the new rules, scoffing at this kind of exercise as utterly useless. Indeed, excellent pilots who later continued in their trade for decades found themselves initially taken in by this logic. Karl E. Voelter, later employed by the Federal Aviation Agency as head of disaster relief, recalls his own experience. In 1928, Voelter still flew for hire with passengers in Indiana, of course without a license, because other pilots had advised him not to take the tests and "get tied up with that outfit."[23] At this point, Howard Rough and Harold Neely, both inspectors with the Aeronautics Branch and working out of Detroit, apprehended Voelter, grounding him for two weeks. The young aviator reports that he was "scared as hell" as he studied for the impending exams. Voelter's anxiety was uncalled for as he easily surmounted the rigorous paces. During the flight test, Voelter observed his frightened inspector as the sideslipping to land on the "hanky" was completed accurately. Voelter's debut with the Aeronautics Branch turned out favorably and fostered a lasting respect for this authority by the pilot. Undoubtedly this story could be repeated for numerous other pilots; the theme reflects the gruelling task of finding and testing so many individuals and airplanes in these first years of the new service.

THE AIRWAYS

Issuing licenses and inspecting aircraft occupied a most important function of the Aeronautics Branch, but equally urgent was the task of supervising airways as entrusted to the Bureau of Lighthouses. Here, in fact, some precedents for operation existed. For example, the airways section of the Army Air Corps, already in 1923 under General William Mitchell, began to publish descriptions and sketches of airports in addition to air-marking facilities which happened to be available.[24] This section, under Lieutenant Burdette S. Wright, continued its work, especially for the army "Model Airways" extending from Washington, D.C., westward via Dayton, Chicago, St. Louis, and San Antonio. Tickets were issued for travel, primarily to congressmen and army personnel. Radio facilities of the Signal Corps were used for reservations as well as valuable weather reports and forecasts, the Weather Bureau providing at definite times each day the data on winds aloft which was relayed to the stations on the airways. Several of the employees involved in this work later moved over into the Aeronautics Branch and its successors. Then, too, the celebrated transcontinental airway of the Post Office Department provided an excellent model of operation when it was transferred to the Department of Commerce on June 30, 1927, as specified in the Air Commerce Act.[25] Extending the 2,612 air miles from New York to San Francisco, the airway was equipped with lights, except for the segment from the western terminus to Salt Lake City, and included 17 radio stations, 612 electric and acetylene gas beacons, and 92 intermediate landing fields equipped with beacons and boundary lights. The 146 Post Office employees maintaining the transcontinental line also were transferred to the Department of Commerce. Work on approximately 2,080 miles of lighted airways, excluding the transcontinental, gained top priority throughout early 1927. In fact, $300,000 of the Aeronautics Branch's initial appropriation went toward lighting aids on these airways; additional funds allotted for fiscal 1928 were made available for similar use in February, 1927. Priority routes for lighting were the following: St. Louis–Chicago, Dallas–Chicago, Salt Lake City–Pasco, and Los Angeles–Salt Lake City.

Maintenance operations on the airways were organized under the existing district system in the Lighthouse Service, sixteen licensed pilots and twelve engineers overseeing repairs and inspections. Always a problem because of the immense areas involved, maintenance encompassed personnel working out of strategic centers located, in most cases, on more than one airway, specifically, at Staten Island, Buffalo, Milwaukee, Salt Lake City, and San Francisco. As a case in point, men at Salt Lake City cared for the routes from Omaha to Reno, Salt Lake City to Pasco, and Pueblo to Cheyenne. Elaborate preparations went into the selection and construction of the intermediate fields which covered about 40 acres and were located 30 miles apart between airports, much of this preliminary selection being completed by aerial survey reflecting the best flight country. An ideal site would have sea-level elevation, landing strips about 400 feet wide and not less than 1,800 feet long, with two directions providing four directions for landing. Higher elevations necessitated longer strips to compensate for the lessened air density and reduced engine efficiency. The majority of fields were of an L or T shape, fairly level, with good drainage, clear approaches, and close to highways. In the beginning, federal officials allowed rental fees of $8-to $10 an acre per year for these fields.[26]

The airway beacons, located 10 miles apart and between the intermediate fields, were erected on towers of galvanized steel 50 feet high, with a 24-inch standard revolving light using a 1,000-watt electric lamp and a parabolic mirror. Sun relays or astronomic clocks controlled the lights where commercial electricity was available; elsewhere, caretakers operated a 2-kilowatt engine generator. The Aeronautics Branch rented plots of 15 by 60 feet at the annual rent of $25. Special lights served unusual areas such as buttes and passes. Helping the flier to orient himself were concrete arrows at the base of each tower pointing along the direction of the airway; beacon numbers also helped and were painted in black figures on a chrome-yellow background at the feather end of the concrete arrow or on the roof of the powerhouse.

Lighting at the intermediate fields, that is, beyond the beacon, consisted of white boundary lights 300 feet apart, with green range lights showing the approaches, and red lights placed on all obstructions. As a further aid, the wind cone (providing the direction of the prevailing wind) could be lighted internally to show from the air. Bear in mind, naturally, that all these lighted aids proved effective only when weather conditions permitted the pilot to see the field. Marking of the fields for daylight traffic consisted of a large white circle, 50 feet in diameter, and runway indicators, 20 feet long and 2 feet wide, at the intersection of runways, showing the landing directions. Employing private contractors for the installation, which cost an average of $5,500, the Aeronautics Branch first purchased the towers, beacons, and other equipment. Maintenance of the lighting equipment and the fields proved to be a formidable task performed by the Lighthouse Service, which employed an airway mechanician in charge of each lighted airway. These men used panel trucks and tried to service each field and beacon once a month.

At those fields not on the transcontinental line, all weather messages were sent and received via telephone. Already the United States Weather Bureau had begun to expand greatly its observational and forecasting service to aviation, as dictated by the Air Commerce Act.[27] Hence, twenty-two new upper-air observational stations and fifteen stations already existing provided data twice daily. Likewise, the maintenance personnel at Aeronautics Branch locations where no Weather Bureau officials were present provided local observations.

DEVELOPING THE RADIO

Little headway had been achieved by mid-1927 in the realm of radio-range beacons except for the installation at Hadley Field (New Brunswick), New Jersey, although plans called for another such navigational aid at Cleveland, Ohio. Departmental officials, including Ira Grimshaw, exerted a timely influence on the development of radio as an aid to aviation. Research on the radio came within the jurisdiction of the Bureau of Standards, which primarily made use of a station at College Park, Maryland; the loan of the former station WCAP at Washington, D.C.; and, later, the radio-beacon station at Bellefonte, Pennsylvania. A DH airplane equipped with a 1-kilowatt, radiotelephone transmitting set, provided the basis for test flights in December, 1926. During the next May, contact by radiotelephone to an airplane was maintained for 100 miles during a flight from Washington, D.C., to Detroit. The experts agreed that the directive radio beacon with visual indicator, radiotelephony to airplanes, and the radio-marker beacon were all ready for additional trials.[28] Though not yet perfected, these and other experiments with radio provided several joyous moments during the early months of regulation. Secretary MacCracken recounts his surprise at the office one day when two-way contact had been obtained with a pilot traveling between Baltimore and Washington, D.C.[29] Fortunately, the performance was repeated successfully for representatives of the press who heard MacCracken on this occasion order the pilot to return his Ford trimotor to Bolling Field. This type of experiment, though occurring only sporadically, provided researchers

with an incalculable stimulus, to say nothing of the favorable reaction from the public.

AIR INFORMATION

The second new administrative division within the department, this one having to do with air information, assumed a variety of tasks, all geared to encourage and promote aeronautics.
One of the most important duties involved the publication of a
semimonthly, mimeographed summary of activities known as the
"Domestic Air News," which listed newly licensed pilots and airplanes, new beacons or intermediate fields, location and change
in status of airports, amendments or additions to air regulations,
and short feature stories concerned with aviation. In addition,
this division also began issuing a series of special airway bulletins
(112 in the first fiscal year) of a more technical nature, covering
aerodynamics and other fields as progress was recorded.[30]

A further effort to improve flying through increased public
contacts reflected itself in the area of air mapping, which faced a
great increase in demand at the time. Maps used by the military
were sold as well as the thirty-seven strip flight maps completed
by the department's Coast and Geodetic Survey. Mappers asserted that to do a thorough job, four months would be required
for each map, and, with an increase in manpower, they aimed at
completing the maps for ten more routes within another year.
Small in scale, reading 1:500,000, the maps provided the pilot
with such necessary data as: highways, railroads, streams, and
the side of the road where power lines were located. Maps obviously gave the pilot a valuable tool for determining his location
in cases where the earth remained visible to him. Similarly,
painting of the names of communities or other marks of identification would prove useful and became a long-standing promotional activity of the Air Information Division. One oil company
boosted this program by air-marking most of its stations in ten
states.[31] Public relations in this division encompassed also the
many direct contacts of branch personnel with the aviation industry and necessitated the compilation of a wide range of facts
and statistics for later publication or departmental use.

Not only did the federal authorities encourage the development of additional scheduled airlines in this country, they also
promoted the increase in production and export of airplanes and
engines. A trend in this direction had been apparent during

1925–1926, with the United Kingdom and Russia the chief buyers, each importing over $270,000 worth, the latter case occurring during the period (1917–1933), in which the United States withheld diplomatic recognition from the Soviet Union.[32] The gap in scheduled airline operations between the United States and Europe continued to plague the most enthusiastic American supporters and gained early attention of the Air Information Division. Congressman J. Mayhew Wainwright of New York expressed his concern over the lead held by European countries in the amount of air passenger traffic, between 60,000 and 70,000 per year.[33] In 1926, airlines in the United States carried 5,782 passengers; this figure increased to 8,679 during the next year.[34] This deficiency appeared well on the way to being remedied in the summer of 1927 with the initiation of regular airmail operations between Chicago and San Francisco by the Boeing Air Transport Company. National Air Transport's regular schedule connecting Chicago and New York opened in the fall. Although the Kelly Act was promulgated in 1925, the Post Office Department continued flights of the airmail until September 9, 1927, finally relinquishing the entire field to the competitive bidding of private contractors.[35]

However, the major influx of passenger service had not yet started even though, in 1927, the publicists in the Air Information Division could point proudly to the many encouraging innovations at hand for passenger service and comfort. At least manufacturers had turned to the production of cabin-type aircraft, with upholstered seats and ample leg room, resembling the better automobiles of the day. Pilots in this craft enjoyed a heated cabin and sliding, or hinged, glass windows; safety features, such as brakes on the wheels, oleopneumatic and oleospring gears on the landing gear; the new fuselages of welded steel tubing replacing wood and wire; and a major elimination of fire hazard through use of gear-driven pumps. Other planned innovations featured the trend toward monoplanes, reduction in the weight of the power plant, air-cooled engines, and the use of exhaust manifolds which reduced the noise. Increases in comfort entailed the allowance for greater space in the new transport aircraft of 1927, which carried 600 gallons (3,600 pounds) of gasoline for a trip of 400 miles, not to mention a few hundred additional pounds of passengers and baggage.[36] The famous Dutch engineer, Anthony Fokker, had arrived in 1925 with his large, 3-engine planes with 200 horsepower per engine; a cruising speed of 80 miles per hour; carrying 2 pilots and 6 passengers; and a modest load of mail.[37] Unfortunately for the American aviation industry, high cost remained as a major deterrent to expansion. Just as cost factors checked the American public from purchasing as many airplanes as the manufacturers desired, so the price of air travel, averaging 12 cents per passenger mile in 1926, prevented a major influx of passengers. By 1930, the average rate had been reduced to 8.3 cents.[38] Yet the tantalizing reality of the true benefits of the trade emblazoned itself in the news when one realized that competent fliers could travel from New York to Miami overnight or reach the Golden Gate from New York in just over thirty hours. Fog continued to plague the aviator, but departmental attention had already been focused in this direction, along with the financial support of the Daniel Guggenheim Foundation. During the first six months of 1927, weather caused the vast majority of defaulted trips, specifically, 623 of the 685 failures out of 5,272 scheduled operations.[39]

ACCIDENTS AND SAFETY

Air accidents, though certainly not offering the favorable type of publicity sought, had to be investigated by the Aeronautics Branch with the statistics retained by Air Information. At the outset, the cause of individual accidents was not released to the public for fear of legal implication, but the causes of accidents became a part of later summaries which listed the type of cause, type of aircraft operation involved, and the total number of accidents in the various categories. As a case in point, the first annual report listed 25 fatal accidents during January–June, 1927, for miscellaneous flying (all nonscheduled). Thirteen of these mishaps involved pilot error; 3, power failure; 2, weather conditions; and 7 were attributed to structural failure. Practically all these accidents occurred with unlicensed pilots and uncertified airplanes, killing 15 pilots and 28 passengers.[40] In contrast, only 2 pilots and 1 passenger lost their lives during the same one-half year on operations of the contract routes for airmail; here, 2 accidents caused the fatalities and both were related to adverse weather.

Accidents not involving fatalities also came under the scrutiny of Ernest Jones, Chief of the Air Information Division, as indicated in the incident of September 16, 1926, when Lindbergh abandoned his mail plane on the Chicago–St. Louis route near Ottawa, Illinois, reaching the ground safely by parachute but losing the airplane, which cost $7,500.[41] Jones asked the Post Office officials for details and checked with the Weather Bureau on reports of dense fog at Chicago but clear conditions at Peoria. According to Lindbergh's own account, he jumped only after both the main and reserve fuel tanks had run dry. He had made unsuccessful attempts to land at Maywood, his destination, and he failed to pick up the governmental beacons west of Chicago along the transcontinental route. Without radio, pilots at this time could not learn of fields that were clear once they had started the flight.

Aeronautics Branch officials busied themselves with the mass of details necessary to bring about the regulation of air commerce, as described above. A far more exciting panorama of events within the aeronautical world unveiled itself during these same months to present the average American with a sensational realization of what airmen knew all along—aviation was becoming increasingly safer and would take its place in the ranks of the foremost modes of transport. Aeronautical pioneers risked their lives not only because of mechanical deficiencies but, in rare instances, just to prove that man flying in a machine was not an ill omen released by the gods. British Sir Allen J. Cobham, launching a transworld flight in June, 1926, encountered just such tragic reaction when an Arab fired upon the DeHaviland over Basra, killing Cobham's mechanic, A. B. Elliott.[42] To be sure, Lindbergh and his many fellows were record-seeking pilots who did not start but rather advertised a development already begun in the United States.[43] Nevertheless, the heritage to American and world aviation resulting from transatlantic and other flights in 1927 has been so great that, exaggerated as it may seem, the feats remain. And the new regulators of the Aeronautics Branch followed the pulsating drama, exerting influence and offering suggestions at the proper time in order to assure the country of its prime benefits from such famous exploits.

LINDBERGH PREPARES

The perseverance of "Slim" Lindbergh in his preparation for the successful conquest of the Atlantic represents but a continuation of the daring and skill he displayed as a barnstormer and airmail pilot. That he lost two DH's for his company carrying the mail perhaps caused his fellow pilots and Assistant Secretary of Commerce MacCracken quite a bit of anxiety; nobody, however, who actually knew him would question his flying ability.

MacCracken, though saddened by Lindy's parachute jumps, begged William Robertson not to ground Lindbergh, action which would surely jeopardize the prospects of gaining prize money for competitive flights the next year.[44] Taking risks, to Lindbergh, constituted a natural hazard of flying in this stage of operations. So intent was Lindbergh on completing the New York–Paris trek that he advised the builders of the *Spirit of St. Louis* to fix the landing gear so that it could be dropped in flight, saving weight for longer range. The contest committee of the National Aeronautic Association, administrator of the Orteig prize ($25,000) for the Atlantic hop, ruled against the idea of dropping the landing gear. Lindbergh complied as work continued on his plane in February, 1927, for projected test flights in April. Aviation enthusiasts' pulses quickened as the race widened to include R. E. Byrd, Rene Fonck, Noel Davis, C. Nungesser, and C. D. Chamberlin, among others.

HELPING LINDBERGH

In late April, Young, then Chief of the Air Regulations Division, Aeronautics Branch, arrived in San Diego to inspect the new airplane. A chief inspected his subordinate in this instance as Young, a major, commanded the reserve squadron at Richards Field, Kansas; Lindbergh was a member of the squadron. Impressed, as usual, with Young's dry humor, Lindbergh asked about all the new civil air regulations pertinent to his projected flight, but he could not be sure in all cases exactly when Young was jesting. Young advised the young adventurer that the *Spirit of St. Louis* would be given the license N-X, *N* representing the International Code letter assigned to the United States, *X* standing for exerimental—allowing for various modifications without prior Aeronautics Branch approval. Young saw no difficulty at all in obtaining rapid approval of the airplane. Indeed, airplane license N-X 211 arrived before the fuselage and wings could be assembled.[45] Lindbergh earned a transport license, No. 69.[46] Meanwhile, crashes had slowed the undertakings of competitors Fonck, Byrd, and Floyd Bennett, Chamberlin, Davis, and S. H. Wooster; the Frenchmen Nungesser and F. Coli disappeared attempting a Paris to New York flight. True to its verbal promise, the Ryan Company of San Diego finished the airplane for testing on April 28, which allowed Lindbergh and Donald Hall, the engineer, to spend the next eight days maintaining a careful check of the performance under all types of load conditions and brief flights over the nearby Pacific. There followed Lindbergh's harrowing night flight over the mountains on his journey eastward ending in St. Louis some 14 hours and 25 minutes later, a new record. Upon landing, Lindbergh's associates presented him with an envelope containing his pilot's license (No. 69), jesting that it fit Slim perfectly, right side up or upside down—it did not matter. During the mad rush of preparations in New York prior to takeoff MacCracken flew up to look at the *Spirit of St. Louis.* Immediately, Lindbergh requested permission to fly without navigation lights, here again cutting down on precious weight for fuel. MacCracken granted the favor with the observation that Lindbergh probably would not run into much traffic the way he was going.[47] After this visit, the Aeronuatics Branch retreated to a role of well-wisher or silent partner in this drama, as Lindbergh nervously waited for the opportunity to leave in order to win the race over his two most formidable candidates—now Byrd and Chamberlin, in a Fokker and Bellanca, respectively.

In Washington, D.C., MacCracken received inquiries as to Lindbergh's intentions but replied that he had no knowledge of Lindbergh's plans for the next few weeks.[48] Such was not the story after the first successful, nonstop flight between New York and Paris had been recorded. The Aeronautics Branch took an active part for aviation in the promotional follow-up. To those who suggested that Lindbergh be given a post in the government, MacCracken replied: "There is no position which the government could offer that could in any way compare with the financial rewards offered by private enterprise, even in the field of aeronautics."[49] However, MacCracken rightfully withheld complete and unqualified praise when somebody suggested that the inventor of the *Spirit of St. Louis* should be given a medal: "I can scarcely agree with the sender that the inventor of the *Spirit of St. Louis* is especially worthy of a medal . . . there were other important considerations, as for instance, the earth indicator, compass, navigation instruments, etc., which played their part in helping Captain Lindbergh to ultimately reach his goal."[50]

From then on, one might believe that the Aeronautics Branch had evolved into a lecture and travel bureau, clearing and arranging for many of Lindbergh's personal appearances during the ensuing months after his arrival from Europe. Governmental officials, of course, saw much for jubilation in the gigantic boon to aviation resulting from the solo hop across the Atlantic. No prize or reward could be given from the department, but Secretary MacCracken, upon the suggestion of R. L. Faris, Coast and Geodetic Survey, presented Lindbergh with an autographed proof of the first airways map ever issued to commercial aviation by the government. It covered the airway from Kansas City to Moline, Illinois.[51] More often than not the Aeronautics Branch was asked for autographs from Lindbergh and would cheerfully comply.[52] Performing such services can bring the risk of charges against the government for showing favoritism to one individual or business. MacCracken displayed extreme irritation at allegations in one leading newspaper implying governmental involvement in talks with Lindbergh on the part of industry promoting future air transport lines. MacCracken stated that the story would be harmful to commercial aviation and, in turn, was assured that this would not happen again.[53] Practically all types of business and professional organizations appear in the files of requests for speeches by Lindbergh. In many instances, MacCracken or other department officials would accompany the famed pilot to the gatherings, helping to arrange interviews and satisfying the autograph seekers. Lindbergh seems to have been quite willing to comply with all possible requests, with the exception of dances or balls. MacCracken advised one sponsor of a military ball: "There is not the slightest chance of getting him to attend a Military Ball. He seems to have an unusual horror of dances."[54] There were also a few refusals of a different nature, especially when the schedule became too overburdened.[55] The opening of new airport facilities constituted a natural desire to have Lindbergh present at such dedications, local officials expressed contentment if only they could receive Lindbergh's approval of their future plans for installations.[56] On the historic flight to Mexico in December, 1927, MacCracken again extended his very cordial advice, describing places of interest, adding the suggestion that Lindbergh photograph the Mayan areas, using planes loaned by the Mexican government.[57]

Lindbergh certainly captured the fancy of aviation fans as well as the reporters covering his many public appearances after the "conquest" of the Atlantic and Mexico. One newsman concluded, "Lindy is all right."[58] He quickly added that MacCracken ranked as about the closest friend Colonel Lindbergh had in Washington. Lindbergh's incidental aids to air navigation became numerous, sandwiched in between his long flights, speeches, and other gestures. Prior to his Mexican flight, he gave a helping hand to his old associates at the Curtiss–Robertson

Aircraft Manufacturing Company by flying its men over the St. Louis–Chicago route. Lindbergh aided their efforts in finishing a new strip map of the region by adding his suggestions and revisions for sites to locate beacons and extra fields.[59]

FLYING WITH LINDY

A veritable deluge of requests to fly as passengers with the air hero reached the Aeronautics Branch beginning early in the spring of 1928. Some had to be turned down.[60] Most of the requests seemed to please Lindbergh; he once said, "It would give me great pleasure to carry any of the members of the House of Representatives. . . . It will be possible for me to take from eight to ten passengers at a time."[61] Similar encouragement reached the Senate.[62] Already Secretary MacCracken had assured those interested that Lindbergh would turn the *Spirit of St. Louis* over to the Smithsonian Institution.[63] Families representing all walks of life attempted to get into the same airplane with their idol, congressmen being just as anxious. MacCracken's clerical staff kept busy, not only arranging the rides, but also acknowledging the many notes of thanks afterward. To one congressman, MacCracken replied: "I was pleased . . . and trust that their grandchildren enjoyed their ride with the Colonel."[64] Lindbergh would fly one airplane full of passengers while another airplane was being loaded, maintaining this schedule often from sunup to sundown during March. One old lady waited and waited, using a campstool. Someone stole her stool, but she left the scene in serenity after getting her flight.[65] Precautions were adhered to as all passengers had to wear parachutes; the women must wear short skirts in order to prevent entanglement of the clothing with parts of the air machine. MacCracken later claimed that these rides definitely sold flying to Congress, seeing the Capitol for fifteen minutes with Lindbergh at the controls.

PLAYING POLITICS

Perhaps Lindbergh could be thankful for the assistance of MacCracken and others, for it is claimed that he appeared so shy upon his return from Paris as to brush off an offer of some $50,000 for endorsing products in advertising.[66] The tutelage extended by MacCracken and his associates, however, appeared to produce results for the department in at least one outside activity not related to aviation—partisan politics. Not that this temptation would prove easy to overcome, especially during a presidential election with former Secretary of Commerce Hoover carrying the standard of the Republican party. Late in September, 1928, the Republicans became interested in Lindbergh's stand. As one leader in Minnesota wrote, "I think Smith will carry St. Paul by a considerable vote. Even our strong districts in Minneapolis are showing considerable Smith sentiment. . . . Get Lindbergh to endorse Mr. Hoover. . . . Lindbergh's father was always a Republican until he fell for the Non-partisan gag. . . . Between MacCracken and others . . . it would cinch Minnesota."[67] And to MacCracken, the same politician wrote, "I cannot urge you too strenuously to have Colonel Lindbergh issue an endorsement of Mr. Hoover."[68] MacCracken answered, "I thought your father's suggestion a good one also and had heard something to this effect before. In the meantime the press had carried the announcement of Colonel Lindbergh's endorsement of Mr. Hoover. Thanking you for calling this to my attention. . . ."[69]

The Aeronautics Branch gained valuable outside support for its role in promoting Lindbergh's activities. Daniel and Harry Guggenheim and the National Aeronautic Association all agreed with the government's participation. During Lindbergh's post-Paris trips here a department plane, piloted by Phil Love, usually landed ahead of Lindbergh. MacCracken himself accompanied the young flier on the Ford tour; others from the department did so at other times.[70] It was the Guggenheim interests that had been willing to promote Byrd's Atlantic flight in a Fokker. Then, too, aviation benefited from all the challenges of 1927 (the Atlantic crossings) and from Lindbergh's achievements and the achievements (and even the failures) of all the other competitors. As usual, Lindbergh was accorded the majority of plaudits. But MacCracken knew of Byrd's plans and followed with keen interest his activities. In 1928, Byrd remained in correspondence with the head man at the Aeronautics Branch, advising him of his departures.[71]

MEETING WITH INDUSTRY

Rounding out the magic year 1927, Aeronautics Branch officials arranged a conference with a selected representation from the aviation industry. Thirty-eight leaders attended the initial session on December 1, the delegate lists reading like a "Who's Who of Aeronautics."[72] This first in a long series of such meetings came at a most opportune moment for two reasons. In the first place, basic rules had been placed into effect by the

Aeronautics Branch, which now toiled vigorously to force pilots, mechanics, and manufacturers to obtain licenses for men and airplanes. Now there could be amendments or additions deemed necessary by the industry and the government, discussion of which seemed highly imperative before further regulation should be imposed. MacCracken still argued that public confidence must be nurtured while aviation eliminated the image of the barnstormer as the sole example of modern aviator.[73] A second basic reason for the conference lay in the significant improvement in the public view toward aeronautics as the layman found himself caught up in the tide of excitement over the exploits of Lindbergh, Byrd, Chamberlin, and those accorded less publicity. A minority of pilots felt cool toward further controls or even to a suggested handbook, which was considered on the fifth day of the conference with 300 in attendance. Chamberlin desired to be left alone, expressing fear of possible political control from the Department of Commerce.[74] Certainly many uncertainties lay ahead for the Aeronautics Branch. But the groundwork was completed, the promotional aspect had gained considerable momentum, all without upheaval in the aviation industry.[75]

BRINGING ORDER THROUGH FURTHER CONTROLS

AMERICANS, despite the brief national frenzy emanating from the aeronautical conquests of 1927, displayed for the most part rather casual interest in the development of aviation during the ensuing five years. The layman might concern himself with the fancies of a world without war—witness the pious vision of the Kellogg–Briand Pact—only to see his dream erased in 1931 via the Japanese invasion of Manchuria. If he were too dull in mind to consider foreign relations, there was always the stock market to shock him into the bitter realization that all was not well within the "greatest democracy on earth." And to many of those who could not afford the luxury of the stock market, the traumatic experience of unemployment, coupled with the loss of meager life savings, rendered incomprehensible deeper thoughts of scientific achievement.

HOOVER'S SUPPORT

Against this backdrop ridden with doom, the Aeronautics Branch surmounted its most difficult challenge and forged ahead with programs of advice and control which enabled this country to enter the thirties unsurpassed, in certain aspects, by the aviation in even the most advanced European countries. Politically, the change in administrations bringing Herbert Hoover to the White House merely strengthened, if anything, the position of the Aeronautics Branch. After all, it was Hoover who continually suggested the correct procedures to Calvin Coolidge when it came to aeronautical concerns. The aviation interests were grateful indeed that Coolidge listened to his cabinet member, even though Coolidge is said to have commented, "That man has offered me unsolicited advice for six years, all of it bad."[1] Coolidge's "wonder boy" or "miracle worker" undoubtedly incurred this evaluation from his boss in part for his vigor but also for his political rivalry and easy capture of the Republican presidential nomination in 1928. It is correctly argued that Coolidge proved less interested in the ambitious reforms of his Secretary of Commerce than did Warren Harding.[2]

Consistent leadership of the Aeronautics Branch entailed far more than a sympathetic President; this was plainly evident in the preceding chapter as typified by the personage of William MacCracken, Assistant Secretary of Commerce for Aeronautics. When Hoover assumed his duties as President, MacCracken soon retired to the more lucrative financial rewards of the business world, leaving behind his capable lieutenant, Clarence M. Young, who accepted the promotion to the vacant assistant secretaryship. Young, a warm friend of Hoover, continued to serve most capably in this new capacity until the Democratic landslide took effect in the executive departments during 1933. Because of a continual increase in the number of services performed by the Aeronautics Branch, a major change in leadership occurred in November, 1929, at the next highest level. At that time, three key positions, Director of Air Regulation, Chief Engineer of the Airways Division, and Director of Aeronautic Development were established to aid Major Young.[3] Gilbert G. Budwig became Director of Air Regulation, serving the public in all matters pertaining to licensing and inspection. F. C. Hingsburg took over as Chief Engineer, and aeronautical development was entrusted to Harry H. Blee.[4] Additional positions augmenting the increased operations of the branch during the Hoover administration will be mentioned later with the description of the appropriate activity.

DEPRESSION CUTS

Immediately, a word of caution might be in order since the mention of expansion may give the reader an erroneous impression. The Great Depression, though exacting its toll rather late, did indeed curtail the young organization, beginning in fiscal year 1933. Total appropriations rose from the $550,000 in fiscal 1927 to the peak of $10,362,300 in fiscal 1932, before plunging in 1934 to $7,660,780.[5] Acquiring the necessary money from Congress inevitably constituted a veritable risk for the best of scientific and political minds in Washington, D.C., especially in areas of endeavor still considered by congressmen as frills or dangerous experiments. Aviation encountered a bit of this dilemma at the outset. MacCracken well remembered his earliest encounters on Capitol Hill with Congress and particularly General H. M. Lord at the Bureau of the Budget. MacCracken solved this impasse through his friendship with William Abbott, a former law partner in Chicago, now employed in the Budget Office. The next hurdle proved to be the subcommittee of the House Appropriations Committee where MacCracken at first counted on friends, including George H. Tinkham of Massachusetts.[6] That MacCracken was able to secure fabulous increases in funds each year during the last half of the famed Coolidge economy is a striking tribute to the effectiveness of this midwestern lawyer-aviator. Major Young performed with equal persuasiveness, though not without moments of extreme anxiety. Such was the case in 1929, his inaugural test before the House Subcommittee on Appropriations, when Congressman Milton W. Shreve reminded Young of the ease with which Congress could eliminate $1 million from the proposed figures.[7] Fortunately, the threat died. Depression cuts in personnel were handled by Young in such a manner as to retain his professional staff, cutting some 500–600 part-time caretakers at the intermediate landing fields up to February, 1933.[8] At the time, the branch employed some 2,050 persons in air navigation tasks alone.

LIFE AT HEADQUARTERS

Personnel problems confronted the leadership of the Department of Commerce in connection with aviation as well as other areas. Politicians in the South exerted pressure in Congress to embarrass Secretary Hoover over the racial question in 1928, charging that Hoover brought Negroes out of the basement jobs at the Department of Commerce to allow mixing with other more desirable positions so that he might woo the votes of northern Negroes.[9] Hoover wisely ignored the challenge. Employed in such delicate areas of information, in the true legal sense, branch employees periodically heard their superiors warn against discussing the contents of official communications. Sometimes the news leaks consisted of pure gossip, as in the case when clerks in the mail and files sections received a memo bemoaning the revelation of salary data for married clerks: "If you feel guilty, ask me and I will tell you."[10] Personnel had to be reminded not to use the telephone or telegraph for private messages.[11] Great care was exerted to avoid abusing the franking privileges on the part of employees in their correspondence with the private agencies seeking data on aviation from the department.[12] All types of amusing incidents arose, one involving the opinion that the Department of Commerce could accept holders for pilots' licenses as gifts donated by private concerns. Yet the same holders could not be sent on to the pilots in franked or penalty envelopes.[13] The requests for information from newspaper reporters, friends, relatives, and general gossip-seekers always consumed a large amount of time at the Washington headquarters. Statistics on the past performance of pilots often posed rather difficult decisions, legally and sometimes morally or otherwise, over public release. Finally, policy dictated the issuance of information telling ". . . whether the pilot was denied a license for failure to pass the flight tests or the prescribed theoretical examinations."[14] Furthermore, the public could be told the name of a pilot, his type of license, and the number of solo hours to his credit. As to accidents, only a statistical record went to the public without divulging the pilot's name but permitting the place of the accident to be shown as well as the type of aircraft flown.[15]

Life at the central office in those days had its lighter moments, easily understandable with a total roster of just over 150. There was the time when branch files were scattered along Washington streets, a copy of one application for a pilot license ending up in front of the fire station on Twelfth Street. Someone had broken into the President Theater where the old files had been stored.[16] During the first year or two, license applications reached Washington in such leisurely fashion as to allow for much discussion among the clerks. Watching their "favorites" from the initial application through the inspector's approval, the office girls assigned the easy-to-remember numbers to woman aviators and thrilled as their choices successfully passed "graduation." One official commented, "Sometimes I wonder if the issuing of pilots' licenses will ever become a routine job. I think not."[17] One early applicant wanted to learn to fly by summer so he could make a transcontinental flight.

In Washington as in the field, the paramount concern of the Air Regulation Division evolved around the necessity to widen the activities of the inspection and licensing sections. Budwig replaced Ralph Lockwood as Chief of Inspection in May, 1928. Budwig, a former barnstormer and test pilot for Post Office airplanes, claimed 5,730 hours of flying time.[18] The supervising air inspectors, as they were originally called, controlled all the inspections within their districts with nine districts in the nation. For example, E. A. Cutrell, who was in charge at Chicago, controlled operations in Illinois, Wisconsin, Minnesota, Iowa, South Dakota, and North Dakota.[19] R. H. Lees, Jr., was stationed at Kansas City, from where his men served Missouri, Nebraska, Kansas, and Colorado. Other supervisors included: H. F. Rough, Detroit; Leo Wilson, Atlanta; George Vest, Philadelphia; and W. O. Sargent, Garden City, Long Island. Inspectors, beyond the initial tasks of issuing licenses to the thousands of private pilots, expanded their activities to embrace the supervision of airline operations. At times unknown to the pilot, an inspector took a seat with the passengers during a regular flight while, in other cases, the inspector would sit with the pilot. Airline inspectors, added in 1932, operated from three field headquarters in the nation. In 1929, three types of inspectors served in air regulations: aeronautical, aeronautical engineering, and aeronautical schools inspectors. Then, forty-five men assumed a variety of inspection tasks; fifteen had been assigned to factory inspection. Already, competition with higher salaries in industry caused the branch difficulty in securing enough expert inspectors who were guaranteed one year of work at the outset followed by a probationary period.[20] One early difficulty confronted by inspectors in the field involved the many clerical tasks necessitated by the record files. That inspectors' duties proved important might be easily discerned from the fact that in 1928 only 50 per cent of the aircraft accidents occurred in licensed machines, and in one-third of those checked, the equipment was used contrary to regulations.[21] Working some ten to fifteen hours per day, the average inspector could examine three to four aircraft in that time, all for his annual salary of approximately $4,000. In 1932, the salaries ranged from $2,400 to $4,600.[22] The military in this country maintained its own inspection force, including one man in each factory at all times. All accident investigation fell to the duty of the branch's inspectors. The task of the inspector that proved to be the most dangerous involved the flight test by the applicant for a pilot license. Through 1929, three inspectors lost their lives in this capacity.

POWERFUL INSPECTORS

Stories of unpleasant encounters with early branch inspectors have become legend among veteran aviation officials. Comparing the supreme, if not sometimes tyrannical, authority of the old inspector with the "kid-gloved" approach of the 1960's, one official recalled his youth and the exploits of Inspector Jack Fenner of Chicago. He and other inspectors allegedly would take a license away from a pilot on the spot, sometimes for minor infractions.[23] Then there was the case of an inspector who took out his pocketknife and proceeded to cut and tear the fabric along the wing, saying, "I don't think this is strong enough." One inspector reportedly snorted, "I don't like that plane and I'll tell you why—I just don't like it." Another present official of the Federal Aviation Agency recalls that one inspector told the pilot, "I think you need new struts." Though the owner and others argued that the struts were all right, the airplane remained idle at the field thirty days until the struts were replaced. Undoubtedly, some stories and rumors have waxed brilliantly through the years. But there are apparently too many existing accounts sworn to as evidence to deny that the inspector was feared and respected as he applied the rules of safety from the federal arm of government.

Inspectors decided who should fly and what aircraft achieved airworthiness, basing their findings on the exactations arrived at by colleagues who, along with the inspectors, established the norms for the flight tests and the important written examinations for the aspiring pilots. Through 1928, the rate of rejection averaged 10 per cent, the majority occurring, as surely anticipated, among the student pilot group. The four classes of license were: private, limited commercial, industrial, and transport. Effective December 1, 1929, the branch ruled that it would assume the authority to designate exactly which type of airplane each pilot could use in carrying passengers for hire, definitely a response to the fact that one-half of the accidents investigated showed evidence of pilot error. The licensing and inspecting procedures entailed a continual reexamination of pilots. In 1932, about one-half of all pilots renewed their licenses every six months, the rest once yearly, in all cases at no additional cost to the government for the physicals.[24] By the spring of 1932, it was estimated that fully 80 per cent of the nation's 10,000 airplanes had been licensed. The backlog of license applications plagued inspectors. For the year ending on June 30, 1928, some 3,000 licenses each had been issued to pilots and mechanics, while only 2,000 of some 4,700 applications for airplanes were completed. In addition, 4,000 students received permits during the fiscal year. Personnel in the licensing section increased from 10 in 1927 to 25 a year later. Inspection and licensing stood within 30 days of being current in the summer of 1928, a vast improvement over the 6-month backlog one year before. In fiscal 1929, the licensing chores doubled because of natural growth and more rigid examinations. Student applications increased by 477 per cent, and renewals in all classes increased almost threefold to 42,000 licenses—transfers and renewals accounting for 29 per cent of the section's work. Depression cuts forced the reduction of the inspector force by six. But a new service, the inspection of flying schools, was added. The Air Regulation Division was continually handicapped by the problems of transportation, often assigning four inspectors per available plane. In 1931, the airline inspection force was organized into crews of two inspectors and one maintenance inspector each and located at New York, Chicago, Dallas, and Los Angeles. Another innovation placed four engineering bases for flight testing at New York, Detroit, Kansas City, and Los Angeles. By 1932, all interstate schedules of the air passenger lines had been analyzed by the Branch's inspectors who recommended a number of changes in the basic regulations.[25] Aviation enthusiasts could keep track of the growing number of licensed pilots through the pages of the "Domestic Air News." Ninety-five per cent of the civilian pilots applying in fiscal 1928 qualified for some class of license, as measured by the physical standards of the exams.[26] All licensed planes in the United States were required to affix the letter N on the wings and rudder, the N standing for this country. Additional letters also painted on the airplane stood for: S, solely for governmental purpose; C, commercial license, except for gliders; X, solely for experimental work; G, licensed gliders; R, for restricted purposes.[27]

THE LICENSE

The procedure for obtaining a pilot license involved much paper work and rigorous tests, if implemented correctly by the federal personnel. Application forms included the familiar question about one's race. If the aviator desired a private pilot license, he should have sturdy heart, lungs, and kidneys, among other physical attributes, in order to pass the physical examina-

tion. His flight test required: three satisfactory landings to a
full stop; a series of three gentle and three moderately steep
figure-eight turns; a spiral in one direction from 2,000 feet with
the engine throttled, landing in normal landing attitude by
wheels touching the ground in front of and within 500 feet of a
line designated by the examiner. Spin tests for light aircraft were
no longer obligatory.

More stringent procedures confronted the transport and
industrial pilot who after performing the same maneuvers as
the private licensee, must also complete the following:

> From 1,500 feet, with engine throttled, a 360-degree turn, fol-
> lowed by a landing in normal landing attitude, with wheels
> touching ground in front of and within 200 feet of a line desig-
> nated by the examiner; from 1,000 feet . . . a 180-degree turn,
> followed by a landing . . .; a series of three gentle and three
> steep figure-eight turns, and 720-degree steep power turns in
> both directions. A spiral in one direction from 2,000 feet . . .
> emergency maneuvers, such as spins, spirals, sideslips, climb-
> ing turns, and recovery from stalls . . . and a flight over a tri-
> angular or rectangular course at least 100 miles in length, ended
> by a landing at the place of take-off within five hours from the
> beginning of the flight. This flight shall include two obligatory
> landings, not at point of departure, when the craft must come
> to rest. Upon the presentation of satisfactory proof that the can-
> didate has made solo cross-country flights over . . . at least 100
> miles within one year preceding . . . his application, this flight
> will be omitted. In addition the applicant will be required to
> make cross-wind landings and take-offs.[28]

In case of failure, applicants were allowed to reapply within
ninety days for the transport and industrial classes, forty-five
days later for the private and glider licenses. The problems of
the glider confronted branch officials as they issued licenses for
this popular craft. Three classes of license for gliders were:
student, noncommercial, and commercial. For the latter type,
flight tests stressed general and moderate banks, 360-degree
turns, and precision landings.[29]

Written examinations, another hurdle confronting all pilot
applicants, varied, too, in difficulty according to the class of
license. Early in the life of the Aeronautics Branch, sample
questions were published for the benefit of the new learner or
the veteran unlicensed pilot. A summary of April, 1930, is
typical of these helpful aids.

How do you recover from a tail spin? How do you tell when a ship is about to spin? State the possible causes for the following: Nose heaviness, left wing heaviness, excessive vibration. Name three causes for a loss of oil pressure. What is the minimum altitude in flying over a football game? Your compass course is 274 degrees, the deviation is 4 degrees west, the variation 3 degrees west. What is your true course? How would you know if the wind shifted while you were flying a compass course from one town to another? How do you 'track' a propellor? What is the international radio distress signal? What is the rule regarding overtaking aircraft? Name the four basic types of clouds. Why is it dangerous to fly close to thunderheads? What causes bumpy air? Define: stagger wire, thimble, turtle back, walking beam, routed spar. What method is used to protect the inside of steel tubing in a fuselage against rust? Name four reasons for an air-cooled motor to overheat, the lubrication system functioning perfectly? What are convection currents? How many coats of dope should be applied to the fabric of a newly covered wing? May an unlicensed pilot in an unlicensed ship carry pay passengers from one state to another?[30]

Over 250 such questions had been compiled for use, assuring a frequent change in the exact questions for any one group of applicants.

MEDICAL EXAMINATIONS

The other major factor contributing to the success or failure of the applicant had to do with the physical examination. Here, as related in the previous chapter, the branch immediately hired medical experts at the central office to organize the necessary corps of medical doctors throughout the nation to examine all applicants for pilot licenses. Here in the Medical Section of the Air Regulation Division, the standards of proper fitness were changed from time to time as new research revealed physical defects which possibly contributed to air tragedies. Careful attention went into the selection of these cooperating doctors. Medical Section personnel interviewed approximately 200 physicians during fiscal 1928. In that year, 366 medical examiners completed 12,188 physical examinations, including 6,567 trained pilots, 1,242 reexaminations, and 4,379 students. Considerable difficulty was encountered within the next year as physical examinations increased by 250 per cent; the number of examiners was almost doubled. In December, 1928, thirty-five of the doctors attended a conference at Washington, D.C., at their own expense, and a conference was held the next year in conjunction with the annual meeting of the American Medical Association at Portland, Oregon. The branch's medical director attended the First International Conference on Sanitary Aviation, held during May, 1929, in Paris. On the same trip, he consulted with his counterparts in aviation regulation in England, Germany, and Italy. Because of the continued occurrence of accidents (many attributed to pilot error), the Medical Section requested tougher examinations in fiscal 1930, including a most stringent reduction in the number of exceptions, or waivers, granted to applicants. Within a year, the Medical Section had caught up with its backlog of work and turned further attention to research on the relation of physical defects to the causes of air accidents.[31] Preliminary studies already reflected the fact that existing physical deficiences hampered pilots and student applicants later. In September, 1931, the Medical Section reported that in 4,227 accidents studied, physical defects in the pilots were considered in 17 per cent of the mishaps. It was estimated that 7 per cent of the current transport pilots had some physical defects; this type of pilot being involved in almost 12 per cent of the fatal accidents studied. Approximately 16 per cent of student applicants had physical defects; often vision was from 20/40 to 20/50.[32] Officials proudly reviewed fiscal year 1932, which showed possible physical defects as involved in only one airplane accident.

Standards of vision constituted one of the most crucial areas of concern among the medical experts. Often the examiners checked pilots only to find the wrong correction used in the goggles. Assistant Secretary Young warned pilots, especially the beginning students, that the lowest vision allowed in either or both eyes without correcting lenses was 20/50. If goggles were used, the correction had to be ground into the lenses. Eyesight requirements were liberalized for student and private classes in October, 1931, to permit acceptance of the applicant whose vision showed correction to 20/30 or better with glasses or goggles, in addition to requiring depth perception of more than 30 millimeters. The branch received 473 applications from students affected by this change, 63 of these later advancing to private-pilot status.

Ocular imbalance, general physical defects, poor neuropsychic makeup, paralysis of various types and degree, and stiff joints constituted the majority of deficiencies accounting for the rejection of pilots. Of all the newcomers, approximately 31 per cent who were considered physically fit obtained their licenses (private class or better) within one year. As to frequency of physicals, Young pointed out to federal senators that twice a year was not too often; some private companies required more frequent physical checks on employees. No formal educational requirements had been prescribed for the pilot license, but officials contended that a considerable degree of intelligence was necessary in order to pass the written flight tests.[33]

As demonstrated frequently in the past, "Not all who wish can fly." Good eyes, nervous stability, quick reaction and coordination composed the major prerequisites, "literally to see out of the corner of his eye."[34] Experts said that the ear was not as important to flying as formerly thought. Another differentiation was of prime note—the fainters and the nonfainters—with classifications of ability varying with heights of flight. One group reasoned that some persons could perform well without oxygen at 8,000 feet, some at 15,000 feet. Use of oxygen would allow survival at heights of 40,000–45,000 feet, according to the theorists of 1927; interesting conclusions, indeed, for the participants in the space age of the 1960's. At any rate, the "flight surgeons" at the outset of federal regulation served brilliantly to provide this nation with pilots who could be considered physically able.

ENFORCING THE RULES

Enforcement of the Civil Air Regulations rested with the Secretary of Commerce, as detailed in the Air Commerce Act. During the first year of regulation, a vast majority of violations could be dealt with by simple reprimand, specifically, in 121 instances out of violations totaling 224 for the year. More serious were the following results applied: 65 civil penalties, 22 suspensions, 2 revocations, and 5 denials of pending licenses. Chief among the types of violations figuring in the cases were: (a) acrobatics over prohibited areas, (b) flying low over congested areas, (c) flying licensed aircraft without a pilot's license, (d) flying aircraft without identification numbers, and (e) flying aircraft without navigation lights or other required equipment. Cooperative meetings of aviation and governmental employees provided occasional forums seeking to alleviate the burden of violations. Leading these efforts were representatives of insurance companies covering private pilots, the National Advisory Committee for Aeronautics, the Federal Patents Committee, and the newly appointed Accident Board within the Aeronautics Branch. The problem of enforcement proved to be a most tenuous undertaking since pilots and aircraft were not always to blame for the rising volume of public complaints. Especially true were the instances of low flying, many of which entailed only the necessity of executing a landing or takeoff within the pertinent rules. In fiscal 1929, violations totaled 493, with the collection of fines in the amount of $4,525, necessitating 6 public hearings and 12 cases referred to the Department of Justice for further prosecution. Over 40 per cent of the violations for the next fiscal year involved acrobatics or low flying.[35] As the total number of violations increased, it appeared that more penalties and fewer reprimands resulted. Popular young pilots, sometimes those who later built tremendous reputations and exerted dramatic and beneficial influence on American aviation, faced the embarrassment of some type of civil penalty. James Doolittle fit into this category as he paid a fine of $100 in 1930 for ". . . violating the Air Traffic Rules by acrobatically flying an aircraft over an established airport and violating the Air Traffic Rules by acrobatically flying an aircraft elsewhere at a height under 1500 feet."[36] The fine was mailed to the Secretary of Commerce following the collision of his plane with an army plane whose pilot had bailed out. Another important task falling to the Enforcement Section carried an international responsibility because this section, in conjunction with the Department of State, arranged all foreign visits of United States aircraft.[37] Advice and data were also collected for the International Committee of Technical Aerial Legal Experts. Numerous violators expressed ignorance of the rules, hardly a valid excuse. Continually the branch issued clarification of its rulings, for instance, that unlicensed pilots could fly unlicensed craft for pleasure—intrastate or interstate—and could carry passengers and cargo for hire if only in intrastate flying. But an unlicensed pilot under no circumstances could fly a licensed airplane, not even for pleasure. The need for strict obedience of all air traffic rules was stressed on many occasions in the "Domestic Air News" and its successor, the *Air Commerce Bulletin*, complete with diagrams and descriptions of the appropriate procedures in various situations and locations. A persistent source of irritation to the Enforcement Section and other branch officialdom was the failure of airmen to report all forced landings.[38]

TESTING ENGINES AND AIRCRAFT

Though its checking of aircraft was completed by members of the Inspection Section, still another facet of the Air Regulation

Division—the Engineering Section—drew up the regulations pertaining to all new aircraft and parts. Basically, the goal uppermost in mind embraced the question of airworthiness when the airplane left the factory. Specific procedure included: (a) analysis of the manufacturer's drawings which included stress analysis, (b) inspection of the materials to be used in the construction, (c) later examination of the airplane to see if all specifications of construction had been followed, and (d) determination of maneuverability and other flying qualities. At once, branch authorities realized a difficulty in finding competent aeronautical engineers because of the newness of the industry. Furthermore, those who could be interested often held strong biases that prevented a genuine test of all innovations. When a company's product passed all four tests, a certificate was issued by the Aeronautics Branch; this procedure applied to aircraft, engines, and propellers. To facilitate matters, the branch published, in 1927, *A Handbook for Airplane Designers*.[39] Nine approved-type certificates were issued during the first year of control, followed by 38 in fiscal 1928. Tremendous impetus the next year caused a deluge of testing in the Engineering Section with a backlog of several weeks. Employment of university professors in the summer helped expedite the testing of stress analysis. All major new inventions in aviation brought added chores to the section, such as the case in 1931, when the autogiro gained approval. Constant attention was given to the problem of speeding production without detracting from maximum efficiency.

Definite rules of procedure applied to manufacturers asking for approval of aircraft, the following rules reflecting several types of warning offered:

(1) Hard wire should not be used for the control systems.

(2) All fittings must have adequate protective covering.

(3) Watch particularly for longitudinal balance—against nose or tail heaviness—and lateral balance—no wing heaviness.

Directional balance existed when no foot pressure was necessary on the rudder bar or pedals to keep the plane directionally set at cruising speed. Flight tests for all phases of operation were conducted at 90 per cent of the rated engine speed and under all power and load conditions. The airworthy plane would return to straight flight after "disturbed" if it were directionally stable. Methods to use for the approval of engines and propellers were described. Further revisions and amendments were added from time to time, outlined in *Bulletin* 7-A, issued in August, 1932. For example, the service ceiling was defined for transport aircraft as the altitude at which the maximum rate of climb of the fully loaded airplane is 100 feet per minute.[40] Copilots did not have to be checked out on the type ship they operated, but the federal inspectors offered such help if needed.[41] Members of the Engineering Section examined all aircraft implicated in accidents thought to have been caused by structural defects.

Rigorous tests were applied to all engines sent to the department for approval. The actual testing operations took place at installations owned by the Army, Navy, and the Bureau of Standards, one engine of each new type being scrutinized in a fifty-hour test. The backlog of testing proved embarrassing in December, 1928; new airplanes already approved could not be used until the engines proved their worthiness. Congressmen were assured that this nation did not need the standardization of engine design as a way out of the dilemma. Actually, the detailed methods used in engine testing appeared to be quite efficient; the large amount of time necessitated for complete observation of one engine caused the serious delay. For example, a stopwatch could be employed in obtaining the time required for consumption of five pounds of fuel. In one typical year, the Bureau of Standards expended $50,000 on engine testing.[42] The three torque-stand testing units, located at Arlington, completed 52 checks in fiscal 1930, 26 engines succeeding, 23 failing, and 3 being withdrawn. The commonest failures reported were: the crankcase, crankshaft, cylinders, piston seizures, and exhaust valves. Failures continued to run high among the new types of engine, but even then, governmental experts pondered the merits of increasing the severity of their tests. The Army Air Corps would not accept engines unless they passed a 100-hour endurance check, at least 50 hours of it at full throttle. Meanwhile, in fiscal 1931, 5 of 32 new engines tested for the branch were wrecked before completing 5 of the required 50 hours; over 50 per cent of those tested in the next year failed.[43]

FLYING SCHOOLS

Granting licenses to pilots and mechanics, in addition to the awarding of type certificates for airplanes, could be aided somewhat if the original instruction given to new student pilots were kept at a commendable level. Essentially, this problem touched upon the rapid increase of flying schools in the country and began right after World War I, but no solution appeared until after many tragic lessons of reality struck home. One flying-school promoter lied about his previous experience, was convicted, and sent to jail in 1927.[44] Advertisements representative of some of the questionable schools offered the complete course of ten hours for only $100. Colonel Charles Lindbergh, in warning against such methods, reminded aviation adherents that the military required 300 hours of instruction.[45] Officials considered the situation alarming in early 1929, as the branch moved to impose greater controls. Only two flying schools existed in 1926; by February, 1929, some 250 enterprises lured the unsuspecting public, both good and inadequate types of schools included.[46] On February 28, 1929, an amendment to the Air Commerce Act, promoted by Senator Hiram Bingham, became law. It provided the Aeronautics Branch with definite authority to inspect and regulate the instruction and equipment of the flying schools. Schools would then be rated after their voluntary submission to the examination of the federal authorities. Various regulations soon appeared. For example, never could more than 10 airplanes be used for instruction per 100 acres of area. Within less than a year, over forty flying schools met with approval.[47]

By no means did all of the activity in the Air Regulation Division come to be directed toward issuing licenses and certificates and seeking out offenders. Much effort was extended to apprise airmen of the current rules and regulations, as well as to offer helpful hints designed to avoid accidents and generally improve the nation's air service to the public. Safe altitude figured as one of the foremost concerns, with early recognition of 500 feet as the absolute minimum, except for landing and takeoff. Stunt flying must be conducted at a minimum altitude of 1,500 feet above the ground.[48] Pleading for the control of stunt flying, the influential Colonel Lindbergh saw the need for a "Society for the Prevention of Cruelty to Airplanes," alleging that air accidents were usually caused by stunts or general inexperience, especially reflecting itself in the tragic urge to take up friends.[49]

THE AMATEURS

Two deaths in as many months in 1930 caused a prohibition against the towing of gliders by other aircraft without permission. The problem of gliders and the multitude of incompetent amateurs attempting to use them plagued the branch which, to be sure, recognized the need of trained glider pilots for national defense as well as for pleasure. The first type of glider met branch approval the next summer with a *G* letter and number provided. Immediately, licenses for glider pilots were issued, the first to Young and the next one to Budwig, Director of Air Regulation, while forty-six others gained licenses, all of the commercial type.[50] Youngsters often attempted to catapult the glider off the ground or used other improper methods. Deficiencies accruing through several years of regulation caused the branch in 1932 to propose the following list of requirements for airplanes during daytime: an instrument to show the degree of bank and turn, compass adequately damped, airspeed indicator, climb indicator, suitable altimeter or other instrument for altitude, free air thermometer, accurate clock or watch, complete set of engine instructions, all accessories listed in *Bulletin 7-A*, ash containers for smoking, and maps showing 75 miles beyond and on each side of the route with all navigational aids listed. Furthermore, a waiver of the 500-foot minimum altitude would be considered where 2 miles of visibility was present in the daytime; if sight between beacons existed at night; or if directional radio were in operation. All the foregoing exceptions were conditioned on appropriate local terrain.[51]

AIRSPACE AND JUMPERS

Restrictions of airspace gained serious attention at an early date; President Hoover reserved airspace over seven harbors in the United States and its possessions.[52] In 1931, a minimum altitude of 1,000 feet was decreed for aircraft flying over federal or state penal institutions. Airplanes landing and taking off from beaches caused the branch to remind pilots of the urgency of warning the public by the use of flags, signs, or other means. One pilot caused a flock of wild geese to scatter, the result of which brought a stern reminder from both the Department of Agriculture and the Aeronautics Branch that this action constituted several violations.[53]

The art of parachute jumping caught the imagination of both the adventurer and his public audience, presenting the Aeronautics Branch and its successors with many unpleasant incidents, when something went wrong. Should the drop endanger life or injure property, the responsibility rested with the pilot and parachute jumper.[54] Effective on August 1, 1930, an auxiliary parachute was also required. No further rules covered this operation; permission from the Aeronautics Branch was not necessary. Parachutes were inspected and awarded certificates of approval by the Aeronautics Branch, also effective during the summer of 1930. Jumping was declared illegal over congested areas; over any open-air assembly of people; over any established airway, landing field, or within 1,000 feet horizontally thereof. And the chute must open at a height of at least 1,500 feet.[55] Special occasions came under the category of space restrictions, such as in 1932 when flight below 1,000 feet over Los Angeles was prohibited and no flights over the Olympic games village were permitted. Similarly, prohibitions applied on March 4, 1933, when the District of Columbia became a restricted area from 9:00 A.M. to 5:00 P.M. during the inauguration of President Franklin D. Roosevelt.[56]

CONTROL OF TRAFFIC

Airway traffic control, another area of utmost urgency to the maintenance of safety in American aviation, remained outside the scope of federal control until well into the first administration of Franklin Roosevelt. In fact, the system of control here was instigated by private enterprise. The British led the world in airway traffic control, the field at Croydon—the London airport— serving as the model.[57] Already in 1928, a system of signal lights had been devised to replace the old procedure of hand signals. In contrast, at Chicago where seventy to eighty daily landings and takeoffs were recorded, three signalmen were on duty between 6:00 A.M. and 9:00 P.M. Using three flags, the "traffic cop" stood in the middle of the x-shaped runways giving his messages. The "green-go" sign was given by a blue and white striped flag, the red flag meant "stop", while a white flag pointed to the runway that was in use. All other traffic gave precedence to airplanes carrying mail, except for ships in distress. At this time, federal rules specified that pilots must land "up the wind." Even then, aviation leaders pondered means to avoid future airport congestion. The Secretary of Commerce issued uniform field rules in 1929, and the City of Cleveland initiated its own system of air traffic control in 1931.[58]

The new projector, or gun as it became known, was available for air traffic control by 1931, with its candlepower allowing the pilot to discern between the red or green light up to 6 to 8 miles on a clear day.[59] Airmen could learn of the existing local rules at various American airports from the pages of the "Domestic Air News" and the *Air Commerce Bulletin*. For example, in 1928, rules for St. Joseph, Missouri, indicated that after take-off from north and south runways, a left turn was required; the right was obligatory if taking off from the south and west runways. Mail planes had the right-of-way over all traffic, and stunting or low flying was prohibited over the airport.[60] Pilots found these instructions absolutely imperative in order to comply with regulations and to insure their own safety. Unhappily, terrain and other factors prevented national uniformity in turns following takeoff and other procedures.

TIPS TO PILOTS

Watching aviators during inspection and reading about countless other situations led officials of the branch to arrive at a number of conclusions in the form of general advice. One difficulty, they found, rested with the reluctance of pilots to trust their flight instruments as against their own physical reactions and inclinations (according to one pilot's theory as explained to Assistant Secretary MacCracken).[61] The worst offense seemed to be the failure to trust direction in temporary blind flying, a defect resulting from the human ear misinforming the brain. Another difficulty was sensed by a former Bulgarian pilot, who advised fellow airmen never to turn back when the engine quit as it could produce a disastrous stall from the loss of power.[62] Troubles on takeoff occurred frequently enough for inspectors to recommend a series of procedures to follow:

(1) Check gas and oil levels, the safety belt—not too tight.

(2) Use all traditional checks—signal switch off and contact—and use wheel blocks.

(3) Warm engine gradually then throttle wide open, checking fuel pressure to be sure that all valves are wide open.

(4) Check mixture control position, that of the radiator and cowling shutters, and the carburetor heaters.

(5) Set the stabilizer for balance at cruising speed.

(6) Last precaution—move the control stick and rudder. In taxiing, avoid intermittent bursts of throttle and check again at full throttle upon stopping in order to detect possible "fouled" plugs. Then glance at the ailerons to see that they are in neutral position.

(7) The next step involved the only time that pressure was considered necessary on the control stick, raising the

tail of the plane gradually by forward pressure on the stick.

(8) Great care had to be exerted in maintaining a level attitude until flying speed was attained. Inexperienced pilots often allowed the plane to drift across wind instead of holding the plane into the wind.

(9) On bad surfaces—mud, plowed fields, high grass, or snow—the pilot must hold the tail down to prevent nosing over, after first letting some air out of the tires.

(10) Stalls often occurred from attempting to become airborne too rapidly.

(11) Once, poor judgment occurred when a pilot's engine worked satisfactorily but he failed to use enough speed to rise into the air, because of the dead air at that field's altitude of 3,000 feet.

(12) If the engine fails, land straight ahead.

(13) Loss of 200–500 feet is common in recovery from a spin.

(14) Several pilots forgot the technique to use in recovery from a spin, neutralizing the elevator and rudder controls.

(15) Others caused accidents by executing too steep banks.

(16) Careful attention must be given to air commerce regulations when splicing aircraft cable.[63]

Faults in landing approaches also figured in the advice provided by governmental experts. For example, a common error involved gliding too slowly or too rapidly, while in other cases pilots failed to allow for drifting. In situations calling for spot landings, the pilot must land directly into the wind. When cross-wind landings were necessary, the plane should be crabbed into the wind or a wing dropped into the wind. Other pilots encountered difficulties with sideslips from which recovery is made by applying the bottom rudder and, as the nose drops, the low wing is lifted by use of the aileron control. The plane is banked with the nose level or slightly above level, and the opposite or top rudder is applied. Too many pilots overlooked the fact that a plane loses altitude quite rapidly when sliding down in a sidewise attitude.[64] Not all the pointers offered fliers had to do with mechanical and technical problems, for pilots even received a warning against dropping burning cigarets or cigars—a violation of the air commerce rules. Furthermore, brush fires had apparently originated from such action.[65]

INVESTIGATING ACCIDENTS

The investigation of air accidents fell to the Aeronautics Branch under the specifications of the Air Commerce Act, although a special unit, the Accident Board, was not added to the branch until the spring of 1928. Meeting at first only on one-half day each week, members from the start received accident reports at the rate of twice the number they could process.[66] Assigned to these duties were a flight surgeon, two pilots, a lawyer specializing in air law, and an aeronautical engineer. Three members sat with representatives of the Army Air Corps and Naval Air Service as a subcommittee of the National Advisory Committee for Aeronautics. Immediately, pressure from insurance companies, airplane manufacturers, airline operators, and others involved in accidents bore heavily on this exacting type of operation which, to be effective, must be entirely free of outside influence. The initial reaction within the branch embodied an extremely cautious approach whereby as little information as possible would be forthcoming insofar as any single accident was concerned. Bearing this in mind, it would be impossible to report any percentage valuation assigned to the various contributory causes of an accident. This policy met spirited protest in some quarters but withstood efforts in Congress, in 1929, to force the Secretary of Commerce to publish the cause of each accident.[67] Two accidents prompted senatorial action. One tragedy occurred when an unlicensed pilot took a licensed plane without permission and later crashed, killing his two passengers. The second involved the crash of a transport into Mount Taylor, New Mexico, during a severe thunderstorm. A year later, Senator Sam G. Bratton of New Mexico offered a bill which would have transferred regulation of aeronautics to the Interstate Commerce Commission and would force the publication of the causes of air accidents.[68] Several other bills asked for similar action, all of which were opposed by Senator Bingham, the long-time friend of the Aeronautics Branch. Attorney General William D. Mitchell condoned the interpretation of the Air Commerce Act's authority by the department, adding that the real purpose of the outcry for public announcement rested with the hope for aiding litigants, a move which could hamper unbiased opinions of accident investigators.[69] Bratton's resolution passed the Senate, 42 to 23; a report to the Senate was recorded a year later.[70] Yet, the branch policy remained unchanged. In reality, no policy would please everyone; criticism reached the department against the publication of causes of accidents in general without mention of individual cases. Especially irritating to the ears of other pilots or to those aviators involved who survived a crash, were charges of pilot error. Assistant Secretary Young let it be known, too, that weather played a major role in a majority of accidents. Fires in the air were considered rare and seemed to be decreasing in number.[71] Branch investigators did not look into military crashes, as NACA and the military employed their own specialists. One forward-looking measure was instigated in 1928 with the joint military-civilian use of a single form for accident reports. At one point congressmen questioned the testing of airplanes in a dive with the throttle wide open as practiced by the military inspectors, one plane crashing because its wings fell off. Branch officials indicated they did not require this test, that is, with the throttle wide open.[72]

Whenever accidents occurred in these early days, the question of the need for parachutes inevitably arose. The Army required use of parachutes; the Navy made it optional. Civil air regulations held that acrobatics alone necessitated use of parachutes because, as Young viewed it, reliable engines, suitable airways, and competent pilots eliminated the need.[73] If the pilot and other crew members performed well in avoiding major catastrophe, the Accident Board quickly acknowledged this feat, as in the case in February, 1933, at Bakersfield, California, when a Trans World Airways plane was landed while aflame.[74]

During 1930, the Accident Board established a threefold classification of investigation:

(1) Accident, including fatalities or severe injuries or major property damage.

(2) Mishap—little damage and no severe injuries. For this category, no inspection of repairs was necessary before further use of the equipment.

(3) No accident—difficulties encountered while not in flight.[75]

All accidents resulting in death or serious injury were investigated personally by a branch official; many of the others could be scrutinized via correspondence. Structural defects, common in accidents during earlier years, produced fewer difficulties but still plagued the industry. Manufacturers were advised by the branch that, where failures occurred, faulty landing gears caused 77 per cent of the trouble.[76] Shock absorber units needed greater attention, and propeller blades should be checked against any abrupt change in cross section. Failures in airplane design, detected long after satisfactory inspection failed to reveal such errors, always forced perplexing decisions. Young faced one such dilemma in April, 1931, and decided to ground the other thirty-six airplanes similar to the one which crashed killing the popular Knute Rockne, football coach at Notre Dame University. A wing had been ripped off the plane, which had been approved by the branch inspectors.[77]

DEBATING ECONOMIC CONTROL

Issuing licenses, enforcing regulations, and investigating accidents all fell within the jurisdiction of official duties performed by the Aeronautics Branch. During the Hoover Administration, efforts were extended to force passenger rate controls or other forms of economic regulation. Economic regulation had been considered previously, for Young was asked his opinion of the matter in March, 1932, before a Senate subcommittee. Young felt that such action would be premature but hoped that if such regulation ever materialized the Interstate Commerce Commission would perform the rate fixing.[78] Airmail rates, one facet of federal control over aviation, existed but remained within the province of the Post Office Department. Priority of mail-carrying planes has already been mentioned. Indeed, congressmen, on the way to the air races at Los Angeles, attested to once having to give up seats to mail sacks in the middle of the night at Omaha.[79] As to rates paid for carrying mail, President Hoover lamented that this field of control had been much neglected under his predecessors, Postmaster General Harry S. New assuming the attitude that all that mattered under law was the delivery of the mail. Consequently, scores of transport companies sprang up, operating short or long segments on the airways. Hoover declared, "We were threatened with a permanent muddle such as had resulted from our chaotic railway development. . . ."[80] Hoover scored the exorbitant profits made by certain operators, as some contracts ran to $3 per mile, while great speculation existed in the securities of certain aviation companies. The incentive to add passenger service could hardly be expected to emerge when business confined to airmail could be so profitable. By April, 1930, Congress passed the Watres Act, which allowed for a revision of the entire airmail procedure. President Hoover together with the Secretaries of Commerce, Navy, Army, and the Postmaster General met and decided to move for cheaper mail contracts, reducing the cost to a net total of $1.26 a mile for the government.[81] Furthermore, these conferees, in a move to create order out of the chaotic route segments, laid out their ideal of four major east-west transcontinental lines and eight major north-south lines for the nation. Similar encouragement from the President and the Postmaster General helped to create mail contracts—through Pan American Airways—to Cuba, Honduras, Nicaragua, Costa Rica, Panama, Colombia, Ecuador, and Peru (service on a three times per week basis). Young represented the Department of Commerce and met with the other committee members, along with Colonel Lindbergh, spending two days at the Rapidan Camp in discussion of methods for the encouragement of commercial aviation and its adaptation to national defense.[82] Undoubtedly, the new arrangement led to probing on the part of many airline officials into the widespread opportunities for passenger service.

SERVICES AND PROMOTIONAL ACTIVITIES

ALL THE IMPORTANT OPERATIONS mentioned in the previous chapter have to do with air regulations and their enforcement. A second major facet of activity within the Aeronautics Branch encompassed the operation of the air facilities, duties which were assigned to the Bureau of Lighthouses during this era. In the first place, adding to the mileage of both lighted and unlighted airways constituted a major goal—a successful one, too, as the total of lighted routes reached 18,100 miles by the end of Herbert Hoover's term, supplemented by 900 miles of unlighted airways.[1] This represented a gain in lighted routes of 8,000 miles in four years. Politics, always a threat to effective performance of technical and scientific functions within federal agencies, constituted a menace to the branch. Naturally, congressmen depicted progress to their constituents in terms of new airway mileage, addition of lights, and other improvements. Senator Gerald P. Nye, the colorful North Dakotan, queried Assistant Secretary C. M. Young about the whole procedure of selecting new routes. Young admitted that he had not flown from Bismarck, North Dakota, on into Montana to determine the region's needs.[2] Young further contended that new airways had been added upon the recommendation of an interdepartmental committee consisting of three members each from the branch and from the Post Office Department. Senators also complained about the absence of routes between Buffalo and Detroit and between Fort Wayne and Columbus. Construction procedures were spelled out for new airways, many unusual aids proving necessary such as the use of burros in rugged terrain.[3]

An analysis of the Airways Division up to the spring of 1933 reflects the tremendous strides in the quantity and quality of navigational equipment, primarily in the field of radio where the aural-type radio-range beacon, two-way radio, and teletype communications were all adopted, at least on a limited basis. In the case of the radio-range beacon, aviation experts undertook a means of finding their way without the familiar flash of the beacon light. The radio-range beacon transmitters, located just off the landing field, consisted of two loop antennas crossed at an angle of 90 degrees, both working on 290-kilocycle waves but modulated at two different frequencies.[4] Branch researchers labored to switch from the aural reception of the radio-range signals to the highly desired visual method of reading the indicator on an instrument panel. However, the change, although successfully tested, took many years to accomplish. In October, 1930, a visual radio range, developed three years earlier by the Aeronautics Branch, was installed at Bellefonte, Pennsylvania. In Hoover's last year in office, all but one of 99 radio-range beacons in operation were of the aural type.[5] Meanwhile, 95 radio-marker beacons had been installed, another innovation of this era.

THE RADIO RANGE

Perhaps the best way to describe the radio-range beacon and radio markers in operation would be to tell how they could be used by the pilot whose airplane was equipped with the proper receiving instruments. In flying along the radio range, the pilot sought a pathway varying in width from 3 to 10 miles along the beam extending over 100 miles. The radio-range beacon emits two figure-eight space patterns, their axes at right angles to each other, with a cone of silence directly over the beacon. The aural signals, received in the plane via earphones, were given in the dot-dash code, using letters N and A. Along the "on" course, the two merged to give continuously the letter T in code. The experimental visual type instrument gave the position via reed indicators or pointers on the instrument panel. Consider the case of a pilot in the fall of 1932 taking off from Chicago, his destination Cleveland.[6] With the receiver tuned to the Chicago radio range, he picked up the southerly range, heard the monotonous T interrupted by the dot-dot-dash-dot—identification signal for

Chicago—given twice in succession. He followed the right-hand flying rule by steering a few degrees south, periodically checking the radio range by his compass. He must increase the volume of his set to get the weather broadcast (by voice), which interrupted his range signals. All the while, the pilot flew "over the top," without the benefit of land observation. Changing from the Chicago to the Goshen range, he first received the *A* signal, indicating that he was north of the Goshen range, until the *T* assured him of reaching the true course. This procedure was repeated throughout the flight. The radio-marker beacons at McCool, Helmer, Archbold, and Vickery provided the pilot with special voice broadcasts of weather. Marker stations also reported the flight "over" for the teletype record between Chicago and Cleveland. Upon reaching Cleveland, the pilot located the airport via the cone of silence and reported his arrival and expected landing to the control tower. The pilot received this data: wind direction and velocity, ceiling, visibility, aircraft on the landing area and in the air, and the proper time to land. The landing was completed by tuning in on a range aligned with the airport (taking up the magnetic heading), passing the cone of silence over the radio-range beacon again, and breaking through the ceiling to sight landmarks en route to the landing field. The danger of multiple radio-range transmission by some beacons confronted airmen, especially in rugged terrain and mountains. This phenomenon persisted into the 1960's, affecting flights at very high altitudes. Frequent compass checks, familiarity flights around the beacon, and crossing the various range courses at known distances from the beacon, enabled pilots to grope their way with somewhat more assurance. Other modes of compensation were explained, such as changing from the Raleigh to the Richmond radio beacons whose ranges did not intersect. All pilots engaged in scheduled interstate passenger traffic had to demonstrate their ability to fly entirely by such instruments and were tested in flight with outside visibility barred until they lowered to an altitude of 200 to 300 feet. One hundred pilots had passed this critical test by September, 1932. Orientation tips included suggestions for eliminating compass spinning resulting from repeated turns of the plane. A series of right-hand turns proved most satisfactory.

Aid from the radio-range beacon at Boston enabled planes to steer a course from ships 200 miles at sea. Pilot testimonials were collected by the branch to show the effectiveness of the new devices. Their major defects seemed to be the breaks in reception necessitated by the voice weather reports.[7] At Lexington, Nebraska, a branch radioman stood outside his building and relayed messages by radio to a pilot whose plane landed safely in the fog. One airman reported all aids in good order during the rain and overcast between Columbus, Ohio, and Kansas City, Missouri. Another flier persuaded beacon personnel not to interrupt the signals for weather reports while he successfully landed in a squall at St. Louis. The ability to cut in with voice broadcasts prevented accidents at times, for the radiomen could advise the pilot to fly around a known thunderstorm or proceed to another airport. The radio operator's data came from reports and known positions of other aircraft in his area. Remote control of radio stations, including the radio-range beacons, became a reality at seventy locations at the end of the Hoover Administration, allowing transmission from 1 to 15 miles from an airport by use of telephone circuits. This innovation eliminated the need for additional antenna towers, always a landing hazard. The automatic systems performed 100 functions, rendering unnecessary the relay of weather maps by messenger to the fields and the manual operation of the field obstruction lights.[8]

WEATHER BROADCASTS

In addition to the radio beacons and voice radio broadcasts, the collection and dissemination of weather data improved dramatically. A typical report read: Bellefonte—overcast, raining, ceiling 2,000 feet; visibility 5 miles; wind southwest 20; temperature 41; barometer 3004 (thirty-zero-four inches of mercury). There followed a one-minute break for beacon signals after which the local upper-air data were transmitted. Though the results did not always reflect such, operators were instructed to enunciate clearly at the rate of 90–100 words per minute.[9] Conflicting times of transmission plagued the pilot who needed more than one station's hourly reports within a short time, a deficiency remedied in 1932 by assigning terminal fields in one chain called the "red" group with the transmission time of 50 minutes after the hour; the intermediate stations reported 5 minutes later. Another chain, the "blue" group, reported on the hour and 5 minutes after; the third or "brown" chain of stations reported their weather 10 and 15 minutes after the hour. The whole system was tied into the ground collection of data through the speedier methods of the teletype (this first type recorded its data on tape), begun on the New York–Chicago route, at an average cost of $70 per mile for leasing the teletype. An experiment, successfully conducted in 1932, led to the production every 4 hours of page-type weather maps via teletype at 78 airports.[10]

Such auspicious beginnings with the radio led to wide enthusiasm on the part of Aeronautics Branch officials and aviation interests in general. Unhappily, however, much remained to be accomplished with all these innovations in order to assure anything resembling a flawless performance. To make matters worse, the vast majority of airplanes at this time did not have the necessary receiving equipment with which to benefit by the radio navigation aids. Even with radio, interruptions for weather broadcasts and the effects of static (rendering the aids inoperative at the most critical times) left much to be desired in the way of improvement.

AIRWAY MAINTENANCE

Maintenance of the federal airways continued to be accomplished along the lines similar to those already described. Lighted airways averaged approximately $213 per mile to maintain, as reported in 1932.[11] The branch authorized, as before, the construction of additional beacon lights by private enterprise if the request had received the prior approval of local areonautical authorities; a famous example was the Lindbergh Beacon, added in 1929, atop the Colgate-Palmolive-Peet Building in Chicago.[12]

Supervision of the widespread activities in the field of license and inspection, as well as the patrolling of airways to check on navigation aids, required constant use of government-owned airplanes, each averaging over 300 air hours of use per year. Inspectors used thirty-nine planes in early 1933; the other ten belonged to the airway service for patrolling. Two employees, one in a 1927 airplane, the other in a new 1932 model, had lost their lives on duty. The old plane was caught in bad weather without modern instruments. Each new government plane was overhauled after 250 continuous hours, followed by another overhaul after 1,500 hours.[13]

IMPROVING AIRPORTS

An effort to stimulate the development of suitable airports led, in 1929, to the establishment of an Airport Section in the Airways Division at Washington, D.C. Fostering the uniformity of airport field rules, the branch called a national conference at

Washington, D.C., during December, 1930.[14] Uniform field rules were published, and a rating scale was inaugurated to encourage widespread compliance. The Pontiac, Michigan, municipal airport received the first rating from the branch, A-1-A, the highest type.[15] Airport owners sought the ratings voluntarily, 648 towns doing so during fiscal 1929, of which 636 were visited for a complete study of airport facilities and management. Denver, Colorado, gained the second A-1-A, rating and seven others attained the honor in 1931. Ratings of C-1-X and D-2-X were assigned to seaplane landing areas, while, in addition to A-1-A, other land ratings included: A-T-A, A-2-X, and C-2-X. The rating awards continually increased with 244 issued during fiscal 1933. The requirements for the A-1-A rating included: land space of 2,500 feet in all directions, an additional 500-foot boundary around the field, circle marker, boundary lights, rotating beacon, obstruction lights, radio towers, floodlights, repair facilities, fueling, housing and food for the crew, food for the passengers, first-aid and firefighting equipment, meteorological instruments, hangars of minimum dimensions—80 by 100 feet—and at least eight employees.[16] Few early airports in this country could match the telescope loading canopy and colorful Spanish architecture of the airport at Mills Field, Los Angeles. A check of passenger facilities in the summer of 1929 disclosed the first exclusive airport hotel, a thirty-seven room structure, at Oakland. The Aeronautics Branch issued a valuable guide to airport management. To relieve a company or municipality of constant damage suits or claims, contracts for airfields specified crops which might be raised there to offer the least interference with the landing of planes. The airport company owned the crops.[17] Several conferences with members of the National Board of Fire Underwriters aided the Airport Section officials in their plans for minimum standards.[18] Warnings of unusual obstructions were issued to airmen, the eighty-seven lightning rods north and east of the airport at Bakersfield, California, as a case in point.[19]

Efforts to improve American airports came at a time when even the most rabid aviation enthusiasts here realized the inferiority of our airports in comparison to many in western Europe. Dr. F. L. Hoffman, flying actuarial consultant with the Prudential Insurance Company, wrote widely during this era on the bright potentialities of aviation in America and was convinced of the safety afforded by this transportation. Moreover, Hoffman expressed deep concern over the meager existing facilities, both in the airplanes and at airports, for passenger travel. Traveling along most of the major air routes in the country, Dr. Hoffman often found himself wedged between mail sacks without straps or guard rails and alighting at tiny airports grossly lacking in facilities.[20] During one trial flight, adverse weather forced down the mail plane at Bellefonte, whence Hoffman journeyed by train to Chicago. Before proceeding to the West Coast, Hoffman flew to Minneapolis and back to Chicago. He found the Chicago airport far inferior to any second-rate European airport, not to mention such high-class fields as Croydon, Le Bourget, or Tempelhof. Chicago Municipal Airport lacked restaurants, rest rooms, information booth, public telegraph and telephone, and waiting taxis. There were only ten hangars, a shanty, and one brick building. Fortunately, Chicago had as its manager the kind and considerate J. A. Casey who contended with thousands of sightseers each month in addition to the mail flights and passengers. In fact, Hoffman was unimpressed also with the airports at Boston, Hadley, Minneapolis, Omaha, North Platte, St. Louis, and Phoenix, to mention a few cited in his reports. He did enjoy the excellent hangar and landing field at Elko, Nevada; the airport at Buffalo, New York, operated by Colonial Western Airways; and the Ford airport, complete with mooring mast, at Dearborn, Michigan. Hoffman pointed to the glaring deficiencies in American airports; he believed that municipal authorities or private groups owning landing facilities ought to seek the advice of the Aeronautics Branch for better planning.

PUBLIC CRITICISM

Criticism of airports represents just one aspect of the difficulties confronting American aviation during 1927–1933. The Aeronautics Branch could not escape these shortcomings because part of its legal heritage rested with the encouragement and development of aeronautics. Again, Dr. Hoffman stressed other faults as a few of the industry's ills: high passenger fares, poor schedules, and poorly located airports. Many of these difficulties had been improved before the advent of the New Deal. Passenger planes carrying at least twelve paying customers naturally afforded better service than the mail plane with little or no room. As usual in the case of complaints addressed to governmental agencies, some bordered on the ridiculous; one outcry from an irate farmer bemoaned the loss of his chickens due to airplanes flying overhead.[21] Mention has already been made of the congressional attempts to force the branch to publish the causes of each air accident. Attendance of branch leaders at professional meetings came under the close scrutiny of one legislator.[22] A seemingly perennial move in Congress sought the transfer of the Aeronautics Branch to the Interstate Commerce Commission. Young countered with the suggestion that the best way to help the Aeronautics Branch was to let it alone. Congressman John L. Cable of Ohio disagreed and, in 1932, introduced another bill favoring the transfer to the ICC.[23]

AIRLINE WOES

Further woes befell the branch concerning labor problems within the airlines, as indicated in a case in which Century and Pacific Air Lines dismissed those of its pilots who had objected to unfair treatment. Presently the branch inspectors disqualified 50 per cent of the replacement pilots hired and taught by the airline.[24] The Air Line Pilots' Association (ALPA) constantly sought aid on behalf of its members from the Department of Commerce. Sometimes relations with both airlines and pilots could become strained as was the case in 1931 when Young sought airline approval for a series of conferences between branch officials and employees of the airlines.[25] The representative of Northwest Airlines expressed surprise that anyone would object, but one official of American Airlines offered this advice: "Experienced suggestions . . . we feel should be obtained from us and not from our employees."[26]

Colonel Young and his staff labored diligently to overcome these and other criticisms, insisting that branch employees, too, would abide by all regulations in their own flying. When Young and Inspector Neely crashed (uninjured) in their airplane near College Park, Maryland, they invited the same publicity and inspection as anyone else would receive.[27] Noticeable among the pleas against reduction of appropriations for the Aeronautics Branch in 1932 was the telegram, introduced in the Senate by Hiram Bingham, from David L. Behncke, President of the Air Line Pilots' Association.[28] Behncke, a veteran of night airmail flights between Chicago and Omaha, realized the great contribution rendered aviation in the first six years of federal regulation.

UNRELIABLE INSTRUMENTS

Another periodic complaint presented the entire question of the government's role in the nation's economy or, putting it differently, How much aid should be extended to the aviation industry? On the one hand, pilots often complained about having to pay for the medical exam in getting or renewing their licenses. At the same time, a portion of congressional sentiment lent support to the theory that industry should pay for engine testing performed by the branch, even suggesting that the maintenance of the air navigation aids be borne by the users—the airlines. Congressmen, expressing interest in the question of federal maintenance of air navigation facilities and whether private companies could operate these aids, looked at private aids on two airways—Phoenix to Los Angeles and San Antonio to Big Spring, Texas.[29] Young, replying to the charges that the railroads considered aid to aviation as unfair treatment, considered his organization's work as similar in theory to the governmental support of water traffic. Furthermore, he added, "No one owns the air."[30]

Added to the many innovations in radio aids and teletype was a continual effort to produce better equipment and improve the existing methods and materials used in aviation. Early recognition of deficiencies existed. Compasses would spin when most needed; lag developed in the altimeter. Bank indicators, too small at best, often froze. The airplane's instrument panel vibrated excessively; grouping of the instruments needed standardization. Temperature gauges should read either in Centigrade or Fahrenheit.[31] The Bureau of Standards studied these and other such suggestions as eliminating the noise from engines and propellers. Here, officials concluded that mufflers could not be profitable while a manifold system might help.[32] Farmers and neighbors complained to no avail; two suits for injunctions against airport managements were filed. Turning to another problem, authorities had long realized that death and injury in a crash often occurred not from the impact alone but from a resulting explosion and fire. Investigators tried to construct a crash-resistant fuel tank, using rubber tanks up to 200 gallons in capacity. Immediate conclusions reflected pessimism, estimating the need for approximately 1.4 pounds of material per gallon of weight to insulate the tank for a drop of just 20 feet onto concrete.[33] More optimistic were the accomplishments with instrument-landing aids for overcoming fog as an obstacle to aviation. The Guggenheim Fund extended its financial support. Using a low-power, radio-range transmitter, Lieutenant J. H. Doolittle completed a number of "blind" landings in 1929 at Mitchel Field, Long Island. Aeronautics Branch tests were conducted at Newark and on the West Coast; Marshall Boggs lost his life in these tests.[34] Boggs, Assistant Chief of Airway Regulations, had worked diligently on the problems of fog and instrument flying and had obtained from the National Air Pilots' Association (forerunner of the ALPA) a list of former airmail pilots most experienced in bad weather and night flying.[35] Needle pointers, lined up perpendicularly to each other at the center of the panel, signified a true approach to the runway. An improved airway beacon, a deviometer, and an ice-warning thermometer were all produced by branch personnel.[36] Research projects also encompassed experiments in a wind tunnel, welding of joints, propeller flutter, and an effort to construct an interior of an airplane with soundproofing sufficient to reduce noise to that of a railroad car. Young insisted, upon questioning by congressmen, that no duplication in research existed between his organization (research completed for the branch by the Bureau of Standards) and that of the National Advisory Committee for Aeronautics.[37]

AIR HEROES

The transcontinental and transatlantic flights of 1927 inaugurated a long list of similar endeavors with the Aeronautics Branch maintaining its interest and help as before. After much support from the public to extend control, the Aeronautics Branch began exerting stronger supervision in December, 1932, over transoceanic flights, the major change entailing closer inspection of local preparations prior to the flight: pilots must be able to fly solely on instruments, standard equipment rules applied, no unlicensed craft or pilot could be used, all other branch rules applied.[38] Previously, not all preparations were checked by the federal inspectors. Sometimes the tragedy of unsuccessful experimental flights struck close to branch employees. Carl Ben Eielson who, late in 1929, lost his life in a flight off Siberia, had been an inspector for two years with the branch.[39] Eielson was on leave at the time of his flight from Point Barrow to Spitzbergen. Unhappily, the federal authorities had neither men nor airplanes in Alaska—a neglected domain—to search for the lost pilot.[40] In a happier vein, branch authorities took a great interest in special awards and ceremonies, offering suggestions for candidates, when needed, for such honors as the Polar Medal and Silver Wings of Peace.[41] William MacCracken represented the department at a number of functions pertaining to aviation, including memorial ceremonies at Kitty Hawk.[42] Upon request, the federal regulators made special allowance for some flights, such as the case of Lady Mary Heath, who asked, "if you could see your way clear to allow me to make this flight without loading my poor little machine with all this electrical equipment."[43] Permission was granted on condition that she give advance notice of her takeoff. Smithsonian Institution officials expressed appreciation to Young for his aid in getting the Texaco "Eaglet" glider sent to the museum following its transcontinental flight (towed by an airplane).[44]

Friendship and aid from several of the nation's leading fliers rendered the tasks of the branch all the more pleasant. The famous Amelia Earhart, in 1929, served as aviation editor of *Cosmopolitan* Magazine and was a frequent correspondent with Young about her own flying career. Young prized an autographed picture of Miss Earhart.[45] In the spring of the same year, this enthusiastic aviatrix ventured into a new field of air conveyance and enjoyed the results, as reflected to Young: "You are generous to take time to commend my feeble efforts at air propaganda. I wonder if many industries are as misunderstood by the general public as aviation? . . . O, well, why be brutal? I 'glid' or 'glode' the other day, and liked it, as I always thought I should."[46] The air regulations staff sent a wire to inform Miss Earhart she had passed her license exam.[47] R. E. Byrd sought advice from Young for materials to use in a lecture before the NAA at Chicago: "Due to my long absence from the country I have not yet been able to entirely catch up with the march of events."[48] Personal sympathy was extended to fliers losing close friends or associates in enterprises geared to test and explain the future of air transportation. Byrd received such condolence upon the death of Floyd Bennett.[49]

INTERNATIONAL ACCORD

Cooperation with fliers and governments of other nations was sought at all times. Aeronautical leaders in The Netherlands received aid from the Aeronautics Branch regarding rules and possible routes to follow for a flight through the United States and Central and South America.[50] Van Lear Black led men of the Royal Dutch Air Service from London to the Dutch East Indies, receiving honors in the United States at fetes attended by branch officials.[51] Later, the same flier advised MacCracken of a flight to Chicago with nine Fokker-type craft. The United States and

Canada continued their accord with a new reciprocal agreement in 1930.[52] Elsewhere, our State Department and other foreign offices continued the search for international security during this era; in aviation the suspicions remained apparent even when flight over a country was allowed.

NO "OPEN SKIES"

From the beginning, rules of flight in foreign countries were channeled via the Department of State.[53] A perusal of travel restrictions collected by the branch for the aid of American airmen discloses, for example, that the "open skies" plea of the 1960's did not apply at this earlier time. Great Britain decreed that all cameras must remain sealed during flight over the Isles. The Union of South Africa allowed cameras but no arms. Germany condoned special or tourist flights if they met these points: registration, liability insurance, clear markings, and exclusion from the petroleum zone at Hamburg. Advanced permission must be obtained for trips over Japan and Siam, none being allowed over fortified zones, a clear tip-off for later war movements by Japan. France prescribed special licenses before allowing photographing of its land.

International rules for aviation received attention here and in Europe and South America. Adding to the discussion at Versailles (1919), conferences were held at Havana (1928) and Warsaw (1929). Of interest to the defense and reciprocal accord of this hemisphere was the achievement at Havana. Ratified by the Senate on February 20, 1931, this International Convention on Commercial Aviation, adopted at the Sixth International Conference of American States, recognized the right of innocent passage without discrimination. At the same time, each nation retained complete and exclusive sovereignty over the airspace above its territory and territorial waters.[54] The twenty-one members of the Pan American Union promised to use distinctive markings and carry a certificate of airworthiness and a list of passengers—with names, addresses, and nationalities—all to serve for better identification. MacCracken attended the Second International Conference on Air Navigation in Warsaw. Much confusion arose over the full implications of this Warsaw convention, necessitating additional conferences in the post-World War II era.[55] For example, the question of air charter was not adequately mentioned.[56] The United States officials took an active interest in the discussion of air activities by sponsoring in

December, 1928, an International Air Congress at Washington, D.C. Thirty countries sent official delegates.[57] Americans continued to express amazement at the ease with which the leading European countries extended subsidies for both the manufacture and regulation of aviation, France spending $80 million during its fiscal year ending in March, 1931.[58]

STATE LAWS

Lawmakers and federal aviation leaders remained unsatisfied with international talks and the domestic status of air law. One critic explained it: "Now the givers of our law have a new plaything, aircraft, and the whole sky as a playground. . . . Wherever constructive thinking is required of lawgivers, the principle of *laissez-faire* is likely to prevail. The result is nearly always a sorry one." [59] Forty states had promulgated eighty laws embracing phases of aviation, in addition to the federal acts. Only eight of these laws mentioned minimum altitude. Complete lack of uniformity existed concerning liability, the courts tending to base responsibility on the determination of negligence. Twenty-nine states and territories required planes operating within their borders to have federal licenses. Three states issued their own licenses, but only two states employed their own inspectors.[60] One leading editor commented, "The individual cannot stop flights over his land . . . too few laws to exert a restraining influence on inconsiderate or foolhardy fliers." [61] Indicative of the deep concern over coordination of aviation activities was the branch's conference at Boise, Idaho, during July, 1929. Top-level officials of eleven states heard experts outline the problems confronting aviation.[62] Negotiations with American Indians played a role, too, in the expansion of services provided to aviation. Beacon lights plus an intermediate field were needed on the Winslow–Albuquerque section of the Los Angeles–Amarillo airway, requiring formal negotiations with the Zuni, Acoma, and Lagunas Indians. In each case, the entire tribe participated in the proceedings. Though most of the Indians understood English and one chief was a university graduate, proceedings were conducted in the Indians' native language.[63]

GETTING ADVICE

Advisory committees played an important role in the formulation of aeronautical regulation; indeed, NACA epitomized this type of valuable criticism and support. Interdepartmental in thought and personnel, the Air Coordinating Committee (ACC) also proved useful, with its representatives of the Departments of War, Navy, and Commerce.[64] In 1930, aircraft manufacturers accepted 75 per cent of the branch's proposed amendments in regulation, although less agreement and little action resulted from other talks on air traffic control, airport zoning, and marking of obstructions.[65] Air-marking campaigns, aided by local communities and businesses, helped keep the operations alive although nationwide appeal appeared to be sadly lacking. Little Rock, Arkansas, promoted a "Mark Your Town Week," and a unique publicity offer entailed free paint from the Sherwin-Williams Company and free brushes from the Wooster Brush Company for some 100 communities in Ohio. The Pennsylvania Railroad also marked its key stations. Wichita, Kansas, earnestly sponsored a campaign of air marking.[66]

Aeronautical development constituted yet another separate type of activity, at least on paper, within the Aeronautics Branch. However, the foregoing descriptions of the many activities within air regulations and the Airways Division have pointed to an endless number of ways development could be accomplished in the everyday activities of the federal regulators. In all facets of regulation and development, the Aeronautics Branch leadership fostered cooperation with the aircraft industry and, at the same time, reminded this industry of its obligation to furnish the branch all statistics requested.[67] The Air Information Division and the Publications Section codified all possible information of use to airmen, manufacturers, and airlines in the form of airway bulletins, the *Air Commerce Bulletin,* and the *Weekly Notices to Airmen.*[68] By 1930, individual requests for aeronautical bulletins averaged from 25,000 to 30,000 per month.

BOOSTING AVIATION

The branch commenced work on sectional maps of the United States during this era, completing those for Chicago, Detroit, and Milwaukee. The Coast and Geodetic Survey continued to produce the scale of 8 miles to the inch (1 to 500,000), color, strip maps, finishing twenty-two by 1930. Proudly summarizing the gains in aviation, the branch could report in 1929, that the abstract of assessments at Denver, Colorado, for the first time showed the value of airplanes above the figure for horses.[69] In the first six months of 1930, airplane production in the United States included 493 biplanes and 271 monoplanes, all with open cockpit. Elsewhere it was noted that traffic agents were busy for the first time. Even a cargo of precious queen bees was transported safely by air from Florida to California in less than two days. Passenger fares for humans in 1930 ranged from 8 to 15 cents a mile. In addition to carrying bees—and other passengers—the air carriers gained the public spotlight when Hollywood's Rod La Rocque received the trousers to his dress suit by air from the West in one day, just as the gangplank went up on the ship carrying him abroad.[70] Hollywood itself furnished air transport with an average of fifteen reels of film each day, many of these flights at first covering areas without beacons or radio-range facilities, such as a long portion of the Miami–New York flight.[71] As business improved, airmen attempted to allay public fears of airsickness, pleading that poor ventilation in the plane, not the performance of the craft or pilot, often could be at fault. Improvement was promised.[72] Railroad lines sought to augment their service with air-minded passengers by selling "part-air" and "part-train" tickets, for the transcontinental trek that featured two nights by train and air travel during the daylight hours of the two days.[73] Life insurance rates, regarded as too high, gained more scrutiny from the Actuarial Society of America as it culled the files of the Aeronautics Branch again in 1930.[74] One leading newspaper attributed the difficulties with insurance to former President Warren Harding, who allegedly felt that a three-year term policy would suffice because all military fliers would fall within that time.[75] The absurdity of this assertion could be ascertained by a glance at the list of fliers manning the airways at the close of 1932 with records of 1,000 to 5,000 hours to their credit—10 airline pilots out of approximately 400.[76] Better years lay ahead for aviation at the end of the Hoover Administration, and the status was hardly as bleak as an assertion by Charles L. Lawrence, President of the Aeronautical Chamber of Commerce. To Lawrence, aviation had declined because, for the first time in six years, it was not mentioned in the President's general message to Congress nor in the budget message.[77] Perhaps the federal authorities were preoccupied with the general economic crash and forgot aviation.

One of the proudest moments in the early years of the branch came in January, 1929, when the prized Collier Trophy for 1928 was awarded to MacCracken, Young, and the entire staff of the Aeronautics Branch. On behalf of the Collier committee,

James P. Murray presented the award, stating, "I believe I can appreciate the big job you have put across in organizing and causing to function, so well, the Aeronautics Branch of the Department of Commerce." [78] Director Young expressed the joy of his staff in winning the prize offered annually since 1911. [79]

THE NEW DEAL'S IMPACT

HERBERT HOOVER, after years of helpful guidance to aviation as Secretary of Commerce and as President, relinquished the burdens of state in March, 1933, to the ambitious, smiling, reassuring Franklin Delano Roosevelt. The Aeronautics Branch and aviation in general fared well under the messianic leader of the New Deal. For that matter, all the presidents beginning with Hoover have displayed a genuine interest and support of the federal role in civil aviation. Though the vast majority of the nation's industry existed in a state of shock and financial insecurity, the aviation business generally had experienced a boom since 1927.[1] Nevertheless, much remained to be accomplished in the way of government regulation and development to bolster this business with better navigational facilities, including airports. Developmental techniques utilized during the years before World War II stressed aid to the private pilot and the manufacturer of small aircraft.

In the field of aviation the New Deal offered little variation from the approach toward all other segments of this country's economy. Theoretically, federal support was available to those who desired assistance and who would police their own industry in order to pull the economy out of its low ebb. At the outset, the Aeronautics Branch felt the economic pinch in the first year of operations under Roosevelt. However, the new projects and the impetus of the relief programs soon offset such limitations. Accompanying the helpful measures of the New Deal, however, were serious differences of opinion which characterized the

1933–1938 era as one with quarrels over administrative reorganization, party politics, and disagreement within the Aeronautics Branch and its successors, as well as widespread congressional charges of inefficiency and unwise policy on the part of the branch leadership. These controversial subjects will be taken up individually later in this chapter.

ADMINISTRATION AND PERSONNEL

C. M. Young, Colonel Harry Blee, and Director Gilbert M. Budwig resigned from the branch, whereupon the New Deal politicians went into a huddle to select new top leadership. Several candidates possessed backing. James C. Edgerton counted on Senator William G. McAdoo, and Major J. Carroll Cone rode on the smiles of Senator Joseph Robinson. Rex Martin of Peoria felt certain of support from Speaker Henry T. Rainey of Illinois and other midwestern congressmen. However, Eugene L. Vidal of South Dakota gained the job on September 20, 1933, through his friendship with Elliott Roosevelt and Amelia Earhart, Mrs. Roosevelt's heroine.[2] Vidal, West Pointer and football star, had served five years in the Army Air Corps. He had been a coach and real estate agent and spent a year with Transcontinental Air Transport before joining the Ludington Line as president. The Ludington Line, successful with passenger service since 1930, touched at Newark, Camden, and the Hoover Airport across the Potomac from Washington, D.C. Ludington had lost its effort to gain a share of the airmail contracts from the Post Office Department in 1931, although its bid far undercut that of the postal favorite, Eastern Air Transport.[3] Not that fraud proved evident; small lines of 200 miles simply did not fit the designs of the Post Office planners. Rex Martin joined Vidal as Assistant Director for Airways, while C. I. Stanton became Chief Engineer in the Airways Division. At the conclusion of the first Roosevelt term, Vidal was succeeded by Fred Fagg, Jr., of Northwestern University. Fagg had served as a pilot in World War I attached to the British night-bombing squadron. He moved to Northwestern in 1929, founding the Air Law Institute and the *Journal of Air Law*.[4] He also had been coauthor of aeronautical legislation enacted in the state of Illinois. In the spring of 1938, Fagg resigned to return as Dean of the School of Commerce at Northwestern. Roosevelt's third director, Denis Mulligan, had already been with the Bureau of Air Commerce for several months, primarily as a legal expert.[5]

FIGHTING THE DEPRESSION

Vidal inherited from the economy measures of the Hoover era the problem of reduced personnel and reduced general appropriations. In his initial appearance before federal legislators, Vidal reported on savings in many areas of service, including the elimination of some forty-five professional employees. Fifteen of the sixty branch airplanes were stored, travel funds slashed by more than one-half, use of teletype curtailed, wind-tunnel experiments shifted to NACA, engine testing eliminated (factories to do their own), seventy-three emergency fields abolished—all to the glee of William B. Oliver of Alabama, Chairman of the House Subcommittee on Appropriations.[6] In his next breath, however, Vidal outlined a program of increased expenditures, including airport construction and additional airways, aided for the most part by such relief measures as the Civil Works Administration (CWA) and the Public Works Administration (PWA). Total regular appropriations ranged from $5,172,500 in fiscal 1934, to $11,575,970 in fiscal 1938. For the same two years, personnel totaled 1,750 and 2,806.[7] In addition, 70 to 80 persons found work with the bureau on the PWA and WPA rolls. Restoration of the salary cuts of 5 per cent constituted but one of the added needs.

BUREAU OF AIR COMMERCE

As the growth of aviation reflected itself in the nation, the Aeronautics Branch was accorded increased attention within the Department of Commerce. For example, on July 1, 1933, the airway construction and maintenance duties, performed heretofore by personnel of the Bureau of Lighthouses, were transferred to the Aeronautics Branch.[8] Just one year later, the name Aeronautics Branch gave way to the more accurate title, Bureau of Air Commerce.[9] The change in title brought a realignment of administrative segments within the bureau, the head of all activities gaining the title Director of Air Commerce, instead of Director of Aeronautics. The three former divisions became merged into the Air Navigation Division and Air Regulation Division, while the duties of the former Aeronautic Development Service were absorbed in the new divisions; and the bureau director assumed control over smaller units known as the Aeronautics Information Section and the Administrative Section. Research was placed under a Development Section, and other sections were added for airport marking and mapping.[10] Finding the ultimate in organizational arrangement proved to be a perennial chore in the bureau and its successors. Another reorganization took place in 1937 with the establishment of seven divisions: airways engineering, airways operations, safety and planning, administrative, information and statistics, certification and inspection, and regulation and enforcement.[11] A policy board of the seven division heads advised the director and assistant director along with a special advisory board to the bureau made up of representatives from the aviation interests outside the government. Interdepartmental committees continued to be used for various personnel concerns. In 1934, one committee agreed with Director Vidal that the rate of flying pay should remain unchanged in the Department of Commerce.[12] At this time, veteran Aeronautical Supervisor Howard Rough succeeded Major R. W. Schroeder as assistant director, Schroeder moving to United Air Lines as vice-president. Another former inspector, Frederick Neely, became head of Information and Statistics, and C. I. Stanton headed the Airways Engineering Division.[13] Another administrative quandary, decentralization of field activities, came under periodic scrutiny of the bureau. Pleas for decentralization had been heard during various phases of the Aeronautics Branch and Bureau of Air Commerce, especially after times of crises such as major airline accidents or congressional investigations.[14] Charles C. Rohlfing, reviewing the situation, maintained that the need for regionalization did not appear to be necessary earlier under the splendid personal leadership of Young. As the organization grew, separate district field offices supervised nine general inspection districts and six airways districts. Effective May 1, 1938, the bureau established seven regional offices, appointing mostly former inspectors—six had been with the bureau since 1928—to head these offices. Original appointees (in order of the regional number) were: John E. Sommers, Newark; R. C. Copeland, Atlanta; Harold R. Neely, Chicago; L. C. Elliott, Fort Worth; Leonard W. Jurden, Kansas City; J. S. Marriott, Los Angeles; and R. D. Bedinger, Seattle.[15] The actual implementation of the regionalization materialized under the advent of yet another general reorganization to be described in Chapter 7 under the activities of the Civil Aeronautics Authority.

INSPECTION, REGULATION, AND ENFORCEMENT

Activities under this category continued to be implemented much the same during 1933–1938 as they had been prior to the beginning of the New Deal. A drastic departure from the previous routine occurred early in the Roosevelt Administration, when the inspection patrol system was abolished temporarily, leaving this assignment to the bureau's airline inspectors. Abandonment of engine testing passed on to the industry itself a laborious, earlier governmental service.[16] Part of the cut in the inspection force proved to be false economy soon followed by pleas before Congress for additional strength.[17] Especially lacking were maintenance inspectors. The airlines continued to offer free transportation to bureau inspectors on duty whenever seating space permitted. To the casual observer, the vast inspection duties of the bureau went on unnoticed, but New Deal cuts brought consternation to aviation circles. The United States had approximately 10,000 of the world's 14,000 commercial airplanes in 1937; an inspection corps of merely 60 men was detailed to this airline task, compared to 120 men in 1932.[18] Rapid inspection of emergency situations drew praise from headquarters, such as the complete inspection and report filed by 1:58 P.M. on the day that a pilot went into a spin at 3,500 feet, bailing out successfully but wrecking his aircraft at 9:30 A.M.[19]

Careful study of current regulations covering pilot licenses led to several modifications including the abolishment of the old solo-pilot license in September, 1933. Four months later, the federal authorities established the new grade of license known as amateur pilot, attainable following twenty-five hours of solo time. Liberal in its application, the student could apply toward the amateur license all flying time after his initial ten hours as solo time whenever accompanied by his instructor.[20] Colonel J. Carroll Cone, Assistant Director of Aeronautics, at the same time extended the life of the student-pilot license from one to two years. Standard exams were continued for licensed pilots of lighter-than-air craft, including the physical examination; the flight check; and written questions on navigation, meteorology, engines, and all air commerce and air traffic rules. The flight test necessitated correct handling of a powered dirigible, semidirigible, or nonrigid balloon in landings and takeoffs.[21] Airline (airplane) pilots were required to take a new physical examination every ninety days. Starting in June, 1935, student pilots had to pass an oral questioning before taking their initial solo flights. The question of illness among pilots long concerned inspectors and medical examiners who decided in November, 1935, to require civil pilots who were ill for twenty or more days to obtain a new physical if the examiner deemed this necessary. Previously, airline pilots could have been incapacitated for two months without a physical exam before returning to duty.[22] Innovations in regulation featured the certificate of authority (safety), allowing airlines to operate.[23] Throughout this era, aviation interests let their wishes and suggestions be known to air regulations employees, even though new rules did not always result from this honest concern. In 1934, David L. Behncke, representing the Air Line Pilots' Association, informed Major Schroeder, Chief, Airlines Inspection Service, that Pan American Airways carried radio operators as copilots, a doubtful practice in the light of several recent bad accidents: "This does not seem to have acted as a warning!"[24] Thus began a never-ending feud between crew members and airlines over the proper type and number of personnel constituting the operation of commercial aircraft.

VIOLATIONS CONTINUE

The necessity of strict enforcement of all air regulations persisted as a monumental task for the Bureau of Air Commerce, as it had been under the Aeronautics Branch. A rash of accidents involving amateur and student pilots led the authorities to apply a minimum penalty of one year's suspension of a license for each violation. For the two years ending on June 30, 1935, 82 accidents had been recorded in which the amateur or student carried passengers, 31 of the mishaps causing death to the pilot, passenger, or both.[25] Thirty-seven fatal violations during January–June, 1935, included 16 cases of illegal acrobatics and 8 more instances of low flying. What appeared to be so unthinkable was the fact that not one of the tragedies might be considered an accident in the true sense of the term. One student continually buzzed several children and a farmer until crashing to his death, while another met death after requesting a group of school children to mark how close to the school door he could drop a letter from his plane. The letter was found in the wreckage. Attempting to salute bathers in a river, a crop duster met disaster by striking a wire. The excitement of his initial solo flight caused one student to continue in the air beyond the designated flight around the field, whereupon his air show for the benefit of friends at a picnic featured a final turn at 100 feet (a violation), an inevitable crash, and a broken neck. Enforcement studies and analysis of students, amateurs, and private pilots constituted just one aspect of police work. All reported violations of commercial operations came under close attention. For example, the failure to submit flight plans, often the fault of the ground crew for not carrying the plan over to bureau personnel, was cited seven times against American Airlines during September, 1936–April, 1937.[26] Deviation from required altitude reports composed another segment of the analysis. Exceptions existed, of course, when some daring feat captured the public fancy, a case in point following the exploits of Douglas Corrigan who, "pretending" to be lost, completed the solo transatlantic hop to England in 1938. When asked what he would do to Corrigan, Denis Mulligan reportedly commented, "It is a great day for the Irish."[27] Officially, Director Mulligan attempted to explain his feelings about Corrigan in a reply to one person's unfavorable reaction toward the transatlantic flight: "The Department already has suspended the experimental aircraft certificate issued Mr. Corrigan. . . . while the Bureau of Air Commerce is concerned . . . the successful accomplishment . . . proves his skill and courage."[28]

MEDICAL ADVICE

Constantly exploring new leads to determine the effects of flight on humans, the experts in the bureau's Medical Section worked in harmony with the inspectors and regulation makers in licensing and certification. Upon requests in 1934, the doctors allowed special flights for acrobatic maneuvers designed to attempt correction of certain physical defects if the patient's physician so advised. However, use of a compression chamber was recommended as an easier method to explore.[29] Dr. R. E. Whitehead, Chief of the Medical Section in 1937, completed a personal tour of Pan American Airway's Pacific division, seeking all possible information on the comfort of passengers and crew.[30] He noted the ease with which food was served on trays placed on a lap pillow; cotton for the ears to cut down on noise and chewing gum to equalize pressure were also provided. The vibration seemed to be less than on a train, although the cabin of the flying boat became stuffy and uncomfortable before landings and again for a short time after takeoff. Cabin temperature fell to 64° F. at an altitude of 8,000 feet, the rear seats receiving the least heat. The Pan American hotels on Midway, Wake, and Guam provided excellent comfort. The return flight from Manila to Honolulu, at 12,000 feet, involved too long a flight—twelve hours—at that altitude, causing headache and requiring the use of oxygen.

Using the latest in medical equipment, the Medical Section undertook intensive studies in aviation medicine at Kansas City in 1938, focusing its attention on such problems as: deprivation of oxygen, aniseikonia, personality types, susceptibility to anoxia, emotional stability, and proximity to major or minor psychotic breakdown, as well as other related matters which might arise.[31] The bureau received aid for the project from the Harvard, Dartmouth, and Columbia universities, and the Johnson Foundation via the University of Pennsylvania. Grave concern was expressed by several leading aviation authorities, even outside the bureau, over the belief that the development of aeronautical instruments had far overshadowed the attention directed toward the scientific testing of pilot fitness. Available, but apparently not used as much as their promoters liked, were instruments utilized by the military to check on the optical fitness of pilots just before and right after flight tests. Requiring only ten minutes, such examinations could, if continued periodically, keep abreast of the effects of age and other factors.[32]

NEW REGULATIONS

As aviation progressed with faster aircraft and with an increase in number of commercial flights, new and more elaborate air regulations became absolutely imperative. Most noteworthy of the new rules added during 1935 were:

For night flying, multiple-engine planes, capable of flying on one engine in an emergency over terrain where landings were rough, must be used.

Airlines had to get bureau approval of their entire operational divisions, using the suggestions in the bureau's operations manual.

Planes used in instrument flying must be multiengined and have two-way radios in good operating order.

Guarding against fatigue, pilots must fly not more than 1,000 hours per year, 100 hours per month, and not over 100 hours for any 4 consecutive months. They could not fly over 8 hours in any 24-hour period, nor over 30 hours within 7 days.

Dispatching procedure and the personnel of the airlines involved had to be approved by the bureau.[33]

The introduction of instrument-landing approaches caused another set of minimum ceilings to be imposed at airports for this maneuver, the minimum at Chicago being 400 feet while 100 feet provided sufficient space at Indianapolis.[34] Fixed altitudes for flights in the various directions came to be standard procedure as a part of air traffic control. So far as altitudes were concerned in 1936, all eastbound craft flying east of north and south (compass segments) must fly at uneven altitudes, 1, 3, 5, 7, and 9 thousand feet. Airplanes flying west of north and south flew at the even altitudes. In crossing, pilots had to ascend 500 feet. The original procedure had been reversed to allow the westbound pilots to fly lower in the prevailing west winds, yet not be too close to the ground.[35] Designation of various colors for airways was an innovation in 1937, the five transcontinental routes represented in green, the seven north-south primary routes as amber, and most of the feeder routes in red.[36]

STRUCTURAL QUESTIONS

Inquiring congressmen were assured in 1934 that the air regulations imposed by the Department of Commerce did, indeed, include the question of airspeed. The Boeing 247 airliner had been authorized a top speed of 182 miles per hour at 5,000 feet and a cruising speed of 152 miles per hour. United Air Lines voluntarily reduced these speeds to a maximum of 156 miles per hour pending tests which showed vibration in the tail assembly. A strengthening of the elevator torque tube corrected the flutter.[37] Several of the planes had been involved in fatal accidents allegedly because of structural failure.

The bureau recommended a number of points to the aviation industry supplementing the actual structural codes or rules. Airplane instrument panels lacked any semblance of standardization or logical order. Moreover, convenience of the pilot should be taken into account.[38] The suggested bureau model contained a magnetic compass at the top of the panel with two rows of instruments below. The upper row contained the radio compass, airspeed indicator, turn-and-bank indicator, and climb indicator—all just above the bottom of the windshield. On the bottom row would be found the cone-of-silence marker light, altimeter, and directional gyro. The horizontal tachometer and thermometer could be located elsewhere. The panel background of green, instead of black, reduced glare. Structural requirements were published in detail, along with their rationales.[39] Elaborate instructions warned the pilot (and/or owner) of icing hazards to aircraft, especially the fact that formation of ice in the carburetor can be quite slow, allowing the plane to reach full throttle before detection. Excessive heat applied was deleterious to the anti-knock quality of the fuel. Pilots were urged to maintain carburetor-intake air at above 90°F., which involved only a small loss of power. Except in unusually cold or damp weather, the preheater control should be closed.[40] Further difficulties had been encountered in the form of interference with the compass. The bureau suggested use of a "growler" devised by T. R. Hurlbut, mechanic on one of the flight-check crews. The "growler" was a U-shaped electromagnet operated on 110-volt alternating current and used to massage all members of the fuselage and engine mount.[41]

Another safety question concerned the proper number of exits on passenger airliners. In 1935, it was decided to require one exit at least 17 by 24 inches for each 7 passengers on all planes seating over 15 passengers. Furthermore, the emergency exits could not be located in the plane of rotation of the propeller or propellers. Ballast was not used on planes of under 5,000 pounds gross weight.[42] Carbon monoxide, long a source of danger to the automotive industry, plagued aviation as well and manufacturers received the advice to supplement bureau inspections of aircraft with their own to help detect this danger.[43]

Many inquiries reached the bureau about lightning's hazards, a subject invariably misunderstood by the layman. Past experience indicated that lightning struck large dirigibles oftener than airplanes. Strikes on planes usually carried from wing to wing or nose to tail. Gasoline tanks, housed in the metal of the skin on the DC–2, were considered protected. Under artificial experiment, lightning could not stop the engines or other important parts from operating. Passengers, located between the metal sheets—20 feet apart—remained safe.[44] From instances of lightning strikes, authorities concluded that headphones could be worn safely by the crew during electrical disturbances. Trailing antennas on the plane would probably be destroyed. Though several balloonists had been killed by lightning strikes, some had survived strikes only a few feet away. Strange episodes or even tragedies occurred before aeronautical leaders realized the serious effects of some nonrelated items to flight. Suspicions led to thorough tests in 1937 of the effects of camera light meters on the compass; results of these tests showed that a light meter held 4 inches from the compass led to a 180-degree swing. Findings indicated that meters farther away might cause less drastic but still serious deviations.[45]

Regulations, as before, empowered the director to impose restrictions on airspace also. Notable cases included the prohibition of flight without permission over the Century of Progress Fair at Chicago, and a ruling that kept all planes 1 mile from the German airship *Hindenburg* while it was in flight and ½ mile away while it was moored.[46] The inauguration of a later feud between military and civil interests began in 1935, with President Roosevelt's executive order declaring airspace reservations over army and naval reservations and other military locations.[47] Though of a different nature, complaints about air races and shows continued to harass bureau heads, who declared that all craft must be maintained 50 feet apart, no craft reaching 200 feet horizontal to the grandstand and, during acrobatics, no plane approaching 500 feet toward or over the grandstand.[48]

THE CALL FOR PARACHUTES

A number of air crashes intensified a campaign on the part of a few journalists and well-wishers to insist upon the adoption of civil air regulations embracing the use of parachutes for all passengers and crews. Though not original, the arguments gained more space in newspapers during this 1933–1938 era. Typical of the rationale favoring parachutes was the series of articles appearing in the *American Mercury* during 1934–1937.[49] Parachutes, according to this line of reasoning, would be no more cumbersome or frightening to passengers than drills aboard a ship with life jackets and lifeboats. This plan called for parachutes located under each passenger's seat, along with a trapdoor. The pilot manipulated the controls which could eject the passengers in rotation, their chutes opening automatically during the descent. Author Kenneth Brown Collings contended that costs of the parachute ($250), expensive changes in design for the trapdoors, and the reduced payload caused by the added weight of the chutes embodied the real opposition of airline operators to his plan. Especially applicable to this type of rescue operation would be cases in which the pilot was lost without a place for landing, knowing in advance that his plane eventually must be abandoned or maneuvered into a crash landing. Citing the example of the Trans World Airways (TWA) crash of 1935 near Kirksville, Missouri, Collings maintained that all passengers, among them Senator Bronson Cutting of New Mexico, could have been saved by the use of this plan. To the author, the airlines were reacting similarly to the nation's railroads during the late nineteenth century when railroads were forced by legislation to accept modern safety devices; Collings wished that the Bureau of Air Commerce would force the use of parachutes onto the air industry.

The airline operators argued that pilots might be tempted to unload their passengers before exhausting all possible emergency measures and lawsuits might ensue if the pilot got to earth successfully without his passengers. Then, too, passengers could well fear air flight if they felt the pilot might at any time hurl them into space. An extensive study of the crash involving Senator Cutting led Senate investigators to conclude that the use of parachutes on commercial airliners could not be justified.[50] In the first place, parachutes were not infallible and, secondly, there was in most instances, insufficient warning before the crash. On a lighter side, while no regulations resulted demanding the use of parachutes, the bureau continued its careful scrutiny of parachute rigging, granting licenses for such tasks to ten women in 1933.[51]

Trouble with gliders occurred again, leading to careful outlining of specifications for manufacturers and operators who had to obtain an airworthiness certificate from federal officials. Home-built craft were also covered by this regulation.[52]

AIRWAY TRAFFIC CONTROL

Perhaps the most noteworthy innovation in the regulatory activities of the Bureau of Air Commerce evolved with the gradual federal sponsorship of airway traffic control, begun during July, 1936, at Newark, Chicago, and Cleveland; all three originally operated by the airlines.[53] Much of the credit for working out the detailed arrangements of this control must rest with Earl F. Ward, who was employed by one of the leading air transport companies. Ward soon became chief of airway operations with the bureau.[54] Relying essentially upon pilots' reports from check points, Ward inaugurated the system for his own company, with the aid of Glen A. Gilbert, Bureau of Air Commerce. In April, 1935, long after the bureau and industry leaders became alarmed over the hazard of air collision, the air-carrier operators and the Director of Air Commerce met for a series of conferences. It was decided in November, 1935, to allow the companies' flight control officers to handle the duties of airway traffic control. Later the Bureau of Air Commerce acquired the operations at Chicago, Newark, and Cleveland, while on July 6, 1936, new operations appeared at Pittsburgh, Detroit, Washington, D.C., Los Angeles, and Oakland.

Airport traffic control depended entirely upon the pilot's use of the proper radio receiver and transmitter on the plane. In the daytime with a ceiling under 3,000 feet or visibility of 5 miles or less (or with regard to any other local rules), the pilot maintained a course along the right-hand side of the airway (odds and evens for altitude added later), making use of beacon lights, if visible, or the radio-range course, during the last 25 miles of the approach.[55] At 10 miles, a typical pilot report might read: "Smith National Airlines NC–73 (or the trip number) calling WAPS . . . go ahead." Upon acknowledgment, the pilot reported his position, estimated arrival time, and asked for any other desired information. The airport controller gave him the proper runway, direction and velocity of the wind, relative position of other planes in the vicinity, and such other data as requested. "O.K." was the standard form of acknowledgment. After landing, the pilot kept his receivers on for any further directions from the control tower. "All clear for takeoff" greeted the pilot who had been granted permission to leave the airport. Bureau officials scrutinized interline safety agreements on messages and data used in air traffic control in the attempt to obtain uniformity.

Air traffic control of planes outside the vicinity of the airports entailed a constant watch that was based on radioed position reports and required flight plans.[56] Large maps and wooden tabs with pointed ends to show the direction of the flight had to be revised constantly as the index to a wall map listing positions and altitudes of all airplanes under the control station. One controller, with headphone and a long cord, moved around the room, checking the teletype reports (Schedule B), and posting the positions on the wall. Estimates of the future positions were included. All the data must be entered on record sheets affixed to clipboards on the table. The wooden ship markers with a slip of paper listed the name of the airline, trip number, time of departure, and altitude. Markers were moved forward every fifteen minutes (regardless of new reports), with the estimate of distance covered. Original chief controllers were: John L. Huber, Newark; Homer F. Cole, Cleveland; Glen A. Gilbert, Chicago; and Harry D. Copland, Detroit.

Numerous changes in procedure had to be introduced from time to time in order to keep abreast of increased traffic. In

October, 1937, a "black" teletype network for meteorological data and a "white" network for nonmeteorological information were introduced. *Aeronautics Bulletin No. 1* was revised to explain changes to all pilots. Also printed were definite holding procedures spaced at 1,000-foot intervals and at altitudes up to 6,000 feet. In March, 1938, regulations allowed a takeoff for instrument flying when ceiling and visibility were reduced to 300 feet and ½ mile if cleared by a trained operator in air traffic control.[57] At this same time, the width of airways was reduced to 10 miles on each side of the center line. Acrobatics could now be performed on the airways if necessary precautions had been taken. Color designations for the various airways were also revised to include green, amber, red, and blue (replacing the red for secondary airways).

RECKLESS FLYING

Ward kept in close contact with his control managers to educate the airline operators and pilots concerning their responsibilities to air traffic control. Responding to H. F. Cole's report of faulty operations, Ward noted, "Nothing we can do except throw a scare by investigations."[58] Complaints arose steadily in the mid-thirties over delays and encroachments against civilian craft by army aircraft.[59] Waiting on an army plane constituted a mere irritation; other airline officers encountered far more serious treatment. Especially frustrating was the experience of Bruce E. Braun, Operations Manager for Chicago and Southern Air Lines. Believing army aviators had not read of air regulations, Braun reached a point near desperation: "God forgive them they know not what they do."[60] On this same day, planes of Chicago and Southern, TWA, and American had all been endangered at St. Louis by an army bomber: "It is not my intention to threaten on this thing, Jake, but I am giving you the straight goods when I tell you that the first collision that occurs between an army airplane and a transport, I am going to give this entire file to the Associated Press—so help me—if it completely destroys our passenger business."[61]

Braun had previously conveyed the seriousness of other near misses to Army Air Force (AAF) leaders without satisfaction: "Many of our passengers are old riders and are fully conversant with the present regulations governing air traffic on a civil airway."[62] Braun alleged that frequently army and navy aircraft operating between New Orleans and St. Louis crossed before his company's liners as the commercial ships let down out of an overcast. He sought the advice of Major James Doolittle, who believed Braun should write to the AAF headquarters. Military planes, now using the civil airways, constituted a real menace to the airline pilots, according to N. B. Sangree, assistant to Director Vidal.[63] Delta Air Lines complained about the antics involving nine army ships near Shreveport, Louisiana. The station manager at Newark, New Jersey, reported a sudden appearance of army bombers that resulted in mass confusion. Another unreported army flight, consisting of approximately eighteen planes, forced a TWA pilot into a sharp right turn to avoid a collision east of Cambridge, Ohio. Five months later, TWA reported its pilot coming within 300 feet of an Army BT–9 northeast of Camden.[64]

The bureau itself cited instances of improper procedure in the military. In one case, an army plane left Pittsburgh eastbound after filing a flight plan calling for an altitude of 3,000 feet, an impossibility considering the terrain, and without any consideration of the presence of other aircraft legally following other altitudes. The pilot had to leave his declared altitude to get over the mountains. Earl Ward of the bureau became quite upset: "We need a conference between the military and the Department of Commerce."[65] Not all military leaders ignored this serious problem, one which was to plague the civil aviation interests in the country without legal correction until the late 1950's. One army official promised that his fliers would report positions whenever using the area around Chicago extending to Columbus, Ohio.[66] Generally speaking, however, bureau officials believed that the majority of army pilots were uncooperative, failed to advise the civil authorities of a flight plan, and would not observe the rules governing the nation's airways. Ward's staff compiled a list of all violations detected, forwarding such data to the proper military officials in the hope that proper disciplinary action would be in the offing.[67] Little improvement resulted. The Air Line Pilots' Association expressed deep concern, understanding the difficulties in the matter confronting the bureau's frantic appeals to the military.[68]

INSPECTORS OR CONTROLLERS?

A disagreement over the apparent importance of air traffic control (that is, in relation to other activities of the bureau) arose during appropriations hearings before the House in March,

1936, between Director Vidal and Assistant Director Cone. Vidal extended top priority to an item of $100,000 for additional inspectors; Cone wanted the sum for air traffic control.[69] The bureau encountered difficulty in obtaining and training air traffic controllers, turning to former pilots as the most logical source of recruits. Ward trained the men at this time. Each station employed 4 persons with a relief man for the operations which originally accounted for a 16-hour day, only to be extended in 1938 to 24 hours.[70] Bureau personnel followed the flight plans each airline gave to the airports. They did not follow airport control operations which were still handled by the airlines. Assistant Cone estimated the need for 350–500 men if the bureau would assume the control duties at the airports, a change he did not favor. Four men from each of 5 airlines formed the traffic control crew of 20 at Newark. Congressmen were assured that a pilot could not be forced to leave a field against his will, though one dispatcher told his pilots to ignore all weather reports as they were wrong most of the time anyway. The airline employees serving as airport controllers had to obtain certificates from the bureau before assuming their duties.[71]

AIRWAYS OPERATIONS

Indispensable to the advancement of commercial aviation were the improvements in the navigational aids to flying. Essentially, the bureau, during 1933–1938, had first to recover from the appropriations cuts in order to resume its steady increase in construction of new airways. Secondly, increased vigor went into the shift in emphasis from use of beacon lights to that of radio-range beacons, the all-weather approach to guidance along the airways. Learning to fly the beam presented the newcomer with a distinct obstacle: "No pilot can be said to be accomplished who is not capable of flying a plane by instrument and radio methods."[72] In training, the pilot under the hood learned to fly by compass without losing altitude or changing speed or direction. He must time himself while executing turns of 90, 180, and 360 degrees, adding time spirals between altitudes of 500 to 3,000 feet. Next he executed shorter turns of 12, 20, 30, and 40 degrees. At 3,000 feet, he was told to find the radio beam and identify the correct leg, realizing that the beam width was 1,500 feet at 4 miles from the field, and narrowing like a funnel on toward the airport.

As before, congressmen pressed for additional facilities in

their own areas but were assured that new construction met approval only after the consent of the Post Office authorities with an eye to the mail routes. Director Vidal met vast criticism from Congress in 1936 for expending funds previously allocated for airway construction to other facets of bureau operations.[73] After long study of the immediate and long-range needs of aviation, an airways modernization program calling for $7 million was announced in 1938, of which $2 million would be expended on new airways.[74] Improved airplanes and radio beacons led the bureau to decide upon 50-mile intervals between intermediate landing fields, with the hope that radio facilities at each field would be satisfactorily heard at a distance of 25 miles. Unlighted landing fields had amber lights on the beacon at the field. As formerly, the bureau did not purchase sites for intermediate fields because of the many changes made in the airway locations; emergency fields totaled about 300 throughout this era.

RADIO AIDS

The expansion of airways proved to be only as effective as the dependability of the navigational aids available to the pilot. Here, little innovation appeared during 1933–1938, though research and experiments conducted at the time reaped great dividends in later eras. The question of obsolete radio equipment plagued Director Vidal, who informed congressmen in 1936 that worn-out radio aids operated by his personnel differed little from outmoded home radio sets. Many of the existing radio aids became obsolete overnight in 1934 when use of improved radio for guidance came to be considered ready for widespread installation. Vidal had requested $1.5 million more than the appropriation granted for radio aids in fiscal 1936. The combination of voice and direction signals via the radio beacons gained serious attention, the bureau establishing an experimental unit at Elizabeth, New Jersey, in 1933. Two years later, a similar study was under way at Pittsburgh. Pilots complained that static from rain or snow often prevented reception of the combined radio signals in the airplane's receiver.[75] Bureau radio operators suggested the use of code in transmission during poor reception as easier to hear than voice. In one instance at North Platte, Nebraska, code messages between pilot and station arranged for gas, oil, and food upon the landing of a congressional party, an impressive feat witnessed by the holders of the purse strings.[76] Unfortunately, such an auspicious example could not be cited as typical. To provide emergency means for radio-equipped planes, all airport stations were ordered in 1936 by the Federal Communications Commission to maintain continuous watch on the frequency of 3,105 kilocycles reserved for calling by itinerant aircraft.[77] Fan markers were given distinctive, keyed signals to clarify better their differentiation from other equipment. A further aid was offered by D. M. Stuart, bureau radio engineer, in the form of a transmitter emitting a high-frequency beam vertically to indicate the cone of silence by turning on a light in the plane.[78] Promising improved transmission and reception, bureau radio leaders experimented with ultrahigh frequency radio, beginning in 1937.

The ultimate goal of radio aids required the refinement of the instrument, or so-called "blind" landing, tested on flights at College Park, Maryland, and Newark. Blindfolds were used during some landings. Other experiments were centered at Indianapolis and elsewhere, while Assistant Director Rex Martin, in 1935, began a study of twelve airports for possible adaptation to the "blind-approach" techniques, using the system of transmission perfected by the Army Air Corps.[79] Instrument approaches could be made at Chicago and Indianapolis with ceilings of 400 feet and 100 feet, respectively. The early "blind" landing, always a source of rumor and consternation, indeed provided the ultimate test of nerve and skill plus luck on the part of the successful pilot; failure meant certain tragedy, pilots realizing the treacherous business as they sometimes caught a first glimpse of the ground at 50 feet or less. Amateurs, old-timers, everyone, had their own ideas about what constituted the best system, according to Irving Metcalfe, bureau senior aeronautical engineer: "You can't throw away an empty whiskey bottle without hitting somebody who's just invented a blind landing system."[80] Prior to 1938, six plans had been flight-tested in this country. None had won undisputed favor. Another experiment looked to the future development of the omnidirectional navigation range. Reed College and Purdue University obtained contracts for this work in 1938.[81]

An instrument-flying trainer was purchased by the bureau in 1935. The famous Amelia Earhart, employed by the Bureau of Air Commerce in 1935 for $1 a year, served as an aeronautical expert in testing a Lear radio direction finder. Weighing 30 pounds and 7 by 9 by 15 inches in size, the instrument received ordinary radio direction and periodic weather reports at the same time.[82] The close rapport between the bureau and Miss Earhart continued as Director Vidal closely followed her latest endeavors. Many telegrams passed between the two: "Heartiest congratulations Mexico City to Newark flight last night. Anxious for your report on radio compass and the aids to navigation on Department of Commerce airways."[83] Within three months, Miss Earhart resigned from her job with the bureau: "I wish to be free to pursue my commercial aviation activities without any possibility of embarrassment or misunderstanding, which might arise from this official connection, informal and insignificant as it is."[84] Development of the radio compass, an Army Air Corps invention, provided the major basis of the bureau's instrument landing system in 1935. Captain Albert F. Hegenberger was detailed by the Department of War to help the bureau adapt the instrument for its use. This instrument weighed 45 pounds, and the receiving set's selector could be moved to the frequency of a known station, whereupon the needle pointing on the instrument board indicated the direction.[85]

WEATHER INFORMATION

Meteorological data, already mentioned as so important to the pilot, again provided the key to success or failure of many flights, this information being relayed from the Weather Bureau to the pilot via the personnel of the Bureau of Air Commerce. Winds aloft at 12,000–13,000 feet were added to the weather reports in 1933. Weather forecast technique was changed to provide broadcasts from twenty-six stations every four hours (beginning in summer, 1934) with the use of symbols for weather conditions—clear, cloudy, broken clouds—on the teletype. Motorists were advised that they too could pick up these weather broadcasts on a car radio. At this time the Weather Bureau was in the throes of a policy battle over the implementation of new theories known as air-mass analysis, the major value of which would affect aviation a short time thereafter.[86] The use of code and abbreviations on teletype saved one-half the time of verbal transmission, allowing twelve seconds for one weather report. For example, on the Washington–Atlanta airway, the coded report for Washington might read: "WA AG 1341 ES WA Ø/Ø60/8 95/69 ⬊6 998." Translated, this reads: "Washington, ceiling unlimited, high scattered clouds, lower scattered clouds at 6,000 feet, visibility 8 miles, temperature 95, dew point 69, wind northwest at 6, barometer 29.98."[87] Variations of these abbreviations and symbols have been retained to the present. Transmission of the teletype was increased from 40 to 60 words per minute; voice transmission by radio remained at 100 words per minute. As in all phases of its widespread activities, the Weather Bureau encountered much criticism of its reports and forecasts when faulty but received little praise when accurate. Undoubtedly, much improvement remained to be seen in this science, but Weather Bureau personnel did not deserve the assertion of Assistant Director Martin before a congressional committee in 1937, which implied that some of his own personnel exceeded the Weather Bureau in weather reporting.[88] He did admit that the Weather Bureau kept a watch on its own inaccuracies with a constant eye toward improvement. Offenders in both the Bureau of Air Commerce and the Weather Bureau faced the threat of suspension. The collection of upper-air data via airplane observation (Apob), which was inaccurate and dangerous, characterized the obstacles to better aid for aviation until the perfection and use of the radiometeorograph shortly after this period.[89]

Users of radio and weather data were polled to determine their choice of terminology or symbols. Reaction dictated the retention of the term "unlimited ceiling" in the radio broadcasts.[90] Many users believed that a better job of staggering the radio broadcasts could be accomplished.[91] Then, too, many key locations suffered yet from the lack of two-way radio facilities, rendering use of radio-range beacons, instrument landings, or weather broadcasts entirely impossible. The Des Moines airport felt this glaring deficiency.[92] Pilots affirmed, upon questioning by bureau officials in an extended survey early in 1936, that Air Commerce and Weather Bureau personnel both lacked alertness to change, forecasters often issuing the "fair and warmer" type of report appreciated by farmers, not fliers.[93] Pilots urged more attention to wind shifts, feeling complete uncertainty whenever ceiling and visibility dropped under 2,000 feet and 3 miles. Observers should be licensed and face severe penalties for inaccurate reports. Despite all the airways radio aids, the pilots cited lack of dependable weather reports along with interruption of radio-beam signals (on the loop-antenna type radio) for weather reports as top offenders barring air safety. They cited also the need for further air traffic control. Thickness of fog and the air roughness just above it were also data crying for attention. In support of the Weather Bureau, the pilots warned their colleagues not to heed the (airline) company forecasts but to use the Weather Bureau's instead.

POOR AIRPORTS

Airways operations improved only as radio aids and services could be expanded. But the nation's airports woefully needed increased funds and careful planning. Here, emergency funds of the New Deal helped fill the gaps. Previously, local communities had built the airports; the government had merely lent advice and inspected the completed facilities. Now, appropriations could be had for improvements and construction—the long-awaited type of direct federal subsidy to commercial aviation so deplored by the majority of congressmen under Calvin Coolidge and Hoover. By the end of 1934, Director Vidal could report fruitful beginnings in aid which he envisaged as support for the nation's small airports. However, under the Civil Works Administration's guidance, a good share of the projected $33 million went to the larger airports, many of which already had attained respectable status.[94] At the time, CWA engineers worked on 650 new sites and allowed improvements to be started on 550 old locations. Only one employee in the Bureau of Air Commerce maintained liaison with the CWA, a factor justifiably deplored by Congressmen William B. Oliver and Thomas S. McMillan. Continued under the Federal Emergency Relief Administration, other New Deal funds also helped airports. The Works Progress Administration (WPA) carried on 405 airport projects of its own.[95] Air marking of 10,125 locations had also been completed from these relief funds by June, 1938, while the WPA conducted an elaborate national survey of airports during the same year. The nation's capital city, long the target of criticism for inadequate airport facilities accorded to commercial flights, needed a close-by airport and an auxiliary terminal for instrument landings.[96] Despite annual bills before Congress, no action was forthcoming at this time. Meanwhile, the Bureau of Air Commerce simplified its airport ratings, starting in January, 1935, by considering only those fields with scheduled operations and awarding a T rating upon successful examination.[97] Airport problems of all types reached the bureau, even how to lessen the harm incurred by rodents. Bitter experience led experts to warn planners not to build airports on the leeward side of areas heavily affected by smoke and general air pollution.[98]

NEGLECTED AIRWAYS

With attention diverted to the expansion of airways—from 2,000 miles to 23,000 miles between 1926 and 1938—little public heed followed the beginnings of an airways system in a sadly neglected American possession—Alaska. Costs, acknowledged to be high in Alaska, proved to be lower per passenger mile than the fees paid for chartering a dog team. The first aeronautical inspector, Murray Hall, was dispatched there in 1934, but only seventy-nine planes operated in Alaska during 1936.[99] Undoubtedly, the United States suffered early in World War II for not having commenced sooner its establishment of air facilities in Alaska. Another vulnerable territory, the Philippines, could muster even less attention, only two scheduled airlines and no radio in use during 1935.[100]

Maintenance of all airways operations varied from good to bad, depending upon the examiner. Primarily, it would appear that the bureau's major deficiencies lay in the lack of proper equipment, not improper maintenance. At any rate, depression cuts did exact a toll in some areas; C. M. Lample, superintendent of airways at Kansas City, believed conditions in his district to be deplorable, needing two to three years for correction.[101] Not that the top bureau officials had neglected maintenance. Jay A. Mount, Superintendent of Maintenance in 1934, reported the following discrepancies noted on an inspection tour:[102] beacons out of focus, incorrect voltage lamps, receivers and transmitters not properly adjusted, surplus equipment without an inventory, emergency equipment operating continuously due to faulty switches, sheds and foundations in ill repair, and aviation gasolines stored carelessly. The inspection, completed by R. B. Collins, an assistant airways engineer, was documented with photographs. Similar reports reached Assistant Director Martin during the next year, reflecting a spotty record in field maintenance, one which could not be corrected overnight despite Martin's observation: "No one is to gain the impression that instructions can be neglected."[103] Then, too, not all mechanicians involved had such difficult terrain as the Salt Lake–Pasco airway, where the inspections entailed travel by auto, wagon, and seven miles by boat. More sparsely settled than this was the area around the radio station at Guadalupe Pass, Texas, not far distant from the ruins of the depot used by the Butterfield Stage Line operating between St. Louis and California. In 1935, the bureau operator still noticed people spending weeks there looking for buried gold.[104] Maintenance costs per mile, estimated at $220 in 1935, had stood at a similar figure in 1928.

AERONAUTICAL DEVELOPMENT

Not long after his appointment, Vidal expressed pessimism over the status of aviation as he foresaw a three-year program of improvement. Vidal believed military aviation practically undeveloped and commercial aviation, other than the airlines, depressed.[105] Another type of subsidy granted to commercial aviation came with the drastic change in program allowing the expenditure of federal money to develop new aircraft. Director Vidal had no desire to see the airplanes of 1934 built in quantity; his aim was to lead the trend to safer aircraft via bureau design of the craft.[106] This New Deal measure also ordered the bureau to release publicly the causes of air accidents. From the beginning, Vidal's efforts looked to the desired increase in private flying through the marketing of safe but cheap aircraft for the potential user. J. H. Geisse, Chief of the Development Section, explained to wary congressmen that the bureau, enabled to undertake this work by law in 1934, purchased experimental types of planes. Using the NACA laboratory, the bureau built planes on contract, including a tailless plane ($12,500) and a direct-control autogiro. Vidal supported his use of regular appropriations for work on a flivver plane, noting also the transfer of $100,000 from the Department of War for developmental activities. Vidal's approach met antagonism from the start; influencing congressmen proved to be nearly impossible, because private industry had produced all the nation's aircraft before the New Deal. In one verbal exchange, Congressman Robert L. Bacon noted that private enterprise had developed the finest plane, the Douglas DC–3. Vidal cautioned that, while the Douglas was excellent for speed, comfort, and handling in the air, it was nevertheless, the most difficult of transports to handle otherwise.[107]

Vidal and his subordinates also sought the three-wheel undercarriage for aircraft, an aid to landing in strong wind and bad weather. In the competition for contracts, the Hammond Aircraft Corporation of Ypsilanti, Michigan, won the bid in 1935 for a small plane with visibility like a car and the safer landing gear. A second contract went to the Waldo Waterman firm at Santa Monica, California, for work on the tailless plane, adding the feature of detachable wings and rear-wheel drive. Most progressive of all was the award to the Autogiro Company of America, located at Willow Grove, Pennsylvania, for a wingless, direct-control autogiro, equipped also for operation on the highway.[108] Geisse flew the tailless plane to Washington, D.C., from the West Coast. Cruising at 90 miles per hour, this two-seated monoplane had a ceiling in excess of 12,000 feet. Geisse, a veteran of 300 hours with the army in 1917, had not owned a license again until 1934.

Though not delivered, Vidal hoped for a transport plane for small airlines, capable of carrying 5 passengers, 2 pilots, 400 pounds of baggage and cargo, able to cruise for 1,000 miles, and to clear a 50-foot obstacle in not over 1,500 feet of takeoff. The autogiro, with an 80-horsepower engine, was delivered to the front door of the bureau in 1936. Geisse was particularly proud of the Hammond plane, informing Assistant Secretary J. M. Johnson of the preferential treatment the plane would be given in insurance rates: "As you know, the Hammond Airplane was the first project of the Development Section."[109] The plane was spin-proof, operated with two instead of the usual three controls, and Geisse contended that a novice could take it off land. While Vidal thought in terms of a $700 flivver plane, the manufacturers dangled 120 different types of airplanes before the public, only 12 in the $1,500 range.[110] Vidal was able to divert approximately $500,000 of PWA funds toward the developmental work. Designed for the pilot and one passenger, the flivver plane would have an open cockpit on top of the wings and land at a speed of just 25 miles per hour. Vidal's promotional imagination, quite laudable and sincere in spite of so much criticism, called for a transatlantic airway complete with "islands" 550 miles apart along the thirty-ninth parallel and urged the establishment of additional seaplane bases throughout this country.

Government-owned aircraft, while a necessity, remained the subject of much painful debate because of congressional parsimony. At the outset of the depression-caused economy drive, fifteen of the bureau's planes went into storage and the hours of flight were restricted.[111] Colonel Cone complained of the situation before congressmen: "Many of the ships we do operate we would not license or permit anyone else to operate."[112] The bureau asked for twenty-nine new aircraft. Additional funds were forthcoming as the fleet of small ships was enlarged, and a Lockheed 12–A, called "a flying laboratory" by the bureau, was also purchased in 1937. Carrying six to eight people, the craft had a cruising range of 1,000 miles and speed of 213 miles per hour.[113] In answer to legislators, bureau leaders contended they did not need their own autogiros, though this craft was considered excellent in searching for lost planes. Several different types of small craft made up the bureau fleet; the all-metal Curtiss-Wright coupe, the Waterman tailless plane, the Weick W–1, a Hammond, and a Stinson were included. Ironically enough, government employees could travel by air only if the Secretary of their department signed the approval.[114]

PROMOTIONAL ACTIVITIES

Other promotional endeavors of the bureau also looked to the improvement of American aviation. New Deal funds, under the CWA in 1934, came to the rescue of the lagging program of air marking. Later, WPA money fostered air marking; 7,505 markers in 27 states during one 8-month period attested to the notable progress in this field. Roof markings were given the attention of bureau experts, including three women—all with transport licenses—the Misses Louise Thaden, Bentonville, Arkansas; Nancy Harkness, Boston; and Helen McCloskey, Pittsburgh. In 1936, Blanche Noyes, one of the initial ten American women to earn a transport license, joined the bureau as an air-marking pilot; she remains with the Federal Agency still (1966). Miss Noyes, who had been taught to fly by her husband, contended with a fire in the baggage compartment of her plane during her first air race in 1929. Fortunately, she landed safely in Texas. In 1930, she gave John D. Rockefeller, Sr., his first and last airplane flight; the famous entrepreneur reportedly enjoyed the experience.[115] As might have been expected, the bureau took an active role in the famed but ill-fated attempt to have industry police itself: the National Industrial Recovery Act. The elaborate though futile codes were the result of the concerted efforts of Director Vidal and Cone of the bureau, and personnel from the Air Line Pilots' Association, Harvard University, Brookings Institution, and other aeronautical researchers.[116]

The bureau's attempt to foster aviation also featured exhibits for the public, such as the government's radio-aid display at the Century of Progress in Chicago.[117] A radio laboratory was retained in Chicago until May, 1937. President Roosevelt took time to acknowledge support of a fund in memory of Miss Earhart in 1938 and willingly expressed gratitude to Orville Wright for his early contributions.[118] Director Vidal also served on committees and foundations honoring such aeronautical pioneers as Wright and Wiley Post.[119] The response to requests for money was not always heartening, and congressmen in turn learned that, as a business, civil aeronautics in the country did not equal the candy bar industry.[120] In the realm of publications, on July 15, 1933, the *Air Commerce Bulletin* became a monthly issue instead of twice monthly. Weekly notices to airmen continued to aid with detailed information about airport regulations and other pertinent data for pilots. A silent motion picture, *Safety on the Federal Skways,* was released by the bureau in 1935 as a public service. Among the new special bulletins issued to aeronautical interests were No. 27, *Aeronautics Radio,* and the revision of No. 1, *Civil Aeronautics in the United States.* Detailed in its valuable data, Bulletin No. 1, for example, explained traffic control procedures at various airports.[121] The sectional maps of the United States, a service provided to airmen, continued to be produced with seventy-six of the eighty-seven available by summer, 1936.

INTERNATIONAL DEVELOPMENTS

On the international scene, the United States added to its list of reciprocal agreements with foreign states during this era and continued to extend special aid to flights of foreigners to this country. The *Graf Zeppelin*'s trips were examples, the Aeronautics Branch representatives meeting the ship on its arrival from Latin America at Miami on October 23, 1933, en route to the Century of Progress Fair at Chicago. Dictator Benito Mussolini ordered decorations for ninety-nine Americans who aided the flight of General Italo Balbo. Included were Martin, Assistant Director, and William T. Miller, a district manager, both of the bureau.[122] The gratitude of foreign authorities toward the bureau was continued, but awards or decorations had to be turned over to the Department of State until the persons involved had been separated from federal employment.[123] Visiting officials from eleven Latin-American nations, provided transportation by Pan American and Eastern, inspected bureau facilities and those of the Weather Bureau during air navigation week in October, 1935. On another phase of the international scene, a French questioner was assured that the bureau had nothing to do with apparent efforts to lure American pilots into duty in the Spanish Civil War.[124] The French officially congratulated the Bureau of Air Commerce on the speed record set by pilot Howard Hughes.[125]

Not so pleasant was the tightening, already in 1937, of privileges accorded foreign pilots entering Hitler's Germany. Each plane must land at a commercial airport having facilities for examining baggage and passports. This ruled out flights without intermediate landings.[126] Meanwhile, airline companies, both here and abroad, pressed and probed for authorization to serve on both sides of the Atlantic Ocean. Secretary of Commerce D. C. Roper acknowledged Pan American's request for scheduled flights to Bermuda. By late in the thirties, this energetic company stretched its operations across the Atlantic. At the same time, the German line Lufthansa began experimental flights to the United States via the Azores. While the war clouds gathered abroad, some apprehension emerged in the United States about foreign sources learning of our experiments with the various instrument-landing systems. Bureau leaders saw no effective way to keep such information out of foreign hands.[127] On the brighter side, Canadian officials, in addition to the reciprocal flight agreements, contacted their American counterparts for advice on all matters pertaining to fire risks in aviation. The bureau described its system as one which utilized the standards of the fire underwriting companies, augmented by the bureau's own rules for airport fire-fighting equipment.[128] Martin, after completing visits to England, Germany, France, Holland, and Italy and taking the *Graf Zeppelin* trip from Friedrichshafen to Rio de Janeiro, rated Pan American's service better than that of its European rivals. Martin especially liked Pan American's route between Miami and Rio and urged Americans to look to South America instead of Europe for exports in air trade.[129]

Unquestionably, the advent of air carriers capable of providing overseas service came at a time when suitable arrangements among the leading nations of the world to provide genuine, reciprocal privileges to foreign airlines were lacking. World War II merely postponed the decision making for a number of years. Many aeronautical experts hoped for freedom of the air which would allow competing lines from various nations to schedule service in foreign lands. However, little could be accomplished in this direction. Only four of the thirty-one nations concluding the Air Navigation Conference of 1919 had actually ratified the convention; the United States was a nonratifier.[130] Meanwhile, a certain amount of bickering prevailed among nations. Policy displayed by the United States to 1938 could not be considered entirely consistent. Canada received favorable treatment on the

Seattle–Vancouver route but not on any other exclusive route. Secretary Roper frowned on any competition against Pan American in the Caribbean area, refusing the Royal Dutch Airlines (KLM) privileges at Miami in 1937. Encouraging Pan American to negotiate on its own for rights in Latin America and the Pacific, the United States, however, dealt on a government-to-government approach for transatlantic service. Portugal awarded Pan American a monopoly on U.S. carriers there in 1937. On the other hand, Great Britain continually delayed a move to acknowledge American efforts to complete Pan American's route to Europe. An air agreement between Britain and the United States, signed in 1935, specifically excluded air routes without consent of each party.[131] Lufthansa asked the United States for landing privileges, but Germany offered nothing in return. This transatlantic bargaining delayed scheduled air service for several years before the war in 1939.[132] Indeed, freedom of the air became a joke in a struggling world. Similar events transpired in the Pacific, where the Chinese granted no foreign landing rights at Canton for fear the Japanese would ask for the same. The United States refused British and Dutch stops at Hawaii for military reasons. A noticeable lack of Japanese-American air accord existed.

COOPERATION AT HOME

From the many instances of discord revealed in near misses involving military and commercial planes, one might gather that animosity ruled supreme between the two forces. Such was hardly the case, regardless of the dangerous lack of civil control over military aviation. Mention has already been made of the Army Air Corps experiments with instrument landings and the radio compass. Bureau employees extended every possible aid to army pilots when the occasion arose. During April, 1934, bureau employee Edwin F. Flagge noticed two army pilots in fog attempting to follow the highway near his home. With the aid of another radio operator, Flagge managed to guide the lost pilots to the airport. Bureau men at Oceanside, California, had the opportunity to aid in the rescue of pilots in three navy seaplanes forced down offshore. Branch men summoned a police car to high ground along the shore from where T. C. Cunningham, an airways keeper, used the headlights to signal two destroyers via Morse code where to proceed to get the planes and airmen. Nonmilitary airmen enjoyed similar help when in dire circumstances, as in the case of a Weather Bureau pilot taking observations up to 17,000 feet (the dangerous and temporary Apob program). The Fort Worth radio range proved of great value in guiding the aviator out of the overcast which had been reduced from a report of "unlimited" to just 200 feet within ten minutes.

Speaking of aid, bureau officials always cited their help to motorists who benefited by the radio information, much of it in the form of weather information from the Weather Bureau. In cases of emergency, others could be of assistance to the Bureau of Air Commerce, one instance being an emergency flight completed by United Air Lines for the wife of a junior radio operator stricken with appendicitis. Bureau field personnel reflected on numerous anecdotal episodes descriptive of the quick thinking necessary to provide optimum service during as much of the day as possible. A radio operator at Des Moines refused to despair at a sudden breakdown of the radio-range beacon transmitter, for he fashioned a temporary repair consisting of rubber bands, changed often, until the faulty spring assembly could be soldered. At any rate, pilots continued to hear the station's identifying signal.[133]

Cooperation sometimes proved elusive when most needed. To the consternation of central office leaders, the caretaker at an emergency field near Red Rock, Arkansas, refused aid to a customs agent of the Treasury Department sent to check on suspected planes.[134] Officials of the National Archives sought and received permission to look over the confidential files in the bureau's field offices.[135] With the growth of bureau activities came the unpleasant task of obeying subpoenas to provide data in court, a practice often abused by lawmakers concerning federal technical officials such as the Bureau of Air Commerce and the Weather Bureau.[136]

Coordination of federal activities with those of the states again left much to be desired. Late in 1937, Assistant Secretary Johnson asked the state officials attending their convention to meet the federal authorities halfway; the Department of Commerce would be cooperative.[137] Ruffled feelings persisted, however, especially following a California court's ruling in 1937 contesting federal authority in intrastate flight.[138] Though the extent of cooperation varied from time to time, on the whole, improvement could be seen. Governor Henry E. Horner of Illinois, as a case in point, assured Director Vidal that he would allow no acrobatics and would assure a safe demonstration for Aviation Day in Springfield.[139]

Extensive use of advisory committees, both of the interdepartmental and nongovernmental variety, enhanced the operations of the Bureau of Air Commerce. Monthly meetings were conducted with the advisory board, an interdepartmental body, and periodic sessions with all aviation interests helped with airways operation.[140] True, the results sometimes proved disappointing, to no one's surprise, considering the challenge of gaining full accord from so many separate interests. At least the theory was laudable. Hitler's antics in Europe brought another problem close to bureau interests, indeed, to all aviation leaders seeking national defense. The question of training young men in aeronautics at the land-grant colleges came before Congress in 1938, but Representative Ross A. Collins of Mississippi, among others, feared such practice would kill too many young men.[141] The bill failed to gain support at this time.

ACCIDENTS, DISMAY, AND REORGANIZATION

AS NOTED EARLIER, the same law allowing the bureau to contract for aircraft manufacturing activities also forced the publication of causes in the case of individual air accidents, along with compulsory public hearings during investigation of serious cases. Contrary to the early belief, public reaction to the new policy appeared quite favorable.[1] The "probable cause" became a watchword in American aviation circles, even though blaming the dead pilot in many cases led to sharp denial by fellow pilots and congressmen. By and large, however, it seems as if the bureau personnel detailed to accident investigation performed their tasks as conscientiously as possible. The argument between inadequacy or malfunction of the navigational aids on the one hand versus human failure—crew, dispatchers, control tower— on the other appeared inevitable, even as it remains today. Un- happily for the bureau, tragedies involving quite famous or influ- ential persons furnished a sensational glow to the reporting of these same mishaps, usually to the detriment of aviation in general. That commercial and private aviation interests were able to overcome this renewed assault on the baby of the trans- portation world is fitting tribute to the tenacity of the industry and the Bureau of Air Commerce, its silent partner.

THE CUTTING CRASH

Damaging to the public faith in flying and exhibiting the technological and human limitations present in aviation was the crash of the TWA Sky Chief near Atlanta, Missouri, on May 6, 1935, killing Senator Bronson Cutting and four other people while seriously injuring eight.[2] Six days of hearings, testimony of thirty-four witnesses, and more than 900 pages of records displayed the bureau's keen intention to ascertain the reasons why this DC–2 fell. Though not listing a definite cause, the ensuing report identified contributing factors: (1) the Weather Bureau did not predict the hazardous conditions that developed, (2) the company gave improper clearance of the flight at Albuquerque, and the pilot erred in continuing the flight while knowing the plane's radio was inoperative, and (3) the company's ground crew at Kansas City was at fault for not directing the pilot to a field with better weather conditions. The bureau's Accident Board reported that the pilot turned to avoid fog in a depression, the wing dragging into the ground. Sensing the emergency, the pilot's dying declaration explained that he was out of gas. The pilots were commended by the bureau for heroic efforts to counteract this impossible situation. Secretary of Commerce Daniel C. Roper remained firm in support of his bureau: "I am convinced that the accident was due chiefly to bad weather conditions."[3]

Other violations came to light, but could not necessarily be labeled as causes of the accident. Airline management was negligent in these cases since Pilot Harvey Bolton had not taken the quarterly medical examination and had been absent from the particular airline division over six months without seeking new approval from the Bureau of Air Commerce. Copilot Kenneth Greeson did not hold a scheduled air transport rating (continuous flight exceeding eight hours). The TWA dispatcher at Kansas City should have grounded the plane at Wichita, since he knew, when the pilot was over Wichita, that the ceiling was below minimum at Kansas City and the pilot would not have the minimum forty-five minutes of fuel reserve. Finally, the Sky Chief carried out instrument flying without two-way radio operation, the plane's transmitter not functioning on the required night frequency when the company cleared the plane at Albuquerque. Secretary Roper concluded: "Department of Commerce navigation aids and personnel . . . were functioning properly at all times during the fatal flight."[4] For a time Director Eugene Vidal considered undertaking punitive action against the airline for its share in the violations of air commerce regulations.[5]

The repercussions from the Cutting crash, as it became known, proved quite embarrassing to the bureau, even though hardly justified. Friends in Congress jumped to the conclusion that Cutting died because of faulty mechanical aids operated by the Department of Commerce. The inadequacies of the radio-range beacons, such as the phenomena of multiple course and the interference of static in poor weather, bore on the Cutting tragedy just as in any similar case. This did not prove that the bureau's aids at Kirksville, Missouri, the nearest station, caused the fatal crash. Vidal, in further defense of the bureau, asserted that TWA failed to claim anything wrong with the navigational aids until months after the accident, one TWA official testifying that he flew the same course on the night of the crash and found the beam operating correctly.[6] Furthermore, the company knew that Kirksville possessed only a minor facility, a radio marker. John H. Wigmore, law professor at Northwestern University, deplored the congressional attitude toward the bureau concerning the Cutting crash: "The report is deeply disappointing. . . . It gives the impression of bias against the Bureau of Air Commerce."[7] Widespread responsibility for violations must be shouldered, according to one reasonable interpretation of the Cutting tragedy: "Too much credulity is required to believe that the petty violations leading up to this disaster had not been going on for a long time. Not to have known this is as bad as to have condoned it by a policy of easygoing enforcement."[8]

POST AND ROGERS

Famed aviator Wiley Post and beloved movie actor Will Rogers became the victims of another air disaster, this one occurring on August 15, 1935, at Walakpi, Alaska. Engine failure on takeoff at 50 feet of altitude was followed by the plane falling out of control to the water. Both men were killed instantly. Extreme nose heaviness of the craft, confirmed by statements made earlier in the trip by Post, prevented landing of the plane without the engine operating.[9] Cause of the engine failure could not be determined, but icing of the carburetor was suspected.

OTHER TRANSPORTS FALL

Crashes of transport aircraft, spectacular because of the horror elicited by the increased toll in the case of larger aircraft, revealed a wide variety of causes. United Air Lines lost a Boeing 247–D near Cheyenne, Wyoming, on October 7, 1935; all twelve aboard perished as the plane undershot the field by 1,000 feet of altitude.[10] The Accident Board members admitted their inability to ascertain the causes of some accidents.[11] On January 14, 1936, mystery shrouded the loss of an American Airlines DC–2 near Goodwin, Arkansas; all fourteen passengers and a crew of three died. Wild rumors, as usual, ran rampant complete with telephone calls to the bureau. One individual claimed he talked to a man who alleged the pilot, Gerald V. Marshall, had a weakness for liquor.[12] Investigators failed to determine why the plane was flown at the illegal altitude of approximately 500 feet for the last 13 miles or why the crash occurred. Pilferers made off with much of the wreckage, thus hampering the study. Repugnant, indeed, were the number of crank letters, many in longhand, received at the bureau from laymen claiming that they ". . . knew what was causing all these air crashes."[13] But valuable clues seldom emerged.

An unusual development resulted from the loss of twelve out of fourteen aboard a TWA DC–2 which crashed near Uniontown, Pennsylvania, on April 7, 1936—the company charging, at first, the existence of a faulty beam. The bureau attributed the probable cause to the poor judgment of the pilot in using visual ground methods, instead of ascending to determine his position by radio and the failure to follow the right-hand side of the west leg of the Harrisburg radio-range course.[14] One private radio engineer wondered why the airlines closed their eyes to the additional safety available through the use of a radio compass: "It is my belief that the Department of Commerce should share no part of the criticism for that accident."[15] He grew weary of seeing the bureau cast in the role of scapegoat.

Sometimes fate wielded its ugly hand in the form of human mistakes, as in the case of the crash taking the lives of ten aboard a Stinson on September 5, 1936, at Pittsburgh, Pennsylvania. The cause was failure of the fuel supply because the selector valve had been pushed inadvertently to the "off" position.[16] Mechanical failure might have caused another crash, the altimeter still reading 200 feet after a plane undershot the field at Newark, although a faulty report of barometric pressure could have provided the margin of error.[17] Occasionally, the private citizen displayed a keen understanding of the situation, much to the relief of harassed bureau personnel: "If the newpapers had taken the same trouble that you have taken, I am quite sure that the facts would have been presented to the public in such manner as to cause no apprehension to men like yourself."[18] Such was

Assistant Director Rex Martin's reaction in a case involving alleged failure of a radio beam. Cooperation of airline personnel with the bureau existed despite differences of opinion. American Airlines reported striking an object at 6,600 feet over the airport at Lafayette, Indiana, believing that it was not a bird. Investigation followed without success.[19] Assistant Secretary J. M. Johnson promised Colonel E. V. Rickenbacker of Eastern Air Lines better aids to aviation if the airlines improved their operation.[20] Rickenbacker quite fairly realized in a later investigation that it would be unreasonable to criticize the Weather Bureau for poor observations while the promising radiometeorograph remained in the testing stage. Indignation resulted when bureau leaders heard of another incident in which a pilot attempted a takeoff with the aileron block in place.[21]

The loss of Pan American Airways *Hawaiian Clipper* on January 11, 1938, near Pago Pago, Tutuila, Samoa, prompted one layman to suggest that a bomb caused the crash and that the prime suspect would be a Chinese aboard who was bearing treasure: "Remember the Panay."[22] In reality, the probable cause was fire and explosion caused by the dumping of fuel while in flight. Accidents involving a low fuel supply prompted David L. Behncke, Air Line Pilots' Association, to remind Director Vidal of the pilots' opposition to the bureau ruling which changed the 35 per cent reserve fuel requirement to a forty-five-minute reserve. This was insufficient protection, according to Behncke.[23] Senator Harry S. Truman, an ardent aviation enthusiast, attempted to console the father of two victims in the crash of a TWA plane at Pittsburgh, Pennsylvania, on March 25, 1937: "I did my best to clearly explain to them that I could not see there was any negligence on the part of any TWA employees."[24]

Accident investigation data, the subject of much controversy and possible lawsuits, were guarded quite carefully from the public, a continuation of the policy begun even before the bureau announced the probable cause of individual accidents.[25] Some general information, for instance bureau station logs, could be seen following accidents by officials of the airline involved. However, investigation notes and interviews as well as the public hearings could not be taken into court as evidence. Bureau officials exercised extreme caution in the use of data on accidents before the Senate Committee on Commerce investigating the Cutting accident.[26] The desire to cooperate with state aeronautical authorities led Director Vidal to believe that an exception should be allowed in one request for a pilot report from the future director, Fred D. Fagg, Illinois Aeronautical Commission. No hearing had been held.[27]

THE DC-3

Development of the famed DC-3 was begun in 1934 and the plane was initially flown in December, 1935. This airplane was in the foreground as a transport carrier by 1938. These new liners also met disaster, one operated by United Air Lines (UAL) falling, according to the Accident Board, because of improper dispatching into bad weather which created static preventing the determination of position.[28] Radio failure associated with bad weather also contributed to another UAL loss near Newhall, California, on December 27, 1936. Faulty navigation and inability to follow the radio range on leaving Missoula, Montana, led to the crash of a Northwest Airlines plane near Kellogg, Idaho. An Eastern transport crashed at Daytona Beach, Florida, because it struck a wooden pole (erected without warning) on takeoff.[29] A Christmas (1936) disaster (static adversely affecting the radio reception) befell a Western Air Express Boeing 247-D near Salt Lake City; all aboard perished. Another DC-3A of United was lost near Hump Ridge, Utah, on October 17, 1937, all nineteen aboard dead, because an unpredicted cold front brought static conditions which prevented receiving intelligible radio signals. Structural failure, uncommon to be sure, occurred in the loss of a Northwest Airlines Lockheed 14-H on January 1, 1938, near Bozeman, Montana. The failure of the upper vertical fins and rudders was due to flutter. The failure of a cylinder barrel, causing a fire fed by the right engine's oil supply, led to the crash of a UAL DST-A with nine dead near Cleveland on May 24, 1938. A change in wind direction and a sharp increase in velocity, unknown to the pilot, produced confusion over position with reference to the Fresno radio range and the crash of a TWA DC-2 near Wanana, California, on March 1, 1938.[30] Structural failure, among all the causes of air accidents, produced the maximum consternation within the bureau because, inevitably, the aircraft had been inspected and approved by the bureau. Thus, similar to the case of the Boeing 247 in 1934 (already cited in Chapter 5 under air regulations) there resulted dismay over the Lockheed 14, a plane so recently approved, involved in the Northwest Airlines crash.[31] The twin fins and rudders were missing from the wreckage.

THE *HINDENBURG*

Another sensational tragedy brought a necessary investigation from the bureau; this was the fire and destruction of the famous German dirigible *Hindenburg* on May 6, 1937, at Lakehurst, New Jersey.[32] Accident Board officials concluded: "The cause of the accident was ignition of a mixture of free hydrogen and air. Based upon the evidence, a leak at or in the vicinity of cells 4 and 5 caused a combustible mixture. . . . The theory that a brush discharge ignited such mixture appears most probable."[33] Dr. W. J. Humphreys, noted researcher with the Weather Bureau, supported the theory of the brush fire (St. Elmo's fire), after the landing ropes came into contact with the ground. No evidence of sabotage could be found. Two navy aerologists, both witnesses, disagreed over the danger existing in a potential gradient from a thunderstorm which just had passed over the station. F. W. Reichelderfer (Chief of the Weather Bureau beginning in 1938) considered the conditions favorable for a steep potential gradient, while F. A. L. Dartsch felt the potential gradient not serious. The *Hindenburg,* successful in thirty-four ocean crossings the year before, had complied with all regulations of licensing, certification, and authority before the fateful last journey costing the lives of 13 out of the 36 passengers and 22 from the crew of 61. The lack of safety precautions in authorizing such equipment might seem fantastic to the observer in the 1960's. However, use of the highly inflammable hydrogen and the outer cover of cotton and linen—coated with cellon or aluminum powder—did not seem to disturb the aeronautical experts of that early day. One leading journal reflected upon the offer, which was rejected, made by President Franklin Roosevelt to sell Germany some of our helium.[34] This misfortune sealed the fate of such dirigibles.

THE "PROBABLE CAUSE"

Before it became obligatory to state the "probable cause," expressions of bewilderment were commonly heard. But even in 1938, Senator Pat McCarran could not understand one crash because it occurred at Cleveland, the finest and largest airport in the world.[35] The bureau and Cleveland's airport had absolutely nothing to do with this crash. With so many accidents on record, one might easily be misled to forget the improvement in safety achieved by the airlines. Between 1930 and 1936, the fatality rate per passenger-mile decreased by five-sixths.[36] Despite this progress, a number of feature-seeking reporters grasped upon the instances of tragedy to portray a story of fear to the American public over the status of civil aviation. In the main, these journalists honestly expressed their views if they feared the use of air transport. Used correctly, a few candid observations of this variety could prove harmless if oriented toward the promotion of better congressional appropriations for improved navigational aids. But linked to the unfavorable publicity was a perennial movement in Congress to change the status of the Bureau of Air Commerce, ranging all the way from the transfer of its duties to the Interstate Commerce Commission to the establishment of an independent agency to consolidate all matters of federal control over aviation now shared by the bureau and the Post Office Department.

One school of thought held that the Northwest crash at Kellogg might have been caused by the lack of oxygen for Pilot Joe P. Livermore. The bureau denied his widow's charge against the airline of "pilot pushing."[37] The article cited the comedy of errors, including the following of wrong legs of beacons. One medical authority expressed concern because the bureau had not studied the lack of oxygen in air tragedies, a possible cause of pilot error. Formerly, the bureau advised use of oxygen above 18,000 feet, then lowered it to 15,000 feet; but American and TWA told their pilots to begin use of oxygen at 12,000 feet. *Fortune* offered the suggestion that the good safety records of Eastern Air Lines and Northwest might be due to considerable low flying—5,000 to 8,000 feet. The author went so far as to ask if Pilot Bolton— in the Cutting crash—might have had anoxemia.

JUST AND UNJUST CRITICISM

In the realm of unfavorable editorial comment, the *American Mercury*'s Kenneth Brown Collings appeared as a devastating and exaggerating critic of American air transport: "Speed is the fetish of present-day existence. . . ."[38] Collings warned that pilots die at the rate of 25 per 1,000 a year, compared to the normal rate of 3 for the general population. Commercial pilots loved their jobs and generally denied that flying was dangerous. Collings scorned "blind" flying, and in particular, the refusal of airline ground personnel to advise customers of possible bad weather ahead. It was hard to discern the truth: "Our trouble with aviation is that dead pilots tell no tales; and live pilots don't always tell truthful ones."[39] In 1937, Collings admitted that flying was a bit safer: "From the standpoint of safety some improvement has been registered—but not enough to justify uncontrolled paeans of praise."[40] The hazards of flying stood at forty times greater than that of normal occupations. Collings steadfastly asserted that the *American Mercury* remained "the only magazine sufficiently free from advertising influence to discuss this vital subject honestly and frankly."[41] One ray of praise credited the airplane designers with preventing damage from lightning, one airline incurring sixty strikes in one year without serious results.

The bureau's aeronautical development project demonstrated, according to its leaders, the honest attempt to reverse an alleged statement by Henry Ford that flying was 90 per cent pilot and 10 per cent airplane.[42] Airline practices which allegedly caused pilots to push themselves too hard, together with charges of politics and ineptitude on the part of the Bureau of Air Commerce, prompted the sensational attack on air problems, early in 1937, by *The Nation:* "Flying as it is done today on our air lines in bad weather is 90 percent guesswork." Safety must be promoted by the Bureau of Air Commerce, "yet this vital Bureau is a political pasture. . . . No hope [exists] in Roper or his gang in the Commerce Department."[43]

Citing the keen rivalry among pilots, one interpretation blamed the airlines for basing salary adjustments largely upon the record of completed flights despite weather conditions.[44] Dispatchers allegedly persuaded copilots to take off if the pilot refused to gamble with weather hazards. This writer, Marquis Childs, also contended that the Department of Commerce under Secretary Roper had become too lenient toward the aviation interests. The bureau performed as judge, jury, and prosecutor. Worst of all was the niggardly approach of Congress toward the Weather Bureau's needs for improved equipment which would enhance aviation forecasts. Childs, along with several other interested correspondents, likened the woes of the aviation world to the troublous beginnings of the railroads in this country. Indications lent support to the assumption that even Director Vidal would not object to the removal of accident investigation to a separate group.[45] One of the sharp battles confronting the bureau and the airlines persisted in the fact that the vast majority of Americans who could afford to fly did not.[46] Sixty-six deaths in ten months did little to allay public reluctance and presented a clearly defined challenge to the industry and its governmental sponsors.[47]

The storehouse of loose talk about "blind" landings prompted one reporter to accompany the flight of a Boeing 247–D from Washington, D.C., to Pittsburgh. Despite Pennsylvania Central Airlines' record of no accidents during this period, over rugged terrain, the reporter uneasily witnessed a blind landing at Pittsburgh, in which the pilot, Jack Neale, first saw the ground at approximately 50 feet.[48] Much criticism fell to airline dispatchers, and companies were urged to select people for this crucial position from the ranks of former pilots. In a study of seven typical accident reports, one author concluded that pilot error was a factor but urged the Bureau of Air Commerce to help the pilot against unfair pushing by the company.[49] The Air Line Pilots' Association affirmed the charge of exploitation leveled against the operators, offering affidavits—one from a pilot's widow. Though Rickenbacker incensed the bureau by calling its radio ranges "revolving ranges," no evidence of faulty ranges could be discerned in this particular analysis.

A difference of opinion arose over personnel allowed to partake in the accident investigations and hearings conducted by the bureau. Spokesmen for the Air Line Pilots' Association (ALPA) contended that the pilot, not the airlines, should be represented.[50] The bureau upheld its right of allowing one person from the company involved to participate, contending that this was a bureau decision, not the ALPA's. Several other matters of disagreement apparently aggravated relations between the bureau and the ALPA during 1936–1937. Behncke complained that experimental work conducted on the airways constituted a hazard.[51] The ALPA questioned the height of radio towers, but the bureau replied that regulation of this nature belonged solely to the Federal Communications Commission.[52] Both J. Carroll Cone and R. W. Schroeder found themselves "too busy" to accept the invitation to attend the ALPA convention in Chicago.[53] Behncke chastised the bureau for blaming pilots too often for the cause of accidents, claiming that mechanical failure actually caused the crash of a Chicago and Southern plane on August 5, 1936. Behncke scorned blaming of pilots when no cause could be determined. Director Vidal denied any evidence of engine failure and assured Behncke that the bureau would be honest in blaming pilots when it was due.[54]

The ALPA questioned the mechanical airworthiness of certain Delta aircraft in 1937, but the bureau reaffirmed its belief that no failures existed: "It would be appreciated if . . . you would furnish us with specific information as we have a report that the instances mentioned are false rumors."[55] Similar disagreement arose at times, amid wild rumors, over the leadership of the Air Transport Association of America (ATA) and the bureau. Some aviation sources charged that Colonel Edgar S. Gorrell, leader of ATA, coveted either the position of Secretary Roper or Director Vidal. Gorrell flatly denied the rumor in letters to both officials: "We have no quarrels; I do not seek your job."[56] Bureau leadership assured Gorrell later the same year that Dr. R. E. Whitehead, Medical Director, had condoned the 100-hour maximum flying time for pilots.[57]

THE ALPA vs. THE OPERATORS

The ramifications originating from a strong pressure group representing the pilots in the form of the ALPA struck home to the airlines, too, as job suspensions and accident causes ended up with varying results. William A. Patterson, then Vice-President of United Air Lines, described his differences with the ALPA to the bureau: "During the past few months every time a pilot has been dismissed by us because of suspicion of his lack of judgment, based on fact or theory, it leads to constant controversy with the ALPA." Patterson also rendered an opinion on an accident involving UAL: "We have come to the most definite opinion that this was the failure of the human elements."[58] Other controversies arose over the Cutting crash and the question of flight time. Here, military pilots entered a suggestion: "Due to untrue statements propagated by one Dave Behncke of the Air Line Pilots, TWA pilots are being subjected to a condition that is not conducive to their well being."[59] The writer appeared to be most unhappy about the bureau's suspension of the waiver of flight time limits. Washington Hoover Airport, long understood to be inadequate and a hazard, became a constant source of consternation to the ALPA which demanded proper safety restrictions there and better information for pilots about alternate fields such as Bolling Field.[60] In its many contacts with different aircraft, noting their weaknesses and brightest assets, bureau officials had constantly to be wary of company reaction to decisions. Stinson Company authorities complained of misinformation and derogatory remarks made by bureau officials about Stinson aircraft.[61]

SAFER AVIATION

Despite all the criticism, Bureau of Air Commerce personnel pointed with pride to statistics comparing civil aviation since the advent of federal control in 1926. By 1938, aircraft firms had trebled, licensed airplanes had increased five times, and the number of pilots by elevenfold.[62] Student pilots numbered 527 in 1927, but over 38,000 fell into this category eleven years later. The annual income from airmail increased from $750,000 to $21,000,000, and the number of passengers carried from 8,679 in 1927 to 1,267,580 in 1937 and 115,255 during June, 1938. Safety progress had been recorded, for in scheduled airline service, the number of miles flown per fatal accident climbed from 1,467,622 in 1927 to almost 13,000,000 in 1937. Miscellaneous flying (mostly private) also witnessed a marked degree of improvement, with miles flown per passenger fatality rising from 285,174 to 1,009,768. The daily average miles flown in the miscellaneous category increased from 11,830 at the end of 1926 to 234,922 twelve years later.

HOUSECLEANING AND REORGANIZATION

Criticism from the press, the ALPA, and air operators harassed the Bureau of Air Commerce but did not alone effect major changes in the structure of the organization entrusted with the inspection and regulation of commercial and civil aviation in this country. Rumblings in the halls of Congress, usually present to some degree regarding the performance of any government agency, did, in this instance, bring about drastic alteration relative to the Department of Commerce. In the early days of the New Deal, the major attention in Congress concerning aviation was focused on the so-called frauds in the airmail. Involving the Post Office Department, this issue did not touch upon the Aeronautics Branch (Bureau of Air Commerce) except that agents of the two departments did work together in implementing the regulation of commercial aviation. Nonetheless, the investigation of the Post Office Department's rewarding of airmail contracts to air carriers did bring up another pertinent question. Why, argued Senator Pat McCarran of Nevada and others, could not the activities of the two departments pertaining to aviation be consolidated into one independent agency, thus relieving Post Office and Commerce from all responsibility toward aviation? In fact, Senator McCarran introduced a bill into Congress during March, 1934, which basically would have accomplished this very change. The time was not ripe, however, and four more years of criticism and argument proved necessary to effect such a novel manipulation within the executive wing of government.

Meanwhile, congressmen watched closely the difficulties confronting the Bureau of Air Commerce, the basic issue of reorganization into a separate organization always an alternative "waiting in the wings" ready to assume a leading role. More often than not, the alertness of congressmen to affairs within the bureau could be measured by the frequency of their own adverse experiences in flying on commercial airlines, supplemented by the usual despair over the sporadic series of major catastrophes. As already mentioned, the crash killing Senator Cutting (May, 1935) resulted in continual pressure from the legislators toward the bureau for improvement of its services, even though proof of bureau inefficiency in this tragedy could not be substantiated. Interested congressmen sent questionnaires to the airline operators in an attempt to ascertain the status of airway and airport facilities. The replies indicated the need of better radio-range beacons (no fault of the bureau at this time), improved lighting at many airfields, rolled fields after snowfall, and more accurate hourly weather reports.

At this time, practices of the Interstate Commerce Commission were described as greatly superior to those of the Bureau of Air Commerce, qualifications for air inspectors being described as inferior to the five years of experience required of ICC inspectors. Navigation aids, then allegedly just 55 per cent effective, should be operated at 98 per cent efficiency. The loose talk in Congress included a doubt that any of the bureau inspectors could obtain a job with an airline company: "There has been no lack of funds . . . recklessly wasted and inefficiently spent."[63] Congressman Robert L. Bacon of New York charged that funds had been expended for new construction, instead of maintenance and repair of old facilities. No longer with the bureau, Jay M. Mount, according to this theory, had been too revealing in his criticism of existing navigational facilities to his superiors. Understandably, congressmen, hearing of irregularities, jumped to the conclusion, erroneous indeed, that the bureau was entirely responsible for airplane crashes.

The charge of partisan politics was also injected, Republicans labeling New Dealers as the only employees accepted by the bureau. Mount's testimony before Congress left his audience with the belief that all was not well in the Bureau of Air Commerce. For example, Mount reported that the radio-range antenna was improperly connected at Washington, D.C., affecting the reliability of the radio ranges. Here, also, he found weak tubes in the transmitter reducing the distance range of the station. Furthermore, the transmitter had been improperly tuned, and a defective condenser caused a hum in the transmitter amplifier, impairing the quality of speech in the broadcasts. To remove the bureau from politics, Congressman Bacon urged his colleagues to effect a transfer to the ICC. Congressman Thomas S. McMillan of South Carolina defended the administration and the bureau, pointing out that the bureau's own poll of users reflected general support as to the accuracy of facilities.[64] McMillan asserted that many of the complaints about inadequate service were made before the Democratic era. During appropriations hearings, Director Vidal encountered spirited opposition to the prevailing methods by which the bureau expended funds, that is, using maintenance funds for construction of new facilities.[65] Both friend and foe on the subcommittee chided Vidal for this activity. Vidal argued the necessity of this practice if new airways were to be completed on schedule.

Again, Vidal's pet research on new aircraft for private flying came under fire, actually covering an item for which no funds had been allotted during fiscal 1936. Vidal, favoring the addition of inspectors before increases for air traffic control, opposed his subordinate, J. Carroll Cone, who argued for the reverse priority before these legislators who were already wary of bureau policies. Meanwhile, the famous Senate investigation led by Royal S. Copeland of New York gained notoriety after some eight months of more-or-less secret findings. The special investigation arose out of the Cutting crash. Rex Martin, Assistant Director of the bureau, violently denied the testimony of several witnesses before this subcommittee of the commerce committee. Martin reacted to the elaborate charges of his former subordinate, Jay A. Mount.[66] Mount had testified that the Kansas City–Burlington radio range, the one involved in the Cutting disaster, was in error and had sent the plane eighteen miles off course. After Mount's dismissal, the bureau hired renowned pilot Howard C. Stark to investigate the radio beams. He later disappeared (January, 1936) in flight somewhere near Salt Lake City.[67] Senate Investigator Charles H. Dolan contended that the bureau economized to a hazardous extent and blamed too many crashes on either the weather or airline personnel. Jack Frye, President of TWA, charged the bureau with changing its beacons without notifying the airlines. Director Vidal defended his employees, declaring that his inspectors should not be charged with negligence. As for politics, only fourteen men had been replaced in the past two and one-half years. The battle continued, with Vidal and Copeland debating the merits of existing radio aids before another Senate group. Here, comparisons of past accidents, both civil and military, were cited. Vidal and Assistant Secretary Johnson maintained that the army airmail accidents were not caused by the deficiencies of radio. Copeland and Colonel Gorrell of ATA contended that poor radio beams caused most accidents.[68]

This bitter testimony, all recorded during 1936, indicated that some change would be necessary if the ruffled nerves of influential congressional leaders who steadfastly agreed with the bureau's other critics at this time were to be placated. However, Director Vidal did not budge from his firm conviction about the lack of guilt of his subordinates in relation to the series of crashes which continued to plague American aviation. Vidal received the backing of Assistant Secretary Johnson on February 8, 1937, at the next session of appropriations hearings in the House. Both pleaded for leniency in the use of allocated funds, suggesting the bureau should be able to expend at least 5 per cent of each item appropriated for any other activity, after obtaining approval from the Director of the Budget Bureau.[69] Johnson also requested additional funds for Vidal's developmental projects. Both leaders attempted to reassure committee members of the serious efforts being directed toward improved safety on the airways. At a recent conference on aeronautics, representatives of all types of interest decided upon a priority list for a modernization program. Immediate steps to be included were: installation of auxiliary means of navigation by all airlines; directional and homing devices on all airliners; better navigational training for all airline pilots; near future installation of the air log and the antistatic loop antenna on all airliners; simultaneous ranges only on all airways; more detailed and accurate radio maps; promulgation of air traffic control (ATC) radio equipment and rules; pilot training on the Link trainer for all airlines; expediting the installation of airport approach lights; and expansion of safety research and development within the Bureau of Air Commerce.[70] Longer-range requests called for cooperative studies looking to the improvement of: all radio equipment, blind-approach systems, emergency ground direction-finding devices, three-wheel undercarriages and steeper glide paths in aircraft design, use of two first pilots for more efficient navigation, competitive flying, takeoff accelerations, and better weather data. Participating in the conference were officials from the following groups: ATA, ALPA, Independent Operators Association, Aeronautical Chamber of Commerce, National Association of State Aviation Officials, National Board of Aviation Underwriters, Weather Bureau, Army, Navy, Marine Corps, and Coast Guard.

Despite the effort to concentrate attention on future improvement, committee members brought up the perennial question of accidents related to inadequate navigational facilities. Here for the last time, Vidal maintained opposition to Senator Copeland and his committee, which had lashed out against the bureau. Vidal pointed to bureau findings which revealed the causes in 18 of 26 recent air crashes involving factors other than radio, all 18 taking place when the pilot could see the ground. Stunting, ice on the wings or in the carburetor, generator failure, and engine failure on takeoff figured in these accidents.[71] In all, the modernization program called for 330 projects worth an estimated $10,500,000, the bureau asking for $5,000,000 in 1937 to cover about two-thirds of the projects. Admittedly, bureau morale had lessened because of a shortage in manpower reflected by the accumulation of 20,478 days of annual leave over the past two years.

VIDAL IS FIRED

Director Vidal no longer headed the bureau when the Senate held its hearings on appropriations. The handsome, well-dressed, sincere midwesterner resigned from his post during the first week in March, 1937. The usual excuses and niceties filled the nation's press over the ouster, but apparently once the decision was reached, Vidal felt relieved to step down. Curious reporters heard from Copeland that Vidal was all right, but the system caused his downfall: "He is an amiable gentleman. He has a good background. Our fear is that he is too amiable, that he is lacking in iron, positiveness, and determination."[72] Copeland futilely denied other maneuvers within the bureau resulting in less important tasks for Colonel Cone, who was transferred to Europe to study aviation regulation there: "He came through without criticism. I wish I might be able to say as much about some others in the Department of Commerce. I cannot do so."[73] Martin went to Latin America for study of aviation.[74] Obviously, Copeland was happy over this move, as he was, indeed, over the selection of Fred Fagg as the new director. Commerce Department officials maintained that Vidal resigned voluntarily, but even the most candid observer could not deny the existence of political and personal pressure. Among old-timers in the bureau's namesake today (Federal Aviation Agency) one hears the same verdict on Vidal: "He became too heavily involved in politics." With all candor, it would appear that Vidal could have remained an effective head only if Martin, Cone, and Secretary Roper had allowed him complete reign over his bureau, as, of course, should have been the case. One business journal had correctly predicted Vidal's resignation, assessing the real blame for the situation to the politicians' moves for the original appointment of Cone and Martin, both aspirants to Vidal's post as director. Two days before stepping down, Vidal ordered shielded antennae on all planes by November 1, 1937, and direction finders in use by January 1, 1938.[75]

Within a month after the housecleaning, Senator Copeland boasted of the complete amity present within the department, bureau, and the commerce committee over the accomplished reorganization in the direction of greater efficiency and safety.[76] Finally, it must be asserted that Senator Copeland epitomized a fitting example of vigorous detective work and sincere appreciation of the deficiencies inherent in civil aviation in the mid-thirties. The official report of his committee's broad investigation covering the status of civil aviation appeared in March, 1937. Both praise and condemnation of the Bureau of Air Commerce could be found.[77] American scheduled airlines, uncontrolled by the military, achieved a better safety record than elsewhere. But the bureau must not engage in scientific, experimental, or developmental work, which directly invaded the province of the National Advisory Committee for Aeronautics. Furthermore, as cited elsewhere, Copeland outlined the elaborate modernization needs for navigational aids. Copeland, aided by colleagues Bennett Champ Clark, Vic Donahey, and Wallace H. White, Jr., vigorously urged more airway aids for the private fliers who, even in the lowest ebb of flying during the Great Depression, carried twice as many passengers as did the scheduled airlines. Finally, Copeland reported progress already accomplished in the bureau to comply with the committee's suggestions. If any criticism could be laid against Copeland, it would certainly be his unwavering support of Colonel Gorrell and the interests of aviation operators under the strong ATA.

In fact, Senator McCarran labeled Copeland too partial toward Gorrell.[78] The Copeland Committee, after proclaiming that aviation would become safer with the administrative juggling in the bureau and implementation of the modernization program, apparently remained satisfied with the retention of air regulation by the Department of Commerce. But the drive for more permanent alteration—be it creation of a separate agency or transfer to the ICC—continued unabated.

RIVAL BILLS

While Fred Fagg attempted to rejuvenate bureau operations and morale, Congress offered a wild scramble of bills which would affect the bureau. By summer, three rival approaches appeared. First, Senator McCarran pressed once again for the transfer of bureau operations to the ICC. On the surface, it looked as if this move would meet little opposition; it held the blessings of the ATA, the ALPA, a large segment of the press, and both House and Senate committees dealing with commerce. Although quiet prevailed, it could be assumed with the aid of later developments that President Roosevelt looked with favor on McCarran's approach. The second camp embraced friends of the Post Office Department who rallied around the efforts of Senator Kenneth D. McKellar of Tennessee to suggest a transfer of the bureau to the Post Office, irrational as this might sound now to the reader.[79] The third position, weakest in 1937, favored creation of a separate agency for all air control activities. Apparently, Postmaster General James A. Farley avoided the fray, letting Solicitor Karl Crowley fight the battle for the Post Office.

Meanwhile, the possibility existed that transfer of the Bureau of Air Commerce to the ICC might still result in the ultimate retention within the Department of Commerce because of rumors suggesting a move bringing the ICC within Commerce. Certainly unanimity did not prevail among the various private interests. Some airline operators argued, with apparent justification, the danger of placing aviation control under the railroad-minded leaders of the ICC.[80] Unfortunately, the politicians refused to assess the true nature of the dilemma at hand: "In essence, right regulation depends on right men—which brings it back to personnel again."[81] As the next session of Congress opened, yet another organization found support in its bid for a share of the aviation spoils. The United States Maritime Commission asked permission for control of overseas air-route development.[82] Meanwhile, Senator McKellar managed to prevent passage of the McCarran bill in the first session of the Seventy-Fifth Congress (1937). The measure, Senate bill 2, found its major support from Harry S. Truman of Missouri and Burton K. Wheeler of Montana since McCarran was in a hospital at the time McKellar launched his filibuster.[83] McKellar charged illegal lobbying on the the part of an ICC employee in seeking aviation duties. Truman assured his colleagues that this bill merely intended to accomplish what earlier efforts failed to do in 1935 (Senate bills 3027 and 3420); extensive hearings had been conducted on the present measure. Wheeler told newsmen it was time to get aviation out of politics and lashed out against the Bureau of Air Commerce for sloppy enforcement, vacillating policies, and punch pulling. Furthermore, four-year political changes had not aided this organization, which remained afraid of the airlines and in dire need of career men.[84] Wheeler's stand was received as a welcome boon to aviation.

McCarran, back to fight for his pet bill in the third session which opened in January, 1938, found a surprise in the offing, thus altering his whole recommendation of the past few years. Instead of forcing the issue with McKellar to the bitter end, Administration leaders found that President Roosevelt desired harmony through compromise.[85] A concerted effort by McCarran to resolve the differences of the many bills in Congress set the tone of further reaction by fellow legislators. Specifically, McCarran, aided by Senator Copeland, asked for a skeleton bill allowing for a separate agency to regulate aviation.[86] In the House, Clarence F. Lea of California sponsored a bill (H.R. 9738) creating a new agency. He gave the majority report of the Interstate and Foreign Commerce Committee. The minority members called for the ICC to gain the regulation, citing the support of this procedure in former years, along with President Roosevelt's earlier public support of the ICC. Congressman Carl E. Mapes of Michigan led a desperate last-minute attack on the Lea bill, recalling the wide variety of professional groups which had condoned the proposal to extend the authority of the ICC over aviation. Lea answered by pointing out the current situation with airmail controlled by the Post Office, mail rates by the ICC, and the Bureau of Air Commerce regulating other functions. His bill would unify all three functions in one place and also instigate economic regulation—a new venture, except for airmail control—over aviation. Lea provided for an independent authority to implement this economic direction, possessing quasijudicial and quasilegislative powers. To handle airways navigation, inspection, and licensing, an administration would be appointed. A third segment of the reorganized federal control would investigate accidents and make recommendations in the interest of safety. Moreover, Lea contended now that members of the ICC did not want the added responsibility of aviation duties.

Obviously, ICC officials could not buck the White House, a factor carefully and conveniently neglected by the debaters. The idea of an independent agency could hardly be considered new; the Howell Commission had recommended such reorganization already in 1935. Pilots expressed some concern over the Lea bill, hoping for an air safety board, not a one-man division, one which might help prevent as well as investigate accidents.[87] They also feared possible exclusion from existing labor legislation. Congressman James W. Wadsworth, while supporting the bill, expressed worry over the proliferation of governmental agencies. After passing the bill, the House vacated its proceedings in lieu of McCarran's bill (Senate bill 3845) which meanwhile had been adopted in the Senate. In conference, the House yielded on minor points of administrative organization within the new agency, and the measure, Public Law No. 706, was enacted on June 23, 1938. Apparently, Truman would have yielded on some points to the House; McCarran held fast to obtain the law he originally introduced several years before. One concern had to do with the inclusion of a number of civil service jobs, a point included in the successful Senate version.[88]

With the passage of the new law, the Department of Commerce lost, for the time being, its twelve-year hold over civil aviation. Senator Alben Barkley of Kentucky introduced a report summarizing the activities of the Aeronautics Branch and Bureau of Air Commerce during 1926–1938, noting the vast extension of airways and fine leadership of the incumbent Secretary and the Assistant, Roper and Johnson.[89] Such polemics hardly seemed necessary if one considers the fact that the major functions, innovations, and improvements emanating from the bureau during its most recent years had little to do with the physical position within the Department of Commerce. Keeping this in mind, legislators, executive department leaders, pilots, airline operators, and bureau personnel looked anxiously to the future for any change, one way or the other, for better or for worse, under the tutelage of an independent agency. One factor struck all involved as a certainty; the economic control over aviation would involve a new and perhaps baffling avenue of approach to the question of how far government should proceed in the regulation of private enterprise.

FIGHTING REORGANIZATION WHILE
FOSTERING PROGRESS–1938-1941

YEARS OF CAREFUL PLANNING introduced faster and safer airplanes, along with improved navigational aids during 1938–1941. But the federal regulators of aviation found themselves caught in a struggle with politicians who could not make up their minds about the structure of the new Civil Aeronautics Authority (CAA).

To implement the Civil Aeronautics Act of 1938, President Franklin D. Roosevelt had to fill a number of key positions, all now outside the jurisdiction of the Department of Commerce.[1] Presidents seldom please everyone with their choices for such posts; and these proved to be no exception, slanted as they were toward political qualifications instead of scientific and technical expertness in two instances. E. J. Noble, a Yale graduate and army officer in ordnance during World War I, gained the chairmanship of the new authority. A liberal Republican and founder of the Life Savers Corporation, Noble owned one airplane and two autogiros. Authority member Harllee Branch had left the *Atlanta Journal* after thirty years to campaign actively for Roosevelt in 1932, whereupon Roosevelt made him Executive Assistant to Postmaster James A. Farley and then Second Assistant Postmaster General in charge of airmail (routes, contracts, and operations). Oswald Ryan, qualified author and scholar and formerly of the Harvard law school, served as General Counsel of the Federal Power Commission during the last year of the Hoover era and all of the Roosevelt regime until named to the authority.

Another professor, Robert H. Hinckley, originally taught languages at Brigham Young University before turning to politics. Beginning with emergency relief work in Utah, he then became Assistant Administrator of the Federal Emergency Relief Administration in 1935, followed by service in the same post with the Works Progress Administration in 1935 and a position with the WPA for eleven western states. Long interested in aviation, Hinckley aided in the establishment of Utah-Pacific Airways in 1928 and was one of the initial paying passengers on UAL's flight west from Salt Lake City. Iowan and Yale graduate George Grant Mason, Jr., fifth member, left his position of the last five years as President and General Manager of Compania Nacional Cubana de Aviacion (Cuba). Previously, Mason had been First Secretary of Pan American Airways (1927) and at various times provided the Bureau of Air Commerce with much support and data on aviation in Cuba and the Caribbean area in general. Mason also served on the United States delegation at Brussels for the Fourth Conference on Private Air Law. Now with the authority, Mason was concerned with the CAA's foreign problems. These five members of the authority assumed economic control over American aviation, with bureaus of economic regulation and safety regulation to carry out their wishes.

A career federal servant of twenty years became administrator, thus supervising the all-important functions of the Bureau of Federal Airways. For this task, Roosevelt chose Iowa-born Clinton M. Hester from Montana, who served overseas in World War I and earned the A.B. and LL.B. degrees from Georgetown University. Hester held membership in NACA and had worked for the following organizations: Emergency Fleet Corporation, Department of the Interior, U.S. Shipping Board, Office of Alien Property, and the Attorney General's office. While the authority assumed quasilegislative and quasijudicial functions, the administrator possessed independent executive responsibility to the President. In the field, the authority and administrator set up offices within the same regional structure.

A third integral part of the new order, the Air Safety Board, operated outside the above structure and was concerned solely with the accident investigatory functions. Heading the Air Safety Board was Sumpter Smith, a lieutenant colonel in the Air Corps and Alabama National Guard, also with the federal WPA, and holder of an active transport pilot license. Thomas O. Hardin became the Vice-Chairman on the basis of a long record in aeronautics beginning with service in the Air Corps during World War I. Employed by various airlines during 1927–1938, Hardin was senior pilot with American for the six years before his appointment to the Air Safety Board, and his log showed over 10,000 hours of flight. Hardin was also First Vice-President of the Air Line Pilots' Association. The original third member of the Air Safety Board was C. B. Allen, selected in April, 1939. Allen had been aviation editor for the Republican *New York Herald Tribune*.

As in the case of the Bureau of Air Commerce, administrative changes frequently occurred. For example, Noble moved to the Department of Commerce in April, 1939, and was replaced as Administrator by Hinckley (authority member). Edward P. Warner, distinguished aeronautical expert, took Hinckley's place on the authority. Immediately after the new CAA assumed control of the former Bureau of Air Commerce (Department of Commerce) and the Bureau of Air Mail (Interstate Commerce Commission), confusion arose over the relationships among the various segments of the new agency. Furthermore, the public and some politicians never appeared to have mastered the true distinction of duties assigned to authority, administrator, and board. Answering a friend's plea for increased aid to private flying, Administrator Noble admitted at once: "Our problem of organization is terrible."[2] In almost two years of operation under the new organization, the various activities entailed the employment of 4,841 regular workers distributed as follows: authority, 748; administrator, 3,194; Air Safety Board, 76; and general services (legal, secretarial, supplies) to all three, 518.[3] In their confusion about nomenclature, congressmen expressed impatience over the budgetary requests, fearing unnecessary expansion of staff and program. The legislators had to be reminded that the act did not transfer the clerical and legal staffs to the CAA from the Department of Commerce and the ICC. Moreover, the act necessitated the additional staff to perform the new functions of economic regulation—competition, mergers, rates, and loans.[4]

At least part of the responsibility for questioning the new CAA rested with a popular magazine's account erroneously asserting that the CAA had more employees than the airlines which were being regulated. Armed with a refutation offered by Colonel Edgar S. Gorrell, President of ATA, Republican Congressman Charles Halleck of Indiana reminded his colleagues that the CAA employed only 560 in its regulatory phases while the ICC counted

2,599 employees for its regulation work. Moreover, the airlines employed 13,500 people. The vast majority of CAA employees provided airways operations. The distorted charges undeniably promoted an unsuccessful move in the House to reduce salaries and further embarrass the infant agency.

COMMERCE REGAINS A SHARE

The three-headed organization of federal control over aviation gained little time to display what performance could be accomplished before executive manipulation exacted further alterations. The Reorganization Plans III and IV of 1940, extremely controversial and opposed by the majority of aeronautical and congressional leaders, reassigned the functions of the administrator to the Department of Commerce, Civil Aeronautics Administration, effective June 30, 1940. The five-man authority and the Air Safety Board were combined and remained a separate agency under the new title Civil Aeronautics Board (CAB).[5] Partial responsibility for the continued rift over the administrative structure of the CAA must rest with the ill feelings generated during the fight to remove the activities from Commerce prior to 1938. For example, proponents of the ICC resumed their campaign to allow the ICC control over all transportation rates.

Complaints of divided responsibility reached the ears of President Roosevelt.[6] Presidential friends in the Department of Commerce undoubtedly encouraged the return of their "wayward son." That little wisdom might be discerned from the return made little difference to the New Deal's chief pilot who now displayed the typical FDR spirited defense of a sudden, pragmatic move. Calling his opposition "spinach," Roosevelt asserted during a press conference that the three members of the Air Safety Board fought among themselves all day long.[7] Transfer of the CAA to the Department of Commerce would bring the aviation duties closer to the Weather Bureau—under the same reorganization transferred from Agriculture to Commerce—as well as presenting the benefits of a Cabinet seat. The man soon to run for an unprecedented third term also claimed better unification for national defense under such a plan. Turning to the new CAB, Roosevelt foresaw the economic regulation and safety aspects now under uniform control. In fairness to the President, it would appear that the authority and Air Safety Board lacked over-all direction. However, there appears to be no evidence that they could better serve the nation under Commerce than as an independent agency. Certainly the blessings of Cabinet rank filtered down only remotely to the CAA; agencies under a department do not necessarily operate more efficiently within that department than as separate entities.

Congressmen on both sides of the aisle reacted intensely against the triumph of Secretary of Commerce Harry L. Hopkins in getting the President to secure the reorganization. Congressman J. Thorkelson of Montana labeled it the: ". . . Administrative Sabotage of the Civil Aeronautics Authority."[8] Thorkelson, an experienced pilot, warned of the inefficiency of the department. Aviation's true friend, Senator Pat McCarran, lashed out against Roosevelt's claims of Cabinet urgency, likened the reorganization to a "whitewash" of the old Bureau of Air Commerce, and reminded all concerned of the general opposition to the plan outside the government. Joining McCarran were Congressmen Clarence Lea of Minnesota, Robert B. Chipperfield of Illinois, and Ben Jensen of Iowa, all of whom pointed to the lack of rationale for the FDR plan. Congressman Lindsay C. Warren of North Carolina offered the defense of the plan and pointed the finger of blame at Hardin and Allen of the Air Safety Board. Allegedly adding oil to burning waters were Hinckley and Hester, both with the CAA. According to Congressman Warren, Colonel Smith could not get along with Hardin and Allen. Warren scoffed at Hardin and Allen for using government printing to publicize arguments against the reorganization. Hardin's flying ability was questioned, particularly because of an alleged case of poor judgment in getting lost in Indiana during a flight from Washington, D.C., to Nashville.[9] President Roosevelt instructed the Budget Bureau's administrative management division to study the relationship of the Air Safety Board to the entire authority. Delays of over one year in reports to CAA were cited as arguments proving board inefficiency.

Congressman Everett M. Dirksen of Illinois, while not closing his eyes to the apparent friction, failed to see the need to burn down the barn to clean out a few people. His primary concern lay in the absence of support for the measure among industry, pilots, public, insurance companies, and organized labor. Dirksen, lamenting the apparent influence of Hopkins, affirmed the great flying ability of Hardin. Dirksen and John J. Cochran of Missouri clashed over the abilities of Administrator Hester, who admittedly had no flying experience but had over twenty years of experience as a civil servant. Democratic newspapers, including the *Memphis Commercial Appeal, Kansas City Star,* and the *Nashville Tennessean,* opposed the reorganization. Perhaps Congressman Lea pinpointed the whole question when he contended that trivial incidents caused the whole fight, one such case involving the use of WPA funds without proper authorization to aid in the work on airfields. David Behncke's ALPA steadfastly assailed the switch. Lea's resolution against Reorganization Plan IV gained victory in the House (232 to 153) on May 8, 1940. The battle shifted to the Senate, where McCarran found the support of Harry Truman and Bennett Champ Clark, both of Missouri; James J. Davis of Pennsylvania; and Warren R. Austin of Texas. Truman, lamenting the fact that he hated to be accused of being gullible or playing politics because he had earlier favored Roosevelt's proposals concerning aviation, objected to this change.[10] He advised retention of the CAA in its present condition in order to allow it time to finish its job and prove its worth. The *St. Louis Post Dispatch* likened FDR's maneuvers to those of Caesar, because Hinckley of the authority was enticed into accepting the reorganization in return for a promotion to the Department of Commerce. Roosevelt's forces rallied in the Senate behind Claude Pepper of Florida, Alben Barkley of Kentucky, Scott Lucas of Illinois, James F. Byrnes of South Carolina, and Francis T. Maloney of Connecticut. On May 14, 1940, the Senate killed the rebellion against Roosevelt with 34 favoring the resolution and 46 opposing it.

Administration forces won out; the reorganization became reality. But the opposition continued its onslaught against the distressing situation which materialized at a most critical juncture when the country was preparing for national defense and a possible showdown with the Axis military regime. It can hardly be denied that this administrative shuffle offered little in the way of morale building within the CAA and new CAB. One editor contended that Assistant Secretary Hinckley, now in charge of Commerce affairs concerning the CAA and Weather Bureau, had lost all confidence among CAA personnel as the result of his sudden shift favoring FDR's reorganization despite his colleagues' unified opposition. *American Aviation,* citing its previous unbiased praise of Hinckley, now told of his fallen image and the ill respect manifested toward him in the CAA. The sudden resignations of Dr. E. S. Adams, Chief of the Medical Section, and Richard S. Boutelle, Director of the Bureau of Safety Regulation, constituted just two major examples of a continuing White House purge led by Hinckley. Holders of twenty lower-echelon positions in the CAB and even two secretaries felt the axe; others remained uncertain of their future. During the next eighteen and one-half years, the correct titles of the two entities remained the Civil Aeronautics Administration and the Civil Aeronautics Board. As Hinckley moved on to Commerce, General Donald H. Connolly, of the U.S. Army Engineers, became administrator. Branch became Chairman of the CAB.[11]

REGIONAL RUMBLES

The status of the CAA-CAB in relation to Commerce was not the sole administrative problem during 1938–1941. As outlined in Chapter 6, the decentralization process resulted in the establishment of regional offices. From the outset, CAA leadership sought uniformity in policy and operations among the regions but often found this an elusive goal. One CAA expert lamented the rumors from Washington, D.C., about contemplated changes in jurisdiction, all of which proved damaging to morale in the field.[12] Decentralization should bring more powers of decision in the regions, thus relieving the central office of such minor details as granting approval before each airport was qualified for use in scheduled commercial operations. H. W. Anderson, Chief of the Aircraft Inspection Section, recalled his early days with the organization, when "fair-haired" boys ran the inspection of aircraft and were by no means popular. Now inspection had improved, but the inspectors lacked adequate pension and retirement benefits. Those killed on duty left scant compensation to relatives. One has only to review the official correspondence of the CAA to discern the undercurrent of friction prevalent in varying degrees among leaders of the regions and the central headquarters in Washington, D.C. In an effort to bring unity and rapport into the agency, Howard F. Rough, veteran and respected inspector with the predecessors of the CAA, took over the position as Director of Regional Offices in January, 1939.[13] Rough queried his regional managers to uncover cases of criticism and internal friction. J. E. Sommers of the first region considered much of the discord as originating from the lack of coordination among the various sections in the CAA in Washington, a case in point being the private flying and inspection divisions.[14] Sommers offered one remedy, pointing out that extensive travel throughout the regions by top CAA authorities in Washington might enlighten these officials to the problems involved and

provide better mutual understanding. Apparently, many of the
top leaders neglected visiting the regional offices, as reflected by
testimony before a congressional committee in May, 1941.[15]

A few months earlier, Sommers had been accused of attempting to garner a disproportionate share of funds allocated to
the regions.[16] One complaint aired widely in the regions concerned the resentment of older employees at seeing new units
created within the CAA with higher salaries for new workers and
seemingly unlimited equipment for the new enterprise.[17] Manager L. C. Elliott, fourth region, Fort Worth, disclosed his mis-
givings about the regional arrangement: "In all frankness, I
feel that some of the sections in Washington have failed to fully
grasp the Regional picture and are still inclined to follow the
policies of independent action which naturally carries to the
field."[18] Earlier in 1939, Elliott had reassured Rough that the administrative difficulties in his region could be traced to one individual, a carry-over of the political favoritism of the old Bureau of
Air Commerce: "while at one time it was generally known that a
political endorsement was the primary requisite for obtaining employment."[19] Here, and in cases involving other regions, the rules
of Civil Service that were intended to protect employees apparently made it most difficult, if not impossible, to remove from
office troublemakers who cleverly watched their own activities so
as to hide behind such protective measures. Leonard Jurden,
Regional Manager at Kansas City, believed, too, that the existing
regional organization had been ignored by Washington officials.[20]
A trip made personally to regional headquarters in Atlanta,
Georgia, led Rough to advise his own superiors of the reticence
on the part of the regional manager to exercise firm control over
his men.[21] A glowingly optimistic reply to Rough's inquiry about
personnel troubles came from R. D. Bedinger, Regional Manager
at Seattle. Bedinger considered this happy state of affairs due to
the absence thus far of personnel from the Air Safety Board and
air traffic control in his region, in addition to the establishment
only recently of a private flying section.[22]

Staff morale in the field could be measured also according
to the ease with which the personnel found adequate housing.
Difficulties undoubtedly arose in other portions of the nation
before World War II, but the Chicago area presented Rough with
the most concern. Both operational staff and clerical workers
complained bitterly about the housing shortage and high rents.[23]
One CAA communications operator desired a minimum of three

rooms at twenty-five dollars a month for his family of three growing children, a need impossible to fulfill in a country now caught in the price spiral brought on by defense construction. Chicago also failed to provide adequate office space for the various CAA operations; again the midwestern area seemingly caused the most worry. Authorities contemplated moving several offices out of Chicago to South Bend, Grand Rapids, or Milwaukee, in an effort to awaken Chicago governmental and aeronautical interests to the graveness of the situation. Another shortcoming—low-paying jobs in the CAA—occasionally brought to mind the stark reality of unpreparedness on the part of a widow and children when forced to face the future alone. The death of a communications operator in Newark led Regional Manager Sommers to advise Rough that a contingency fund available for such cases would be far more important than merely a flower fund which was not much help in this instance for the penniless widow and three children.[24]

BOLDER REGULATIONS—1938–1941

Administrative details entailed many knotty dilemmas. At the same time, the CAA and CAB progressed notably in the realm of regulations before the attack on Pearl Harbor. Inspecting and licensing aircraft and airmen, the core of all regulatory activities, provided a number of headaches during an era featuring a significant increase in aviation usage. Complicating matters, these events were transpiring against the backdrop of European war and America's precarious existence as a neutral nation that yet was overwhelmingly in sympathy with Hitler's victims. To the reader untrained in the intricacies of federal agencies and the field of aviation, the means employed to regulate airmen and aircraft might seem beyond comprehension. Essentially, the entire process depended upon CAA inspectors who, as before, tested the merits of craft and men; issued or denied the proper certification or license; or recommended disciplinary action, when appropriate, to officials within the enforcement section of the agency. Forming another integral portion of the process was the provision for amendments and additions to the Civil Air Regulations. Here again, changes arose primarily from inspectors' suggestions, along with the findings of the important accident investigators in the CAB. The quality of over-all CAA-CAB regulatory operations depended solely upon the ability of inspectors, together with the cooperation of aviation manufacturers and the airmen at the controls. The actual details of inspection remained essentially identical to the descriptions outlined in earlier chapters. Changes became necessary with the introduction of more powerful aircraft.

A SAFETY RECORD

Certainly the efficiency of inspection and licensing had something to do with the amazing and unparalleled phenomenon reflected in the perfect record of safety without accidents and fatalities on the air carriers from March 26, 1939, to August 31, 1940.[25] Chairman Hinckley, Administrator Hester, and Air Safety Board Chairman Hardin issued the following NOTAM (Notices to Airmen) during this marathon at the end of the initial twelve months:

> Heartiest congratulations to all airline, Civil Aeronautics Authority, and Weather Bureau personnel upon completion of an entire year of airline safety. This is one of the outstanding achievements in the history of transportation.[26]

President Roosevelt echoed his warmest pleasure: "The news is indeed gratifying . . . my heartiest congratulations to the air lines and to your own personnel in the Civil Aeronautics Authority."[27] Colonel Charles A. Lindbergh relayed his sentiments to Hinckley: "It seems clear that the air lines have passed their period of infancy."[28] Even the most optimistic aviation adherent could not hope for a complete absence of further tragedy on the airways. But the unprecedented, spotless record came during a most opportune era when the administrative reorganization, based on charges of petty politics, had cast a shadow over the operations of the former Bureau of Air Commerce.

COMPLAINTS vs. INSPECTIONS

Safety record notwithstanding, complaints were registered against other phases of CAA inspections. One inspector in the Newark region drew a reprimand for indicating the same grade on the examination given to 120 students, much to the chagrin of A. S. Koch, Acting Director of the CAA's Bureau of Safety Regulation.[29] In another instance, alleged leniency in the rerating of flight instructors brought firm but tactful corrective measures. Curtailing the number of errors on inspectors' reports continued to plague the Bureau of Safety Regulation, one regional manager suggesting a drive for accuracy through competition among the regions.[30]

Overworked inspectors probably considered filling in forms and other types of paper work the least important tasks they must perform. That most inspectors faced an insurmountable work load proved to be common knowledge among aviation leaders. For example, Inspector Daniel C. Moulten was confronted by as many as twenty-three pilots for tests on a single day. Moulten worked in several midwestern communities including Evansville, Vincennes, Paducah, Owensboro, and Huntingburg. Community leaders in Evansville complained of a three-month backlog there.[31] Visiting Evansville one day each month, Moulten often labored long after dark in an effort to reduce the waiting list. Authority officials told Congress that Moulten's case was the typical situation throughout the country. H. W. Anderson, Chief of the Air-Carrier Inspection Section, exerted major influence in strengthening the core of inspectors, sending his men to Indianapolis for two weeks of "flying under the hood."[32] Further improvement resulted from the purchase of a DC–3, now used by the CAA as a flying laboratory complete with a new azimuth indicator developed by CAA personnel.[33]

The prewar shortage of inspectors continued, and fifty-three qualified mechanics aided with inspection duties to help fill the void. Low pay scales did not alleviate the problem. By 1941, the qualifications of the various inspectors stressed experience and age limitations—depending upon the specific job—between twenty-one and forty-five.[34] Flight supervisors needed 1,000 hours of flying and a valid commercial license, while the maintenance supervisor had to possess a mechanic's certificate for engines, aircraft, and parachute rigging. Citizenship was required of inspectors, and all could expect a salary of between $3,500 and $3,800 per year. Unfortunately, the inspector failed at times to secure the cooperation of pilots during regular air-carrier flights. The ALPA registered complaints against what it termed "inspectors barging into cockpits."[35] Similar accusations have come more recently from the same organization. Placing a further burden on the inspectors, some pilots obviously attempted their flight examinations before attaining sufficient competency, forcing the inspector to act as an instructor during the test flight and wasting the expert's time.[36] Striving to maintain high standards, CAA leaders realized the manpower shortage hindered their fight against allowing the inspections to become a mere rubber-stamp operation.[37] As do educational authorities, inspectors perennially guarded against the stealing of examinations for later use. Disclosure of such practices by several individuals and personnel of certain aeronautical schools led the CAB, upon request by the CAA, to issue a special regulation against this illegal activity.[38]

Public reaction to CAA inspectors, when of the unfavorable variety, often resulted in written charges reaching congressmen. A resident of Hibbing, Minnesota, informed Senator Joseph Ball of Minnesota that CAA inspectors had not visited Hibbing for several months to inspect reconditioned planes. Administrator Connolly, after investigating the matter through Regional Manager H. R. Neely, denied the charges.[39] One inspector drew the wrath of pilots for not following the prescribed order in testing and failing over 50 per cent of his applicants.[40] No indication was given as to what he should have done in case, say, even 80 or 100 per cent of his aspirants proved to be incompetent. Members of an air service located at Mansfield, Ohio, complained bitterly over a visit by two CAA men, who landed in poor weather (ceiling about 2,000 feet and visibility 1 mile), off course by 30 miles, and without the proper sectional maps for the area: "We had 18 students on the ground at the same time and a considerable amount of our effort in trying to impress the seriousness of complete preparation was lost because of such bad procedure."[41] The writer claimed that the CAA men would not identify themselves. Congressman Dirksen received a complaint about an assistant aeronautical inspector from Chicago, who visited Peoria as part of his duties, apparently resenting this assignment and taking out his ill feelings on the applicants of Peoria.[42] A dentist in nearby Eureka recalled his encounter with the Peoria inspector. His request to be given the examination as soon as practicable in order to return to a schedule of patients brought this answer: "I don't give a goddamn . . . you'll take the exam when I get ready."[43] Following considerable delay, the pilot successfully completed the examination with the admonition not to take up passengers for another week. Though not representative of the entire corps of inspectors, such actions on the part of a few officials seriously damaged public relations for the CAA. Most definitely the old spirit of authoritarianism among inspectors died a slow and painful death.

Not all complaints, to be sure, warranted serious consideration; often new inspectors demanded strict compliance in cases where undue leniency had formerly prevailed, resulting in a deluge of protests to Washington, D.C. A veteran pilot in Rapid City, South Dakota, summed it up this way: "We have probably been spoiled in this territory. . . ."[44] Inspectors there allegedly mutilated a plane during tests. The accused inspectors, Gordon R. Matthews and Vaughn R. McNulty, defended their actions and submitted a thorough account of discrepancies found. At Brookings, the inspectors noticed wings that had been rebuilt without use of a straightedge or tram rod, while the ribs were out of alignment and there was a broken strut fitting.[45] Pilots reportedly lacked instruction in executing the "figure eight" at Huron. Considerable difficulty was encountered at Rapid City in readying one plane for the inspection flight; the cowling was off, the landing-gear shock cord weak and full of oil, and gear bolts showed excessive wear. Moreover, the aileron jammed in full right-stick position. The mechanic had not connected the front carburetor support, because he did not know its function. Finally, the gas line lacked a flexible connection between the gas filter and carburetor. Other planes appeared with similar deficiencies. Elsewhere, an aeronautical instructor in Oakland, California, exasperated because one of his students waited six months without learning the results of his written examination, aroused sympathetic action from Koch, Chief of Certification and Inspection.[46] Aviation enthusiasts in Portland, Oregon, petitioned the CAB, though the problem concerned the CAA, for an increase in the number of inspectors in order to eliminate the bottleneck in aviation expansion there and elsewhere.[47] The CAA replied that 100 new inspectors were being sought for immediate duty.

Not all aviation shortcomings were laid at the doorstep of the CAA, as those men testing for industry also faced the charge of improper qualifications. An expert summarized one situation: "All twenty-eight of these dreamers take up the time of the Engineering Department of the CAA."[48] On the other hand, one airline head charged the CAA with certifying unqualified mechanics, bringing forth a promise from the CAA to improve the quality of the written examination.[49] Speaking about maintenance of high standards, top CAA leadership realized the difficulties involved, particularly now that the plea for national defense had resulted in a rapid increase of the number of young Americans seeking flight training. Revisiting the operations of aviation schools and spot-checking their students during instruction was a more difficult assignment than rerating a pilot already established.[50]

Personal inspection of air carrier operations, both of pilots and mechanics, resulted in much useful information and warnings for all CAA inspectors via a monthly news letter. Early in 1940, inspectors received notice of corrosive action caused by one deicing fluid, and, at the time, the Lockheed 10–A craft did not operate satisfactorily over the Seattle–Billings division because of excessive icing. Winter operations of Northwest Airlines and Pennsylvania Central Airlines came under close scrutiny; the latter line had just recently begun to use DC craft.[51] Harrowing experiences occasionally dramatized the skill of CAA inspectors and industry's own personnel. CAA and TWA experts tested a Boeing 307, entering a thunderstorm at approximately 15,000 feet, whereupon the No. 4 engine backfired, probably from icing.[52] Shortly, Nos. 3 and 4 (each on the right side) both stopped, but no feathering action was taken in the hope that the ice would break sufficiently to restart the engines. At 700 feet, No. 4 came on sluggishly; a rough landing followed with only minor damage after the agonizing five minutes of reckoning.

CAA inspectors often responded willingly to CAB requests for special investigations of airline operations beyond the routine of accident studies. Acting Chairman Warner commended the CAA for its thorough check on National Airlines' maintenance activities.[53] Occupied with its own backlog of applications and smarting under criticism from Congress and the public, Koch at least once voiced his disapproval of the CAB's request for the use of three experts. Rivalry between the CAA and CAB, however, scarcely could be regarded as a serious matter at this time. Petty differences arose periodically within the ranks of CAA inspectors, for instance, between the air carrier personnel and those in the general inspection section (concerned primarily with private flying) in the Atlanta region.[54] In checking on airline operations, CAA personnel reassured the ALPA in 1940 that Pan American and Panagra pilots were not exceeding the 100-hour monthly maximum for overseas flights, Panagra showing but 1 violation of this type in the period March, 1939, to February, 1940.[55] However 12 violations were detected in domestic operations, where the 85-hour limit was still in effect. The increase in Pan American's business necessitated the stationing of a CAA inspector at Lima, Peru, for the purpose of licensing pilots and helping the

Federal Communications Commission (FCC) by checking on radio communication employees.[56]

In all relations with the public, CAA leadership stressed the necessity for inspectors to maintain silence concerning points of legality and responsibility.[57] Chairman Noble believed that ALPA President Behncke should likewise refrain from unfair public criticism prior to a scheduled hearing.[58] The reorganization creating the CAA in 1938 brought about the obligation to provide a hearing even in cases where a student or beginning pilot had been refused a license by a CAA inspector, a privilege not accorded under the Bureau of Air Commerce to a disgruntled or offended person.[59]

VIOLATIONS

The most naive observer could hardly deny that airline personnel occasionally violate the Civil Air Regulations, indeed, just as motorists often abuse the rules of the road without always ending up as a fatality statistic, as a victim of arrest, or with a possible fine. Whenever inspectors noted violations, the enforcement section of the CAA assumed the responsibility of taking action, whether or not fines (civil penalties) were invoked. Pilots must be considered human beings. But to authorities the simplest violation always loomed as a potential cause of fatal accidents. Therefore, pilots guilty of the most trivial errors could expect notification, at the least, if their mistakes had been detected. Failure to report a change in flight plan appeared again and again as the most frequent abuse in these days. One marvels at the patience displayed in some cases on the part of the CAA toward a pilot with several violations, minor as each case seemed.[60] Monthly summaries of violations were recorded for each airline. Numerous instances of $100 fines appear in the records. If revocation of a certificate were deemed appropriate, the CAA advised the CAB to undertake such action.[61] The government collected approximately $15,000 in fines during 1940. Airways and airport irregularities constituted a major portion of one survey of violations compiled by the CAA and publicized for its employees and all aviation interests.[62] Covering the first eight months of 1940, the study revealed 151 takeoffs and 76 landings without permission, 92 instances of disregarding CAA radio messages, and 103 examples in which the pilot taxied without authorization from the control tower. Airport personnel were urged to force violators to spend time in the control towers, write new license examinations, or, in severe cases, to deny them use of the airport for ten to thirty days.

The usual number of license suspensions for acrobatics and other illegal procedures occupied a vast amount of time for the compliance personnel. One student pilot lost his license for thirty days after he exhibited his prowess in acrobatics at less than 500 feet and without a parachute.[63] Acrobatic flying at low altitude caused nearly one-half of all fatal accidents in private flying during November, 1939.[64] The manager of the Illini Airport, Urbana, Illinois, faced suspension of his limited commercial-pilot certificate for ninety days after allegedly giving flying instruction without a valid instructor's rating.[65] The Southern Aviation School, New Orleans, encountered suspension of its certificate, the action stemming from a flight instructor and a student flying dangerously low over the Coast Guard station at Biloxi, Mississippi; the use of planes not approved for the Civil Pilot Training program; and the falsifying of records.[66] Violations occurring on the ground caused their share of damages and headaches for the CAA. Welding in storage hangers and smoking around aircraft apparently led to several fires; the failure to have metal aircraft grounded properly and the lack of ample current capacity in wiring led to other blazes.[67] To remind airline operators of the many errors which might lead to trouble, CAA authorities made use of the popular *Civil Aeronautics Journal* (successor to the *Air Commerce Bulletin*) for disseminating these warnings and such advice as "keep all safety belts in good repair."[68]

CIVIL AIR REGULATIONS

Invaluable experience gained through inspection duties, along with detection of deficiencies—both human and mechanical—led CAA and CAB officials to revise the Civil Air Regulations continuously. The sixty-one amendments of 1941 included the following:

(1) All transports must be equipped with full-feathering propellers as a means of stopping engine rotation in flight.

(2) The crew must be supplied with oxygen when flying at 10,000 feet or higher for thirty minutes.

(3) Planes of over 10,000 pounds are required to carry radio communications and a recorder of altitude while in flight.

(4) The aircraft a pilot can fly will now be designated by horsepower, not by weight.[69]

Sometimes the notices issued to airmen contained humorous items, though tragedy lurked nearby. Airmen at Newark, New Jersey, were advised: "It will be appreciated if pilots will refrain from landing on these beaches."[70] Bureau of Safety Regulation personnel warned all pilots not to "press" themselves, particularly after a miss on the first landing attempt, likening the ensuing tense reaction to that of a golfer who missed the ball on his first swing.[71]

Following its long-established policy, the pilots' professional organization, the ALPA, submitted periodic suggestions for the Civil Air Regulations.[72] Better relations evolved between the CAA-CAB and the ALPA after the reorganization in 1938. Hester and other authority officials even went to Chicago for a conference with ALPA boss Behncke, who expressed delight at the results—a far cry from the days of undeclared war under the Bureau of Air Commerce.[73] Shortly afterward, the ALPA expressed hope that proper action could be initiated to eliminate the smoke from the city dump at Newark, long a hazard to flying.[74] Apparently the "smog" problem, still unsolved because of industrial disinclination in the 1960's, proved too much for the CAA and ALPA at the time. Military flights along civil airways, a problem cited earlier, continued to harass pilots and federal authorities, primarily because of the collision hazard.[75] Fear of collision in the vicinity of airports also reached the CAA, TWA reporting such acute possibilities while descending or climbing in the Akron and Pittsburgh areas.[76]

Another branch of air regulations work, centering in the Medical Section, launched a series of profound studies designed to ascertain fitness of pilots. New vision tests for pilots included the reading without difficulty of towns and cities on their charts in the different colors indicating varying altitudes—green, white, and brown—and the ability to read the titles on a card 18 inches from the eyes.[77] Encouragement to aviation medicine resulted from the continued interest of the Mayo Foundation which undertook at its own expense a study of pilots' physical examinations correlated with their flight performance.[78] Recent winners of the Collier Trophy for aviation, the Mayo experts previously conducted tests of Northwest Airlines pilots in ascents up to 40,000 feet at the rate of 4,000 feet per minute, stressing after the experiments the need for pilots to use oxygen, even to the extent of inhaling it prior to flights.[79] The UAL Clinic at Chicago already required a rigid annual examination of its pilots including the Schneider Index, a circulatory efficiency test checking the cardiovascular system under rest and exertion. On the rating scale of —4 to +18, most pilots scored 12 to 16.[80] Eye tests featured the search for night blindness—the exhaustion of visual purple. Witnesses of the space age of the sixties might be surprised to learn that German scientists already in 1940 indicated the possibility of securing the pilot on his back or stomach while in flight so that the circulation might endure greater speeds.[81] Despite the importance of the Medical Section's work, not all CAA leaders were satisfied with its current organization at the Medical Science Station in Kansas City.[82]

As the new authority took over air regulations in 1938, the aviation industry reached the threshold of widespread support for the four-engine aircraft. Not all theorists yet accepted the practicality of the successfully tested DC–4 and the Boeing 307 Stratoliner; orders for the two giant ships had lagged, ostensibly because of the added expense. Curtiss Wright then challenged the four-engine supporters with plans for a larger, two-engine plane (each engine with 1,500 horsepower) supercharged and capable of flight at 20,000 feet.[83] During 1940, CAA engineers approved the first engine of 2,000 horsepower.[84] Because of the increased work load, delegation of some duties to the airlines was approved, e.g., balancing of aircraft and minor repairs without inspection. Engines long constituted a major subject of deep concern in the CAA which cited poor maintenance and operations for 28 of 64 engine failures in a CAB study made during 1939.[85] Amendments to the Civil Air Regulations included the requirement of an independent oil supply for each engine.

The scheduled airlines occupied an ever-growing amount of study, yet regulations governing private flying also won consideration during this era. In fact, one of the early actions of the new authority came in September, 1938, with the establishment of a private flying section. Grove Webster was in charge.[86] Interest in private flying lagged in the United States when compared to the number of flying clubs in Europe, for example, in Czechoslovakia. On the other hand, American regulators did not seek more leniency in order to foster private flying. Indeed, the original age minimum of sixteen was raised to eighteen for licensing of private pilots, though student and solo ratings could still be awarded at sixteen.

A sharp rise in interest toward parachuting in this country brought consternation to the public at times of tragedy. But the CAA stood firm with its regulations, especially the ruling that delayed jumps (the free fall) must be completed above 2,000 feet. The same provision applied to use of the popular Bat Wing parachute, except that here the chutist must have completed ten or more earlier delayed jumps.[87] Enthusiasts continued their zeal for this sport despite the above restriction which prevented attempts to better an alleged Russian record of fall from 26,575 feet to 600 feet above the ground, a mark accomplished in 1934. A distraught father, upon the death of his thirty-eight-year-old son in his first jump, inquired about the legal responsibility. He was informed that CAA authorities had evidence of the son's intention to attempt the dangerous delayed jump.[88] Parachute rigging again received the close attention of authorities, one rigger losing his certificate for ninety days because of "carelessness and inattention."[89] Such problems as those outlined above posed a major challenge to CAA inspectors and rule makers who collectively made up the bulwark of governmental authority in aviation concerns, an authority always designed to provide competent fliers navigating airworthy machines.

SAFETY, ECONOMIC REGULATION, INCREASED FACILITIES–1938-1941

ENGAGING in political turmoil over the rightful owner-ship of the Civil Aeronautics Authority and confronting the many woes of inspection and licensing the nation's airmen and planes required a great deal of attention during 1938–1941. Meanwhile, momentous developments transpired in the realms of accident investigation, economic regulation (a new duty), and improved airway facilities. The CAA and CAB shared in the progress recorded before Pearl Harbor.

CAB–ACCIDENTS AND SAFETY

Reorganizations in 1938 and 1940 centered the responsi-bility for accident investigation with the same authorities. The title Air Safety Board simply reverted to the Bureau of Safety under the CAB in 1940; in each instance a body independent of the Department of Commerce controlled this all-important func-tion. The Air Safety Board established field offices at New York, Chicago, Fort Worth, and Los Angeles. Mention has been made of the splendid record of no airline fatalities over the seventeen months beginning late in March, 1939. Nonairline mishaps, the majority of which could have been avoided, brought forth a reiteration of safety axioms for the private flier. Sixty-two per cent of all fatalities during three months of 1938 occurred because of failure to keep the plane's nose down. Stalls often could be avoided by maintaining a sizable margin above stalling speed when flying in gusty air. Failures of other sorts included: inadequate gasoline supply upon takeoff; nonuse of safety belt; inability to land straight ahead when engine failed on takeoff or forgetting to do so; instrument flying without training. Two pilots died attempting to fly without instruction of any sort. A favorite mechanical observation read: "An aircraft with a misbehaving engine should be kept on the ground."[1]

One departure announced early by the Air Safety Board embraced the policy of investigating a larger share of all air accidents, striving to have a personal representative look into all air carrier mishaps, at least 15 per cent of all nonscheduled aircraft accidents. The remainder would be investigated by questionnaires. Before, only about 15 per cent of all accidents were personally investigated.[2] The laboratories of NACA, California Institute of Technology, or Massachusetts Institute of Technology (MIT) performed analysis of engines for accident investigation. Unhappily, the goal of investigating was not met during the first year, even though CAA personnel aided the Air Safety Board, the two directly surveying slightly less than one-third of all accidents. Chairman Thomas O. Hardin noted that, although carelessness and negligence seemed evident in quite a few cases, investigators proceeded cautiously, knowing that insurance policies were cancelled if negligence or violations entered the official reports.

The accident reports submitted by the Air Safety Board and the CAB present all varieties of meticulous effort on the part of dedicated investigators, with the aid of CAA inspectors, to arrive at an honest opinion of what went wrong. They placed the blame where it belonged. Laboring day and night in rugged terrain, with or without valuable clues, the investigators could win the admiration of an experienced detective. CAA men, aiding the CAB, put in a total of 524 man-hours within 4 days following the crash of a Pennsylvania Central plane killing 21 passengers near Lovettsville, Virginia, on August 31, 1940—the crash that ended the 17-month record without fatalities.[3] Despite the long record of lightning strikes causing little structural damage to aircraft, the CAB listed lightning as the probable cause of the Lovettsville crash, asserting that the flash might have temporarily blinded the pilots, after which the plane abruptly dived 5,000 feet to the ground at over 300 miles per hour and at an angle of 30 degrees. Turbulence and lightning constituted the only two major possibilities.

Once every so often, a near tragedy occurred without death

or injury, as in the case of the Mid-Continent crash at Sioux City, Iowa, on June 11, 1941. The pilot, according to the probable cause, had received an inaccurate weather observation from the company radio operator prior to making a downwind landing. Failure of the airport lights contributed to the mishap which resulted in the pilot trying a ground loop to the right and ending up 200 feet past the runway in a plowed field.[4] Ineffective brake action probably caused the crash of a DC–3 at Denver, Colorado, on June 10, 1941. The crew of an Eastern Air Lines (EAL) plane, whose right engine caught fire while in flight, successfully brought the craft down without loss of life at Montgomery, Alabama, on October 18, 1938. A series of accidents involving Pan American aircraft brought quick CAA reaction: "It may be that a check-up should be made on their pilot personnel in order to determine their competency."[5] Flying boats had been involved in several accidents during the previous two years, one caused by engine failure on landing at Rio de Janeiro on August 13, 1939, another occurring at Sao Luiz, Brazil, two years later; Pan American Airways (PAA) lost another flying boat at Guam, and one disappeared in the Pacific.

BIZARRE REPORTS

Accidents involving private pilots continued to include bizarre reports of all types—two killed when the pilot lost control striking a wing to the ground while hunting coyotes, another couple seriously injured after the pilot lost control at 50 feet above ground while shouting to a farmer for directions (better to drop a note), several accidents caused by loose control sticks (inexcusable). Plagued for years by souvenir hunters at accident scenes, the Air Safety Board gained a regulation, effective September 7, 1939, making it illegal to disturb wreckage in which death or injury was involved.[6] Unfortunately, looters still persisted. The individual accident report, that is, a report for each crash, was suspended early in 1940. Among the many accidents reported in private aviation, one involved an apparent suicide in which the pilot took an unlighted plane from an unlighted airport and deliberately flew into a hangar wall.[7] The collision hazard increased with the frenzy of national defense maneuvers in 1941, and civil airmen were told to look out for the military: "You must watch for them. That is your patriotic duty and responsibility."[8] The "open season" on civil aircraft had arrived.

CAB—ECONOMIC REGULATION

Prior to the changes brought about under the Civil Aeronautics Act of 1938, the Post Office Department contracted for airmail rates while the ICC set, and revised, the rates payable to the mail carriers. Now the Civil Aeronautics Authority assumed these duties along with other new chores:

(1) Certificates of public convenience and necessity would be issued before any company engaged in air transport.

(2) A "grandfather clause" under the law allowed airlines that were providing adequate service before May 14, 1938, to receive their certificates without much difficulty.

(3) Applications for new routes must be made with public hearings provided.[9]

A second category of new duties covered the all-important rate-making powers of the authority (the CAB after the next reorganization in 1940). Every carrier now posted its tariff of rates and rules before the authority's criteria of "just and reasonable, nondiscriminatory and nonpreferential." Hearings and notices were announced prior to changes, all of which must have authority (CAB) approval. To October 31, 1939, 64 of 74 requests were allowed, all at a lower rate. Practically no complaints had been received about passenger and express rates. Another economic duty designated the authority as responsible for allowing or disapproving airline consolidations or mergers.

Before World War II, the authority (CAA) and the CAB witnessed the airlines' rise from a point of economic chaos in 1938— primarily because of the reckless bidding for mail contracts, according to the experts—to financial success beginning with a sharp rise in passenger business since August, 1938.[10] The Bureau of Economic Regulation within the authority, and later the CAB, instigated prehearing conferences in order to eliminate many details from the formal hearings. To obtain a true picture of the traffic requirements concerning requests for added service, the bureau conducted surveys of station-to-station traffic, including origin and destination statistics, all of which aided greatly in deciding the merits of applications for nonstop flights.

The initial certificates granted under the "grandfather clause" went to PAA's route from Charleston, South Carolina, to Fort Worth.[11] PAA obtained permission for its long-anticipated transatlantic service on May 19, 1939, for two round trips per week on northern or southern routes. A day later, on the twelfth anniversary of Charles Lindbergh's hop to Paris, the PAA flying boat *Yankee Clipper* left Port Washington, New York, for Lisbon —via Horta, the Azores—and then on to Marseilles, France. The action on the northern route stemmed from cooperation with the State Department in obtaining reciprocal agreements with the United Kingdom, North Ireland, Canada, and the Irish Free State, whereby British and U.S. carriers would operate across the North Atlantic with a maximum of two round trips each week.[12] The war undoubtedly delayed further inauguration of European efforts to obtain certificates for service to the United States; several such applications were approved—British Overseas Airways Corporation (BOAC) and Air France—others were on file with the CAB. Imperial Airways, Ltd., was authorized the London–New York route for one flight per week beginning on August 4, 1939. Later BOAC took over the Imperial permit. Airline operators felt keenly the rising competition inherent in the new routes and services sought of the CAB. PAA early requested photostats of all such applications.[13] In other international action, the authority cancelled Germany's 1938 application for dirigible air service to the United States with a sister ship of the *Hindenburg,* obviously for lack of prosecution of the service.[14] Prior to the fall of France in June, 1940, Air France Transatlantique tested six-engine (800 horsepower each) flying boats, planning one trip every three weeks to La Guardia Field, New York.

The authority's International Division, in close harmony with the State Department, dealt with the complicated problems of air transport on the worldwide basis. Further help came from an interdepartmental committee on civil international aviation, a group made up of assistant secretaries of the executive departments. Neutrality legislation forced PAA to terminate its northern-route flights at Foynes, Eire.[15] Likewise, the southern route had to be terminated at Lisbon. Public response to the transatlantic hop proved to be sensational, a waiting list of 100 or more names often existed, and a third weekly flight was sometimes approved. American Export Airlines (AEA) received a temporary certificate—for the war emergency plus sixty days— to operate between New York and Lisbon, via the Azores. AEA used the new Sikorsky S–44 flying boats to fly nonstop. Pan American's activities gained approval for extension to Leopoldville, Belgian Congo, primarily to carry spare parts and return with our military air-ferry personnel. In the Pacific, PAA extended its operations from San Francisco to Auckland, New Zealand (fortnightly), via Los Angeles, Honolulu, Canton Island, and New Caledonia, plus service between Manila and Singapore, and operations to Alaska. Furthermore, a 1939 conference with Canadian officials brought approval of several American lines' service to our northern neighbor. Additional PAA flights shortened dramatically the travel time between Miami and Buenos Aires—three and one-half days—and to the Canal Zone. At this early date, several airlines exercised their right of appeal to federal courts. Of 7 early cases, the CAB won 3, 2 were dismissed, 1 concluded by common consent, while another was decided in part for the board, in part against. A key victory was the board's decision, backed by the court, to allow competition on the transatlantic service.

Applications for mergers invariably drew extreme interest not only from aeronautical interests but from the business world in general, for the current governmental attitude toward monopoly versus competition was at stake. Consolidations involving large operations gained primary attention, a case in point being the authority's denial of UAL's attempt to purchase Western Air Express (operating from Salt Lake City to Los Angeles).[16] On the other hand, during 1941, the CAB approved all requests for mergers. In the UAL-Western case, the authority overruled its examiner's favorable report toward merger, though an exchange for planes with sleeping equipment was allowed. TWA was denied the request to buy Marquette Airlines. The CAB held no general control over airline expenditures;[17] but the financial statements concerning airlines were not considered confidential by the board, much to the chagrin of some businessmen, one of whom disliked the public scrutiny of his procurement of twenty-three air transports for the war-ravished British in 1940.[18] The authority originally threw up its hands in dismay, with justification, over the route problems in Alaska, and decided to grant temporary certificates until such a time as a more complete study of the needs might be ascertained.[19] Nonscheduled operators drew the grace of exemption from CAB certification, also pending further study. All loans and other financial aid to airlines had to meet with authority (CAB) approval, even in cases where the loan originated with the Reconstruction Finance Corporation (RFC). A consolidated tariff for local and joint passenger service was announced by the CAB on July 15, 1940.

Airmail, long a major thorn in the regulatory functions of the federal government, provided little difficulty during 1938–1941. The brighter picture involving airmail had begun prior to the reorganization in 1938. During fiscal year 1938, the government had paid the operators $15,712,000 compared to Post Office revenue of $15,301,000, a deficit eight times less than the figure in 1936.[20] Competitive bidding under the rules of 1934–1938 resulted in bids ranging from 1 mill to the maximum of 33 cents per mile; the Bureau of Air Commerce had no say in the matter. Congressmen, Post Office, and CAB officials looked toward the day when mail receipts would exceed the government payments to operators. This happy situation occurred on PAA operations during fiscal 1941, gross receipts totaling almost $1 million above payments.[21] Airmail rate making involved numerous complicated factors, the aim being to consider the need of the operator as well as the desires of the Post Office for mail delivery. Surveys indicated that 94.5 per cent of airmail traveled over 325 miles. A constant review of each company's profits and financial activities would be necessary if the principles of this operation were carried to the ultimate. However, little difficulty arose over this point before Pearl Harbor.

WAR IN EUROPE

World War II in Europe, with the few exceptions previously explained, brought about an almost complete halt in new commercial operations which had reached the threshold of epoch-making proportions. Certainly the suspicions and rivalries outlined in the description of the 1934–1938 era continued until war ensued. Just when the State Department considered western hemispheric accord cemented by the Act of Havana (1938), Chile decided to suspend part of the agreement by requiring all U.S. aircraft to obtain permission for travel there.[22] At home, CAA personnel had to be reminded in 1940 to keep the Canadian code secret.[23] German and Italian influence in Latin America became a source of major concern in 1940, with Air France operations there coming under the Axis control. Increased activities by PAA represented the United States' attempt to counteract the trend.[24] Within the next year, CAB authorities reported progress in attempts to gain cooperation with Mexico. Correspondence with warring nations continued during the period of American technical neutrality; just before World

War II, authority officials labored diligently to obtain permission for landing facilities during one of Howard Hughes's flights.[25]

While the CAA-CAB directed efforts in the realm of national defense, one journal, *The New Republic*, editorially cautioned the nation against Nazi sabotage in the airplane factories, especially the plants delivering aircraft to the military. German workers in American plants, according to this article, loudly celebrated the fall of Czechoslovakia, slipped aircraft blueprints to visiting Germans, distributed Nazi propaganda leaflets, and deliberately produced faulty planes.[26] The editor begged the Federal Bureau of Investigation (FBI) and military intelligence to investigate Nazi influences in the country instead of collecting data on "Reds." The CAA and CAB suspected little difficulty in sabotage from the alleged Nazi sources because of the unparalleled safety record compiled by the commercial airlines during this same period.

ALONG THE AIRWAYS

Providing radio communications, landing fields, and the supervision of airway and, eventually, airport traffic continued to be the responsibility of the CAA's Bureau of Federal Airways. Mention has been made of the $7 million program of modernization launched during 1937–1938 by the Bureau of Air Commerce; the improvements, long-range in nature, formed an integral portion of the authority's efforts to give the country safe airways. Expansion proved to be the keynote, even before the nation began its defense in earnest against the Axis in 1941; lighted miles of airways increased by over 20 per cent between 1939 and 1941. When Howard Rough left the leadership of the Bureau of Airways to supervise the regions, C. I. Stanton assumed this responsibility. Stanton, a civil engineer and graduate of Tufts College, was a flier in World War I and a test pilot for the Post Office before joining the Aeronautics Branch as one of the first airplane and engine inspectors. Except for an interval of four years, Stanton had been with the CAA and its predecessors continuously.[27]

The following table well illustrates the advances in the airways facilities during fiscal years 1927–1940.[28]

The simultaneous ranges, the first installed in 1938, drew immediate praise from pilots and airline operators. TWA's personnel acknowledged the improved operations at Kansas City,

AIRWAYS FACILITIES

Type	1927*	1940
Mileage	4,121	29,903
Personnel	134	3,288
Expenditures	$294,533	$14,982,509
Costs per mile	$506 (1928)	$499
Lighted fields	124	300
Beacon lights	719	2,304
uhf fan markers	20 (1939)	101
Combined broadcast and radio range	9 (1933)	83
Radio range, full power	1 (1928)	17
Radio range, medium power with full voice	2 (1932)	138
Costs of communications per mile	$32 (1928)	$167

*Programs beginning after 1927 indicated with date in parentheses.

St. Louis, and Wichita, although the Indianapolis range was still not properly adjusted.[29] CAA patrol pilots advised all radio operators to decrease slightly the voice modulation because of existing interference. Some aviators complained that they did not know just when to expect the voice broadcasts, one pilot experiencing icing at 1,000 feet and failing to hear the CAA operator's attempts to contact him.[30] The Memphis range was considered "fuzzy" during an instrument landing rendering the American Airlines approach unsafe. Airways officials earned the warm praise of R. S. Damon, then Vice-President of Operations American Airlines, for replacing the radio-range tower at El Paso within nine days after it had been struck by a falling aircraft.[31] These reports greatly facilitated the CAA's check on its communications which like any other mechanical apparatus at times could fail. In fact, human error entered the picture on more than one occasion, being considered a factor in leading to the crash of a UAL liner near Salt Lake City on November 4, 1940. The radio range's east leg had swung far to the east into the mountains; the CAA cited the failure of the communications operator to monitor the range in order to detect the malfunction.[32] Communications chiefs often labored under the handicap of performing their own maintenance duties during this era.

Radio communications aided the flier along the airways, yet the true ability to land aircraft in unfavorable weather did not materialize until the perfection of an instrument-landing system (ILS). Long sought after, this system as described in earlier chapters went through rigid tests, first in 1929 and later at Indianapolis, before the CAA authorized the installation of the famous ILS radio aid in 1941 at New York, Chicago, Kansas City, Cleveland, Fort Worth, and Los Angeles.[33] The type of system finally adopted consisted of: a runway localizer range (vhf) course for lateral guidance, a glide path or landing beam for path of descent, and two marker beacons for showing the progress of approach to the landing field. Each was on a separate frequency (75 to 110 megacycles), providing a straight glide from an altitude of 600 feet to the runway. Other developments in radio communications included the construction on Long Island of station WSY which could be heard halfway across the Atlantic Ocean.

Use of the airways in the nation had swung heavily in the direction of the military before Pearl Harbor, 80 to 85 per cent of all traffic according to CAA figures.[34] This unexpected development produced many problems for the CAA which had, meanwhile, advanced its competency in the realm of air traffic control under the Air Traffic Control Section of the Bureau of Federal Airways' Airways Operation Division (the reader will note the difficulty of acquainting himself with the names of CAA subunits). Control centers were added at Fort Worth, St. Louis, Salt Lake City, Atlanta, Seattle, Cincinnati, and Kansas City, bringing the total in service to fourteen with nine new centers planned for fiscal 1942. Apparently even CAA personnel had difficulty in remembering the nomenclature, for the Chief of the Airways Operations Division asked Earl F. Ward, Director of the Bureau of Federal Airways, to remind people of the Airport Traffic Control Section.

The exacting labors of controllers grew more difficult with the dramatic increase in the number of military aircraft. While responsible for assigning both civilian and military planes their proper altitudes, CAA controllers found, not to many experts' surprise, that the military pilots often ignored the civilian traffic regulators even in highly congested areas.[35] Flight personnel and several passengers on a TWA liner noticed with horror a fully camouflaged army B–18 flying at least 6 miles on the wrong side of the airway near Burnett, Indiana. Moreover, the pilot had no approval for flight above 3,500 feet.[36] The records are full of other complaints similar in nature, all occurring before Pearl Harbor. Another pilot failed to contact controllers at Des Moines after landing. The frantic emergency search, conducted at the request of the CAA, finally ended four hours later. Taking off without flight plans, landing without permission under conditions below minimum regulations, and flying without a radio transmitter constituted further military violations called to the attention of army and navy officials. CAA, CAB, and military leaders collaborated in a voluntary effort to establish more realistic air traffic rules late in 1941[37] All aircraft operating on the airways between 3,500 feet above the ground and 17,000 feet above sea level must carry a radio receiver, a transmitter, and a sensitive-type altimeter. A flight plan was mandatory if the pilot entered airspace under the jurisdiction of airway traffic control. In an attempt to aid the military planes, all airspace above 17,000 feet, on or off the airways, was reserved for their use. Finally, the CAB ruled that all pilots—including purely intrastate operators—must hold federal licenses and use a certificated aircraft. Priority of certain airways—green, yellow, red, and blue, in order—aided in traffic control, the east-west routes (green) holding the top priority. In crossing airways, the pilot continued to raise or lower his altitude, whichever applied, by 500 feet.

In 1941, CAA operators took over the traffic control from the airport-managed original systems and faced the formidable task of training many additional controllers at the very time of other high-priority defense operations. From the outset, newcomers received their instruction on the job at the control towers for this exacting and critical type of activity. Here was one branch of CAA endeavor in which any incompetent met speedy dismissal.[38] Airport controllers assumed jurisdiction by contact (visual) operations of activity within 3 miles of the airport, by radio on 278 kilocycles, or by light signals. Director Stanton (Bureau of Federal Airways) appreciated successful handling of emergency situations but considered this ability absolutely necessary to smooth operations. Thus, when his subordinates praised the teamwork between the Washington and Baltimore towers in getting a pilot down in poor weather under rather poor visibility and ceiling, Stanton noted, "It occurred at a time when there was very little traffic."[39]

DIRECT SUPPORT TO AIRPORTS

Under the Civil Aeronautics Act of 1938, Congress proceeded to request of the CAA a six-year program of improvements for the nation's airports.[40] Entailing the expenditure of $560 million, the program provided for the construction of some 4,000 additional airfields (double the existing figure). The first appropriation enabled the CAA, with advice on sites from the War and Navy Departments, to initiate plans for 250 fields with the aid of $9 million in WPA funds. CAA leaders felt handicapped because they could locate only five airport consulting engineers in the nation. Support for the vigorous, new, direct CAA activity in airport construction and control came from the United States Conference of Mayors in 1939.[41] The mayors agreed that municipal airports required this federal support; the local officials would continue to provide the land, buildings, management, and routine maintenance. The reader should remember that this new program was not the first instance of federal aid to airports. The WPA, in over four years ending in 1940, had participated in the construction of 373 new airports.[42] Then, too, a joint CAA–National Youth Administration (NYA) project undertook the establishment of new hangars at twelve locations in 1940.

In addition to all the foregoing, the CAA and aviation in general could well agree with President Franklin Roosevelt that the dedication of the new Washington National Airport provided a key achievement in the federal control of aviation. The cornerstone was laid by Roosevelt on September 28, 1940, at which time the field was over 90 per cent completed.[43] In November, 1938, construction had begun on this 750-acre, model terminal which provided 565 acres of runway and one north-south runway of 6,500 feet—an aviation dream come true with the help of $12 million from the WPA and PWA. The airport, with its turntables for positioning of planes, flush-type underground service pits, and excellent terminal accommodations, was officially opened on June 16, 1941. Furthermore, the CAA, in another departure, became the operator of this airport.

Major Lucius D. Clay, in November, 1940, became chairman of an airport approval board representing War, Navy, and Commerce and charged with selecting 250 sites for new fields.[44] Finally, after much change of heart, the CAA arrived at a new system of numbering runways, effective in the summer of 1941. Now airports must utilize the reciprocal of the magnetic bearings as read on the pilot's compass. For example, the west end of an east-west runway would be No. 27—the reciprocal of 270 degrees; the east end of the same runway would be No. 9 (for 90 degrees).[45] North and south should be numbered "36" and "18," respectively, and airport officials were to use the nearest even 10-degree division for the runways. The old system had involved the use of No. 1 for the runway nearest true north, numbering the remainder in a counterclockwise fashion.

ALASKAN OPERATIONS

Pioneer CAA employees persevered on the American frontier in Alaska for over two years before the Japanese attacked this country. At times these employees wondered if their superiors at Washington headquarters recalled just where Alaska was, let alone the value of the CAA in that remote area. In an effort to bolster sagging morale, the following message arrived for all CAA personnel before Christmas, 1939: "Your first Christmas in Alaska will be more than something to tell your grandchildren about in your old age, for it marks the beginning of orderly aviation progress in the Territory . . . labels each man a true pioneer . . ."[46] The *Anchorage Daily Times* reflected the genuine support of aviation in the territory when it heralded the decision in Washington to make Alaska a separate region within the CAA framework.[47] Marshall C. Hoppin, Superintendent of Airways in Alaska since 1939, became regional manager. A veteran of the Army Air Corps in 1917, he became Airways Extension Superintendent in 1928. Rough, Supervisor of Regions, related the plight of Alaskan operations to his Washington colleagues upon his return from an inspection trip to Hoppin's critical locale. Rough noted that the entire journey had to be taken by air. Hoppin and his staff, wearing overcoats while working, had long labored in a dilapidated railroad station but now had moved into a post office.[48] Praising the caliber of CAA personnel in Alaska, Rough further related the hardships in locating housing (the influx of military families had complicated the problem). Apparently Hoppin's woes concerning lack of attention from Washington lessened, but the distance still caused embarrassment from having to miss conferences and other CAA activities.[49]

One marvels at the ingenuity of the inhabitants and the CAA personnel in Alaska as they devised numerous techniques aimed at defying the inherently harsh weather hazards to aviation. One CAA inspector advocated rubbing of the skis (on planes so equipped) with a burlap cloth saturated with kerosene in order to gain the optimum use of landing and takeoff distances.[50] Airplane travel in Alaska might well be compared in terms of necessity to automobile use in the United States. The air distance (550 miles) between Fairbanks and Nome could be traversed in less than 5 hours; the same trip by dog team covered 700 miles and took between 30 and 40 days. These individualistic CAA men in Alaska complained that headquarters demanded too many reports of all varieties.[51] Freight costs bore heavily on the CAA and CAB, as well as all American installations in Alaska, amounting to the purchase price in the case of shipping a $3,500 house.[52] The CAA was at least functioning in Alaska before Pearl Harbor. American interests in another possession, the Philippines, reflected a complete lack of preparation; no radio facilities for aviation were in operation prior to World War II.

CIVILIAN PILOT TRAINING

One of the most ambitious and commendable undertakings initiated by the CAA evolved in 1939 with the Civilian Pilot Training Program (CPT) authorized by Congress, though $100,-000 of NYA funds had already been utilized to pioneer this program during the previous year. Aiming at the successful training of 10,000 youths by June, 1940, the federal law provided $4 million toward the program which would provide ground training at thirteen colleges and universities and flight training at existing flying schools.[53] The private pilot license normally required seventy-two hours of ground instruction and thirty-eight hours of flying. CPT was a valiant attempt to increase the number of certificated pilots from the low figure of 21,118 from a population of more than 130 million. Under NYA funds, Purdue University enrolled 8 students for 80 hours in the classroom. Ten hours went into study of the Civil Air Regulations and thirty-five hours each were devoted to navigation and meteorology, the flying course following later. The CPT program, aided tremendously in its fight for adoption by the military and the National Research Council, aimed to help the military by eliminating many of the unqualified applicants in the early stages of instruction. The Private Flying Development Division, under the CAA's Bureau of safety regulation, supervised the operation and differed from military regulations in some details. For example, CAA officials allowed the students to wear glasses; the military did not. The army "washout" rate stood at approximately 50 per cent; the CAA aimed for 60 per cent successful completions in its age range of eighteen to twenty-five.

As the plan broadened in scope, courses were divided into

the primary instruction, 35 to 50 hours, and the advanced program consisting of an additional 50 hours. Students paid $40 for the lessons.[54] Flight instructors earned $290 for the 35 hours of training, 8 hours of dual instruction coming at the outset. Various fears expressed by congressmen met reassurance from CAA officials. Negroes could enroll in the training; six Negro schools participated in CPT, a report satisfying Everett M. Dirksen. Congressman James M. Fitzpatrick of New York worried over the possibility of "pinks" at the schools of higher learning affecting the program. Authority Chairman Robert Hinckley replied that CPT enrollees would not be in contact with those at the "tea rooms and cocktail lounges" but would be, according to the testimony of college officials, out helping their country and giving the campuses a patriotic air. The CPT program also enrolled 700 in its early noncollege group. Cooperation of the schools showed itself in many respects, not the least of which lay in the financial outlay of approximately $5 for each $1 of federal subsidy. Immediately, the CPT appeared successful. Morale ran high; only about one or two students from each class left the program.[55] By January, 1941, the program had suffered only seventeen accident fatalities. In May, 1940, regional managers had received direction to attempt the completion of declared quotas before June 30: "Although every pressure must be exerted to complete this program on schedule, extreme care and caution must be taken to see that our safety record is maintained."[56] School authorities found a great deal of interest in the defense-minded training. Cornell College, Iowa, inaugurated a course attracting fifty men and five women.[57] Larger schools, of course, predominated in the list of participants. By early 1941, approximately 200 CPT graduates each month entered the Army, reaping dividends for the War Department which originally had requested the CAA to launch the program. Not all became pilots; many served in other useful military roles such as meteorology and engineering.

Shortly, the second-guessers began questioning the entire role of CPT. Congressmen heard from a few military sources that CPT graduates were advised to forget all they had learned and listen to the military.[58] Navy Commander J. B. Lynch, testifying before a House subcommittee, explained the situation. The CAA trained students in light planes of 30 or 40 horsepower; the Navy started them with craft of 225 horsepower. Furthermore, the CAA made the enrollees promise that they would later enter the military but could in no way enforce this promise. Of 35,000 students in the primary training and 4,300 completing the secondary training (to March 1, 1941), the Navy accepted 783 and 273, respectively. Some men were too old, others too young; a number failed the navy physical. However, Lynch noted that the CAA was changing its physical requirements to coincide with the military standards. The CAA, with no height restrictions, had graduated individuals who were too short to reach the rudder pedals. Minimum heights of 5' 6" (Navy) and 5' 4" (Army) prevailed. A few CPT graduates found trouble at first with the military before its requirement of 20/20 vision without glasses was relaxed. Lynch visualized the CPT's role as that of getting the country air minded, nothing more. Brigadier General Davenport Johnson, Assistant Chief of the Army Air Corps, reported to the same committee that his organization accepted 63 of the CPT's secondary course and graduated 52. On the other hand, he contended that the "washout" rate reached 17 per cent of all CPT men accepted, while the Army's own rate stood at 5 per cent.

Truly it might be said that Grove Webster, acting head of CPT, took an unjustified "beating" at this hearing from the military. Any program so hastily inaugurated would certainly display a number of shortcomings, though one conclusion is certain. The true value of the CPT venture (1939–1941) was struck home dramatically and helpfully to frantic officers of both the Navy and Army in the panic and frustration ensuing for months after Pearl Harbor, before victory appeared a certainty. Then all would agree to the paltry stature of the $37 million which was appropriated for CPT in fiscal year 1941 but questioned during the months immediately before the Japanese struck. Insurance companies, impressed with the undertaking, charged the students only $7.20 for $3,000 worth of accidental death and $1,000 in hospital coverage.[59] CPT's expanded offerings in 1941 included two courses (cross-country and instructor) beyond the secondary training. The cross-country consisted of 32 hours and the instructor course consisted of 120 additional hours of instruction in larger aircraft. The instructor program led to examination for a commercial pilot certificate and instructor rating. Since its inception, 75,000 had taken courses with only twenty-one fatalities. Contrary to the misleading testimony cited above, 7,403 had served in the armed forces. Over 1,200 others worked as military aviation instructors. Needless to say, in a project as large as CPT, the CAA coordination and supervision generated many problems.

Enforcement of strict regulations has already been cited under earlier topics. Generally the public response, particularly from the flying schools involved, embodied praise of the total control by the CAA. A few, as always, rendered complaints against alleged ill treatment.[60]

COOPERATION AND RESEARCH

Much has been related above and in previous chapters about the routine operations of the CAA and CAB bearing on mutual exchanges of data or routine dealings with such organizations as the Weather Bureau, Post Office Department, ICC, and the military in addition to such relief groups as WPA and PWA. That friction arose between the military pilots and the CAA and CAB no one can deny. But far more incidents of friendly cooperation involving the two interests were recorded without fanfare during 1938–1941. However, J. H. Doolittle sought Chairman Clinton Hester's suggestions as to nominations for the annual Collier Trophy, only to find Hester of the opinion that the CAA should remain neutral concerning the nominations.[61]

Training 100 student pilots for the aviation weather service in 1940 comprised a joint Weather Bureau-CAA project, the men all having four years of college with thirty semester hours of mathematics, through calculus, and physics.[62] Officials of the CAA urged Weather Bureau Chief F. W. Reichelderfer to invite other CAA men to learn more about meteorology.[63] The CAA and FCC settled one matter satisfactorily when the FCC assumed responsibility for painting its own towers (obstruction).[64] Congressmen, as usual, expressed disbelief when assured by the CAA that its research activities neither conflicted with nor duplicated the experiments of NACA.[65] For example, the CAA performed the developmental work for NACA on flutter and vibration, icing, engineering instruments, and measurement. Meanwhile, NACA undertook no plans for radio development, a realm already reflecting widespread CAA progress, and improvement in airway facilities. The Army, not the CAA (congressmen learned), attempted to develop a bulletproof gas tank.

Miscellaneous CAA research, much of it a continuation of the pre-1938 era, included the following: boundary lights, a smoke-generating wind indicator, airport drainage and soil stabilization, automatic instrument log, frequency-modulated (FM) and omnidirectional types of radio ranges, FM traffic control transmitters, and a grant to twenty-one universities for predicting the success (skills, judgments, flight ability) of air cadets.[66] A new flight-level indicator, using an aneroid barometer with an altimeter mechanism, promised to provide a greatly improved record of level over the process of continually resetting the old sensitive altimeter. In 1941, at least two congressmen, Jack Nicholas of Oklahoma and Dirksen of Illinois, urged members of the Senate to restore House cuts in appropriations for CAA research and airways facilities, items critical to the nation's defense and aviation progress.[67]

THE WILL TO FLY

Airline travel increased materially during the three years preceding Pearl Harbor; the CAA-CAB role in making flight safe—thus attractive—has already been traced. Promotional endeavors in the realm of publications and air information continued to receive heavy emphasis in both agencies. Then, too, the tremendous confidence in aviation predominant in the military, girding itself for the national defense, furthered the public image toward aeronautics. The airlines themselves learned to cater to the comfort of the public, increasing attention to the important airline hostess job created back in 1930. General qualifications had evolved over the years to stress charm, poise, personality, intelligence, attractiveness, good moral character, wearing of clothes well, and foreign language for international flights. To qualify, hostesses (stewardesses) had to be 5' 2" to 5' 5" in height, 21 to 26 years of age, and weigh between 100 and 120 pounds.[68] Nurse's training, though preferred, was not required for these women who earned from $85 to $135 per month after the original training of two or three weeks.

Publicity for the CAA made up part of the separate building for the aviation industry at the New York World's Fair (1939). A CAA traffic control display, a Link trainer showing flight aids and the ILS (instrument landing system), and a private flying exhibit were all represented.[69] Airport users—commercial, private, or military—benefited continually from the variety of CAA publications, all designed to foster safety and increased utilization of aviation. Over 7 million weather observations at 182 airports went into the publication of the CAA *Technical Development Note* in July, 1940.[70] All state air laws were listed in Civil Aeronautics *Bulletin No. 4*.[71] Other highly informative articles appeared in the *Civil Aeronautics Journal,* one such account summarizing the research on flying in lightning, as prepared by an employee of TWA.[72] The theory stated here indicated a greater fear of the cumulo-clouds in general, not necessarily only during a thunderstorm, and warned to avoid—if possible—these clouds in the zone adjacent to the freezing isotherm of 26° F. to 34° F. But all emphasis on gaining publicity ceased when the Japanese bombs spelled war on a Sunday in December, 1941.

WORLD WAR II–1941-1945:
INTERNAL SECURITY

THE CARNAGE SUFFERED by the United States at Pearl Harbor crystallized immediate and superlative cooperation from the CAA and CAB in the common task—destroying the forces of aggression emanating from Berlin, Rome, and Tokyo. Other federal agencies—the Weather Bureau, Coast and Geodetic Survey, to name examples—also turned immediate attention to the war effort, but nowhere in the fascinating story of America's rise from defeat on December 7, 1941, to victory in 1945 does one find a model exceeding the contributions of the CAA. Here, a civilian organization elicited an *esprit de corps,* which could well be envied by any governmental unit—either military or civilian in character. Despite personnel losses to the very military it helped save, the CAA played a leading role in supplying controllers, trained fliers, communicators, and other technicians for overseas duty. Those CAA leaders and politicians who opposed in the 1960's the tenacious lobbying of the military to obtain the Federal Aviation Agency (the CAA until 1959) as a military unit in time of war should, by all means, point to the efficient record of the civilian CAA during World War II as support for retaining the agency's nonmilitary character.

Luckily, the CAA had already begun a modernization of facilities in addition to its defense-minded projects aided financially by the Army and Navy. In order to launch such expansion, the CAA had increased its personnel during 1938–1941. During the war years, the CAA designed its program for the military while fighting desperately to employ enough men and women to accomplish the required work load. CAA leadership, as in many other governmental agencies and, to be sure, private businesses, encountered the inevitable differences of opinion with local Selective Service officials who possessed the authority to defer or draft eligible personnel for the armed forces. Unfortunately, no general system of deferment for the CAA was devised, leaving the struggle all the more troublesome because of the variations among draft boards. Generally, CAA experts felt harassed by this action, believing with all sincerity that their tasks proved to be as essential to the war effort as any other noncombatant assignment for which deferment was granted. L. C. Elliott, Regional Manager at Fort Worth, declared that local draft boards in his area depleted his personnel through thirty-day deferments which could not be appealed and were followed by the automatic call to military duty. Stressing the existing low morale, Elliott concluded, "I have no hesitancy in putting the blame exactly where it belongs; in this case the local Army representatives. . . ."[1] On the other hand, H. A. Hook, Regional Manager at Santa Monica, reported, "Selective Service has strung along pretty well with us."[2] Losses there proved to be lower than among civilian employees of the Army and Navy. The uncertainty surrounding the draft undoubtedly hurt morale. The CAA did not stand in the way of anyone's attempt to resign for a commission or other choice assignment in the military.[3] However, if an employee remained with the agency, he ran the risk of being drafted and placed in work which he did not relish and without suitable rank. R. E. Sturtevant, an administrator in Air Traffic Control, summarized the dilemma:

> We do not mind where we work, nor for which federal department. However, if the CAA should collapse and our men be drafted into other types of work because their loyalty to this organization has prevented them from accepting enlistments or commissions in the services of their choice, then it would appear that we administrative officers have failed in our duty to the group that composes the very backbone of the organization—the field personnel.[4]

Early in the war, CAA officials attempted to secure deferment of key personnel.[5] A tangible success appeared with six-month deferments for the flight instructors and mechanics engaged in the CPT program. But this achievement proved to be fleeting; local boards began calling up the men, completely disregarding a vigorous appeal for additional consideration from Director of Selective Service Major General Lewis B. Hershey.[6] By the end of 1942, even instructors from schools holding army contracts received the "greetings" for the call to the colors. In October, 1942, Marshall C. Hoppin, Regional Manager in Anchorage, urgently requested deferred status for the CAA in Alaska similar to that ordered for the vital Panama Canal Zone. The reply was in the negative.[7] By May, 1943, Administrator Charles I. Stanton told a Senate subcommittee that the CAA had lost to the draft approximately 800 of its highly skilled communications operators, traffic controllers, and radio maintenance men. In retrospect, it would seem beyond a doubt that Senator Henry Cabot Lodge's expression in reply, "uneconomical," aptly described this phenomenon.[8]

MILITARY STATUS?

The CAA's status in relationship to the military remained an open question for some nine months after Pearl Harbor, apparently until after an exchange of letters involving Army, Navy, and Commerce. The decision to retain the civilian organization was attributed to the following: CAA's long experience, its specialized work, its functions for both Army and Navy, and a belief that the agency would be difficult to maintain and administer under military rule.[9] Brigadier General Donald H. Connolly, then CAA boss, apparently felt that either CAA or military control of all phases connected with aviation would result in the smoothest operation. At one point, even the civilian Weather Bureau became involved. Dr. F. W. Reichelderfer, Chief of the Weather Bureau during 1938–1963, later reflected upon this episode, asserting that Connolly once telephoned him to say that President Franklin D. Roosevelt had authorized the CAA's control of the Weather Bureau. However, just before Connolly's call, Reichelderfer had persuaded the President to allow the bureau to retain its separate entity; this sad news Reichelderfer then relayed to the disappointed General.[10]

MANPOWER SHORTAGES

Classification of jobs, a perennial headache for heads of federal agencies, continued to plague the CAA. Shortly before

Pearl Harbor, the Civil Service Commission had refused to grant an increase in grade to the positions involving flight engineers and factory inspectors.[11] The CAA had not asked for wages comparable to industry but desired at least token increases. Complaints from within the CAA over its personnel dilemma ranged through all levels of work, technical or nontechnical, central office or field stations. The incompetence of clerks in Region One came in for one major complaint.[12] Manpower savings, a theme quite necessarily inaugurated by the Bureau of the Budget for all agencies, met firm resistance from the CAA whose officials maintained steadfastly that they had already effected all possible reduction of staff before Pearl Harbor.[13] Administrator Stanton inherited this problem and asserted, "I find classification is the toughest problem we have to deal with. Every group in CAA feels that its positions are improperly classified."[14] Incentives to serve outside the United States helped to augment the necessary force of CAA experts, all those selected receiving the 25 per cent differential in salary typical of other governmental jobs overseas.[15] By the end of 1943, the CAA had some 556 employees in this category.

As a result of wartime conditions, the CAA assumed a 7-day week and 24-hour day, whenever necessary, for all its field personnel.[16] By late 1943, out of more than 7,000 facilities operated by the CAA, 3,750 were considered indispensable to the war effort.[17] Effective January 19, 1942, the CAA adopted a 44-hour week along with the entire Department of Commerce.[18] Women rendered invaluable service to the CAA, just as they came to the rescue in nearly all sectors of the nation's economy—both public and private. In addition to the more common clerical tasks, women also served as control tower operators and worked at meteorological duties where the CAA performed these tasks.[19] Women comprised 90 per cent of the 4,000 persons trained by the CAA for communications and traffic control to January 1, 1945.[20] Availability of women and newly trained men only to fill the many openings did not always please administrative leaders. Midway in the war, one air traffic control authority believed that the quality of CAA's trainees had slipped badly, with 70 per cent displaying low aptitude in the current program.[21] CAA leaders realized during the initial months of American participation in the war that they had to confront the manpower shortage without the advantage of military conscription applied to the civilian organization. There could be no compulsion to serve.[22]

SAFEGUARDING INFORMATION

Two closely related problems, public relations and security, plagued CAA authorities early in the war. Security on the home front often proved to be most difficult to enforce because of the insular feeling resulting from the remoteness of the battlefields. Of basic concern internally were the efforts to control access to documents which might, if seen by enemy sympathizers, hinder the war effort. Classification of government documents, though not originating with World War II, nevertheless persisted as a cornerstone of security measures. Secret and confidential documents were to be locked up securely when not used by the proper persons. Restricted documents, while not considered absolutely vital to the war effort, provided a handy catchall for administrative privacy—a category too often abused after 1945, as realized by historians who find themselves restricted in the use of agency correspondence. Field employees, and those at Washington also, found it difficult at times to be aware of dangers resulting from rather casual use of CAA documents and sustained harsh reprimands directed toward such willful neglect of duty.[23] The safeguarding of military information constituted a most imperative area of concern, CAA employees receiving the same instructions as the military.[24] Because of security precautions, CAA officials complained to the military of not being allowed the data from their transatlantic cablegrams and requested the transmission of all such messages directly to CAA headquarters.[25] In addition to documents, CAA workers received orders to protect all communications facilities against photographs, this precaution having been effected eleven months before Pearl Harbor.[26]

Another major service to the nation involved the CAA duty of maintaining records on the location of every private airplane in the nation.[27] On the whole, full cooperation was achieved in this direction. Unusual circumstances caused embarrassment, such as the times when independent-minded operators ignored all precautions. One case occurred at "Marshio New Jersey Airport, where the operator said he would take his engines out and warm them up when he pleased."[28] Guards were placed at landing fields. E. J. Robins, Facility Security Officer with the CAA, provided the U.S. Office of Civil Defense personal data on all members of this CAA section.[29] The rigid enforcement of wartime regulations brought a number of court actions and fines against violators. A company engaged in crop dusting was permanently enjoined by the federal court at Vicksburg, Mississippi. Andrew

D. Drumm, Jr., of Fallon, Nevada, saw his plane impounded by the CAA, which filed charges totaling $11,000 against him for flying without a pilot license. He allegedly declared that the CAA and CAB should know better than to interfere with him.[30] A U.S. district court upheld a $2,500 fine against Drumm, sustaining the CAB's legal action, though reducing the figure from the original $11,000. Drumm claimed to have flown without a certificate for twenty to twenty-five years but asserted he had never used the governmental aviation facilities.[31] In another situation, a commercial pilot with 650 hours to his credit flew over a defense plant at Alton, Illinois, relating later that he failed to see a notice against such action posted at the airport. Amazingly enough, the pilot landed safely after he and his passenger, flying at an altitude of 1,000 feet, had been seriously wounded from shots fired by the guards. Time and again, records of the enforcement proceedings read like a tragic comedy—even though in time of war. A commercial pilot lost his certificate for six months after taking off without a flight plan and flying an Army B–25 within 200 feet of an airliner. Another culprit skimmed along a highway in Illinois, narrowly missing a bus. Finally, one pilot performed a low-altitude show with a four-engine plane over a World Series baseball game in New York City.[32] Army bases, considered off limits to commercial pilots, could be utilized freely in case of emergencies. Use of the base might be granted in normal situations upon receipt of a formal request to the base commander, including a copy of the flight plan.[33] In addition, the military air defense zones received all data—flight plans with deviations—for all "friendly" flights of military and civil nature.

Security cooperation with other federal officials brought its amusing incidents. Early in the war, CAA maintenance employees in the East were prevented from carrying out their duties during a trial blackout when detained by cautious air-raid wardens.[34] Meanwhile, all unauthorized or unknown personnel were barred from airways installations. Furthermore, during January, 1942, regional officials decided to leave all beacon lights turned off in potential combat zones where switches were unavailable to turn off such lamps upon fifteen minutes' notice.[35] Instructions concerning radio operation, an obvious first line of concern, were forthcoming shortly after Pearl Harbor restricting the transmission of data for class FM and cone-of-silence markers from the West Coast east to the Cascade Mountains.[36] Jittery West Coast officials warned especially of being alert against subversion in that critical area. Enemy aliens were restricted nationally from air flights by December 11, 1941.[37] From the outset, release of all technical data to the general public was forbidden.[38]

ALASKA AND THE ALEUTIANS

The foregoing description of personnel and security problems involved mainly the domestic area of the United States—the West Coast shortly after Pearl Harbor representing the area of deepest anxiety. Alaska and the Aleutians, especially the latter, proved to be even more crucial because of the actual battle activity at hand. An acute manpower shortage had materialized in Alaska, bringing an appeal from Administrator Stanton to all regional officials in the CAA to help locate volunteers. The 25 per cent pay differential and Civil Service rating of CAF 4 or 5 awaited the brave souls sought by Stanton's day letter: "This opportunity for real war service of first order should appeal to all men willing and able to render vital service to their country in present emergency."[39] The request for additional volunteers persisted throughout the emergency, causing grave doubts as to relying solely on volunteers. However, no alternative existed. New volunteers had to serve without their families, a factor not conducive to optimum morale even under peacetime conditions. In August, 1943, Hoppin confided to Stanton that housing conditions had not been what he had requested while recreation activities must be held out in the snow from early October to mid-May. Hoppin declared: "To find four girls, or four men, who are congenial enough to live under one roof in cramped conditions is indeed a Houdini trick. . . ."[40] Hoppin further contended that his civilians felt hindered by the predominance of military personnel at Ladd Field, leading the CAA boss in Alaska to allow his men to purchase their own uniforms (with the appropriate U.S. civilian labels) at the army post exchange.[41] At small field stations on the Aleutians, it was felt inadvisable to place a CAA civilian in charge of the location at which an army enlisted man also worked because of the war hazard.[42] Another crisis occurred during summer, 1942, when the Alaskan Railroad, under the Department of Interior, was unable to provide commissary services for all CAA personnel, a deficiency overcome by help from the Department of Commerce.[43]

Letters, both incoming and outgoing, were deemed important enough to warrant military censorship. One American employee, not with the CAA, described in a letter caught by censors the exact location of an important airport project in relation to the nearby town and the Bering Sea. Less serious and, indeed, amusing enough was his description of the huge profits made by his employer, Morrison-Knudsen. Other letters described movement of military men and equipment, CAA men complaining of low morale, cliques, and most embarrassing and disastrous of all—the disappearance of a code book.[44] The war situation brought to light further amazing incidents in Alaska, requiring much investigation on the part of the belabored CAA. Those private aviators who had escaped the arm of CAA regulation now found their efforts had been for naught. One mechanic and maintenance man for Star Lines, busy flying freight up and down the Yukon, explained when apprehended: "I worked like hell to get this far—being here in the interior, where the CAA Inspection seldom if ever come I am able to fly without getting in dutch—I haven't a commercial license . . . well its a long story have [sic] to do with a little trouble with the CAA . . ."[45] The man did, however, hold a student pilot certificate. Often the Federal Bureau of Investigation was called upon to aid with more troublesome cases. Chief J. Edgar Hoover summarized one such investigation by revealing the existence of several troublemakers causing numerous difficulties for the CAA. One employee reportedly sold liquor to the natives at Moses Point, while another CAA man was fired in March, 1942, for living with a squaw. The only married employee at Moses Point complained of his fellow workers living with girls at CAA headquarters. One pilot and a dentist allegedly landed there and found CAA employees and local women in a drunken state. Inaccurate weather reports given by the CAA office were reported by a Pan American pilot who experienced a rough landing on skis after receiving a promise of a good field.[46] It would appear that two CAA officials in particular caused this situation at Moses Point. Another internal housekeeping quarrel involved charges leveled by a disgruntled employee against the security practices of the chief of CAA communications at Anchorage. The resultant investigation revealed the fabrication of these charges, a complete retraction in writing, and the return to duty of the guilty accuser after proper cautioning.[47] The CAA did not remain completely free of genuine security troubles, for E. J. Robins, Facility Security Officer at Seattle, reported in 1943 an increase in sabotage activity concerned with the Alaska Projects Depot there.[48] At locations not on the war front or under attack, officials in Alaska kept all radio-range buildings floodlighted to discourage sabotage.[49]

Fortunately the personnel problems and security questions outlined above did not prevent the CAA from performing its tasks well in support of the nation's military forces in the Aleutians and Alaska; the story of these technical activities will be related in Chapter 10. Similar difficulties undoubtedly occurred in other areas of the world where CAA men suddenly found themselves aiding the United States and its allies. Minor frictions became a type of occupational hazard to be endured. For example, Administrator Stanton complained about the Department of Interior gaining jurisdiction over CAA people in Puerto Rico and the Virgin Islands.[50] Anguish over the shortage of manpower led Hook, Regional Manager at Santa Monica, eventually to suggest the conscription of CAA personnel from other regions to serve on Pacific islands.[51] Here again, the job could be accomplished only through the concerted efforts of a few veteran employees who risked grave dangers in serving their nation as civilians.

PUBLIC RELATIONS

In the realm of public relations, considerable restraint was applied. For example, the popular NOTAMS had to be censored for the public and reserved primarily for military use. As ordered by the Weather Bureau, the limitations on the release of meteorological data applied to this type of information utilized by the CAA. Nevertheless, the CAA could still provide the public with much useful information. Field officials were urged to have their staffs answer promptly—in fact, as promptly as inquiries from congressmen—all requests for information from newspapers. In one case involving the *Boston Globe*, an airport office had failed to accord this speedy service.[52] Apparently Washington employees saw a general lack of coordination in policy concerning publications, a deficiency hopefully corrected by asking the Division of Information and Statistics to clear all releases with Floyd B. Brinkley of publications and statistics.[53] Brinkley incurred criticism from newspapers if CAA and CAB news releases reached one rival paper before the other.[54]

Other housekeeping matters of a more routine nature persisted in war as in peace. Bureaucracy inevitably led to snags now and then. Elliott, Regional Manager at Fort Worth, complained in 1943 about receiving elaborate instructions from the budget staff in Washington without their having first cleared the other affected branches and the executive officer.[55] Chain of command as a problem became even more acute with the question of uniformity among regions, a most elusive goal. Essentially, the problem involved informing Washington officials of what was happening in the field.[56] Regional managers, in turn, registered protests against tardy monthly reports and other correspondence from their own field offices.[57] Top authorities in the CAA did not always condone the way in which their subordinates answered public criticism or managed operations in general. J. E. Sommers, Deputy CAA Administrator, reprimanded O. P. Harwood, Acting Regional Manager at New York, for his reply— delayed over two weeks—to the incensed mayor of Fulton, N.Y. The mayor was disturbed because a CAA field representative forgot a promised visit. Sommers declared Harwood's letter was poorly written and "does not in any sense answer his questions."[58] Harwood assured Sommers of no recurrence.

Congressional pressure, cited in earlier chapters, continued to harass the CAA. Senator H. M. Kilgore requested that the Charleston, West Virginia, station be kept open. Administrator Stanton and Deputy Sommers asserted that the question was up to the regional office involved.[59] Louisiana's Governor Sam H. Jones received an unqualified "No" to his request that all of his state be placed in one region.[60] Unexplained was the delay of more than two months in answering this "political" letter. The frank and outspoken Sommers advised his boss in another instance that the airport service (CAA) in Washington, D.C., was attempting to run the Airport Section of the second region (Atlanta) by remote control. Stanton agreed that Washington authorities should give more information and advice to their men in the field, especially after hearing a rumor in the second region that the CAA was "folding up."[61]

The tremendous increase in wartime activity led the CAA to remind its employees to heed all government regulations concerning wage rates and questions of civil rights. Rates for wages on projects were set by the Wage Adjustment Board.[62] By autumn, 1942, all future proposals had to comply with an executive order stating, "Contracts shall not discriminate against any worker because of race, creed, color or national origin."[63] One detects an unusual awareness by the CAA of questions concerning civil rights at this time. For example, personnel officials in

Washington advised all offices to keep track of the employment of Negroes under their jurisdiction.[64]

CHANGING BOSSES

Soon after the United States became actively involved in hostilities, CAA Administrator Connolly resigned in order to return to the military.[65] Veteran leader Stanton took over as acting head. Connolly's new duties entailed a position as a coordinator for the Army's work with the CAA.[66] Another administrative change occurred with the resignation in August, 1942, of Robert H. Hinckley as Assistant Secretary of Commerce.[67] Later, in 1944, Stanton reassumed his position as second in command when Theodore P. Wright became CAA Administrator.[68] Wright, a graduate of Massachusetts Institute of Technology, was an architectural engineer with long experience in aviation. Engaged in navy aviation during World War I, Wright later worked for the Curtiss Airplane and Motor Company and for the federal government with the War Production Board (WPB), Office of Price Management (OPM), and the Aircraft Production Board (APB). His varied experiences included visits to German aviation factories prior to World War II. During his earlier career, Wright had been chief engineer for the Curtiss Company's top aircraft in the Pulitzer and Snyder Cup races and such military aircraft as the Hawk, Falcon, Helldiver, Shrike, and Condor.[69] In 1940, he became a member of the Advisory Committee for the Council of National Defense and was with the OPM aircraft branch which was reorganized in 1943 as the Aircraft Resources Control Office of the APB with Wright serving as the director. Both Stanton and Wright received honors during the war for their service to aviation. Stanton was awarded an honorary Doctor of Science degree by Tufts College, his alma mater. Wright, already the holder of the same degree from Knox College, gained a commendation from Secretary of War Henry L. Stimson for his exceptional civilian service in production of prize-winning designs for warplanes while with the OPM.[70]

WARTIME RULES

Struggling with the many personnel and administrative problems comprised a natural part of the CAA's growth during 1941–1945. At the same time, services on the home front had to be maintained, though here, too, most activity became oriented toward the movement of troops and material for the successful prosecution of the war. One immediate outgrowth of Pearl Harbor was the cancellation of all private flying in the country, a ban lasting until February, 1942. The CAA recorded the whereabouts of all civil aircraft at all times during the war.[71] Clearance from a police officer, possession of an identification card, and restrictions on baggage and cameras were the major defense measures applied to private flying. On the airlines, baggage was to be searched and cameras secured. All planes must be made inoperative unless under twenty-four-hour guard.

CIVILIAN PILOT TRAINING AND WAR TRAINING SERVICE

Turning to the operation of CAA facilities and programs, one finds two major projects under way when the United States went to war—CPT (Civilian Pilot Training Program) and the development of airports. Much has been said in Chapter 8 about the beginning of the controversial CPT program. The CAA trained 435,165 aircraft pilots, glider pilots, and instructors during the life of this important project.[72] Intensification of the CPT program by July, 1942, enabled the student to get his private pilot license in eight weeks instead of six months. For a time, the CAA selected all noncombatant pilots for the Army Air Force. Emphasis on the second-level course of training led to providing civilian instructors for the army contract schools and copilot replacements for the airlines and, after still further training, the transatlantic ferry command and the Pan American African Ferry, Limited.[73] Local Selective Service boards, for once, took a favorable view toward the CAA flight instructors, granting deferments in approximately 95 per cent of the cases early in the war.[74] Here, as elsewhere, women helped fill vacancies. Of some 2,500 women pilots in the country, 104 had become instructors by early 1943. On June 7, 1942, the name CPT yielded quite appropriately to the War Training Service (WTS) which trained 300,000 pilots in just over two years of its existence.

Many air heroes gained their early experience with CAA instructors; for example, Major Joe Foss, Marines; and the late Major Richard Bong, and also Captain Walter Mahurin, both with the Army Air Force. CAA publicists expressed glee over the receipt of pictures showing former CPT men with General James H. Doolittle over Tokyo.[75] Senator Robert A. Taft of Ohio was informed that Lieutenant John Bell of Ohio, a Silver Star recipient in the evacuation of Burma, first trained in CPT at Marshall College.[76] A winner of the Navy Cross had initially been eliminated from CPT for "air sickness" and being tense.[77] Other holders of the Silver Star and Distinguished Flying Cross also had learned to fly under the CAA program. Lieutenant George S. Welch, who learned to fly in a CAA course at Purdue University, received a decoration for shooting down four Japanese planes over Pearl Harbor.[78] Seventeen former CPT trainees were killed in the first three months of combat. Beyond the important training of pilots, the CPT-WTS program offered opportunities in research which were utilized by the National Research Council. Recordings of flight instruction resulted in the publication of the "patter" book, the standardized techniques used by the Navy for its service pilot training.[79] One of the earliest programs after December 7, 1941, entailed the training of 400 transatlantic ferry pilots by the CAA.[80]

High schools throughout the country rose to the occasion by launching some 14,000 preflight aeronautical courses by 1942. Encouragement to aviation study in high school came with the availability of inexpensive textbooks (24 cents to $1.32) secured in cooperation with Columbia University and the University of Nebraska.[81] Enthusiasm for aviation training in high schools varied throughout the country, the Detroit system even providing some flight training for its enrollees.[82] By 1944, over 250,000 high school students participated in aviation courses, gaining advice from the CAA's Aviation Section, which employed thirteen people.

A broad undertaking like CPT-WTS naturally would invite criticism from the public, especially when one's favorite trainee did not gain his niche in the military with great dispatch. Undue delays occurred, and congressmen were beseiged with complaints which were then relayed to the CAA. One disgruntled wife registered her disdain for the program—her husband received no pay while in training, and the CAA would not extend him the franking privilege—by going directly to the "top," addressing her letter (without return address) to Mrs. Franklin D. Roosevelt.[83]

Most serious of the complaints against WTS involved the "sit and wait" period following the CAA training. Officially, of course, the CAA could in no way promise the young pilots immediate military service. Likewise, the military would not promise immediate bomber or fighter pilot positions to WTS trainees. Undoubtedly when delay ensued, the participants felt bitter toward both the CAA and the military. The failure to receive pay while enrolled as reservists also brought criticism, even though the CAA had no authority over this problem. Again, trainees who did become reservists without being called into active duty were called "draft beaters" by those considering themselves less fortunate.[84] To charges that the CAA trained the men then let them go, Administrator Stanton declared that his men often took the graduates (though certainly not compelled by law to do so) to the army officials for enlistment. Nevertheless, the bottleneck grew in magnitude until over 100,000 trainees were idly waiting.[85] Realization of this dilemma brought the caustic Senator Kenneth McKellar of Tennessee to declare that Sergeant Alvin York had become a good fighter without formal education. But McKellar was immediately reminded that York was not required to learn air navigation.[86]

A closed group, the reservists wore surplus Civilian Conservation Corps uniforms and after December 30, 1942, were entitled to receive $50 per month.[87] Though the Army dropped 5,000 from these rolls, it continued to hold 14,000 such reservists on inactive status. This picture truly represented a glut on the pilot-training market by 1943, yet the consequences of this surprise dilemma hardly proved anything but welcome if one considers the vast need for trained pilots for commercial and private flying in this country after the war ended.

Unhappily, the program received too much criticism relative to the value provided to the military. One sour note appeared in the record on February 7, 1944, when an accident cost the lives of an instructor and trainee at Pacific Air Schools, Tucson, Arizona. Senators queried Administrator Stanton about the mishap and learned that the chief pilot apparently sent out flights in bad weather without checking with the Weather Bureau.[88] Company officials maintained that poor weather closed in suddenly after the control tower permitted the flights. R. M. Stewart, CAA Executive Director of Training, reminded the committee that CAA controllers had no responsibility on takeoffs in bad weather, a decision left up to the pilot. Furthermore, Stewart reported the company had had previous maintenance troubles, although it possessed an excellent safety record prior to this accident. Another of the more serious attacks on the CPT-WTS came from Congressman Alvin E. O'Konski of Wisconsin, who declared:

> Born as the result of a shotgun wedding between the Army Air Forces and the C.A.A., it was tenderly reared until its parents

went their separate ways and then, an unwanted child, it was denied its birthright and its members came to know themselves as the 'orphans of the air.'[89]

O'Konski objected strenuously to the manner in which the plan bogged down because of insufficient planes and facilities for the men who were kept idle for seven months prior to their release in January, 1944. Following their release, the graduates were reclassified within two days and sent into army basic training. Actually, the CAA requested a continuation of the WTS program during fiscal 1946, basing its request legally on the grounds that Congress had extended the life of the program through this era. However, the Budget Bureau would not include recommendations for further appropriations.[90] Another facet of the aviation training program involved an "air conditioning" course given during the summer of 1942 at 650 colleges, the CAA reimbursing the schools for each teacher enrolled.[91]

DEVELOPMENT OF AIRPORTS

The second major CAA project already begun in 1938, encompassed the plan to provide better airports throughout the nation. By the spring of 1939, the CAA had completed the initial step, a survey of existing airports, which shocked military and civilian authorities as it revealed the fact that not a single airport was large enough to accommodate all types of existing military aircraft.[92] In summer, 1940, the CAA requested and received initial funds to construct or improve public airports which might be required by the Army and Navy. The Secretaries of War, Navy, and Commerce comprised a board to administer the first supplemental Civil Functions Appropriations Act of 1941, effective on October 9, 1940. At this time the CAA's Airport Section was removed from the Technical Development Section and made a separate unit. Naturally, the airport program gained in strength as war clouds persisted. Construction was completed mostly by private contractors. Three other governmental agencies shared in the responsibilities with the CAA—the Army Engineers in Alaska, the Works Progress Administration at home, and the Navy Bureau of Yards and Docks in much of the Pacific area. Work sites numbered 29 at home; 41 in Alaska; 8 in Hawaii; 2 in the South Pacific; and 1 each in Canton, Palmyra, Puerto Rico, Samoa, and the Canal Zone. The new DCLA (Development of Civil Landing Areas) designation of the program was begun in fiscal years 1943–1944 to complete the work of the old WPA at 30 locations. Under the latter program, approval of the chairmen of the War Manpower Commission (WMC) and the War Production Board was necessary.

By the summer of 1944, President Roosevelt requested that all projects not started under the national defense airport program be deferred. By then, work at 550 locations had begun. Numerous problems, not unlike earlier years in some respects, confronted the airport planners. The number one dilemma concerned the lengthening of existing runways to accommodate larger and faster aircraft. Here, Secretary of War Stimson requested help from Commerce and the CAA in suggesting materials for soil stabilization leading to more lasting pavement on runways.[93] Some of the WPA's bituminous runways had deteriorated. Several universities conducted experiments on the problem of finding suitable chemicals to stabilize the soil. The Airports Section continued to issue advice to city officials requesting help, typically calling for the type of airport possible to build with money raised in a bond issue. However, many airports could not be built or improved since the CAA encountered some difficulty in getting priorities from the WMC and WPB.[94]

Airport managers and CAA controllers garnered many an interesting tale from the day-to-day operations of both large and small landing facilities. At Pratt, Kansas, a farmer sought a claim for damage caused by soil blowing from the nearby intermediate landing field. A CAA official at Kansas City substantiated the claim as justifiable, and Congressman Clifford R. Hope expressed his approval to Administrator Stanton. However, Stanton felt there existed no authorization for such compensation.[95] The CAA hired its own guards at Washington National Airport and experienced a disconcerting episode when one guard died while on duty. No undertaker would touch the deceased, until a coroner had visited the scene, because of the persisting quarrel as to the legal location of the airport—District of Columbia or Virginia. The District coroner issued the necessary papers only after the Veterans Bureau had interceded in behalf of the guard who was a veteran.[96] In an amusing vein, controllers at Washington National Airport could not believe their ears when informed once that there were sheep on the field, thinking the informants reported a "jeep" was there. The animals had wandered away from a railway location.[97] Again, at small airports, 111 accidents among non-air carriers over the two previous winters brought CAA advice not to pile snow in high banks close to narrow runways. Fog at terminals was the topic of a detailed summary of hints, utilizing the spread between air temperature and dew point to predict ground fog of various intensities.[98] Airline management also came in for its share of advice and warning; one case indicating that a UAL DC–3 skidded off a runway onto a highway embankment—fortunately without deaths or injuries—because the UAL manager had failed to keep up with the runway condition, a sheet of ice 3 inches thick.[99] An *Airport Builders' Manual,* published by the Public Roads Administration, provided another service from the CAA. A problem so minor as keeping the grass neatly cut plagued authorities at Washington National Airport where the tough zoysia (Manila lawn) grass, believed to have originated in Manchuria, was introduced. A duty assumed by the CAA's supervisory and inspection staff involved the rationing of gasoline to civilian pilots, a task so cumbersome as to be delegated within five months to retail (bulk) dealers.[100]

Long before the Germans and Japanese surrendered, CAA officials, together with the aviation interests in general, began talking about a new era of airport building just ahead. As one popular news magazine proclaimed, the fields would come first, the planes second.[101] Assistant Secretary of Commerce William A. M. Burden told delegates to the Joint Airport Users Conference that the nation required a billion-dollar airport program calling for simple airparks and geared largely to family travel. For example, Massachusetts would need 36 new sites to complement its 54 existing airports. Minnesota would require 114 new air strips to augment its present 45 landing fields. Private flying smarted under the handicap of the lack of utility inherent in the small plane caused by the scarcity of low-cost airports at convenient locations.[102] Legislation to implement such a rosy future was not forthcoming at this time, even though proponents could cite the federal expenditure of $25 billion for public roads over the previous twenty-five years.

10

WORLD WAR II:
FACILITIES, REGULATIONS

THE CAA's role in aiding the military by providing better airports began in the prewar days. Other more drastic measures became necessary in the area of federal airways projects. Facilities in Alaska had been improved to the point where the largest of our military planes could operate. The air strip at Cold Bay aided in beating off the Japanese attack on Dutch Harbor.[1] The CAA strengthened the Seattle-Alaskan airway by constructing Canadian radio ranges at Comox, Port Hardy, and Masset. Elsewhere, the CAA helped the Seabees and Signal Corps with installations at Umnak, Atka, Tanaga, Oghiuga, Amchitka, Adak, Shimya, and Attu. The northernmost weather station was located at Point Barrow, Alaska, the CAA again cooperating with this venture. In cooperation with the Army Engineers and Signal Corps, the CAA constructed in the Alaskan interior steel towers from 150 to 300 feet in height with diversity antennas providing uninterrupted reception. CAA men helped the military under fire. In one instance, three employees risked their lives to save three crew members from a crashed British bomber, a feat bringing official praise from our ally.[2]

THE PACIFIC AREA

Action in the Pacific brought about many further dramatic endeavors in which the CAA proved indispensable. The Southwest Airway, operated by 10 CAA men, included 12 radio ranges and 4 communications stations. Here the standard radio ground systems required drastic modification for practical use on the many tiny coral islands—mainly because of the rise and fall of tides in the porous coral. Excavation for buildings and towers proved most difficult, not to mention the troubles with tropical pests, infection and disease, Japanese air raids, and shortages of food and supplies. Radio Engineer Frank Geissler, on the initial assignment at Guadalcanal, saw a 1,000-pound demolition bomb miss his foxhole by 200 yards. He reported:

> The radio equipment was scattered all over the island. The ship . . . was torpedoed in the harbor, but the captain pushed her up on the beach before she got too low in the water. . . . Our equipment was in the forward hold and dry. . . . Lt. Hiller, the Liaison officer, and I sifted beach sand for three days locating our tower bolts, nuts, and washers. . . .[3]

Geissler and his associates proceeded to occupy a concrete building with 5/8-inch steel reinforcing rods. Another close scrape came when a 250-pound fragmentation bomb landed close to his tent. The Japanese apparently did not fully realize the extent of CAA-Army efforts in establishing radio aids. The enemy, when talking with captured Americans on Guadalcanal, scoffed at the Yankee effort to fool the Japanese with a "dummy" airport and "dummy" planes. On the contrary, Carney Field became a stark reality contributing to Japanese defeat.

The CAA experts also helped the Navy install radio ranges at Chirikof, Canton, and Sand Point, all in the Pacific. Early attempts to save Midway Island involved the CAA, and only expendable towers and buildings were actually captured when this position fell to the enemy. Early in 1942, at Maui, Hawaiian Islands, the CAA added a third radio range which could be controlled remotely. Another range was added at Honolulu in May, 1942, while the Navy acquired further ranges at Palmyra a year later.

AID FOR THE EUROPEAN FRONTS

For the European front, the CAA maintained the famous Northeast and Crimson airways. Utilizing the former radio-range station at Utica, New York, the Northeast route terminated in Scotland, coming from the United States via Manitoba, Hudson Bay, Baffin Island, Greenland, and Iceland. The Crimson route extended from Central Canada to the British Isles via Southampton Island and the Arctic Circle, functioning on the air by August 21, 1942. Radio Engineer P. L. Copland and Airways Engineer F. H. Cosgrove were assigned to Northeast which was opened on July 7, 1942. Radio Engineer J. S. Turner and Airways Engineer R. J. Alpher manned the Crimson route. Both routes materially aided the operations of the Air Transport Command. Arctic mosquitoes and muskeg swamps greeted the CAA operators in many instances, though the voluntary response for service there, as elsewhere overseas, was most encouraging.

The Allied North African invasion (November, 1942) necessitated establishment of the Southeast Airway made up of 9 key air bases in South America and Africa. The system was expanded beyond Africa—Arabia, India, and Ceylon—to cover 31 radio ranges and 4 radio communications stations by VE Day and was controlled by 42 CAA engineers. Selection of locations for these stations proved to be a major headache because of the difficult jungle terrain of Africa; blasting for foundations in volcanic ash on Ascension Island; the sands of Morocco, Egypt, and Arabia; not to mention the mountains of India. Initially, the rainy season in British Guiana hampered CAA workers. Turner and W. L. Lehman took charge of the radio and airways engineering when this route was opened. Our "good neighbors" to the south who helped with locations included Mexico and Brazil; obviously, the British and U.S. island possessions also became involved. Finally, the vast air-cargo lift "over the hump" (Burma) entailed navigational support from the CAA. General Thomas O. Hardin, who aided in framing the CAA Act of 1938 and was later Chairman of the Air Safety Board, flew the "hump" himself to get the route organized. He indicated that twenty DC-4's or Constellations could do the job.[4]

COOPERATION WITH RISKS

Military "brass" often thankfully acknowledged CAA's radio and airways aids; in general, the cooperation between the two groups remained excellent. However, sometimes a CAA official might question his military brethren's technical knowledge. Such was the case when Regional Manager Marshall Hoppin (Alaska) expressed the belief that some military leaders should read a text on suitable aids to air navigation. He especially scoffed at military use of the medium-power range loop (MRL) as a localizer.[5]

Risking their lives on these overseas assignments, the inspectors, engineers, and communicators with the CAA encountered a most knotty technical problem concerning life insurance—the war-risk rider. In February, 1943, H. A. Hook, Regional Manager at Santa Monica, reminded Administrator C. I. Stanton of this tragic shortcoming in a secret letter. The unprotected CAA men on Canton Island had requested recall after that island had been shelled for a week, one burst hitting just 200 feet from the station.[6] This was not the first CAA installation to have been under fire. CAA people resented the fact that Pan American employees there did have insurance coverage.

Rosters of May and July, 1943, graphically illustrate the widespread overseas functions assumed by the CAA for the military.[7] A total of 379 airways communicators served at 48 stations in Alaska, Hawaii and other Pacific islands, and in the Caribbean. An additional 254 personnel worked in other capacities, all overseas, in the signals division and foreign airways extension. Airways engineers also labored in India, Iceland, Morocco, Canal Zone, Mexico, Greenland, Samoa, Labrador, Solomon Islands, Sudan, Honolulu, Society Islands, Fiji Islands, and Canton Island. W. T. Miller, Chief of the CAA's Air Carrier Division lamented to Stanton about "the new tactics now employed by the Army Air Forces to obtain additional personnel for service with the Air Transport Command. . . . The agreement between the secretaries of War and Commerce not to purge the Administration any more should be carried out. . . ."[8] Stanton backed Miller, refused to release two inspectors, and also explained to the Army the drain on air carrier inspectors who now had to test Pan American and American Export Airlines (AEA) overseas flights.

Now and then individuals offered thanks to field employees of the CAA. One major stationed in the Air Corps, extended particular credit to the communications personnel.[9] A CAA radio engineer in Alaska drew special praise from a top official of the military's Alaska Defense Command. In another instance, personnel of the CAA and FCC collaborated to relay messages bringing aid to an army B–17 pilot in distress in the Gulf of Mexico region.[10] Close cooperation, however, did not mean submission to army control, as Administrator Stanton reflected in his declaration that he did not want his unit on vibration and flutter permanently assigned to one military center.[11] So exacting and demanding did the aid to the military become that one CAA engineer completed fourteen transatlantic crossings in sixteen months to install vital equipment in various combat zones.[12]

AIDING THE MILITARY AT HOME

Overseas contributions to the military effort were augmented by a continual number of aids at home. From the outset, it became apparent that the CAA's airways system would prove invaluable to the armed forces. An executive order of December 13, 1942, authorized the military to take over any civilian aviation system deemed necessary.[13] Difficulties encountered between the military and civilians over airspace led to a clarification of practices, effective April 1, 1943, as announced by the Interdepartmental Air Traffic Control Board (IATCB). This committee passed judgment on any construction, relocation, or approval by the CAA of a landing area for use under security rules. The new regulations reduced the width of airways from the former 20 miles to 10 miles (to give the military more space), forbade the military from conducting training flights along the airways, and permitted pilots to fly in daylight at any altitude under contact rules (when the ground was visible) without approval of a flight plan.[14] In case of disagreement, the IATCB referred its problems to the War Aviation Committee made up of the assistant secretaries for air in War and Navy, the special aviation assistant to the Secretary of Commerce, and the CAB's chairman. At the same time, the CAA, along with federal law enforcement officials if needed, assumed the task of checking the loyalty of 140,000 certified airmen and the location of their 25,000 aircraft and some 2,600 landing fields in the nation. Thorough investigation of 103 cases of alleged subversive activities by airmen in civil aviation led to the permanent grounding of several individuals.[15] The records do not indicate whether the activities represented carelessness or wanton action to hamper the war effort.

During the war, CAA engineers and inspectors participated in the development and flight testing of military aircraft, e.g., the popular P–38 and P–39 fighters, the B–17 bomber, as well as the gliders produced by Piper, Aeronca, and Taylorcraft. Furthermore, CAA authorities contributed manuals and handbooks for the military.[16] In summer, 1945, CAA engineers worked on 66 military projects including 10 types of trainers, 12 gliders, 13 cargo planes, an ambulance plane, an 8-engine wooden craft, and one of stainless steel. Long hours and days went into the testing, failures occurring before successes. Once at Wright Field, stringers in the outer panel failed in testing a C–76 at less than 80 per cent of the design load.[17] Duplication of military-CAA jobs was eliminated in 1943 by having the military conduct some of the actual flight testing.

The Civil Aeronautics Board, always an active partner in the war effort, entered the picture in organizing many phases of civil air transport to the necessary advantage of the military. L. Welch Pogue, then CAB chairman, contended that, in 1943, 50 per cent of his agency's work had to do with the war effort.[18] Asked about any conflicts with the Interstate Commerce Commission, Pogue saw no troubles at all. Another CAB war function involved much advice and planning for the invaluable Civil Air Patrol.[19] In 1943, the CAB comprised 302 employees, 33 of whom were at the field offices. The CAB absorbed the Office of Air Transport Information from the CAA during the war. CAB investigators had no planes, begging rides or driving to the scene of accidents.[20] The CAB ordered a reserve pool of 200 commercial airliners, 165 such planes for scheduled commercial operations and 35 for the Air Transport Command's cargo work. All other planes (over 50 per cent of the existing total must be sold to the government. All planes reserved for the commercial companies were of the DC–3 (21-passenger) type except for ten Lodestars (14-passenger type).[21] Further modification of regulations allowed some use of single-engine craft for mail, cargo, and pilot training. But no charter or special flights could be undertaken without CAB permission. In essence, commercial operators now served almost 72 per cent of the former air mileage with about 51 per cent of the former aircraft. Five classes of travel were established: (1) President and Secretaries of War and Navy, (2) ferrying-command pilots, (3) trips ordered for military personnel, (4) military equipment, and (5) trips for military and diplomatic personnel—still in the essential classification. Employees at the new field offices of the Air Transport Command helped judge priorities. As would be expected, a financial boom resulted for commercial operators now blessed with such widespread military business. After all, military usage of civil airways increased from 39 per cent in fiscal 1941 to 86 per cent during fiscal 1945.[22] Another move aiding both commercial and military interests allowed pilots in training for military cargo duties to serve as copilots on scheduled civil airliners.[23]

As wartime production of military planes increased, the CAB ordered planes returned to the air carriers. During the year September 30, 1943, to September 30, 1944, the air carriers achieved a load factor of 90 per cent while the DC-3s were flown at an average of 1,848 miles per day. Beginning on March 1, 1944, the Secretary of War allowed the CAB full responsibility to allocate equipment among the domestic air carriers.[24] The fleet grew from 324 planes in May, 1942, to 507 on October 15, 1945. The final act in dropping wartime controls came with the Army Air Force's termination of its domestic air priority system on October 15, 1945. As the peak of the CAA's war efforts— considered to be at the end of 1943—was passed, the task of looking to postwar development began. Here, the sale of surplus airplanes loomed as an immediate problem, the CAA supervising the sale of 5,000 such planes during the last seven months of 1944.[25]

In addition to the regulation of planes and airways, the CAA greatly facilitated other facets of the military effort. Radio aids, the backbone of around-the-clock flight, naturally formed a major area of concern with utmost concentration on utilizing the latest equipment for the military. Construction of vhf (very high frequency) radio, planned in prewar days for over 350 sites, was given a high priority and funds by the military, as some of its planes were equipped only with vhf equipment. The Army received the new vhf units planned for the CAA which had to wait till after World War II to get factory delivery of the better radio sets. The radio range and voice communications comprised an all-out effort to combat the static encountered in the present sets using the band of 200–400 kilocycles.[26] The War Department's decision to place the new vhf at 100 airports was helpful to the CAA. Another new device, called a "homing" range, was added at seventy-one locations, this device operating on 50 watts or less with signals modulated at 1,020 cycles per second.[27]

DIRECTING TRAFFIC

Airway traffic control, a task performed by the CAA since 1936, proved to be a most important service for the military as, indeed, was the airport traffic control duty taken over by the CAA shortly before Pearl Harbor. The CAA pioneered an approach control procedure whereby a fan marker approximately ten miles from the airport served as a holding and reporting point from which planes were directed to land at intervals of about 4 minutes instead of the former 15-minute spacing. Army funds enabled the CAA to purchase forty-three such devices.[28] The "stacking" of planes awaiting permission to land began at an altitude of 2,500 feet from which planes were held at 1,000-foot levels. By the war's end, twenty landings per hour could be accomplished even in bad weather. At this time, New York City was the busiest airway traffic control area. Training of controllers became a gigantic task, the CAA offering the preliminary course to 400 trainees during fiscal 1942 in addition to army and navy personnel who participated.[29]

Congress authorized the CAA's airway traffic control wherever the military requested new centers, 9 additional ones being added to the 14 prewar centers prior to July, 1942. Six centers in the Aleutians used military men trained by the CAA. Six senior CAA controllers aided the Air Transport Command in Africa while 11 others went to Brazil in 1944. By the end of the war, the CAA Airway Traffic Control Division encompassed 52 separate tasks involving 3,194 personnel. War and Navy early in the war asked the CAA to assume control of over 100 airport control towers. Furthermore, 450 additional airport transmitters, built to CAA specifications, were procured by the military for other sites. Here, as in airways communications, women played a major role. Despite the female aid, Administrator Stanton expressed dismay at the thought of losing his top 30 male controllers to the Army, frankly stating that only 75 of his airport controllers could be considered competent in adverse weather conditions.[30] Apparently Stanton's suggestion led the Army to assign several of its personnel to CAA airway traffic control centers. Military-CAA cooperation led to CAA adoption of the army jargon "downwind leg, base leg, and approach leg." The CAA's traffic control school at Atlanta featured a miniature airport mounted on tracks hauling the planes around on a ceiling.[31] In 1944, upon request of the military, the CAA assumed control of military CFR (contact flight rule) flight plans, requiring the training of hundreds in airway communications.[32] The CAA was called upon to provide transmission of air-raid warnings and developed a device known as automatic station identification (ASID) to prevent enemy agents from tampering with the system. Radio communications always brought up the problem of the scarcity of radio frequencies, a concern alleviated overseas and in the territories by an integrated CAA-military system. The circuit C teletype transmission, inaugurated before the war, helped greatly in facilitating the 600 per cent increase in radio communications with en route aircraft.

An innovation becoming standard practice was the flight advisory service designed to transmit airways information and weather data to the pilot even before he asked for it. The service was inaugurated in 1943 at twenty-three control centers. Already, the top administrators in the CAA found rivalry between the employees in air traffic control and communications. Often the communicators lamented that they received the tasks which air traffic did not want. A fine line of distinction separated the two areas of endeavor, according to Thomas B. Bourne, the veteran Director of the Federal Airways Division.[33]

Heavier traffic resulting from the war led CAA observers in 1942 to foresee the time when the dispatching of information would become so confusing as to reach a "breaking point."[34] This opinion has been shared for over two decades by aviation men who have seen the fantastic increase in traffic continue its flirtation with a "breaking point." Even in the early forties, the current system of posting incoming data on paper strips and flight progress boards cried for automation, long discussed but not forthcoming. The experimental board at Washington, D.C. —featuring the posting of teletype-written information by the machine operator—failed to gain the confidence of all concerned. Meanwhile, the experts watched the experimentation at Indianapolis for posting with navy radar.[35] Another experiment involved a mobile control tower.

The celebrated airport ILS program suffered a delay of at least two years during the war. Nine CAA systems were operating by early 1945 and ten additional locations were under construction. Moreover, the CAA was installing fifty more systems for the Army, looking ahead to the later commercial adaptation of these operations.[36] Another boost from the military in 1945 produced ten carloads of military radar promised to the CAA for control work within a 25-mile radius.[37] Strengthening of the intercontinental radio station WSY (New York) by early 1943 provided meteorological data and word broadcasts simultaneously on three frequencies, all using a five-figure code.[38]

The hectic concern of war strategy to assign personnel as needed apparently led T. B. Bourne, Director of Federal Airways, to abrupt reaction when fifteen men signed a petition (contents unrevealed) concerning their work. Bourne suggested that this method was entirely unnecessary to express their desire to remain at Washington, D.C., and concluded, "I don't like the petition way of doing business."[39] One gathers from the official correspondence a mixed reaction to the quality of work produced by women assigned to communications systems. Records of high turnover and lack of training marred the excellent record attained by many women in airways communications.[40]

INSPECTION, LICENSING, ENFORCEMENT

The CAA, confronted with heavy demands from the military and riddled by loss of manpower, simply could not satisfy all civilian interests during the war. All in all, the official records show a happy balance between praise and criticism from civilians. For example, the head of South Carolina's Aeronautical Commission complained that his state lacked inspection service, but Alabama's aviation authorities praised CAA service.[41] Administrator Stanton denied a Minnesota official's charges of CAA browbeating and "bullying." Elsewhere, in reply to Congressman Jennings Randolph, Stanton cited time and cost as reasons for moving the inspection and CPT offices from Charleston to Clarksburg, West Virginia.[42] Deputy Administrator J. E. Sommers, cognizant of the demands on his subordinates, reassessed the inspector's woes: "I am wondering if the inspector does not spend more time in making the report than he does in actually making a full inspection of the station."[43] On the other hand, the "new look" for the inspection staff promoted courtesy and patience. One inspector had to be reminded of this approach via a letter of caution from his superiors following his unauthorized action in picking up an airman's certificate.[44]

Airline management did not escape unscathed despite the preoccupation with war promotion. Administrator Stanton frankly reprimanded Chicago and Southern for violations arising from operations six weeks to four months after the lapse of airworthiness certificates. Stanton declared, "Obviously had there been an accident . . . while either of these violations were in process, your company and this organization would have been in a serious embarrassing position and I do not know what the status of your insurance might have been in such a case."[45] Stanton approved a compromise of $100 for Chicago and Southern from the original $600 worth of violations. National Airlines was apprehended exceeding overhaul periods and failing to equip aircraft with proper instruments, a $1,000 civil penalty which one CAA legal expert felt could be reduced to $200—the "rock-bottom figure."[46]

In the field of Civil Air Regulations, the war years could not diminish the concern of safety leaders for the problems confronting the CAA when hostilities ceased. F. M. Lanter, Director of Safety Regulations, outlined these future concerns during January, 1943, in a letter to Stanton:

(1) Expanded jurisdiction over all U.S. airspace.
(2) Extension of certificates of convenience and necessity to all types of commercial aircraft.
(3) Segregation and zoning (tall obstructions) at airports.
(4) Simplification of regulations.
(5) Adequate recordation of aircraft functions.
(6) International transportation.
(7) Universal aviation education in our schools.
(8) State legislation and state-federal-local cooperation.
(9) Varied liability and insurance laws.
(10) Accurate identification of all airmen.
(11) Further emphasis on medical research.
(12) The tremendous impending increase in airmen's certificates.[47]

Lanter, elaborating in this fifteen-page letter, hoped for machine evaluation of flight tests and the centralization of all flight control, instead of allowing the companies to handle a portion of the decisions involved—a condition still existing today. With thousands of examinations on record from CPT, surely doctors could improve on the physical tests for airmen. Higher altitudes and speedier craft necessitated the study of the possible detrimental effects of high altitude on passengers and crew. Current research suggested the taking of vitamin A to combat night blindness among pilots.

Significant amendments to the Civil Air Regulations included the extension of the maximum flying time for pilots, in one month, from 85 to 100 hours, effective on April 29, 1942. Also in 1942, the free baggage allowance for international flights was dropped to 55 pounds, instead of the range up to 77 pounds. Pilots of seaplanes received continual warnings to abide by maritime rules (CAR 60.92)—yielding to the vessel on their starboard right. Even when no CAR was violated, accident investigations prompted the CAA to alert pilots to risky situations

—even to field mice. In a recent fatal accident the right aileron fabric had deteriorated badly along the piano hinge; the wing failed; and during removal of the wreckage, a mouse jumped from the fuselage. Other instances of damage from rodents and wood-eating termites were on record. Dehydrated wing spars caused additional consternation, and the CAA warned those affected to contact the manufacturer since the remedy varied for type of product. Landings continued to haunt aviation, the CAA urging pilots not to be "too proud" to "give her the gun" and go around the field again for a better touchdown.[48]

VIOLATIONS AND ACCIDENTS

Many practices leading to warnings were discovered in accidents investigated by the CAA and CAB. Investigators and researchers continually sought to prevent accidents through promoting safer equipment, revising regulations, or providing hints from veteran fliers. Even so, Dr. W. R. Stovall, Medical Director of CAA, believed there are accident-prone pilots as well as automobile drivers.[49] Too often, carelessness or recklessness entered the picture, as in the case of an army pilot causing a midair collision between his bomber and a DC–3, killing all 12 on the airliner with no injuries to the military crew. The pilot allegedly wished to "thumb his nose" (rock his wings) to attract the attention of his friend, who was first officer on the airliner. A propeller on the bomber tore off three-fourths of the DC–3's rudder.[50] A PAA Clipper, carrying actress Jane Froman among its passengers, fell while landing at Lisbon on February 22, 1943, to become the first U.S. commercial aircraft to crash in Europe. Twenty-four of the thirty-nine aboard died, and the cause was listed as: "Inadvertent contact of the left wing of the aircraft with water while making a descending turn preparatory to landing. . . . [51] Miss Froman and two other entertainers received payments of $20,000 each from the United States Government. Pilot error and faulty company practice were cited in the crash of a PAA DC–3A in the Peruvian Andes on January 22, 1943, killing all but 1 of the 15 aboard. The craft was blown off course by a 20-mile-per-hour tail wind. The CAA's advice that Panagra publish a flight route manual for the area had been ignored twice, with the issuing of verbal advice only.[52]

As always, flying through or near thunderstorms proved most dangerous, an American Airlines plane literally being "pushed" to its destruction by a downdraft encountered at an altitude of approximately 1,300 feet near Trammel, Kentucky. A strong wind probably contributed to loss of lift and prevented recovery of control at about 200 feet above the ground.[53] Two survivors told about the downdraft and severe lightning accompanying the storm. One glider expert offered to airline pilots his own observations concerning cumulo-nimbus cloud hazards, once having noted a rate of climb exceeding 3,000 feet a minute in a mild cloud of that type. Other soaring planes reportedly gained 20,000 feet in five minutes, making it easy to reach the "sharp-edged gust" of 30 feet per second which was listed as the criterion of structural design.[54] Another type of tragedy cost the life of actor Earl Steinmetz who walked into the path of a taxiing airplane while on a movie location at Van Nuys, California.[55] Failure to use a safety belt allowed a pilot to fall from his craft, causing his death and that of his two passengers. In yet another bizarre incident, a pilot and his passenger scuffled in a C–3 Aeronca during their unauthorized air show at 200–250 feet and crashed to their deaths. A Northwest pilot of a DC–3 let down to "take a look" during conditions below minimum, after which the craft failed to respond to the application of full power because of ice on the wings. The result was death for all but 1 of the 15 aboard near Moorhead, Minnesota, on October 30, 1941. The CAA was critical of the pilot and the company's dispatcher at Fargo airport for not deciding to proceed to an alternate field because of such conditions.[56] A collision at the Wichita, Kansas, airport on July 9, 1943, occurred at a time when a controller was allegedly holding a dustpan and cleaning the control tower floor. Glen A. Gilbert, Chief of the Airway Traffic Control Division, was obviously irked by the incident and extended blame to the chief controller if the sweeping constituted a required duty.[57]

WEIGHING THE DC–3

Cooperation between the military and the CAA-CAB did not conceal the fact that military pilots became involved in mishaps as well as near misses. Safety precautions were eased to allow commercial planes a heavier load when in military use; CAB officials contended that the former DC–3 limit of 25,200 pounds gross was a conservative figure. The Army sometimes carried 30,000 pounds which precluded emergency flight on just one engine because of the weight.[58] The question of maximum weight prompted David L. Behncke, President of the ALPA, to oppose vigorously the CAB proposal to increase the DC–3 takeoff weight to 26,200 pounds and the landing weight from 24,400 pounds to 25,200 pounds. Behncke asserted, "What I'm thinking of is the cushion of safety."[59] Heading the organization of 4,500 members (ALPA) Behncke had quit his job as an airmail pilot in 1934 after sustaining a broken leg in a crackup on the Chicago–Omaha run. Charges against the military for near misses continued as in the past with military controllers in CAA towers watching for such action. Returning military air heroes did not always exhibit their skill with commercial and private craft, prompting one leading scientific editor to advocate more rigid CAA control of the new civilians by demanding written and performance tests.[60] The warning appears to have been substantiated, for the CAA-CAB issued bulletins and warnings following a disproportionately large number of serious crashes involving ex-military pilots shortly after the war. Among the titles were: *Air Recklessness, That 500-Foot Regulation,* and *Service Pilots Versus Light Planes.*[61]

A perennial question, that of duplication between the CAB and CAA on accident investigation, appears from the records to have been an area of acute awareness on the part of both parties who tried to avoid such charges. CAA authorities were officially alerted to prevent duplication.[62] Citing an opinion of the Attorney General, the CAA did refuse to allow the CAB use of its files in a board hearing.[63] Upon CAA request, the CAB adopted a regulation against unauthorized reproduction of examinations by aeronautical schools.[64] Queried by the administrator about CAB and CAA duplication, CAA general counsel Webb Shadle personally believed that the work of the administrator was to a greater or lesser degree directed and controlled by the board.[65] Invariably, some members of Congress failed to discern the differences in work performed by the two agencies. That the CAB made the rules while the CAA enforced the rules and maintained the facilities proved to be a separation of duties difficult for laymen to understand.[66]

RESEARCH ACTIVITIES

Researchers continued during the war to study hazards which had caused accidents or near mishaps. Ducks and other birds smashing against aircraft windshields led the CAA and the National Bureau of Standards to foresee "duck-proofed" windshields and to claim at least partial success in their development.[67] John Easton, Chief of the CAA's Technical Development Division, designed a new plastic and glass windshield which reportedly would stop a 15-pound bird carcass.[68] But Administrator Stanton told congressmen of a CAA pilot experiencing the crashing of a buzzard through his windshield at about 3,000 feet. The pilot was dazed and cut but recovered in time. Stanton declared that birds penetrated the glass more easily than bullets.[69] Another long-time dilemma, the search for crash-resistant fuel tanks, gained further interest and appropriations during 1941–1945. Though the same principles were used as in earlier experiments, one gathers that CAA men remained dubious of finding the practical type of rubber tank. Still perplexing to all concerned were the indications that deaths occurred by fire in some accidents considered not "too hard an impact," yet the tanks were damaged enough to cause the fires.[70]

Cooperation on the part of the CAA with the Weather Bureau and the military has been mentioned in the foregoing account of wartime activities. Another innovation, the international ice patrol, helped aviation. Operated by the Coast Guard, the weather ships also provided excellent radio fixes for airliners crossing the Atlantic.[71] The idea of installing weather and radio facilities on the Atlantic had caused much discussion before the war. Suggestions centered on seadromes (like the later ill-fated Texas Towers) or some type of floating airdrome, but fear of German submarines had precluded any formal action. Continuing the rapport between the CAA and the Weather Bureau, a liaison man, Robert W. Craig of the Weather Bureau, was named in June, 1945, to handle relations between the two agencies. Outside parties continued to laud the CAA-Weather Bureau accord, especially the efficiency in obtaining and transmitting the hourly weather reports.[72]

By 1945, licensing of all aircraft and pilots solely by the federal government was accepted in all states except Alabama, Connecticut, Maryland, New Jersey, North Dakota, Oregon, Utah, and Virginia, these states requiring additionally a state license or some form of option from either state or federal sources.[73] According to state officials, there existed no quarrel with the CAA. But the states wished to retain control of intrastate aviation while still adhering to the desire for uniformity among the states.[74]

Many projects in the field of research have already been related in connection with their particular CAA activity.

However, other organizations cooperated in additional experimentation worthy of mention. The National Research Council undertook a thorough study of the selection and training of pilots, granting 67 projects to approximately 40 universities and colleges, the cost totaling $1 million. The government appropriated 70 per cent of this total, the rest coming from the states and institutions of higher learning. The Navy used the study as a type of screening device for potential trainees, and claimed it eliminated 21,000 applicants out of 70,000 who originally sought training. In August, 1945, the National Research Council published final results of the five-year study.[75] Cameras in the cockpit, flying personnel from other countries as subjects, and a special effort to discern tendencies which suggested "poor risks" among our own applicants—all were aspects of the study. A few of the topics comprising individual contracts were:

(1) Measuring skin temperature and perspiration.
(2) Effectiveness of "patter."
(3) Eye fixations and movements.
(4) Effect of distraction lights, biographical data, and predicted success.
(5) A test of decision time, "tension," and maneuvers most closely related to accidents.

CAA authorities used resin in an effort to stabilize soil for runways on the Pacific islands. A mechanical cement spreader was developed in 1943. General Douglas MacArthur and his staff complimented the CAA on its use of aerial photographs to determine the engineering characteristics of airports. Furthermore, CAA engineers designed and developed the first portable airport turntable, of which hundreds came to be used by the military. For the Navy, the CAA introduced the rubber buoy for seadrome lighting and seaplane mooring.[76] New instrument-approach charts for 500 airports were developed in cooperation with the Coast and Geodetic Survey. Also, relief maps were furnished for China, Burma, and India in addition to more thorough maps of the route from Edmonton to Nome. Several projects, not all initiated by the CAA—or if so, unfinished in 1945—still held promise for the future. For example, the anticollision device grew out of military use on night fighters to detect enemy craft; the angle and distance indicator was also a war creation. A stall-warning indicator originated with the CAA.[77] A celestial altitude computer, an approach-zone camera, an artificial horizon sextant, and an improved embossing machine remained untried. Looking ahead,

Administrator Stanton alerted congressmen in 1944 to the gigantic strides to be expected in aviation within three to five years after the war. To be sure, commercial airlines still used 350 two-engine planes, but Stanton foresaw private business exceeding the scheduled lines by 10 to 1, with total activity increasing 20 to 30 times.[78] The surge of interest in aviation could be discerned in 1944 with an increase of 30 per cent in new student pilot certificates (51,000) and 20 per cent more mechanics' certificates.[79] Wartime predictions also looked for jets and planes capable of traveling 2,000 miles per hour.[80] The CAA bided its time until the danger of invasion or enemy activity subsided to renew pursuit of a favorite and invaluable project—the air marking of town names on airports or other prominent buildings. Blanche Noyes campaigned for markers every 15 miles and, at the end of 1943, resumed her CAA flights across the country. The military had demanded the obliteration of all such markers within strips 150 miles deep along the east and west coasts.[81]

THE CAA, CAB, AND ECONOMIC PLANNING

The glowing anticipation of lucrative expansion for the United States and international traffic in passengers and cargo foisted a menacing barrage of alternatives upon the CAB which must sort out the sound and promising business ventures from the crackpot or financially unsound suggestions. Moreover, in the international field, our friends and allies from the war years would certainly seek favors for their own airlines long frustrated by Hitler's advances. In a sense, the CAA had furthered interest and ability among our allies through training of foreign aviators in this country.

The inter-American training program, begun in 1941 by the CAA, included several separate programs at Purdue University; Spartan School of Aeronautics, Tulsa, Oklahoma; CAA's operations at Kansas City; and the Army. Pilots, mechanics, technicians, and interns also spent eight weeks studying English at the University of Michigan. The CAA placed mechanics from some of the programs with U.S. aviation industries for on-the-job training. Officials in the State Department arranged for the selection of students who would enroll in this Good Neighbor defense gesture. By the end of 1943, some 484 pilots and mechanics had completed the training.[82] CAA experts also spent considerable time with Latin Americans who toured air facilities in this country. And U.S. officials, both CAA and CAB, worked in Latin America to survey areas of future commercial service there, traveling by burro and facing torrential rains on the La Paz–Buenos Aires route.[83] Difficult to understand was the reluctance of one aid recipient, Brazil, to accept the now common license (bilateral) for pilots traveling over Brazil.[84] A leading business editor in the United States lamented the training given Brazilians who would then convert Germany's prewar lines at home to compete against American airlines.[85] The same journal envisaged an international fight over air cargo with the major U.S. carriers looking overseas while the British worried over the existence of so many available commercial aircraft in the United States. The CAA even came to the aid of Latin-American trainees here who petitioned successfully for free rides to their homes in Argentina, Bolivia, Brazil, Chile, Ecuador, Peru, and Uruguay.[86] Minor irritations did arise concerning the international programs. For example, Who should pay for the hotel bills of visiting aviation officials when they walked off without paying? William Burden of Commerce believed this the responsibility of the State Department but realized that one could "stretch" the legal basis "to encourage and foster the development of civil aeronautics."[87] The CAA requested $5,000 for entertaining foreign guests, on the basis of receiving one-half that amount for the same purpose during fiscal 1945.

An indication of the tremendous problems confronting aviation could be ascertained from the outcome of the meetings of the International Civil Aviation Conference at Chicago (1944). Burden, CAA; Edward Warner, CAB; Adolf A. Berle, Jr.; and Stokeley W. Morgan represented the United States. An important decision, the "two freedoms agreement," offered planes of each nation the free and unlimited passage through airspace of another. The "five freedoms agreement" stated that for transportation purposes each nation retained the right to authorize routes.[88] Fifty-four nations sent delegates to Chicago; the enemy states, of course, were absent. Also absent were: Argentina, which was not invited; Saudi Arabia, which refused; and the USSR for reasons unstated. Unfinished business abounded, embracing the recognized need to improve radio facilities, establish international standards of safety, and the rights of conducting trade. The New Zealanders, foreseeing the mad competition for air routes, called for the complete internationalization of major routes. Problems of economic routes, even the United Kingdom's balking at the transport agreement at Chicago, had to await post-war settlement.

The CAB had no control over air operations of airlines when their planes did not fly over American soil. Furthermore, it failed to gain control over international rates, a domain held firmly by the International Air Transport Association, wherein one dissent among the fifty-seven operators killed a proposal. *The Nation* described the dilemma facing the CAB and told about the flood of applications for air routes, a great many of which must be turned down "cold."[89] Airlines fought desperately against domination or control by any surface carrier in this behind-the-scenes wartime maneuvering. Though railroads were feared as well, even the Greyhound Bus Corporation sought parallel air-ground routes despite the fact that it owned no aircraft at the time.[90] From the outset, the State Department and CAB announced collaboration on all international applications, State to forward such to the CAB. The CAB, to put it mildly, had always taken a dim view of American surface transportation companies having anything to do with airline operation. Congressman Thomas J. Lane of Massachusetts complained that a steamship line applied in 1940 for rights to fly in the Caribbean area. After a delay of almost four years, the CAB first scheduled then postponed a hearing on the proposal.[91] Pleasing congressmen, of course, invariably proved to be impossible—when one was satisfied, a rival's pet company had probably lost a route. As to actual overseas operations, PAA and AEA service to Eire had been continued, and the British gained the route from New York to Bermuda. Pan American had been refused a line from Los Angeles to Mexico City on the grounds that Cia Mexicana de Aviacion already had this service. American was granted the route from Dallas–Fort Worth to Mexico City, via El Paso and Monterey. In 1942, PAA still operated its Pacific route to Honolulu and Auckland with a new stop at Suva, Fiji; war cancelled all other Pacific trips. In 1944, BOAC gained an increase from two to three weekly flights from Baltimore to Foynes, Eire. In August, 1943, the Dutch line KLM began operation of a route in the West Indies touching at Miami.[92] Pan American resumed its Alaskan operations on August 1, 1944, and on January 1, 1945, began to conduct its regular transatlantic service, while American began its transatlantic runs one day earlier. Groundwork was laid at the Chicago conference for international bilateral agreements which would authorize routes. Immediately after the end of the war in Europe, Deputy Administrator Stanton undertook a mission to London to study CAA war data and the need for CAA offices abroad. Study was also made of the overseas activities of the U.S. Air Transport Command.[93]

On the domestic front, the CAB tackled such knotty problems as airmail rates and passenger fares, holding in abeyance the numerous applications for extended air service. Officials of the Post Office Department and CAA proudly announced an estimated profit of $35 million on airmail during fiscal 1945, exceeding in this one year all the deficits accruing since 1918.[94] For the time being, Stanton could agree with Senator Kenneth McKellar's hopeful plea for a self-supporting aviation agency. Eleven carriers transported 80 per cent of the mail during fiscal 1944, with a service rate of 0.3 mill per pound-mile (60 cents per ton-mile). In two additional instances, the question of "need" was determined by the CAB to allow earnings of 8 per cent after deletion of federal taxes. During 1945, after long proceedings, the compromise of 45 cents per ton-mile replaced the old 60-cent figure for American, Eastern, TWA, and United, whose combined efforts carried 86 per cent of domestic airmail.[95] Board members considered the average mail load as 300 pounds.

Applications for new commercial routes, both domestic and international, awaited CAB attention; the domestic hearings were not resumed until June, 1944. Meanwhile, Northwest looked to expansion in the Pacific to Manila; Northeast envisaged a route to Europe, including Moscow; and Chicago and Southern hoped for a run from Chicago to Java. At home, UAL, TWA, and Eastern applied for routes to Washington, D.C., and points west. The first application filed by a woman was for a certificate to establish a mail and passenger service for sixty towns in North Carolina, South Carolina, Tennessee, and Virginia, using at times the roofs of post offices and promising autogiros and helicopters as well as conventional planes for passenger traffic.[96] A flood of 444 new applications arrived in the four months following the lifting of the ban on new requests (June 21, 1943). For the year ending October 31, 1945, the CAB granted additions of 8,351 miles to the domestic system bringing the total to 66,997 miles. United was allowed into New York from Pittsburgh; Northwest flew from Milwaukee to New York via Detroit; American, Braniff, and Western also gained extensions.

Passenger fares drew much consideration from the CAB

during the war. Citing increases in income as the major reason, the CAB in 1943 asked the eleven leading domestic lines to show cause as to why a 10 per cent reduction would not be in order.[97] Within three months, five airlines reduced fares voluntarily by 6 to 7 per cent. Effective May 1, 1945, UAL inaugurated a reduction of 10 per cent. In transoceanic fares, PAA reduced its Atlantic trip by 17 per cent in 1943, at the same time lowering its Latin-American fares by 10 per cent. At the war's end, fares at home averaged approximately 4.35 cents per mile. Profits realized because of the war enabled eleven airlines to pay dividends in 1944 and ten companies did the same during the following year.[98]

Auditing of the financial books kept by the airlines proved to be a most burdensome chore for the CAB's twenty-five field auditors. Four or five auditors would travel by railroad (with Pullman) to Kansas City and spend twenty-five to seventy-five days covering the accounts of TWA; stops at Cheyenne and Chicago were necessary to check on UAL; PAA, American, and EAL could be checked at New York. Late in the war, auditors for the first time began looking over PAA-Grace's books at Lima.[99] Perhaps the CAB felt obligated to inaugurate more thorough audits of PAA. After all, it had come to light in a congressional subcommittee hearing early in the war that PAA was the lone company not examined that year. Author Matthew Josephson, who claimed that Franklin D. Roosevelt had saved PAA much embarrassment in 1934, again felt that the government needed PAA too badly during 1941–1945 to investigate very deeply; and PAA's President Juan T. Trippe remained unperturbed by the CAB. Admitting the terrific political pressure under which CAB members labored, Josephson added, "Trippe and his great corporation are more powerful by far in political influence than those modestly paid officials who would be called on to do the regulating."[100] In addition to the foregoing duties, the CAB also began its careful examination of the pressure to establish feeder airlines connecting smaller cities throughout the country with the large metropolises. The CAB's decision and the results belong to the postwar era.

(Upper left) General William F. McKee became head of the Federal Aviation Agency in 1965 with instructions from President Lyndon B. Johnson to emphasize the development of supersonic aircraft for commercial aviation. (FAA.) (Upper right) Miss Blanche Noyes, successful early pilot, has continued her flying as an employee for the FAA in the important task of air marking of ground landmarks to aid pilots. (CAA.)   (Lower left) Najeeb E. Halaby served as head of the Federal Aviation Agency during 1961–1965, an era during which the commercial jet airplanes steadily achieved economic success for the airlines. (FAA.)

(Lower right) E. R. Quesada, first head of the FAA (1959–1961), sought tighter regulations governing crews and aircraft in this inaugural of the commercial jet age. (FAA.)   (Left) Airport traffic controllers at Washington, D.C., National Airport observe traffic operations at one of the three airports owned and operated by the FAA. (FAA.)

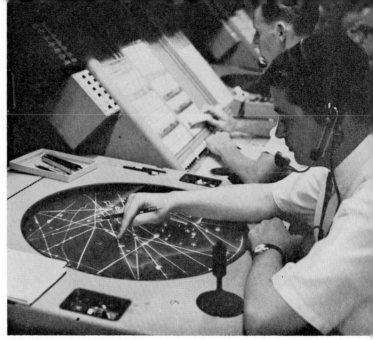

(Above) Tracking aircraft on radar has become a typical safety aid for airport traffic controllers and air route traffic control centers. (FAA.)   (Below) In the middle 1930's these controllers at the Newark, N.J., center were keeping track of aircraft without benefit of radar and other advanced electronic data. (FAA.)

(Above) In 1956 Pan American World Airways officials accepted delivery of the first U.S. jet airliner, a Boeing 707 transport, and obtained a provisional operating certificate from the CAA. Passenger service began in 1959. (Boeing Aircraft Co.)   (Left) James T. Pyle, Acting Administrator of the CAA, at the controls of the Boeing 707 just before his test flight at Seattle, Sept. 24, 1956. (FAA.)   (Below) Instrument panels of the Boeing 707 indicate complex duties of jet-age crewmen. (FAA.)

(Above) E. R. Quesada, first administrator of the Federal Aviation Agency (center in dark suit), took part in the certification ceremonies for the initial DC–8 jet transport. (FAA.)   (Right) C. I. Stanton, longtime Civil Aeronautics Administration official, served as administrator during World War II. (CAA.)

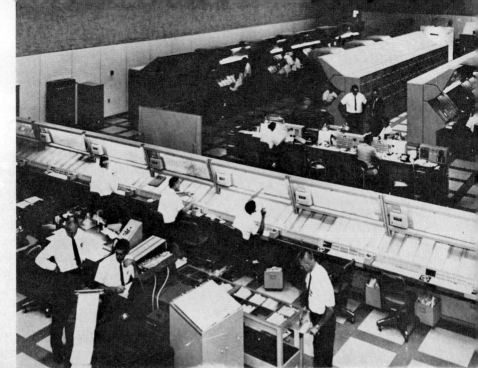

(Above) Increased air traffic and the jet transport have resulted in the necessity of large air route traffic control centers such as this one at Memphis (1965). (FAA.) (Left) Administrator Clinton Hester (standing third from left) inspected the CAA Communications Office at Allentown, Pa., in 1940. (CAA.)

(Right) This Bellanca was used by the Department of Commerce in developing the Instrument Landing System (1933), using the pole and loop antennas. (Department of Commerce.) (Below) This Bellanca instrument panel was used in developing the Instrument Landing System, or "blind landing" as it was commonly called in the '30's. (Department of Commerce.)

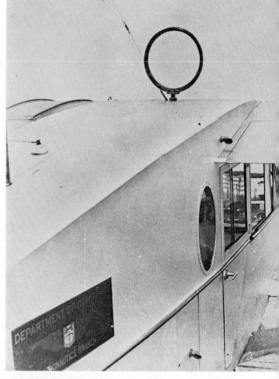

(Above) Airport and approach lighting glow as an aircraft lands at Washington, D.C., National Airport. (FAA.) (Left) Helped greatly by officials of the Aeronautics Branch before and after his famous solo flight to Paris, Colonel Charles E. Lindbergh left Bolling Field (Washington, D.C.) on his thrilling flight to Mexico on Dec. 13, 1927. (Harris and Ewing.)

(Above left) The DC–3 has enjoyed three decades of successful operation in commercial and military circles. (CAA.)   (Below left) The instrument panel of the DC–3 represents one of the most interesting sagas of U.S. aviation. Although rapidly vanishing from scheduled commercial operations, this workhorse continues to hold a place in the skies. It was used for certain duty during the Vietnam action. (CAA.)

(Above) Air traffic controllers maintained an accurate check on the whereabouts of all aircraft in the vicinity of the center at Washington, D.C., Hoover Airport (1939). (CAA.)

(Above) A test jet owned by the FAA runs through a layer of slush on the runway to help measure the effects of slush on landing and takeoff operations. The research is conducted at the FAA's National Aviation Facilities Experimental Center, Atlantic City, N.J. (FAA.) (Right) David D. Thomas was selected as deputy administrator of the FAA in 1965. Thomas, with the CAA and FAA since 1938, is a pilot and former air traffic controller, directing the FAA's Air Traffic Control Service during 1959–1963. (FAA.)

(Left) This radio navigation facility, the VORTAC, transmits radio signals giving pilots their location from the station. Over 800 of these and other radio aids are in operation along more than 350,000 miles of airways in the nation. (FAA.)

(Above) An FAA maintenance inspector reviews drawings
with an airline mechanic during a routine check on procedures at an airline overhaul base. By 1966 the FAA had
certified over 120,000 aviation mechanics. (FAA.)

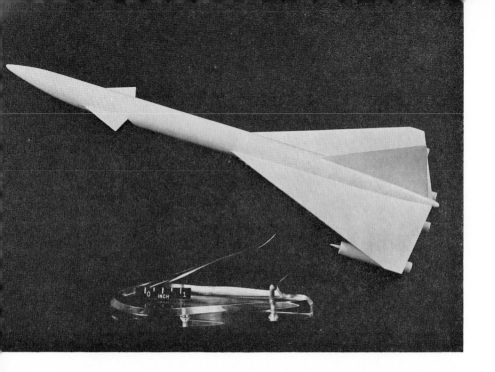

(Above) This model is typical of the fixed-wing designs under consideration in the late '60's for supersonic commercial air transport. (National Aeronautics and Space Administration.)   (Below) This model of the supersonic commercial air transport (SCAT) is shown with the variable sweep wing in the high sweep position for supersonic flight. The FAA continues to push for supersonic passenger service by the 1970's. (National Aeronautics and Space Administration.)

11

POSTWAR EXPANSION, HEARTACHES, SUCCESSES—1945-1959

GUIDING America's civil aviation program through the stages of conversion from war to peace and the long anticipated growth in traffic and equipment proved to be a formidable task for the Civil Aeronautics Administration and the Civil Aeronautics Board. In a sense, the war years aided long-established air carriers—after all, utilizing the alloted equipment to the utmost frequency brought rewards in the form of near capacity traffic geared to the military enterprise. However, this new and exciting era in commercial aviation would occasion a variety of problems and mistakes as other American transport innovations had done in the past.

After VE and VJ days, Americans could anticipate traveling on faster and larger four-engine craft, the likes of which had been used by the military during 1941–1945. Furthermore, hundreds of medium-sized communities would now anticipate the advent of regularly scheduled passenger service serving their towns as well as the major cities served by the trunk lines. Then, too, federal authorities would be confronted with a number of daring, enterprising, and sometimes most competent flying veterans who sought to establish their own passenger and freight services, holding in disdain any and all restrictions on their practice of free enterprise. New and better equipment arrived simultaneously with the trying decisions necessary to implement for civilian use the several wartime electronic aids, the foremost of which entailed various types of radar. The CAA and CAB labored

213

diligently for the most part to solve these tangles but, as usual, produced less than maximum results because of continual political pressure—much of it from Congress—revolving around the perennial question of administrative organization, particularly whether the Department of Commerce should have a voice in the control of aviation. An unusually high rate of turnover in the positions of administrator (CAA) and members (CAB) reflected this unwarranted and unwise political influence concerning scientific and economic matters. Politicians, of course, must not receive all of the blame for changing leadership. In certain instances the rewards of a return to private enterprise or the disinclination to endure further Washington's "bureaucratic whirl" brought about natural attrition.

ADMINISTRATORS, PERSONNEL

T. P. Wright, who assumed the CAA's top position during the war, continued in that status until 1948, though political rumblings were heard against his capable leadership. Republican Senator William Langer, North Dakota, wanted President Harry S. Truman to fire Wright, charging that Wright held interests in the Curtiss-Wright Corporation. Wright immediately sent Langer a copy of his resignation from Curtiss-Wright, dated January 30, 1941.[1] Wright retained Truman's support until tendering his resignation on January 11, 1948.[2] One detects a note of disappointment here over Wright's failure to be offered the job as Assistant Secretary of Commerce for Aviation, though Wright also cited outside offers with higher salaries. Wright became President of the Cornell Research Foundation and Vice-President of Cornell University with the main responsibility of administering the Cornell Aeronautical Laboratory at Buffalo.

D. W. Rentzel, administrator for the next two years (beginning in June, 1948), had served with American Airlines during 1930–1943, advancing to the position of Director of Communications. Rentzel, a pilot, was President of Aeronautical Radio, Incorporated, for the next five years before heading the CAA.[3] Rentzel accepted an appointment to the CAB in 1950, and Donald W. Nyrop became administrator. Nyrop, a graduate of Doane College (Nebraska), later earned an LL.B. at George Washington University and served as an attorney for the old Civil Aeronautics Authority (later the CAB). Nyrop served with the Air Transport Command during 1942–1946 then worked with the Air Transport Association until 1948 when he became Rentzel's deputy in the

CAA.[4] The rapid changeover within the CAB brought Nyrop over to that agency within the following six months, whereupon Charles F. Horne received the nod to head the CAA. Horne, a Naval Academy graduate, received the M.S. at Harvard (1935) in communications and electronic engineering. Returning to the Navy, Horne played a major role in the development of shipboard radar plotting and other communications while participating in the campaigns at Tarawa and Okinawa. He became Deputy Chief of Naval Communications in 1946, serving on numerous committees geared to coordinating technical developments within the military for civilian use, and headed the U.S. delegation to the International Civil Aviation Organization (ICAO).[5] Horne also had been Director of the CAA's Office of Federal Airways. The change of politics bringing Republican Dwight D. Eisenhower to the White House in January, 1953, elevated Deputy Administrator F. B. Lee to the top CAA position. Lee's ouster in December, 1955, touched off a raging debate in aviation circles within Congress. Nevertheless, Lee, a Republican, could not get along with his superior Louis S. Rothschild, Commerce Undersecretary for Transportation, a story which will be related in more detail later in this chapter.

Charles J. Lowen, Jr., Lee's successor, had already received the political blessings of the Eisenhower Administration when he became second in command of the CAA in July, 1955. A 1938 graduate from the University of Colorado and a pilot, Lowen worked in aviation sales until 1942 when he joined the Air Transport Command. For three years after the war he held various administrative positions with Capital Airlines, after which he served Denver as Director of Aviation until 1951. Lowen then went into the automobile business before returning to city government in Denver as Manager of Safety and Excise (1954).[6] Tragedy ended the career of this young administrator; Lowen died of cancer on September 5, 1956, at the age of forty-one. Once again the second highest official in the CAA received the foremost position. James Pyle, born in 1913 and a Princeton University graduate of 1935, worked for Pan American Airways until navy service during 1944–1946. Pyle held all types of pilot ratings and for the next seven years worked in private aviation at Denver. Before joining the CAA, Pyle in 1953 became Assistant to the Assistant Secretary of Navy for Air, concentrating his duties on traffic control.[7] Pyle remained as administrator during the CAA's final years as an appendage of Commerce, which ended in 1959.

It would be sheer folly to condemn the entire leadership of the CAA during 1945–1959 just because the administrators "popped in and out of office like ping-pong balls off a table." Doubtless the frequent shifts brought confusion and lack of continuity in technical programs, hence, less than top performance within the CAA. Lack of agreement between the CAA and Commerce, and between the CAA and the military was responsible for much of this unhappy impasse in addition to congressional interference. These controversies will be taken up later as they pertain to individual CAA activities.

MORALE PROBLEMS

Personnel problems in the CAA during 1945–1958 seemed little different in essence than earlier, or, for that matter, from the type of complaints and difficulties inherent in other governmental offices, human nature being the imperfect entity that it is. Congressmen scorned the low morale in the aviation safety activities of the CAA as related in 1952 by *Aviation Week*. This journal editorially blasted Director E. S. Hensley and Deputy William Davis as the only men of GS-13 rank who were not compelled, by their own choice, to take examinations for reorganization.[8] Referring to the Hensley-Davis clique, the editors cited other journalists' allegations that men in aviation safety smuggled liquor into the United States on aircraft. Bear in mind that the complaints remained anonymous, the critics explaining secrecy as necessary to protect the CAA informants. A random check of such complaints revealed the following:

> The stench of politics, the intrigue, and the petty cabals. . . . The output in work units in Aviation Safety could be equaled by a 9-year-old moron in an iron lung. . . . The men who are tapped . . . are the men who are 'on the team.' . . . If we object, we are transferred, down-graded, demoted in position, and made the subject of gibes. . . . Never has the morale been so low, the prestige so diminished, and the confidence so lacking. . . . Selections are political, despite promises of National Promotion Plan, written examination, oral interview, and group interview. . . .[9]

Nor must one be lulled into the belief that all field personnel of the CAA were beyond reproach. An unsavory case allegedly existed in Pittsburgh, Pennsylvania, reportedly dating back to 1939. Administrator Wright, upon inheriting the problem, asked Commerce officials to investigate. Subsequently, a board consisting of the Department's chief investigator, the chief classification officer, and the CAA's personnel director spent months searching out the facts. The results electrified CAA employees. Dismissals were requested for the regional administrator and the superintendent of safety regulations, both in New York; a CAA man formerly in charge of inspection at Pittsburgh; in addition to one CAA employee and his secretary—both at Pittsburgh. Other CAA officials were transferred elsewhere. The charges were:

   (1) Issuance of airmen's certificates without flight tests for friends.

   (2) Discrimination as to approving aviation mechanical school.

   (3) Collusion on written exams.

   (4) General unsuitability—improper relations with women amounting to public notoriety, in the case of the one employee at Pittsburgh.[10]

The summary of the case indicates that the Pittsburgh employee fought his dismissal for three years. CAA leaders were deeply chagrined by the undercover support extended the accused by some quarters of the CAA: "The effect of this test case on the morale of CAA field personnel cannot be exaggerated."[11] Secretary Averell Harriman wrote Harry B. Mitchell, President of the U.S. Civil Service Commission, that he wanted the individual "out."[12]

Less serious personnel difficulties focused attention on the perennial shortage of trained key employees at one time or another in all types of positions, even those clerical in nature. The federal security program instituted during the Korean emergency, while invoked for the obvious reason of guarding against subversives, led to consternation among officials attempting to carry on their normal business. For example, one had to be careful to employ only stenographers with the proper security clearance (replete with all the bureaucratic delay and red tape) for dictation.[13] One girl had to be cleared in order to record dictation concerning soils and paving of runways. The office of airports at Austin reported a jam in clerical routine because of the high turnover of help and delay in getting new people checked. Veteran CAA leader H. A. Hook summarized the dilemma for his region at Los Angeles: "This classification of 'sensitive' has haunted us ever since the labor market became tight, and now that I have been in the field for four years . . . to study this problem, it is strongly recommended that immediate steps be taken to declassify from the 'sensitive' category all positions except a few which can be truly critical in nature."[14]

Finally, Administrator Rentzel came under pressure for dismissal by some disgruntled interests who asserted that he was incompetent. Typical of the "ammunition" was an account by Drew Pearson describing the occasion when Rentzel sent a CAA plane to fly Senators Homer Capehart and Owen Brewster to a Notre Dame football game, from which diversion Brewster traveled on to fulfill an $800 speaking engagement.[15]

CHECKING PILOTS AND AIRPLANES

A great many of the leading problems confronting the CAA following World War II resulted from the increased usage of the airways by the armed forces. Technology, too, brought its share of new crises. The tremendous influx of military aviators into peacetime aeronautics placed a major strain on CAA inspectors though, of course, this increased activity had long been anticipated. The CAA and CAB authorities reluctantly allowed manufacturers wider leeway in testing planes and engines before formal certification, authorizing 2,000 industrial specialists to perform annual inspections and inspections following major repairs.[16] Not all quarters issued plaudits for this leniency. William T. Piper, of the Piper Aircraft Corporation, reportedly suggested that the CAA should accept a new aircraft only after the manufacturer had ridden in the plane for 500 hours.[17] Indeed, mechanical "bugs" in the DC–6 and the Lockheed Constellation soon after the war led some observers to attribute the difficulties to faulty original inspection by industry and the CAA. One critic informed the White House that manufacturing engineers and CAA men should have discovered the need for changes in a DC–6 delivered to President Truman; changes which necessitated four groups of modifications to make the craft safe.[18]

Administrator Wright, recipient of the Guggenheim Award for aviation in 1945, informed congressmen of several tests performed on aircraft, including the use of sand in filling a plane to determine load factors. Sand was poured onto a wing until the wing separated from the plane, revealing the breaking-point weight. Fuel tanks were "jiggled" until the vibration caused a break. This same test was applied to the wings to ascertain the likelihood of flutter at high speeds. The normal landing load placed on the landing gear could be tested by filling the plane with sand, lifting it 3 to 5 feet off the floor, and dropping it (dead weight).[19] Industry performed many of these tests with spot checks by CAA personnel. Early in 1949, J. J. O'Connell, Chairman of the CAB, testified before a congressional subcommittee that both the industry and the CAA erred in allowing the original placing of the overflow gasoline vents on the DC–6. After two airborne fires, killing all aboard on one flight, the vents were ordered relocated.[20]

Further disagreement between the CAA and CAB ensued over the Lockheed Constellation as CAA officials maintained that Administrator Wright had failed to gain CAB acceptance of his request to increase the test period of the new craft to 500 hours.[21] E. M. Sturhahn, Wright's Executive Assistant, told the House Subcommittee on Appropriations that Eastern, due to Eddie Rickenbacker's decision following the perusal of Lockheed reports, had delayed purchase of the "Connie" until the "bugs" had been worked out. Airborne fires in 1947 led Wright to ground the "Connies" until modification could be made in the supercharger device which pressurized the cabin. TWA suffered most from difficulties with the Constellations; American and United felt the brunt of the DC–6 grounding for six months. The CAB already accepted, at least in theory, the fact that the new models required longer testing because of the many difficulties, both mechanical and maintenance, occurring in the initial stages of operations.[22]

Despite the above reservations, the CAA, under an economy drive invoked from the White House and Commerce, further cut its inspection of the air carriers in 1954.[23] Senator Pat McCarran, long-time friend of the CAA, lamented to Administrator Lee that industry had now been given too much authority in matters of safety: "There are still those in industry who have the same state of mind as the manufacturer who once told a former CAA administrator: 'You can wipe out all pilot regulations for all I care. The more they crack 'em up, the more planes I build.' "[24] Again, McCarran reminded Lee of the bitter fights by manufacturers over changes to eliminate some dangerous flight characteristics of an airplane.

Obviously, the delegation of certain inspection duties to industry proved inevitable after the war. The rechecking of each pilot within an airline every six months was now accomplished by the industry's chief pilot under CAA supervision, meaning spot checking as well as detailing of specific items on which to test the pilots.[25] General agreement on inspection procedures and rules was not always forthcoming. For example, the Army desired to have its planes designed to meet CAA as well as military specifications; the Air Force opposed this stipulation. The CAA, with no axe to grind, watched the controversy from the sidelines, realizing its past difficulties with one military craft, the C–46.[26] Furthermore, the Air Force requested that its contract carriers (nonmilitary) be allowed to operate outside the basic authority of the Civil Air Regulations and that military personnel be allowed to repair civil aircraft.[27] In 1958, disagreement arose in the CAA over the question of engine testing, specifically whether to have decentralization of engine testing or to designate one office for this task. Industry favored the latter plan.[28] Meanwhile, the inspection of air-navigation facilities presented another dilemma because of the need for additional pressurized CAA craft to replace the existing DC–3's and Beechcrafts. Most of the discarded military craft given to the CAA right after the war hardly qualified to meet the necessity of gaining higher altitudes. One CAA inspection crew was lost on January 21, 1948, near Ward, Colorado; the wreckage was located four months later.[29]

The onrushing jet age brought a flurry of activity among inspectors who must learn to fly and inspect the new craft before supervising the certification of these planes and jet pilots. The CAA had the authorization already in 1950 (Public Law No. 867) for the testing of jets. But appropriations were not forthcoming when Administrator Horne asked for White House aid in February, 1952.[30] A jet training program, utilizing a Lockheed T–33 trainer and two F–80C Shooting Stars, was later undertaken at the CAA center in Oklahoma City.[31] Governmental aid to jet testing loomed as one of the most important proposals in the early fifties. Introduction of the British Comet, though this craft was doomed some months after inauguration of flights, spurred on the discussion in Washington, D.C. Senator Edwin C. Johnson, Democrat of Colorado, favored a CAB plan whereby the government would lend 75 per cent of the costs (a maximum of $15 million) repayable in ten years at 1 per cent interest. For every plane sold to an American line, the obligation would be reduced by $1 million. In addition, the CAB would underwrite operation of jet all cargo service for twelve months and a minimum of 2,000 hours of service tests.[32] The target date for commercial jets was set as 1957–1958, a prognostication missed by just a few months.[33] The long-sought legislation enabling the CAB to guarantee loans to aviation companies became law on September 7, 1957 (Public Law No. 85–307).[34]

By summer, 1958, the Fokker F–27 (turboprop) and the British Britannia (jet) had been certified; the Lockheed Electra (turboprop), DC–8, Boeing 707, and Convair 880 were among those for which final approval was pending.[35]

NEW REGULATIONS

Changes in the Civil Air Regulations, always a reflection of the CAA's endeavors to improve aviation's safety record, included a variety of enactments—along with controversy—during the postwar years. Nonairline operations also provided authorities with a number of causes for regulations applying to such activities as: ambulance service, searching for coyotes and for lost persons, eagle hunting, air police, heading off wild game, or determining amounts of snow in remote areas.[36] The expanding number of nonscheduled operations came within CAR control in the following areas: limitations on the amount of flying time for pilots, fuel reserves (forty-five minutes), major overhauling of engines after 1,000 hours, checking out instrument-flying pilots every six months, and strict compliance with all CAA minimum rules for ceiling and visibility. The old minimum flight altitude of 500 feet was amended in August, 1945, to benefit crop dusting, mail pickups, and other special services. No minimum requirement was placed on open country or over water; the 500-foot minimum applied to sparsely settled areas. A minimum of 1,000 feet was invoked over cities and congested regions. Another postwar innovation entailed a written examination over the CAR's before the student pilot's solo flight. The more widespread use of the ILS system—thirty-five in operation by early 1947—necessitated revised rules concerning ceiling and visibility at these locations. The CAA imposed absolute minimums of a 200-foot ceiling and ½-mile visibility for scheduled airlines.

Flight recorders, required earlier (up to June 9, 1944) until a scarcity of necessary materials forced a repeal of the order, were required again, effective June 30, 1948. The type utilized—recorded on 2 inches of tape per hour—indicated continuous altitude of the craft, in addition to all vertical accelerations encountered in rough air or maneuvering. Improvement in the mechanism was still needed. Terrain indicators, showing altitudes of 2,000 and 1,000 feet above terrain, became mandatory equipment earlier in 1948 on a two-year experimental basis.[37] Despite all earlier precautions, accidents in rugged terrain occurred leading the CAA to raise the minimum instrument flight rules (IFR) flying altitude above mountain peaks from 1,000 to 2,000 feet. Simultaneously, the minimum daytime altitude for visual flight rules (VFR) operations was raised to 1,000 feet above the mountains, and the night minimum in unlighted areas over mountains—also for VFR—to 2,000 feet. A military-civilian feud brought the CAB acceptance of both nautical miles and knots, effective July 1, 1952. Another alteration in radio brought the adoption—with ICAO instigation—of the new, phonetic alphabet retaining only "Victor" from the celebrated names American GI's and the public heard—especially "Able, Baker, Charley"—during World War II.[38] Difficulties of translation into other languages, expressed by the ICAO, led the CAB to adopt the term "visual" instead of "contact." Also in 1946, the CAB changed its "see-and-be-seen" rules to require use of the pilot's magnetic heading to determine correct altitude instead of the former proximity to clouds. Other rules pertaining to traffic control will be discussed under that topic.

A controversy arose during the fifties over what the ALPA cited as excessive flying time for pilots on long trips. Senators McCarran, Barry Goldwater, Herman Welker (Idaho), and Johnson (Colorado) unsuccessfully requested a flat eight-hour day for airline pilots.[39] Clarence Sayen, ALPA boss, charged that often a scheduled eight-hour flight actually meant nine hours, citing rare cases in which a pilot was on duty twenty or more continuous hours. During the Korean struggle, the CAB lifted its twelve-hour rule, allowing two-pilot crews to fly continuously for sixteen or seventeen hours. Sayen depicted the pilot as caught in the middle, the CAB advising him to stop the trip if fatigued and the airline threatening discharge from duty if the schedule were not completed.

During the postwar years, the CAA and CAB continued their vigilance in other aspects of a medical nature, receiving congressional criticism, however, for allowing (1946) private pilots to obtain physical exams from their own doctors.[40] To describe a general laxity in medical standards, Senator John Bricker (Republican of Ohio) in 1952 cited the fatal heart attack suffered by a nonscheduled pilot, causing death to twenty-six passengers and two other crewmen. However, Bricker admitted that the pilot flew despite a CAA ruling confining him to company check-pilot duties.[41] Nevertheless, Bricker asserted that the ICC maintained more rigid standards for truck drivers than did the CAA for pilots, now allowing thirty-three diabetics to fly in some capacity.

Bricker's accusations appeared a bit harsh in this instance. The CAA consistently warned pilots of physical deterrents to safety, even citing the use of sulfa drugs and dramamine as being particularly dangerous.[42]

ENFORCEMENT

Violations of the CAR's detected among pilots—private, scheduled, or nonscheduled—or the air carriers continued to occupy a shamefully large portion of man-hours in both the CAA and CAB—shameful because of the lack of responsibility inherent in the violators. In 1948, an airline pilot's certificate to carry passengers for hire was permanently revoked and his pilot license lost for engaging the plane's gust lock while in flight. The plane dived several thousand feet before the copilot brought it under control at approximately 400–500 feet, saving the forty-nine passengers and crew of five. Reaffirming a similar decision in 1939, the federal authorities labeled this case "a shocking revelation of human failure which fortunately is rare among the airline pilots of this country. . . ."[43] The reader of enforcement proceedings listed in the *Civil Aeronautics Journal* could locate each month dozens of examples of action directed against the acrobat, one pilot losing his license for three months after flying low and completing acrobatics over Champaign, Illinois, on October 31, 1948. In fact, the CAA issued pleas for citizens to report to the nearest CAA station any cases of "buzzing" or other violations.[44] Simultaneously, pilots received the perennial warning to file their flight plans. Among the alleged "buzzers" one finds the name of television star Arthur Godfrey, who reportedly "buzzed" the airport tower at Teterboro, New Jersey, losing his license for six months.[45] Later the CAA's regional office in Chicago forwarded charges by Ozark Air Lines claiming that Godfrey "crowded" one of its planes, a DC–3, by flying his own modified DC–3 just 100 feet off its right wing and then crossing directly in front of the Ozark plane.

Suspension of a pilot's license prior to a CAB hearing caused the ALPA to request and gain from the CAA an unprecedented discussion session early in 1957. Involved was Captain Leonard Specht, a TWA pilot, who was cited for "leaving an assigned altitude without proper clearance and allegedly creating a mid-air collision hazard."[46] According to authorities, Specht wanted to move from 14,000 feet to 18,000 feet; a nearby Capital plane was located at 16,000 feet. From the tape, officials claimed they heard: "You get that traffic out of 16,000. I'm going up there. Do you want to run into somebody? You didn't miss me by very much." Obviously, the key question involved whether Specht had declared an emergency. The CAB claimed, after its official hearing, that Specht used his emergency power in truculence and anger. The report charged that Specht had not been confronted with a severe icing condition.[47] Tremendous pressure from the ALPA was brought to bear on the CAB and CAA in this case. Naturally no written proof is available, but one might conjecture that such ALPA pressure had a part in what some observers would consider a light punishment—a six-month suspension of the pilot's air transport rating but retention of the commercial pilot's certificate, enabling Specht to serve as a copilot. During the hearing, CAA controllers resented the cross-examination by CAB examiner S. Thomas Simon who neither condemned nor condoned their actions in the case. To his credit, Specht's prior record was unblemished. The kindest readers' letters to *Aviation Week* referred to the "emergency," while the other extreme called for "the book" to be thrown at Specht.

Airlines came in for periodic scrutiny disclosing numerous violations. Operations of Northeast Airlines, a very rapidly expanding postwar carrier, underwent a two-month check by the CAA in 1958, resulting in the necessity of further instrument-flight training for at least nine pilots.[48] The CAA gained full cooperation from the airline and planned similarly thorough inspections of other carriers. Thirty-day emergency suspensions were imposed on two large irregulars (nonscheduled carriers) in 1955. The charges encompassed operating with unqualified airmen, an excess of pilot flight time, exceeding the required time limits for inspection, and overloading of aircraft.[49]

The CAB checked on another airline abuse—overbooking— along the East Coast, finding only one such violation in a month by one carrier compared to 130 such violations in the same month committed by another airline.[50] Admittedly, the overbooking was usually cancelled out by a much higher number of "no-shows." Indeed, the three-month CAB study revealed a total of 500 over-sales to some 43,000 "no-shows." What bothered the air-minded, then and now, is the fact that no legitimate purchaser should legally be refused a seat despite the possibility that individuals might fail to appear for a trip. The CAB charged that victims were often illegally placated with cash or a free trip on a different flight. The problem of overbooking affected all strata of the

American scene. Legislatively, ticket agents came under CAB control on July 14, 1952.[51] Two formal actions against their tactics followed within a year. Senator Margaret Chase Smith, Republican of Maine, reported, in 1956, being stranded trying to travel between Washington, D.C., and Maine "because there were five oversold reservations waiting for my place."[52] A year later, the CAB charged Eastern and National with deliberate overbooking and Delta and Eastern for misleading advertising.[53] Senator Smith also scored the "too favorable" weather reports issued to the public by the airlines. A Capital Airlines ticket agent received criminal court fines and suspended sentences for allegedly selling fares below tariffs on five occasions.[54] The former president of one airline was fined $22,000 for twenty counts each of falsification of records and granting unauthorized free transportation.[55]

AIRPORTS' SERIOUS LIMITATIONS

Nowhere could the growing pains of 1945–1958 be more dramatically witnessed than in the ground facilities available to aviation in America. The increase of overcrowded conditions in many areas was menacing to airports. In the first place, urban expansion, usually totally without the blessing of community planning, surrounded existing airports which now required greater facilities to service larger aircraft and increased traffic. Second, in several instances, two or more airports serving commercial and military operations in the same city now lacked sufficient spacing for optimum safety, again because of increased speed and traffic.

Few would question the validity of federal aid to airports during World War II. The peacetime continuation of this support from Washington brought a number of headaches. Inadequacy of present airports—lack of ILS and adequate lighting—loomed as a prominent criticism in a special study completed in 1947 by the American Institute for Research, Pittsburgh, under a contract from the National Research Council's Committee on Aviation Psychology.[56] Interviewed were 270 airline pilots, 42 CAA inspectors, and 16 company check pilots. The nonstandardization of cockpits and instruments, along with the absence of vhf radio ranges, also gained prominent mention.

President Truman, an ardent supporter of commercial aviation, showed particular interest in the entire airport program. The Federal Airport Act of 1946 now stressed inclusion of the smaller cities long neglected under the defense-minded previous expenditures.[57] What perplexed aviation planners was the fact that by 1959 the total of $520 million appropriated under the Act had not been expended.[58] Shortly after World War II, an initial note of rivalry appeared with the suggestion that the Federal Works Agency (FWA) and the state highway officials coordinate the airport construction program. Assistant Secretary of Commerce William A. Burden protested to Commerce Secretary Henry A. Wallace, who personally intervened with President Truman. Wallace received the wise assurance that the CAA should direct the appropriations; the FWA and the states could do the actual construction.[59] Wallace correctly pointed to the CAA's role since 1940 in contracting for and supervising construction at 500 airports, costing some $400 million. Usually those experts highly critical of the CAB's economic regulation in general also scored the CAA's airport aid. Two writers called for state planning, concentration on the large airports first, and self-sufficiency of airports.[60]

By 1949, CAA leaders had testified before a congressional subcommittee of the aid program (which was lagging) that sixteen states were not utilizing this support.[61] Over 60 per cent of the funds spent in the three years went to the large airports (Class IV with 7,000-foot runways). Two years later the entire program was jeopardized because of some individual carelessness brought to the attention of congressmen. An investigation was prompted because several employees allegedly allowed their families to ride in government autos.[62] Congressman John J. Rooney (New York), charging boondoggling in the program, criticized the dispatching of one CAA man from Washington, D.C., to Roanoke, Virginia, for the purpose of informing the local airport manager how to cook his hot dogs better.[63]

AIR POLICY COMMISSION

Among the many studies of aviation ordered by President Truman was the President's Air Policy Commission, which reported its findings after more than five months' labor on January 13, 1948.[64] Rickenbacker, President of Eastern Air Lines, considered ground aids obsolete and inefficient, citing the war as the reason. He also felt the airport policy to be a political football and stressed the fact that many airports established for the military were not in sound commercial locations which might lend themselves to strong civilian use. President Truman, cognizant of the stream of complaints regarding airports, heartily supported the establishment in 1949, of the Airport Advisory Committee to make suggestions to the CAA for improved airports.[65] Promising to "pull no punches," the committee issued the following recommendations:

(1) Continue the Federal Airport Act.

(2) State legislation to exempt commercial and privately owned fields from taxes.

(3) Avoid abandoning airports.

(4) Raise the federal share of funds for land purchase from 25 to 50 per cent.

(5) Improve airport-to-city highways.

(6) Require two-way radio for all aircraft at some airports.

(7) Have weather observations taken closer to the end of runways.

(8) Have voice identification at omniranges.

(9) Increase the proficiency of private fliers (use Air Force ratings and require greater skills).

(10) Increase the number of bleed-off taxiways and warm-up pads.

AIRPORT SPACING

Meanwhile, further controversy arose over spacing of airports. In September, 1950, officials in New York City lamented the inadequacies of La Guardia Field and the need of four major airports in the area within a few years.[66] Secretary of the Navy James Forrestal, whose branch of the military used Floyd Bennett Field, promised aid. In addition, President Truman suggested that civilian operations might also use the navy airport. Hubert H. Humphrey, then Democratic mayor of Minneapolis, appealed to the White House in 1946 for all possible influence to settle a controversy arising over the Veterans Administration's acquisition of a portion of Fort Snelling adjacent to the city airport.[67] Humphrey desired 600 acres for the airport, reminding the President's aide, Matthew Connelly, that Minnesota's only Democratic congressman lived in the Minneapolis-St. Paul area. Finally, Minneapolis-St. Paul received 25.5 acres from the federal authorities under provisions of the Federal Airport Act of 1946. Similar grants materialized elsewhere as Rockford, Illinois, gained land from Camp Grant.[68] President Truman authorized the transfer of lands in the Snoqualmire National Forest to King County, State of Washington. A Texas feud arose between Dallas and Fort

Worth, both Class IV airports, but Fort Worth in 1948 was unable to handle four-engine planes.[69] Love Field (Dallas), with 10,000-foot runways, apparently satisfied Dallas whose delegates to Washington disputed the need of a common airport between the two cities. Petitioners from Kansas City, Kansas, sought White House assistance in their hope to regain use of Fairfax Airport—a a ticklish matter involving a five-year lease to TWA. President Truman advised the War Assets Administration to clear up this matter very soon.[70] Litigation, however, continued for some time.

Most perplexing of all the feuds was the question of airports in the Baltimore-Washington, D.C., area. Only after an Eastern airliner and a military plane collided, did the government act to halt military fighter planes from using Washington National Airport. During the summer of 1949, Maryland's Governor William Preston Lane, Jr., informed President Truman of his visit with Thomas B. Bourne, former twenty-year veteran with the CAA, whose firm of private airport engineers now wished to work on the new airport to serve Washington, D.C. Lane, "plugging" Bourne as a lifelong Democrat from the eastern shore of Maryland, was informed that no federal appropriations had yet been allocated for such a project.[71] President Truman, long interested in another major airport for the capital city, believed that few of the big city airports had been planned well. He informed Governor Lane that he disfavored the use of an airport 30 miles from town—Baltimore's brand-new Friendship Airport.[72] Obviously, the Maryland politicians and citizens of Baltimore were chagrined to learn that their fine new air facility would not receive the blessing as the airport to relieve pressure from Washington National. Even suave requests from Senator Millard Tydings would not sway the President from his decision, which seemed to him the only logical choice. In January, 1950, Truman, Rentzel, and R. P. Boyle of the CAA, and R. B. Landry of the Air Force visited potential sites near Washington. Truman gave the go-ahead for a site west of Washington, D.C., known as Burke.[73] Another proposed site, Chantilly, was not visited as it was then considered too distant from the city. Nevertheless, the furor continued unabated with Maryland Governor Theodore R. McKeldin urging Truman eighteen months later to abandon the Burke plans. Truman refused, asserting that the "capital of the world must be adequately served."[74] Truman's special group known as the Airport Use Committee approved the new site in November, 1950. In Congress, Marylanders beat the drums for

Friendship which, they declared, averaged only 17 minutes of "stacking" time though located 30 miles and over 45 minutes driving time from Washington.[75] The Burke site is 14 miles and about 28 minutes from the capital. After expending over $1,703,-250 on the new project, the House voted 128 to 41 to block additional funds in 1952. Senator Harry Byrd, Democrat of Virginia, along with several citizen's groups in Fairfax County, Virginia, opposed the new site.

Under the Eisenhower Administration, a supplemental appropriation of $12.5 million was granted in 1957 for the establishment of a new airport at Chantilly.[76] Meanwhile, CAA officials told congressmen that sale of the land at Burke was being negotiated. Almost a decade elapsed since the original zeal of the Truman era until Congress finally decided where to place the new field. This was certainly not a proud record which left the capital without a landing field for commercial jets in 1959 just because of political rivalry and indecision. The sole consistency revealed that Friendship would not be the permanent second capital airport. Meanwhile, the Maryland delegation entered a plea with the CAB to designate Friendship as Washington's alternate field until the new airport was built. The board investigated but came to no decision during this era. Board members realized that they simply could not force the airlines to use Friendship for nonjet operations any more than they could later force the carriers to retain operations at Midway in Chicago after O'Hare Field was opened.[77] During the Senate debate over the Burke-Chantilly-Friendship case, the CAA's opposition to Friendship was attributed to its position on the main airlanes between New York–Washington and Washington–Philadelphia.[78] Senator A. S. (Mike) Monroney, Democrat of Oklahoma, likened the current squabble to the slowness in establishing the original Washington National Airport. Then President Franklin Roosevelt simply took the matter out of Congress' hands by ordering the WPA to begin the project despite the delays caused by objections of property owners. The property owners and officials of Fairfax County contributed to the delay at the Burke site—the whole issue becoming a popularity contest instead of a question of engineering feasibility. Public Law No. 762 (1950) allowed the Secretary of Commerce to select a site. Senator Spessard V. Holland of Florida, disagreeing with Monroney, stressed the CAA's lack of consideration for the 200,000 people in Fairfax County, the impending jet noise, cutting into the watershed, and the routing of flights over Fairfax High School. The entire matter would arise again for debate, but Chantilly ultimately became the new site.

THE PRESIDENT'S AIRPORT COMMISSION

President Truman realized the need for additional information about the nation's airports as he witnessed the beginnings of the fight over a new field near the capital and in 1952 called upon General James H. Doolittle to head the President's Airport Commission, a temporary investigatory body.[79] Doolittle, then employed by the Shell Oil Company, was assisted on the Commission by Dr. Jerome Hunsaker, Head of the Department of Aeronautical Engineering at Massachusetts Institute of Technology; Administrator Horne, CAA; and S. Paul Johnson, Director, Institute of Aeronautical Sciences, who served as executive secretary. The voluminous file compiled by the group indicates a variety of problems discernible in 1952, many of them embracing aviation in general, not airports alone.[80] All segments of the aeronautical world had an opportunity to correspond with the committee; many individuals were interviewed. Here is just a sampling of the detailed findings:

(1) The ALPA complained of a television aerial right in line with a takeoff lane at Kansas City.

(2) The pilots' spokesman (ALPA) also felt that only the CAA, not a city, had the power to close an airport (Newark had been shut down by the New York Port Authority).

(3) Sayen congratulated the CAA and airport management at Chicago. He favored 10,000-foot runways but deplored single runways in certain instances, e.g., at Denver.

(4) There should be a separation of instrument and VFR traffic.

(5) The ALPA stood firmly against state or municipal control of air commerce.

(6) Sayen lamented the lack of reverse propellers on numerous planes.

Continuing their search for improvement, the President's Airport Commission commended Wold-Chamberlain (Minneapolis-St. Paul) Airport's fire and crash equipment but observed many pilots making unusually low approaches and advised the use of preferential runways (use of separate directions for takeoffs and landings) as well as the relocation of the control tower for better view of all runways. At Milwaukee, local CAA officials advised the closing of a short runway (2,600 feet), which sent traffic over a school with 800 students, obstruction lights for two large smokestacks, and a change in local rules regarding turns in the traffic pattern. Use of a definite runway—wind permitting—precluded planes flying over residential areas at Cincinnati. Noise and no runway marking lights appeared to be major problems at Detroit City Airport, a field recommended for closure to traffic over 35,000 pounds. Trees needed topping at the Paducah, Kentucky, airport which was named after Vice-President Alben Barkley. On the other hand, noise was not a problem at Kansas City; the ALPA also lauded noise abatement cooperation at La Guardia Field, New York.

Low-altitude flying over densely populated areas at Elizabeth, New Jersey, led the New York Port Authority to close the Newark airport on February 11, 1952, following three crashes and the loss of 119 lives. Local citizens had complained bitterly, and the field was reopened only on a limited basis in June, 1952. Despite the aviation world's displeasure over the closing, it would seem that such action was plausible to placate a city harassed in such unusual fashion, even though ill luck had seemingly caused this series of crashes. This hazard, the Commission found, was not restricted to Elizabeth. Experts pointed to the same phenomenon at Chicago and San Diego's Lindbergh Field. C. F. Watkins, City Manager of Alexandria, Virginia, complained of planes legally "turning in" over that city for landings at Washington National. Chairman Doolittle noted that a pilot must not compromise the safety of his passengers to avoid annoying people. Howard Hughes, the controversial TWA magnate, hoped for legislation prohibiting housing and other habitation near runways. Sensible airport planning in the twenties and thirties could have promoted Hughes' dream and prevented most of the nation's complaints about noise around airfields. But without such planning, it would seem foolish to protect those individuals so naive as to live nearby and then complain about noise.

Signed resolutions from the existing Airport Advisory Committee, Airport Operators Council, and the American Association of Airport Executives advised Doolittle to recommend: maximum noise levels in volume and pitch, a general campaign of noise reduction, use of preferential runways, zoning, military use of fields only when necessary, and the impracticality of relocating airports.[81] Dr. Hunsaker alerted Doolittle to the sound way in which Massachusetts had assumed the responsibility for approach and landing patterns; Boston's Logan Airport provided a model. Hunsaker believed that states should take the responsibility to alleviate nuisances and hazards incidental to air access to airports.[82]

Throughout their investigation, Doolittle and his colleagues found CAA officials most cooperative in uncovering problems and suggesting remedies. Former Administrator Wright—summarizing research limitations—bemoaned the lack of reliable devices to warn of fire; cited the need of further research on propellers; and warned of fires caused by carrying of matches, lighter fluids, and certain chemicals.[83] Doolittle, Hunsaker, and Administrator Horne issued their report, *The Airport and Its Neighbors*, on May 16, 1952.[84] Highlights of the lengthy study summarized most of the recommendations already cited, placing heavy emphasis on airport planning and zoning, state and local responsibility along with federal help, priority to runways, altitudes for circling and maneuvering, additional training of flight crews, restriction of military training flights, development of the helicopter for widespread use, CAA certification of airports, and more positive air control.

CONGRESSIONAL INQUIRY

Unhappily, as so often happens, sound advice from advisory committees becomes lost in a maze of bureaucratic bewilderment, in this instance the inability of the military and civilian aspects of aviation to resolve their differences. Additional feuds and sorrows occurred before remedies could be effected. In 1953, Cliff Clevenger, Republican of Ohio and new chairman of the House Appropriations Subcommittee, lashed out against the CAA's airport program.[85] Utilizing a former agent of the Federal Bureau of Investigation to gather their ammunition, Clevenger and his associates bemoaned the unused space in the terminal at Orlando, Florida. They questioned whether the value of burley tobacco for our military troops and allies warranted the new terminal building at Bowling Green, Kentucky, for the average load of three passengers per day. Clevenger ridiculed the justification of projects at Dublin, Georgia, in the name of Veterans Administration (VA) ambulance planes operating there when only one patient had used an airplane in over four years. But in the Senate, McCarran raked Administrator Lee for excluding new airports in the askings for 1954.[86] A proposed cutback in funds providing operation and maintenance of municipal airports brought a strong protest from the American Association of Airport Executives through its president, Walter E. Betsworth, Waterloo, Iowa.[87] The advisory service of the CAA proved even more necessary with curtailment of construction caused by the Korean emergency. Furthermore, many airports without a manager depended heavily on this advisory service.

In all fairness to the CAA, James E. Murray, representing Commerce at the hearing, pointed out that airport development had not proceeded at a more rapid pace simply because interest in private flying had failed to increase as quickly as predicted. By 1956, Arkansas, Colorado, Delaware, Georgia, Nevada, and North Carolina were yet without participation in the funds available under the Federal Airport Act of 1946. A prominent feature of the program brought forth state cooperation; no funds were allocated until a state agency certified the need of a facility.[88] Significantly, O'Hare Field, Chicago, destined eventually to replace the crowded Midway as the world's busiest airport, had already received over $9 million under the Act.

The fourteen-month lag between initiation of proposals and first construction persisted, and political tempers flared. Senator Monroney, bemoaning the lingering impasse over a new airport at Washington, D.C., asserted, "I certainly hope the White House or Assistant President Adams, or whoever is running it, will consider the matter."[89] Monroney reminded his colleagues of the ground-minded (as opposed to air-minded) Secretary Sinclair Weeks, formerly with the Pullman Company. Senator Gordon Allott, Colorado, refuted Monroney's charges against Commerce and incoming Administrator Lowen: "No agency in the United States has been so afflicted with inability to get things done as the CAA has been, at least within my last ten years of active interest in it . . . it has been like the proverbial old lady unwilling and unable to make up its mind."[90] Truly, it would seem, the airport program was caught up in a political hassle. Senator Holland reminded Monroney that most of the 126 airports in Florida aided by federal money could be dug up and returned to pastures. During the same year (1956), the smouldering feud between Willow Run and Detroit-Wayne airports erupted.[91] Seven airlines operated at Willow Run on lease from the University of Michigan. Congressman George Meader of Michigan chided the CAA for denying Williow Run any funds while continuing to expend money ($975,000 in 1956) on Wayne, which the airlines refused to use despite the urgings of the Air Coordinating Committee.

CIVIL RIGHTS AND AIRPORTS

The activities of the airport functions of the CAA were concerned with racial discrimination and segregation during this era. As in other facets of the American scene, violence and mass demonstrations were not yet in the order of events. But constantly alert citizens and the few interested politicians questioned the use of federal expenditures for any facility allowing such practices. Regional officials were alerted to investigate racial segregation practices and warned: "You are well aware of the delicacy of this matter . . ."[92] Administrator Lowen advised one inquirer that the CAA withheld funds only for the portion of a building which was segregated.[93] A warning, formulated at the White House and on the departmental level—in this case, Commerce—during the fall of 1955, was relayed to Administrator Lowen suggesting that funds be refused "for use now or in the future for separate racial groups."[94] CAA and Commerce leaders then met on April 6, 1956, to discuss the tighter policy further. Acting Administrator Pyle, upon receiving a petition from the Louisiana congressional delegation protesting the action, advised Congressman Overton Brooks that no basis existed for changing the policy against segregation.[95] The new policy was issued on April 6, 1956, and its major force could naturally be felt in regard to restaurant facilities.[96] The loophole inherent in this position involved the fact that federal money could yet be given to help any airport, even though a part of the building might be paid for entirely by state or local funds. Administrator Pyle continued to receive complaints but summarized his position in a letter to Congressman Charles C. Diggs: "In the absence of a more specific mandate from Congress . . . we have gone as far as we can consistent with the obligation Congress has imposed upon us. . . ."[97] Obviously, as in the case of school desegregation, the burden of proof was left with the Negro or his white supporters to contest any alleged violations in the courts. The CAA maintained that it had actually adopted the new policy during October, 1955, since no funds had been given since that time for segregated accommodations.[98] At least the CAA had effected a beginning action against white supremacy.

NOISE AND THE PUBLIC

Almost immediately following World War II, complaints increased against noise around airports, a problem recognized by the President's Airport Commission.[99] Henceforth, airline officials were urged to keep planes at a minimum of 1,000 feet until the latest possible moment before landing, in addition to the changing of traffic patterns as already discussed. Irate citizens in New York City organized volunteer plane-spotting teams, watching Idlewild and La Guardia airports and charging the CAA and CAB with negligence for allowing planes to "buzz" so low (100 feet), especially from runway 4-22 at La Guardia.[100] A telegram complaining about Idlewild was sent to President Truman.[101] The whole matter resulted in court adjudication after a local ordinance at Cedarhurst, Long Island, banned low flying below 1,000 feet. The ban's effective date of June 15, 1952, was avoided by an injunction. In 1955, the federal district court in Brooklyn, N.Y., ruled against local restrictions of low flying by citing the Civil Aeronautics Act of 1938, which gave the federal government such authority.[102]

NAVIGATION SYSTEMS AND TRAFFIC CONTROL

Seeking to find an improved system of air navigation proved to be one of the major—if not the biggest—problems confronting federal aviation authorities after 1945. First, the use of military radar during World War II led some observers to believe that this new aid would replace the CAA's expanding instrument landing system (ILS). Such could scarcely be the case, for the two communications facilities simply complement each other in the increasingly difficult tasks of landing planes at busy airports in various types of foul weather and at night. The precision beam radar, ground-controlled approach (GCA), was considered imperative for the large centers; ILS was felt to be basic eventually for all airports with regular commercial schedules.[103] By 1948, too, the CAA requested distance measuring equipment (DME). This would transmit to the plane, from the ground omniranges and the localizer of the ILS, the distance in miles from the plane to the DME. GCA, developed by Massachusetts Institute of Technology (MIT), was placed at New York, Chicago, and Washington, D.C., as a gift from the Air Force. One immediately detects a bit of military–CAA rivalry which prompted President Truman to ask and receive from Congress a bill organizing the Air Navigation Development Board (ANDB) to prevent duplication of projects and decide on navigational aids.[104] Secretary Charles Sawyer prevailed upon Ralph S. Damon, President of American Airlines, to agree to serve as chairman of the body.[105] That there was sufficient room for both ILS and GCA was borne out by time. Meanwhile, in 1948, the Radio Technical Commission for Aeronautics was seeking an all-weather air traffic control system by 1963, as reported to President Truman by Secretary Sawyer.

The next major dispute involved the military ultrahigh frequency tactical air navigation aid (TACAN) versus the CAA's continued use of omnirange (VOR) and the uhf DME. Essentially, the military had carried on development of the TACAN system—spending $325 million. By 1954, the CAA and ANDB used $116 million and had installed 411 units of VOR (since 1946) and 332 systems of DME, first ordered in 1950.[106] The ANDB recommended retention of VOR for ten years but immediate discontinuance of DME. On the other hand, the Air Coordinating Committee, with Rothschild, Undersecretary of Commerce for Transportation as chairman, agreed to retain VOR for ten years but to keep DME for five years while implementing the use of TACAN. The average life of a VOR unit was estimated at seven years. The Air Coordinating Committee, established by executive order on September 19, 1946, consisted of nine representatives—one each from Commerce, Treasury, FCC, Bureau of the Budget, and State in addition to three members from Defense.[107] Congressmen argued explosively over the wrangle, demanding a resolution to force a solution. CAA leaders maintained that VOR/DME was not considered good enough for the tactical requirements of the military.[108] Officials of Mohawk Airlines decided to equip their fleet with DME at a cost of $5,000 per unit at a time when only 340 of more than 55,000 planes in the nation were so equipped.

The installation of other radar continued with inauguration of the air-route surveillance type of radar at Norfolk and Jacksonville. Precision-approach radar was ordered for another 12 cities in 1956–1957, and 85 airport-surveillance radars were ordered during the same two years. The CAA and military cooperated in the use of radar at some 43 locations. Finally, the CAA decided to use the VOR system combined with TACAN to form a distance and direction system (VORTAC) facility for civilian services. As a result, the famous slogan "phasing out," heard so often around Washington, D.C., now could be applied to DME, which had cost $12 million.[109] The price of the new program, geared to three years, was $132 million. The Air Force grudgingly transferred

$21 million to the CAA in fiscal 1958 for use on VORTAC facilities. By summer 1960, the CAA hoped to have in use some 606 VORTAC units. Meanwhile, the ANDB turned its attention to yet another project known as SAGE (Semi-Automatic Ground Environment) for the purpose of forming a radar blanket across the nation. Stations were necessary at 200-mile intervals in flat country and 100 miles apart in the mountains.[110] The total planning toward improved radio facilities was encompassed in the new plans of 1957, which will be discussed later in this chapter. SAGE, which combined radar and computers, brought military aircraft to bear on enemy craft. The CAA studied a modification, which might keep aircraft apart.[111]

THE CAA AND THE BERLIN AIRLIFT

One of the most dramatic testimonials to modern air traffic control involved the United States in a most delicate flareup in the Cold War—the Berlin airlift of 1948–1949. Traffic controllers, trained by the CAA, manned the towers while GCA radar proved its worth in addition to the several vhf OMNIS. All the original controllers dispatched were in the military reserve and had been in traffic control during the war.[112] On one typical day, the group handled 1,000 aircraft and 373 instrument approaches at Frankfurt and 25 instrument approaches at Tempelhof—all with just 10 minutes of delay for "vittles" aircraft. One curious innovation involved the elimination of stacking in the holding patterns; each plane missing a landing would return to its point of takeoff. No C–54 was on the ground over 40 minutes, while the maintenance involved 50-hour checks in Germany, 200-hour checks in England, and 1,000-hour checks back in the States. On the average, 90 engines per month as well as 23 tires per day were replaced on the 206 C–54's during this crisis.

APPROACH SYSTEMS

Personnel of the CAA developed another first in landing aids with the introduction of the slope-line system. The late Jerry Sweet along with H. J. Cory Pearson had worked on the project since 1940. The basic feature of the aid consisted of lights in rows showing the pilot a simple funnel of two rows leading him to the end of the runway.[113] Other patterns showed him when he was off to the right or left, too high, or too low. Inexpensive, the unit consisted of 14 sealed-beam bulbs mounted on a board or metal box 10 feet long and 1 foot wide, placed at an angle of 45 degrees to the ground. Authorities considered 200-watt bulbs sufficient for the unit. Certain limitations were inherent concerning the V-shaped system versus the "straight-down-the-middle" approach which the ALPA supported. It was not practical to install the slope-line technique at many airports.[114] Apparently the British-made Decca system was considered to be inferior to U.S. systems. Past experience had shown the need for a number of carefully explained hints issued by the CAA under the title, *Flying the Instrument Landing System*.[115] Pilots were alerted to allow their radio receivers to warm up for at least 10 minutes before an approach and not to deviate in course over 2 degrees. Pilots were also advised not to be alarmed by momentary oscillations of the localizer needle and that wind direction and velocity have a great effect on descent.

THE "CURTIS REPORT"

President Eisenhower, just as his predecessor, became keenly interested in the controversy over aviation and appointed Edward P. Curtis as a Presidential Special Assistant to study the needs of aeronautics. The final report, *Aviation Facilities Planning*, was published on May 10, 1957.[116] The so-called "Curtis Report" predicated the necessity of doubling airport capacity by 1975 and underscored quite heavily the demand for a single national system of aviation facilities (navigational aids). Division of airspace into various zones, controlled separation at all times, certain space reserved for visual flying, and paths for high-precision interceptor aircraft must all be planned in the immediate future. Curtis urged the creation by statute—the old Air Coordinating Committee (ACC) had no statutory backing—of an Airways Modernization Board (AMB) to advise, test, and experiment on various air aids. The AMB would help select traffic and navigational systems when more than one type existed. Congress responded with the Airways Modernization Act of 1957, approved the same year as Public Law No. 133.[117] Consisting of a chairman appointed by the President—with Senate approval—and the heads of Commerce and Defense, the body would require approximately $30 million for each of its three years. Within a year three, 40-mile wide transcontinental swaths (airways) had been established between 17,000 and 22,000 feet.[118]

Despite all these efforts, the nation's press could well be critical of the delays already caused by the military-civilian feud, that is, laboring without coordination on systems so vital to air traffic control. Perhaps the words of deposed Administrator Lee best summed up the dilemma: "What we need in this government is an organization that can take action and take it promptly—to meet the needs of today and the future."[119] The same editors blamed both Truman (1949–1950) and Eisenhower (1953–1954) for not pushing forward the requests for a crash program in new navigation facilities. Editors of *Aviation Week* assailed inferior performance of radar which allegedly was turned off when it rained because of the interference from "storm clutter."[120] Criticized also were the lag in introduction of new facilities; the existence of five different approach-light systems at U.S. airports; and the operation of both ILS and a multiple, high-intensity approach light installation at London while no U.S. airport used this combination.

The CAA's detailed research on new or improved navigational aids was carried out at the Indianapolis center. Here, in 1957, the elements of VORTAC came under intensive "shake down" evaluations, with plans calling for 1,230 VORTAC and 289 ILS-TAC installations by 1965.[121] At Indianapolis, major research centered also around the dire necessity of a "datamation" system which could file the flight plan, route the data for the air traffic control center, and provide the required data for all stations to follow the plane along its journey. Refinements of radarscopes bright enough to see in daytime and all-weather runway lights provided further tests.

Increased use of the radio facilities—doubling of broadcasts shortly after the war and the introduction of vhf equipment—led to deep concern over the availability of frequencies in the future. In the meantime, the airlines had formed a corporation, Aeronautical Radio Incorporated (Airinc), commanding 45 channels in 2 groups—one at 3,000 kilocycles, the other at about 6,000 kilocycles. In 1946, C. I. Stanton contended before a House hearing that the CAA did not worry about Airinc's domestic broadcasting, a project urged onto the airlines for years by the CAA and FCC. But the CAA did wish to handle all international messages.[122] A few months later station WSY (New York) began issuing wind reports at twenty-five minutes past each hour (at 3,380 kc.), covering 500 to 800 miles of flying routes to Europe, and received much current data from pilots' routine position messages.[123]

AIR MARKING

For the private flier, the perennial question of air marking gained vigorous renewed support in portions of the country. A helping hand came from the following: Boy Scouts, Flying

Farmers (Michigan), women's pilot clubs, state aeronautical commissions, Civil Air Patrol (North Carolina), Standard Oil of California, Texas Oil Company, and the Florida State Road Department.[124] Two pilots credited the marker and airstrip at Gainesville, Missouri (on Skyway One), with saving their lives. Another Skyway—No. 11—provided private fliers with a safe, visual lane 40 miles in width from Pembina, North Dakota, to Laredo and Brownsville, Texas. By 1948, some 4,000 markers existed; authorities claimed the need of 100,000 such aids. Boy Scouts, 20,000 in number, worked on the markings, including the largest in the world—on top of an automobile plant in Chicago with individual letters 50 feet in size. Florida led all states with 165 new markers added during 1950.

Faith in flying and testimonials to the safety of aviation continued to be important assets in instructing the public. Thus, President Truman's flight home at Christmas in 1945 was praised editorially by the *Indianapolis News*.[125] Development of aviation in the country entailed the entire operations of both the CAA and CAB but cried for additional impetus and funds to keep abreast of overseas competitors who enjoyed national appropriations. Commerce officials recognized the Budget Bureau and congressional opposition to separate developmental funds but reluctantly condoned Administrator Rentzel's order for an office of aviation development.[126] Too often the critics visualized only the routine operations, air marking, training, and flight information as all that was required for development. Aviation, despite its gigantic strides in safety and increases in traffic, both passenger and freight, continued to battle the odds against it with amazingly bright prospects for the future. The three major disadvantages remaining late in the fifties were: high costs and rates, the hazards of flying, and interference from adverse weather conditions.[127]

THE FEDERAL AVIATION ACT OF 1958

It was inevitable with all the criticism in and out of Congress during the middle fifties that another of the famous reorganization movements would gain in momentum. One of the prime advocates during earlier attempts, Senator McCarran declared in 1951 that he now opposed further reorganization plans: "Frankly, for 18 years I have watched these reorganization plans. I vote against them [now] all the time. I have never seen one of them that effected an economy."[128] However, he did not rule out increased efficiency, later to be a prime reason for the 1958 law. Before his death in 1954, Senator McCarran proposed a redrafting of the 1938 Act to create an independent CAA and Air Safety Board.[129] For the next three years, congressmen gained the necessary support to remove the CAA from the clutches of the Department of Commerce and realign somewhat the relationship between the new FAA and CAB. Congressmen looked to the Harding Report of December 31, 1955, which recommended a separation of the CAA from the Department of Commerce, for their guidance a year later. The report stated that "certain essential elements of effective government seem to be missing—full-time direction, full disclosure of departmental information and plans, closely coordinated budgetary planning and funding and a unified approach to the Congress in matters of appropriations."[130] President Eisenhower, after announcement of the Harding Report, appointed Curtis as a special advisor to study the question of the CAA and Commerce.

Meanwhile, in 1956, Senator Monroney offered a bill (S. 2818) to establish the CAA as an independent agency.[131] This move, coming at the height of the controversy over the firing of Administrator Lee, was bound to become involved in a partisan tug-of-war. Curtis issued his final report on May 10, 1957.[132] Citing the dire necessity of keeping abreast with aviation's growth, the recommendations offered both temporary and permanent suggestions for improved organizational control. The interim plan called for the creation of an Airways Modernization Board, an independent agency especially designated to aid in the selection of air traffic and navigational systems, after accomplishment of which the AMB would be dissolved. Curtis envisaged the permanent body as an independent Federal Aviation Agency consolidating all the essential management functions for both military and civilian aviation and being staffed by both the military and civilians. Another recommendation called for the CAB to relinquish to the new FAA its role in accident investigation and its writing and amending of the CAR's. Division of airspace into zones, doubling of airport capacity by 1975, official recognition of the two-cent user tax on aviation gasoline, and increasing the Weather Bureau's meteorological research to aid aviation were additional suggestions of the Curtis Report. Back in Congress, the plan for an independent FAA wallowed through another unsuccessful session, despite the pleas of Representative Harry G. Haskell, Jr. of Delaware; but victory was achieved in

1958. Senator Monroney now received support from Senator Goldwater and others interested in aviation for passage of the Federal Aviation Act of 1958, Public Law No. 726.[133] The head of this independent body would be known as the administrator. In brief, the major duties consisted of the following:

(1) Allocate airspace and control its use by military and civil aircraft.

(2) Establish and enforce air traffic rules, military and civilian.

(3) Develop and operate a common system of air navigation facilities for military and civilian use.

(4) The new function recommended earlier by Curtis—to make and enforce safety regulations governing the design and operation of civil aircraft.

Contrary to the Curtis suggestion, the CAB retained its role in accident investigation along with its vast economic regulation of the air carriers. Furthermore, the Act called for special boards of inquiry for major air accidents and special provision for accidents involving military aircraft. One aspect of the law worried certain leaders—the President could by executive order transfer functions to the Department of Defense. The deputy administrator might be a military officer and remain in that capacity. Also explicit in the 197-page bill was the absorption of the temporary AMB by the new FAA. Finally, there could be no change in air navigational facilities—either military or civilian—without the permission of the administrator. The role of the Weather Bureau in continuing its meteorological services to aviation was carefully repeated in the bill. The Act also provided for an extension of the grants under the Federal Airport Act through 1963, increasing the available appropriations from the current $63 million to $100 million ($95 million to the states, $5 million to the territories). Curtis extended his support to this and other provisions of the measure.

Opposition to the final proposal (Senate bill 3880) certainly should not be considered formidable. But the reasons for dissent are interesting. Congressman Meader complained, "We all know that there has been confusion, duplication, overlapping activity, and conflict among the agencies in the executive branch of Government having responsibilities in the field of aviation. . . . This bill will create the exact opposite of that situation. This bill vests dictatorial power in one man. . . . We are creating an aviation czar."[134] Meader feared military control, an apprehension held by many FAA employees who winced at the thought of the several military conscription proposals for the CAA-FAA before and after this law was enacted in 1958. Critics of the initial two years of FAA independence also supported Meader's comments about one-man rule, as will be discussed in Chapter 13. Finally, Meader suggested establishment of some type of bipartisan board, unworkable as this sounded to most of the experts who might classify this idea with Premier Nikita Khrushchev's troika for the United Nations or John C. Calhoun's dual presidency for the United States (1840's). Meader's support within the administration centered mainly in the controversial Undersecretary of Commerce Rothschild, who had opposed the same general solution four years earlier and had clashed on numerous occasions with CAA leadership, as already cited. Meader was reminded by his opponents that Secretary Weeks favored the bill. Meader also utilized conflicting reports of inferior workmanship and construction under the Federal Airport Act as ammunition against the granting of independence. The Michigan solon labeled the CAA as "pitiful . . . timid, bound to the mistakes of the past and either unaware of, or indifferent to the needs of the future."[135] In so doing, Meader actually cited the identical reasons that his colleagues espoused as the heart of their argument for the law he opposed. Aviation interests supported this new bill, seemingly a farsighted departure from the manner in which the CAA had been returned to Commerce, in 1940, after just two brief years of freedom as an independent agency.[136]

The Airways Modernization Board, with its chairman, General Elwood (Pete) Quesada, began its temporary duties in 1958. A flurry of correspondence indicated that Administrator Pyle and Secretary Weeks assured Quesada of all possible cooperation.[137] Quesada told Senate appropriations subcommitteemen that his unit would employ over 100 people, about 15 per cent of them on "loan" from the military; and he wanted $30 million the first year from military and Commerce budgets. Testing facilities were used at the Atlantic City Naval Air Station, and the first order of business involved work on a zero-zero landing system, a dream yet unrealized in commercial operation at the time of this writing.[138]

THE CAB–ECONOMIC REGULATION
AND SAFETY–1945-1958

A GREAT SHARE of the postwar adjustment in civilian aviation came to be guided by the Civil Aeronautics Board. This body continued to grant or deny routes, cooperated with the Post Office Department in the knotty question of mail pay, investigated accidents, and promoted commercial aeronautics through a highly controversial system of direct subsidies after 1945. Decisions of any governmental regulatory agency are bound to arouse criticism. However, the CAB appears to have incurred a dosage of abuse far exceeding its share of federal internal checks on the nation's business. Although part of the criticism is deserved, exactly how much is indeterminable because of widely differing opinions shared by laymen, politicians, scholars, and technicians as to the perfect role of the government in the country's economy.

PRESSURE ON THE CAB

One factor remains certain. The pressure and attempted intrigue brought to bear on CAB members has been and still remains an immeasurable entity. Unfortunately, written records of lobbyists' pleas and blandishments in hopes of receiving favors are too few in number. But few can deny that this embodiment of the American political order played far too great a role in harassing the smooth operations of the CAB. For the written record—and to satisfy those critics who demand a written source for every assertion—evidence does substantiate the existence of lobbyists, great numbers of whom descended upon the CAB offices when serious cases appeared on the docket for consideration.[1] One congressman even suggested that CAB clerks keep a formal record of these visits. In addition to the utilization of pressure regarding matters of routes, lobbyists strove for increases in fares. Senator John Sparkman, Democrat of Alabama, alleged the presence in 1958 of "terrific pressure" to grant a fare increase.[2] Board member G. Joseph Minetti agreed with Sparkman in dissenting against the grant: "No changes in traffic and cost conditions of sufficient import have been presented."[3] Minetti saw the alarming possibility of an increase in coach fares alienating 75 per cent of adult Americans, the segment which did not fly, from flying in the future. Continually the nation's politicians criticized the CAB for yielding to pressure but, at every turn, exerted their own form of exaction from that regulatory body. In 1945, Congressman Walter H. Judd, Republican of Minnesota, led nineteen midwestern members of Congress in a protest against the CAB's possible acceptance of an Orient route from Chicago via Alaska, instead of via the Pacific Northwest.[4]

THE ROLE OF THE PRESIDENT

The importance of the White House in decision making simply cannot be overlooked, this form of persuasion at times amounting to the final decision. In turn, pressure on the President and his aides was unrelenting, at times absurd. President Harry S. Truman's military aide, Colonel Harry Vaughan, lamented to a friend: "I am beseiged by requests from various Chambers of Commerce and other civic organizations desiring economy in some locality other than their own and suggesting that the camp or airport in their own vicinity be continued and made permanent."[5] Such demands, if granted, led to further requests for air service from the CAB. Literally, boxes of official correspondence remain showing the deluge of individual protests sent to the President following practically every decision granting or denying routes. Sometimes the intent was most subtle. For example, Jack Frye, president of TWA, enclosed a copy of *Newsweek,* which excoriated the view held by Senator Pat McCarran and Frye's rival, Juan Trippe, President of PAA, that one U.S. company should serve foreign lands as a monopoly.[6] On a happier note, Edward E. Day, President of Cornell University, thanked John R. Steelman, a Truman aide, for the

CAB action giving a certificate to Robinson Airlines.[7] On at least one occasion, the President's aides cautioned him not to become involved in pending controversial decisions.[8] New routes or renewed services could affect the outcome of the 1952 election and assure the reelection of Senator Joseph C. O'Mahoney, Democrat of Wyoming, if the CAB would only believe one Denver politician who desired the granting of Western Airline's bid for direct service from Minneapolis to Los Angeles, via Casper and Salt Lake City.[9] Late in the same campaign, Truman, from his Presidential train, assured Arkansas Governor Sid McMath that the CAB would make every effort to reach a speedy decision concerning Central's petition to extend service to Hot Springs, Arkansas, for the winter resort season.[10] Another stalwart Democrat, Paul E. Fitzpatrick, Chairman of the New York State Committee, alleged that National's flight—Miami to New York—had left ten minutes early, refusing his confirmed reservations.[11] Here, the CAA and CAB supported National's claim that the flight departed exactly on time. In addition, National earlier had refused a telephone request by Fitzpatrick to hold the plane. Among the passengers on the DC–6 were General and Mrs. Douglas MacArthur.

Members of Congress requested interviews to help their aeronautical constituents gain the President's attention. For example, Senator Tom Connally, Democrat of Texas, telephoned to see if the President would see Tom Braniff, President of Braniff Airways, about the Balboa case before the CAB.[12] Massachusetts Congressman John F. Kennedy, hoped that Truman would have time to hear Langdon P. Marvin, Jr., Research Professor of Air Transportation and Economics at Georgetown University, discuss the potentialities for air cargo.[13] Marvin, after his interview, wrote Mrs. Franklin D. Roosevelt that he was surprised at what an alert and quick mind Truman possessed. Future President Lyndon B. Johnson offered help to a constituent interested in gaining the use of light aircraft for military ground forces.[14] Running the gamut of interest and naiveté, one request from a Kansas woman promised a crashproof airplane utilizing magnetic motors if she could obtain $1 million for research.[15] Another "unusual" approach came from a New Yorker who demanded that airline operations be abolished except for the carrying of mail and fast freight: "People ought not be in such a hurry to die."[16] This pessimist would reintroduce civilian passenger traffic only when air travel became as safe as the New York subway.

Albert E. Payne, Ohio Republican gubernatorial candidate, grumbled because federal authorities refused to allow him to drop nylon hose from an airplane over Edgewater Park, Cleveland.[17] Mrs. Hazel Burnelli, stressing the merits of her husband's aircraft designs, requested an interview at the White House but was politely refused.[18] Burnelli did get a meeting with Secretary Stuart Symington to discuss type designs for air cargo. Aviation industry authorities and aeronautical writers acknowledged the important role of Edwin A. Locke, White House aide, who appeared quite often at CAB headquarters, though one author concluded that Chairman J. M. Landis would retain the decision making in the CAB.[19] Organized labor's leaders also kept a close watch on the aviation industry. In 1948, Walter Reuther, President of the United Auto Workers (CIO), cautioned Truman against the continual mass production of obsolete military aircraft and urged a conference of labor-management-government. Truman replied that he was having a study completed.[20]

The proposed merger of National with Delta, PAA, or EAL in 1948 brought a storm of protests to the White House ranging from pilots' wives to National executives.[21] No merger resulted. ALPA boss David Behncke even complained to Steelman about one National official who aided the scabs, fought the strike against National, but worked against Truman by contributing to the opposition's campaign fund.[22] During the same year, the White House was informed of American Overseas Airlines (AOA) pilots' actions in attempting to buy the airline so as to avoid a pending merger with PAA.[23] The Lions Club of San Juan, Puerto Rico, complained about EAL's possible loss of the New York–San Juan route to PAA. The ALPA, always a vigorous opponent of mergers, appeared before the CAB to protest the request of a merger between Braniff and Mid-Continent.[24] On the other hand, the President received favorable reaction toward some proposed mergers, e.g., Senator Earle C. Clements of Kentucky condoned the uniting of Delta and Chicago and Southern.[25] After the board allowed the merger of Delta and Chicago and Southern in 1952, the President was advised to accept the decision. Truman received one tirade for allegedly promising the late Franklin Roosevelt he would gain the merger of PAA-AOA.[26]

IRREGULARS (THE "NONSKEDS")

The question involving routes and operations of the non-scheduled airlines also gained the attention of the Truman Administration. This dilemma involved much emotional appeal to support the air-minded veterans concerned. Charles A. Carroll, President of American Air Export and Import Company, protested the CAB restriction on "nonskeds" to ten trips a month between any two points.[27] Chairman Landis was consulted by White House staff before a noncommittal reply was dispatched to Carroll.

The White House was apprised of financial difficulties inherent in the tight control over TWA maintained by Howard Hughes. In 1946, files of the CAB, Justice, and State indicated that Hughes would not budge in his restriction on sale of common stock to anyone but himself. A pilots' strike, and the grounding of the "Connies" during the previous six months had definitely hurt the company, though the investigation displayed confidence in the future of TWA, a factor cheered by the *Kansas City Star*. The 5,000 employees of the company were naturally concerned. The CAB, sympathetic to TWA's setback, arranged a loan of C–54's from the ATC if TWA so desired.[28]

CAB LEADERSHIP

White House relations with members of the CAB and the appointments to this body represent a further high degree of interest in aviation on the part of the President. In 1947, Truman initiated a policy of appointing the chairman and vice-chairman to one-year terms; and, as had been the case since 1938, the vice-chairman was selected from the Republican ranks.[29] A year earlier, Truman had appointed Landis, Dean of the Harvard Law School, as CAB head. Landis, a New Deal adviser, had the B.A. from Princeton and the LL.D. and S.J.D. from Harvard.[30] Serving first as a law clerk for Justice Louis Brandeis, Landis then taught at Harvard. He authored several books before accepting posts under FDR on the Federal Trade Commission and Securities and Exchange Commission. In 1937, he became Dean of Harvard's law school. He directed the Office of Civil Defense during the war and in 1943 became American Director of Economic Operations in the Middle East. Resignations during Truman's initial year as President included Edward Warner who then became president of the interim council of the Provisional International Civil Aviation Organization (PICAO), and L. Welch Pogue, chairman since 1942. Truman accepted Pogue's advice in elevating veteran Oswald Ryan to the vice-chairmanship under

Landis.[31] Clarence M. Young, former head of the Aeronautics Branch, served on the CAB for twenty months.

DROPPING LANDIS

Perhaps the most spectacular action generated by Truman resulted from his refusal to reappoint Landis to a new term. Utilizing executive privilege, the President weathered a storm of protests in dropping the last of Roosevelt's early "brain trust." No reasons were given; no comments issued by the participants in the struggle. Landis asked to see Truman again but was unsuccessful.[32] One telegram recorded indignant revulsion against the Landis ouster with the suggestion that Truman hold a conference between those who manipulated his statements and those who guided his actual performance.[33] Within a week, Truman had decided he would seek the appointment of a military leader, Major General Laurence S. Kuter, to head the CAB.[34] Carleton Putnam, President of Chicago and Southern, favored the selection of Kuter and advised Truman that Landis had actually been in favor of mergers, not competition. Putnam had little use for the fallen CAB chieftain.[35] Despite this opinion, later records indicate that Landis disfavored the proposal to create a monopoly for one company to serve the United States overseas.[36] Undoubtedly Landis' apparent vigor and intensity of purpose helped to alienate him from a segment of the aviation industry. Perhaps Landis displayed too much impatience for Truman. One year before his ousting, Landis had asked the President for an announced governmental policy on aviation, saying no legislation could be won unless promoted by the Executive branch.[37] As cochairman of the ACC and a member of the Air Policy Commission, his opinions, farsighted as they appeared, could well have alienated enough individuals to bring about the ouster. Again, Landis also lived in this era of the "fatal gap . . . between military and civil aviation. . . ."[38] Perhaps important to Truman were Landis' alleged personal indiscretions, for which the President had reportedly been pressured to drop him.

NO MILITARY BOSS

The political "winds" in the House appeared favorable to the Kuter appointment if limited to two years. However, where the matter must be won—the Senate—firm and unrelenting resistance cancelled the idea to allow the military representative to head a civilian agency without changing his current relationship to the military.[39] A unanimous vote of the Senate Committee on Armed Services vetoed the proposal. The group still maintained its original position following a visit of congressional leadership in both houses to the White House. Truman commented that over 1,000 military personnel were then serving in the various departments while on duty, but he lost the issue. Joseph J. O'Connell became chairman on April 6, 1948.[40] Member Harllee Branch retired, creating yet another vacancy early in 1948. Truman followed with appointments for Harold A. Jones and Russell B. Adams. Republican Ryan apprised Matt Connelly, White House aide, of the *Denver Post*'s use of an Associated Press account crediting the CAB as accomplishing more with three active members during the changes than with the full complement of five.[41] Interestingly enough, but certainly to be expected, the White House staff kept a record of potential board nominees, the file on Adams showing him as a registered Democrat since 1932.[42]

In 1950, Chairman O'Connell resigned to return to private life and CAA Administrator Delos W. Rentzel was appointed to the post. The choice of Rentzel was heartily approved by Ryan and former member and Chairman Pogue, who believed that industry also backed Rentzel.[43] Rentzel assured the White House staff in 1948 that he possessed no financial ties with the Air Transport Association or other groups.[44] The reorganized board then met at the White House with Truman to discuss its problems. Meanwhile, veteran Josh Lee, a cordial admirer of the President, was reappointed to another six-year term. Lee now showed a tremendous interest in the new feeder services. Change occurred again the next year, with Donald Nyrop moving over from administrator to chairman. In Truman's last months as President, former Senator Chan Gurney, Republican of South Dakota, was appointed to the board with this fond tribute: "You are about the only person on the whole list that I am appointing at this time, but if your Republican colleagues don't treat you right you can't blame it on me."[45] A Yankton, South Dakota, Democrat particularly appreciated the choice of Gurney by Truman. When Nyrop offered his resignation in September, 1952, Truman regretfully accepted and named Ryan as chairman. As one of his last duties, in mid-January, 1953, President Truman extended his gratitude to each member of the the CAB for his service to the administration. He noted Ryan's continuous service since 1938, and Lee's presence on the board when he had become President. Truman had kind praise also for newest member Joseph Adams who, with his eight-year-old daughter, had enjoyed a recent visit to the President.[46]

EISENHOWER AND THE CAB

White House influence on commercial aviation continued to be exerted by the first Republican President since 1933. Dwight D. Eisenhower overruled the board at times, failed to reappoint personnel when his advisers dictated, and exerted an influence not unlike his predecessor. Whenever the White House papers of his eight years are made available, perhaps Eisenhower's role may appear even greater than does a summary available from the present sources. Sherman Adams, top White House adviser—called the "Assistant President" by Democratic detractors—allegedly intervened before the board whenever it was deemed necessary. Senator William Proxmire of Wisconsin, charged in 1958 that Adams, without Eisenhower's knowledge, had discussed the status of North American Airlines (in 1953) with the CAB chairman, delaying the shutdown of that firm.[47]

An editorial in the *Washington Post and Times Herald* asked, "Is it that Mr. Eisenhower just isn't interested, or is it that Mr. Adams, who attempts to ease the Chief Executive's burdens, filters what the President reads?"[48] The *New Republic* held that Adams misled the President about this case just as he was misled about the Dixon-Yates scandal. An earlier House investigation of the FCC had led to the discovery, by Senator John L. McClellan's committee, of a letter from Adams to a California lawyer reporting the contact with the CAB. This incident, simply adding to the mountain of complaints against Adams' practice of conducting numerous talks with regulatory officials, indicates that influence from the White House is important but neither wholly unnecessary nor always sinister. It all depends on the merits of the case involved.

THE CAB RECORD, 1945–1958

Cases of a regulatory nature, whether involving routes, mail, or subsidy, drew excited denunciation from supporters of parties unsuccessful before the CAB and, usually, silence from those favored. In a sense, one could say that it was most difficult to ascertain if the CAB had any true friends during this troubled postwar epoch. The host of problems anticipated before the war's conclusion now struck with full fury—the scramble for new overseas routes, expansion of the "nonskeds," the advisability of raising fares, and making wise decisions as to domestic routes embracing existing trunk lines and the new feeder service.

INTERNATIONAL PROBLEMS

Most pressing were the international tangles concerning routes coveted by all the leading aeronautical interests in the world. Mention has already been made about the establishment of the PICAO, which became the ICAO in 1946, the same year in which four observers from the USSR attended meetings.[49] Truman, anxious to exert all possible U.S. influence toward the success of the ICAO, strongly urged Senator Alben Barkley to push during the current session (1946) for adoption of the convention. However, the international meetings failed to provide definite and responsible means of implementing agreements reached, according to William C. Foster, U.S. Undersecretary of Commerce and Chairman of the Air Coordinating Committee. Foster also called for better coordination of executive and legislative action concerning all such obligations assumed by the United States.[50] Subsequently, bilateral agreements were of utmost urgency, as before, the United States tackling one such knotty problem with Great Britain at the so-called Bermuda Conference of January, 1946. Britain, along with France, India, and Russia had refused to accede to earlier decisions on routes and "economics" (rates). At Bermuda, Britain agreed to the details opening eighteen points to air traffic in the United Kingdom and several Commonwealth locations. Now everyone except the USSR had agreed to the "transit agreement," allowing other countries' planes to stop anywhere for nontraffic functions, e.g., procuring fuel or repairs.[51] Limits on schedules such as existed before World War II were lifted, but no accord was forthcoming on PAA's attempt to lower its Atlantic fare to $275.

The air carriers dealing with international routes had formed the International Air Transport Association—fifty-seven companies originally—with just one "No" vote sufficient to negate any proposal. The CAB held this power of review for the United States. Thus, though it desired control of international rates, the CAB was practically helpless to do so. These foreign negotiations involved Commerce because of the CAA, the

CAB, and the Department of State, with harmony among these bodies absolutely imperative. The CAB informed State that it was restricting issuance of various airman certificates solely to nationals of countries which granted reciprocal provisions.[52] The State officials did not always include the CAA and CAB in their discussions with foreigners, which practice, as pointed out by Secretary Averell Harriman, violated the Civil Aeronautics Act of 1938.[53] The CAA claimed it had no representative at State's bilateral negotiations with China, India, or Peru. Representation of both the CAA and CAB was secured for the next meetings arranged by State with Canada. Commerce adjusted its foreign efforts to requests from the State Department, retaining Roberts Field, Liberia, at the strong behest of Secretary James F. Byrnes in 1947.[54] Later in the same year, Acting Commerce Secretary Foster informed the State Department it could not formalize a proposed agreement with Mexico because too much flight instruction was required of U.S. officials.[55] The transfer from military to civilian (CAA) control over air navigation facilities in foreign lands was accomplished periodically by executive order upon the request of State and Commerce officials.[56] Truman also acted on the temporary assignment of negotiators for the State Department. The Chief Executive also warned—through his aides—against risking loss of goodwill by selling inferior surplus aircraft abroad as had occurred following World War I.[57]

American officials scrambled to obtain foreign accord, while PAA hastened to extend its long existing stronghold internationally. In 1946, the CAB reported that thirteen U.S. carriers served foreign stops, while ten foreign companies held access to U.S. cities.[58] PAA became a world line with stops at Frankfurt, Vienna, Istanbul, and a route across the Central Pacific onward to India. Northwest went to the Orient via the Great Circle, and TWA pushed on from Europe to Bombay and Shanghai. United gained a route from San Francisco to Honolulu.

Leaders close to the watchful eye of American diplomats and aeronautical experts clamored for better services. Operations in the Territory of Alaska, so valuable in war, now demanded further attention. A splendid safety record had been compiled in this challenging part of the globe, much attention being extended to cargo—hardware, perishables, and building supplies—as United States-Alaskan service registered a postwar boom. During 1947, passenger totals there stood at 120,000 compared with under 30,000 in 1938.[59] However, the CAA personnel maintaining facilities there still registered a high rate of turnover, mainly because of the housing shortage. Often three families lived in one-family dwellings. Indeed, low morale persisted as a problem in the outlying regions. Discontent continued, for in January, 1950, Alaska's Governor Ernest Gruening informed Secretary of Commerce Charles Sawyer that the President favored aviation in Alaska but the CAB retarded operations there. Truman called on Chairman O'Connell for a personal investigation and received the support of Secretary of the Interior Oscar L. Chapman who agreed that shortcomings existed in Alaska.[60] One year later the CAA asked its employees: "Would you like to work where you can pan for gold, collect fine furs, catch big fish, shoot your own meat for the winter?"[61] Not everyone answered in the affirmative, but the CAA maintained that the majority of its 1,500 employees in Alaska were happy. Meanwhile, Chris Lample, with CAA since 1927 and a long-time staunch promoter of Alaskan aviation, began in 1948 to manage the airports at Anchorage (where he lived) and Fairbanks.[62] For a former possession, the Philippines, Commerce and CAB officials aided in the proposed agreement submitted by the Department of State.[63]

Aeronautical relations with Latin America aroused the wrath of many critics who disputed the manner in which routes were awarded. Negotiations with Mexico proved unwieldly and embarrassing for Truman and Eisenhower. CAB member Lee advised Truman against reopening negotiations with Mexico in 1952, though his CAB colleagues disagreed. Lee asserted that it would prove far better to weigh each individual proposal for an exchange of routes.[64] A mild ripple of disdain resulted in 1946 from Truman's influence in directing the selection of routes to Latin America. The incumbent PAA lost its monopoly on the Los Angeles–Mexico City run, now sharing this with Western. Eastern, Braniff, and Colonial each added new routes, though PAA's hold on the Bermuda and South American trade was hardly shaken. The brunt of opposition to the CAB's decisions in Latin America was especially aimed in its fury against the lucrative, veteran PAA. In 1950, PAA drew criticism for the CAB examiner's report favoring a merger with AOA, a union effective the same year. This merger involved Atlantic traffic, but the adverse reaction seemingly affected the attitude toward all segments of PAA.

THE MEXICAN TANGLE

In essence, the whole problem involving Mexico originated much earlier. PAA had secured its Brownsville–Mexico City route even before the Civil Aeronautics Act of 1938. In 1946, Truman's effort to allow Eastern, Braniff, and Western into Mexico was invalidated only because the Mexican government refused the arrangement.[65] Reviewing the impasse in 1954, Senator Allen J. Ellender of Louisiana believed that U.S. negotiators were hampered in their efforts by PAA agents who convinced the Mexican officials against allowing further U.S. lines into the country. CAB member Ryan then testified that he honestly could not say if PAA's influence prevented the acceptance of the other companies. Ryan declared that U.S. lines, with their subsidies, might be considered too powerful by the Mexicans. Ryan, who headed the team of American negotiators to Mexico in 1946, asserted that the Mexicans immediately attacked his group for having decided the routes prior to consultation with the Mexicans. Presently Mexico argued for a fifty-fifty division of traffic and frequencies on the agreed routes, a real shock to the Americans. This type of bickering, carried on into the fifties, especially concerned a coveted New Orleans–Mexico City route. Then President Eisenhower intervened by cancelling the U.S. certificates of Eastern, Braniff, and Western. Ryan answered Ellender's query as to how this action could take place: "That is the $64 question, Senator. . . . One day out of a clear sky, we get word of the cancellation of the certificates by the President of the United States. That is the situation confronting us."[66]

HEAT ON PAN AMERICAN AIRWAYS

Senator Harley M. Kilgore of West Virginia objected strenuously to what he termed secret negotiations with the Mexicans performed by PAA and American Airlines, for which each probably received subsidies. Here PAA's vast and intricate system of investments—subsidiaries in aviation, hotels, etc.— came under bitter scrutiny. Senator Kilgore lashed out against the ridiculous practice of allowing PAA to claim losses on one segment of its operations without having all its earnings considered in the same accounting. The problem, according to Kilgore, was analogous to permitting Anheuser-Busch to charge losses from the St. Louis Cardinals (baseball) against the brewing company's federal income tax. CAB officials pleaded insufficient funds to accomplish a full audit of PAA, but Kilgore reminded his listeners: "I have known outfits that had three and four sets of books, one for the public utilities commission, one for the local assessor, one for the directors, and one for the stockholders."[67] Perhaps Kilgore's allegations describe an American business disease more than any specific laxity on the part of the harassed CAB. At any rate, the "heat" was on PAA and the CAB's lack of interest for correcting this so-called favoritism of the past. Naturally, with the airlines the entire problem became enmeshed with the question of subsidies. Columnist Fulton Lewis, Jr., claimed that Ryan and former Truman aide Connelly were the ones responsible for the merger of PAA and AOA against the wishes of the board. Drew Pearson maintained that the PAA had not lost its rabbit's foot in the White House during Eisenhower's administration.[68] The *Dallas Morning News* felt the CAB "ought to get back to the basic consideration of the convenience and necessity of the people, not just for some airlines."[69] It would appear that Ryan disfavored uneconomical competition since he persuaded the President to allow the PAA-AOA merger (1950), instead of viewing the issue merely as a pro-PAA gesture.

Senator Russell B. Long, Democrat of Louisiana, summarized Eastern's dilemma. That company had held a certificate for nonstop traffic from New Orleans to Mexico City since 1946, yet the operation could not be inaugurated seven and one-half years later. However, American Airlines applied early in 1954 for a New York–Mexico City route and received approval from the CAB, whose closed-door, unprecedented, forty-minute session afforded no opportunity for protest. Marquis Childs, writing for the *Washington Post*, explained the action as the result of Air France's similar new service over the same route. Gurney, Ryan, and Denny favored the American grant; Lee and Joseph P. Adams opposed it, seeing neither emergency nor national interest at stake. Senator Alexander Wiley, Republican of Wisconsin, came to the defense of the CAB, stressing the urgency of U.S. competition with the French flag and reminded his opponents that American, indeed, had the sole U.S. certificate (with stops en route) over this very circuit.[70] Furthermore, American had first applied in 1947 for the nonstop service on its existing route to Mexico City. Additional routes were granted during 1956–1957 to Northeast (New York City–Miami) and National (transgulf Miami–Houston). Mexico relaxed its long delaying tactics to sign a two-year agreement with the United States, which mostly benefited Braniff at first. Within another year, Eastern gained a nonstop route—New York–Mexico City—while Northwest and TWA sought additional routes to open up the coveted Florida market.[71]

The Supreme Court came to the aid of the reformers by declaring in 1954 that excess earnings from domestic operations of an international carrier be offset against the international (United States paid) subsidy rate. Justice William O. Douglas wrote both decisions, stating, "If the carrier's treasury is lush, the need for subsidy decreases whether the opulence is due to transportation activities or to activities incidental thereto. . . ."[72] The Court also denied various claims for back mail pay in what the *Aviation Week* termed "The first CAB loss to the Supreme Court." Senator John F. Kennedy led a fight to lower drastically the total amount of subsidy available for allocation by the CAB but lost his effort in 1954. Supported by fellow-Democrat Senator Paul Douglas of Illinois, Kennedy sought a slash of approximately $10 million for our international carriers only.[73] Senators McCarran, Styles Bridges, Irving M. Ives, and Kilgore led the forces defeating the frugal Kennedy's amendment.

THE HOOVER COMMISSION

One of the nation's noblest efforts to instigate true reform at Washington, D.C., now extended the following suggestions to improve the CAB. The Commission on Organization of the Executive Branch of Government—the so-called Hoover Commission—recommended final decisions be rendered within three months in nonhearing procedures. Furthermore, international cases should be subject to judicial review. Alluding to the tremendous pressure on regulatory bodies, the commission warned against conflict of interests and scorned the practice of allowing former CAB members to represent clients before the CAB. Finally, the commission would eliminate the use of examiners in the CAB, replacing them with an "Administrative Court of the United States" for use by all the regulatory agencies.[74] Unhappily the Hoover Commission's effect on bureaucracy has been practically nil, leaving only a dream for casual perusal by the student of government.

ROUTES IN THE PACIFIC

The furor of the midfifties embraced more than proposed service to Mexico and the rest of Latin America. The climax was reached over two other issues—the nonscheduled airlines and another White House-CAB rift, this time over service in the Pacific. On February 1, 1955, President Eisenhower overruled the CAB's unanimous decision by extending to PAA a monopoly on the Seattle–Hawaii run despite the existence of Northwest service on that route since 1948.[75] Another favor to PAA, this time passed by the CAB, disallowed TWA's attempt to compete with PAA over the route—Rangoon–Bangkok–Hong Kong–Formosa–Tokyo. This blow to Northwest led to an eruption of protest in Congress. Henry S. Reuss, representing Wisconsin in the House, called February 1, "Giveaway Day." Minnesota Senator Eugene McCarthy labeled the action comparable to the Dixon-Yates contract. His Minnesota colleague, Senator Hubert Humphrey, led a drive in the Senate to get the President to rescind his action. The move paid off the same day with Ike instructing Gurney (CAB) to give both lines temporary, three-year certificates. This congressional victory had been engineered by leaders from areas served by Northwest, yet there is little doubt that the presidential backdown constituted the only sensible approach to remedy a glaring error.

SELECTING MEMBERS

The incident led the outspoken leadership of *The New Republic* to step beyond this case and castigate the President for the entire manner in which the CAB leadership was selected: "Until a few weeks ago three of its five members were former (defeated) Congressmen or Senators . . ."[76] The same editors pointed at the tremendous persuasion exerted by PAA's Sam Pryor, former Republican National Committeeman from Connecticut, in attempting to get Ryan reappointed to the board. However, according to this version, a wild scramble for a replacement ensued with Secretary Sinclair Weeks and Republican National Chairman Leonard Hall favoring Harold Jones, former board member and our representative to ICAO and a friend of American Airlines. Presently other candidates were advanced by Senator Joseph McCarthy, Republican of Wisconsin; Senator Wiley; and Congressman Dan Reed, Republican of New York. In the panic that ensued, the White House came up with the choice of Ross Rizley, Republican former congressman of Oklahoma, a career politician who had lost in 1948 to Democratic Senator Robert Kerr. Rizley could boast of having been solicitor in the Post Office (1953) and then Assistant Secretary of Agriculture.

The New Republic well described the dilemma facing any new member of the CAB and noted Rizley's lack of experience in aviation: "Whether he will have enough subtlety of mind and strength of character to avoid becoming that industry's tool— no one yet knows. . . . The choice is a common one, under Democratic as well as Republican Administration."[77] The White House reportedly offered the position to Jones but reconsidered when opposition arose among the local service airlines.[78] Senator A. S. (Mike) Monroney offered Democratic support of the choice, feeling that Rizley was a "neutral." Rizley frankly stated that he did not seek the job. In discussing his views on becoming chairman, Rizley declared there would be no strategy conferences or party-line decisions and stated that he favored competition and would not take directions from the Undersecretary of Commerce for Transportation. Rizley dropped a "bombshell" when he declared himself in favor of subsidies for all to carry mail, not solely the certified lines. Later in 1955, Rizley displayed further vigor in bemoaning the attitude of industry and Congress for "the extrajudicial pressures brought on the CAB to favor specific points of view in considering decisions."[79]

Informational leaks from the CAB annoyed Rizley who warned of a vigorous attack on the practice, but he probably realized this type of approach was futile. One leak allegedly involved Albert H. Ruppar, a trial lawyer with the CAB's Bureau of Air Operations, who bought Northeast Airlines stock on August 3, 1956, the day after the CAB decided to give Northeast a New York–Florida route.[80] Ruppar denied any wrongdoing but "left" the CAB and claimed to have sold the stock, losing money on the 1,000 shares. Senator McClellan advised that two leaks had caused a substantial increase in the trading of Northeast Airlines stock at this time.[81] Twenty CAB employees attended the session in which a vote took place to grant Northeast the New York–Miami route. This overruled the CAB examiner who favored Delta. The next day 24,000 shares were traded instead of the normal 500. McClellan termed the people involved evasive and uncooperative. No criminal statutes existed against the practice, and two bills attempting to remedy this oversight died in committee. In March of 1956, the House Judiciary Subcommittee on Monopoly Practices headed by Emanuel Celler (Democrat of New York) called the members to testify about their decisions and operations. Rizley agreed that getting decisions out of the board was most difficult but called it a conservative philosophy rather than a conspiracy. Adams refused to answer Celler under oath, while Harmar Denny denied influence in changing his vote to oppose an investigation of fares after he had talked to Stuart Tipton, then counsel for and later president of ATA. Rizley agreed that PAA was "absolutely dominating the international scene."[82]

Beginning in December, 1953, several party-line decisions led Senator Edward Johnson, ranking Democrat on the Senate Commerce Committee, to allege party voting, only to find the charge denied—as could be expected.[83] The turbulence increased as President Eisenhower was confronted by a major turnover in membership, the first since his tenure began. The first break in the old lineup of Democrats—Rizley, Lee, and Adams—came with the appointment of Democrat Minetti, New York attorney, to replace Lee. Minetti, forty-eight years old, had been on the Federal Maritime Board. Senator Monroney, upset at the loss of two of his constituents—Lee and, soon, Rizley—expressed anger at Undersecretary Louis Rothschild who obtained the appointment of Minetti. When Rizley quit, Wisconsin attorney James R. Durfee became chairman. A Republican, Durfee was formerly Chairman of the Wisconsin Public Service Commission. In 1957, Adams was replaced by Louis J. Hector, Florida attorney and businessman, who formerly had been a special assistant to the Secretary of State. Member Gurney was named vice-chairman, and Denny, the Pennsylvania attorney (a pilot and former representative), continued his service on the board.[84]

NONSCHEDULED AIR SERVICES

Assigning routes and regulating the day-to-day activities of all the nation's commercial carriers involved the perplexities surrounding the tremendous growth in the number of nonscheduled operations after 1945. Only one of fifty-five such carriers with a gross income of more than $10,000 for April–September, 1946, was operating prior to 1945. Many of the total of 737 operators used small aircraft, but 90 per cent of the gross receipts went to those using the DC–3 or larger planes.[85] From the outset the board watched closely to avoid regularly scheduled service by these lines. However, strict enforcement proved most difficult despite a vigorous campaign against the operators in 1948. Enforcement actions uncovered not only nonscheduled air carriers but also PAA, upon complaint of TWA, for alleged illegal operations to Saudi Arabia.[86]

Though the CAB likened these lines to tramp steamers, the American public gained one notable innovation as a result of pressure from the nonscheduled carriers. Air-coach fares were finally recognized and condoned by the board, initially for Capital on the New York–Chicago run in November, 1948. The rate was 4 cents per mile, two-thirds of the prevailing regular fare. Soon Capital and Northwest realized that over 20 per cent of their revenue came from this service.

Gaining board approval for summer, 1949, another noteworthy achievement, special group fares, resulted from these irregular airlines. Religious, educational, and charitable organizations rushed to take advantage of this sensible milestone. The chain reaction continued happily for American travelers who saw the inaugural of the famous tourist rates by the scheduled carriers (transatlantic) in 1952.[87] The irregulars then could handle such flights only if the regular lines became overcrowded. Reduced fares included the family plan which usually applied to travel restricted to a certain portion of the week and basically amounted to a reduction of 50 per cent in the fare of the second member of the family with further reductions for subsequent members. Special round-trip fares for flights to Europe, good for sixty days during October–April, also met CAB approval reducing the price to one and one-third the one-way cost. The in-season rates remained at 180 per cent of one way, applying to eastbound during April–August, and for westbound during July–November.[88] In 1951, to promote the Korean "police action," the CAB allowed the irregulars to receive Defense Department contracts, a necessary action for both parties. The final innovation of the era to promote increased traffic came with the inaugural in 1958 of the economy class which reduced the fare for London–New York from $290 (tourist) to $252.[89] However, those readers who have flown a great distance via economy might wonder if placing three seats on each side of the aisle actually made the loss in comfort worthwhile for this new "sardine class."

In Congress, the irregular operations gained increasing support. In 1948, Congressman John F. Kennedy resented the "kicking around which this Government has given to many of my fellow veterans of World War II, who are engaged, or rather trying to engage, in the business of carrying cargo by air."[90] Kennedy considered it shameful that in two and one-half years the CAB had failed to grant a certificate to these lines but allowed the large carriers to undercut them by 13 cents a ton-mile. The vets held 125 planes for such operations while the scheduled lines had but 60. Kennedy certainly touched upon one of the major dreams of postwar aviation—the increase in air cargo. Secretary of Commerce Harriman wrote Chairman Landis in 1947: "Cargo carrying can ultimately become the greatest incentive for the full development of air transportation."[91] The cudgels for the smaller lines were then picked up by other congressmen. But Pacific Overseas Airlines Corporation's bid for reduced passenger fares on slower planes was blocked by the scheduled lines. Congressman Karl Stefan of Nebraska believed: "There is airspace for all types and all classes of operations . . . the CAB and CAA have at the behest of the big scheduled airlines successfully blocked development in the fields below the mainline operations."[92] Senator Sparkman, refuting the CAB's reluctance because the irregulars used old equipment, pointed to the perfect safety record (July, 1949, to August 29, 1951, the day of his speech).[93] Senator Wayne Morse, Democrat of Oregon, joined Sparkman in rebuking the CAB, emphasizing the role of the non-scheduled lines in carrying food to Alaska. In fairness to the CAB, one must assert that many violations of the CAR's did indeed occur, particularly because overzealous irregulars strained their operations to the limit and would not refuse passengers despite restrictions against a "regular" type of service. However, it cannot be denied that the CAB's attitude toward the entire irregular service—air cargo or passenger carrying—was ultra-conservative, protective of the thriving regular lines, and not exactly promoting the spirit of free competition which might reduce fares and gain new air travelers in the process.

Natural attrition took its toll of the weaker "nonskeds." Ridiculous experiences were reported to the CAA and CAB, such as the occasion when one pilot had to pass the hat among his passengers in order to purchase gasoline. This "shoestring" operation had no established credit and it took three days to complete a transcontinental flight.[94] Then, too, the difference in safety requirements between the scheduled and the irregulars raised numerous eyebrows. For example, the irregulars did not have to have their own communications facilities, a chain of maintenance bases, or route requirements—checking on the pilot's familiarity with the region in which he flew.[95] Of course, it would be impractical to require these rules of the irregular lines. In 1957, the CAB instigated charges against the Flying Tiger line for transporting passengers between Miami and Latin

America at rates below the effective tariff. The tip-off on the the violation originated with a petition from TWA.[96] The action also served as a warning to other companies violating the charter rules by allowing fictitious groups to gain lower fares.

Meanwhile, Senator Sparkman's Senate Committee on Small Business received support from Senator William Langer, Republican of North Dakota, who recalled that the RFC extended loans to the veterans in the irregular carriers after the war. By 1953, most of the substantial lines had survived and merged into the North American Airlines, only to run afoul of the CAB. Langer asserted, "One of the best ways of eliminating subsidy is to permit the nonsubsidy carriers to develop in air transportation so that operating statistics showing actual costs would be readily obtainable."[97] Senator McCarran rallied to the support of the CAB by calling for new legislation—Senate bill 9 of the Eighty-Third Congress, 1953—to enable the CAB to regulate the non-scheduled operations, something McCarran claimed the 1938 Act failed to do. Senator Kilgore, mindful of the legal difficulties confronting the "nonskeds" in West Virginia, backed McCarran in this cautious approach toward the CAB.

LOCAL OR FEEDER SERVICE

Shortly after the war, the CAB warily announced the establishment of the new feeder service connecting American cities not served by the existing trunk lines. Citing aid to national defense and the Post Office Department as reasons, the CAB yet considered the undertaking experimental and granted three-year, temporary certificates.[98] The experts agreed that the smaller airlines would undoubtedly face stiffer competition from the rail, bus, and automobile users than did the established lines. In 1946, there existed 8,641 miles of the new local service. The beginnings were inauspicious from a financial standpoint, 7 of the 13 feeders operating at a loss in 1948—despite federal subsidies. By the same token, the improvement in air transportation for the cities involved plus the initial use of this convenience by businessmen in these smaller cities certainly proved to be worth the financial instability of the operation. One of the key problems lay with the inability of the aircraft industry to produce a plane to replace the old work horse, the DC–3. CAB leadership took the attitude that this craft should be replaced. But as late as 1965, many a DC–3 was still being utilized in local service. CAB policy of caution toward the local service paid dividends later. This partially entailed restricting competition and primarily basing the routes and number of flights on the growth of traffic.[99] In 1955, the "use it or lose it" policy enabled the board to demand an average of five persons boarding a plane from a location per day in order to qualify for a permanent certificate.[100] Furthermore, the trunk lines were allowed to assume a portion of the local service. Another innovation greatly enhancing the local routes was the use of "flag stop" service—landing only if passengers were to board or leave the plane at the location in question.

By 1958, the local service lines had grown in number to 14 systems reaching 413 towns in 44 states. The average length of hop between cities was 81 miles. A major boon to the future of the service now materialized with the introduction of the Fokker-Fairchild F–27, a sleek, new, two-engine, turboprop aircraft.[101] Nevertheless, the changeover from the antiquated, uncomfortable DC–3 was painfully slow; costs were the reason for local airlines not purchasing different craft. Pioneer's attempt to utilize the Martin Pacemaster, a 36-passenger craft capable of speeds to 270 miles per hour, was blocked by the board in 1953, undoubtedly because of the cost burden.[102] One healthy feeder—North Central—obtained a nonstop flight between Duluth–Superior and Chicago, a distance of 414 miles in comparison to the usual shorter trip. A law passed in 1957, Public Law No. 85-307, allowed the board to guarantee loans to airlines. But the CAB lacked a coveted check it long desired, the right to regulate the issuance of securities for all types of carrier. The ICC held this control over the nation's railroads. Furthermore, the CAB's general attitude toward competition had vacillated. Prior to 1944 it had fostered competition then foreswore such a policy, in the main, until the middle fifties when local service was expanded.[103] Another type of craft, the helicopter, finally gained respectable status with certification in 1953. The first attempt centered in the New York area with New York Airways, Inc., serving three airports.[104]

Basic to the problem of the irregulars was the realization that the scheduled lines could not properly develop air-cargo service along with their other duties, primarily because of the directional limitations of their certificates.[105] Temporary certificates for the all-freight carriers appeared to be a ridiculous practice, a type of discouragement to the owners involved. What looked like a major increase in air cargo—a volume rise of 234 per cent during 1946–1949—yet remained only a fraction of 1 per cent of that merchandise moved by the surface carriers. Manufactured products accounted for over 90 per cent of the goods carried by air. Naturally the higher air cost proved to be a limiting factor. Supporters of the cargo haulers saw a thaw in the CAB in 1955 when President Eisenhower signed a five-year certificate for a nonsubsidized cargo operation. Seaboard and Western Airlines, a survivor of the World War II veterans' lines, could now fly from New York, Philadelphia, and Baltimore to Newfoundland, Canada, Ireland, and other points in Europe.[106] Beclouding the general circumstances surrounding irregular air carriers was the lack of agreement internationally on the concept of air charter. In 1929, the Warsaw Convention left the charter question open. A leading Swedish authority saw two major problems. First, is the convention applicable to the contractual relationship between the airplane owner and the chartered? Secondly, is someone other than the chartered involved? One school of thought would acknowledge the applicability of the convention if the owner or chartered was in actual control of the crew.[107] Steps were taken to initiate amendment of the Warsaw Convention at a meeting in The Hague during 1956.

A most dramatic furor arose in 1955 over CAB action toward North American Airlines, a veterans' outfit with nine planes and the instigator of the popular coach fare in America. The CAB had disallowed the use of the word "American" in the carrier's title, only to be reversed by the U.S. circuit court in Washington, D.C. CAB Vice-Chairman Adams dissented in the board's ensuing action revoking the line's certificate: "I dissent from the majority's refusal to accept any settlement short of outright and complete revocation no matter how stringent the sanction might be . . . particularly since the majority has refused even to confer with officials of North American Airlines . . . regarding a possible settlement."[108] Congressmen James Roosevelt and Chet Holifield, both of California, Victor Wickersham of Oklahoma, and John J. Rooney of New York spoke heatedly and eloquently in behalf of North American. Rooney bemoaned the possible destruction of the nation's pace-setter in low fares and challenged the CAB to undertake a true and thorough study of all airline fares. Rooney scored the $1 per ticket fare increase allowed in 1953 (Lee and Adams dissenting). The CAB relented under this fusillade, allowing the courts to review the charges and the validity of federal regulations on which the case was grounded. Holifield considered the real aim to "get" North American for "flying too many people, too often, too cheaply, and without subsidy."[109] In fairness to the CAB, regulations existed against these very practices; what the critics really attacked was the wisdom of this regulatory policy. The CAB's Rizley pointed out that all members agreed to the existence of violations by North American but that such punishment did not fit the crime. Rizley admitted the only charges against North American encompassed a combination whereby this company, in effect, served as a regularly scheduled airline.[110] Some forty-nine of the irregulars had been allowed to fly up to ten trips per month between any pair of locations. Charges arising in 1958 implicating (Sherman) Adams with interceding in behalf of North American were labeled as utterly false by CAB member Denny in a letter to Congressman Oren Harris, Democrat of Arkansas: "North American needed no instruction in the fine art of appealing to the courts."[111]

SUBSIDIES AND RATES

The issue regarding fares raised board member Adams' charge: "In its entire existence this Board has not yet conducted a judicious investigation of air fares in the interests of the traveling public."[112] During World War II the board had acted to curtail fare increases and in 1952 announced a general fare investigation. But all the trunk lines requested a dismissal of this action and the CAB relented by a vote of 3 to 2. In 1945, the air carriers lowered fares to 4½ cents per mile as the CAB agreed to lower the airmail rate ranging from 60 cents to 45 cents, instead of 32 cents. Determination of proper fares, in fact, subsidies as well, depended upon proper knowledge of the industry by the board. To this end, the Comptroller General advised House Speaker Sam Rayburn in 1956 that the CAB should undertake a long-range study of all routes, using the records of the carriers' total operations and requiring annual audits by the carriers. Existing fares were 6 cents for first class and 4½ cents for daytime coach. Such an investigation was ordered by new Chairman Durfee.[113] Meanwhile, North American, now called Trans American, offered for board approval transatlantic fares of $125 to $146.50, allowing the passengers to purchase their own meals at Gander and Shannon and using the DC-6B with 100 seats. Trans American had introduced the coast-to-coast fare of $80 in 1952.

One persistent roadblock to understanding financial accounting resulted from the combination of subsidy and airmail payments to the airlines. Post Office officials, following the arrangement already established in the thirties, paid the airmail subsidy upon the recommendation of the CAB. In 1950, Senator Edwin C. Johnson, Democrat of Colorado, led the fight for separation of airmail pay from the direct subsidy (Senate bill 1431) which would let the CAB, in effect, have a better overview of all airline finances.[114] Supporters did not foresee a reduction in airmail payments, which totaled $125 million at the time. CAB Chairman Nyrop advised President Truman of the separation on October 1, 1951.[115] In the process of change, the CAB accomplished a saving of $4,959,000 in the Big Four mail-rate case (Eastern, TWA, American, and United) by reducing their rates from 63 cents per ton-mile to 45 cents.[116] During 1953, 10 of the 13 domestic trunk lines remained free of subsidy mail pay. On October 1, 1953, the board was made responsible for the subsidy pay while the service mail pay was returned to the Postmaster General. The airmail costs baffled members of Congress who continually queried CAB leadership about the situation. Chairman Gurney explained the handling costs (Post Office) at $81 million while the airlines received $120 million.[117] Gurney figured the transatlantic costs amounted to 85 cents a ton-mile for mail, the same rate as for a first-class passenger. Finally, the CAB allowed the airlines to instigate another experiment—carrying certain first-class mail by air (October 6, 1953).[118] Immediately, the railroad interests protested this competition, even though railroad hauling of first-class mail in 1953 amounted to just 0.4 per cent of the total railroad operating revenues.[119] The majority of the board agreed to let the railroads test their decision in court if they believed CAB action illegal. Member Lee dissented vigorously against his colleagues. Once again the cargo carriers offered to outbid the regular lines, this time to haul first-class mail for 18.66 cents per ton-mile compared to the lowest of 45 cents paid to the passenger lines. Slick Airways, Inc., The Flying Tiger Line, and Riddle Airlines made the offer which was supported by the Postmaster General but rejected by the CAB.[120]

The complications of mail payment also included the problem of rates for international flights. A formula was found in the Merchant Marine Act of 1936, indicating that contracts for subsidy should not exceed ten years. In return for the service, the company should return to the government one-half of all its profits over 10 per cent on its investment. The law allowed the Postmaster General to fix international mail rates, assuming he would follow the rate of the Universal Postal Union (established in 1872). Foreign nations paid U.S. airlines ($11 million in 1951) for carrying their mail; the United States reciprocated with the foreign companies ($2 million) for hauling our mail.[121]

JOHN F. KENNEDY vs. SUBSIDIES

The boon to aviation profits caused by the Korean War led many critics to attack further the program of subsidies, both for airmail and direct aid, as continued by the government. On the other hand, proponents of subsidies considered the aid necessary if the aviation industry were to introduce jet aircraft and test it for widespread commercial use. Much has already been mentioned about the unfavorable opinion in Congress surrounding the interests of PAA. In hearings before the House Appropriations Subcommittee in 1954, Chairman Gurney asserted that there had been no complete audit of PAA prior to December 31, 1950. Then an audit was made in 1952 but without the inclusion of PAA's vast affiliated companies—foreign airlines, hotels, radio stations, etc. John F. Kennedy, a persistent foe of high subsidies since 1949 when he submitted the first bill to separate subsidy and mail costs, echoed Congressman Rooney's sentiments in the Senate. Kennedy pointed to the Supreme Court's stand in *Summerfield v. CAB* which instructed the CAB to consider the entire operation of the airline in determining subsidies. Kennedy further reminded the Senate Appropriations Subcommittee of the promises aired in 1938 for a reduction in subsidies. In 1954, only three trunk lines—Continental, Northeast, and Colonial—remained on subsidy. CAB members testified that they disallowed costs of various strikes against the airlines when deciding on the amount of subsidies paid, a long-standing practice. A year later Senator Douglas entered a plea against subsidies for PAA's hotel chains.[122] Joining the critics, the railroad interests once more voiced their disdain toward aviation subsidies: "No other form of domestic transportation receives a greater variety of outright subsidies and direct or indirect aids than the commercial airlines."[123] Douglas' plea for an audit finally paid off in 1956 when the CAB launched an integrated survey of PAA's domestic subsidiaries for the first time.[124] Member Gurney then expressed his opinion against subsidy for any line even if it reverted back to a position where subsidy might be needed.[125] The CAB alleged that PAA improperly charged depreciation costs, failed to allocate overhaul costs to subsidiaries, and in a number of cases, deviated from the board's uniform system of accounts.[126] These practices, according to the CAB, enabled PAA to receive higher operating costs and an increase of $6.5 million in subsidy for 1954 on its Pacific division. PAA had received $200 million in subsidies since 1938 not including another $300 million in mail pay.

Subsidies remained on the books of several American air carriers (feeders) despite concerted efforts each year by a few congressmen to eliminate the practice. For example, in 1958 Senator Thruston B. Morton, Republican of Kentucky, entered his plea for Senate bill 3887 to eliminate subsidy from domestic trunk lines. He was joined by Senators Strom Thurmond, Wallace F. Bennett, John Marshall Butler, Russell B. Long, and William Proxmire. The effort died in committee.[127] Amazing to politicians and economic experts was the attitude of Eastern's boss Eddie V. Rickenbacker, who in 1949 proudly reminded congressmen that his line operated without subsidy; he claimed the other twenty lines did not because of inefficiency.[128] Rickenbacker announced that over 95 per cent of his company's routes had been opened to duplicate competition; but the key rested with the cost level, 48.19 cents per revenue ton-mile for Eastern during 1947, the lowest of all competitors. Next lowest was United's 51.04; Northeast's ranked costliest at 94.87. As the domestic trunk lines slowly went off subsidy during the early and middle fifties, the international carriers faced a similar challenge, especially from the antagonistic congressional reaction toward PAA which went off subsidy on October 1, 1956. By 1958, only Braniff, of the international lines, remained on subsidy, receiving $781,000.[129]

DECISIONS CRITICIZED

In further transactions, Congressman Samuel N. Friedel of Maryland alleged "skullduggery" in the board action rejecting PAA's Baltimore–Miami run in favor of Northeast which he claimed had no four-engine planes for the route.[130] Smallness did not deter leading politicians from pleading for Northeast's request to gain a New York–Florida route; Congressman John McCormack and Senators Leverett Saltonstall and Styles Bridges opposed the CAB's award of this service to Delta.[131] Edgy solons looked with strong disfavor on the attempt by six leading airlines to effect fare increases in 1957. Congressman Charles A. Vanik of Ohio contended that in one case—Eastern—the increase in passenger miles and net income failed to reflect the need for such a request. Meanwhile, Senator Morse paid a tribute to Joseph P. Adams, the man Eisenhower failed to reappoint to the CAB. Morse lamented, "Aviation has become a blue sky club, and the CAB is little more than the doorman. . . ."[132] In his six-year tenure, this dissenter favored air-coach fares and a general fare investigation. He opposed increases in transatlantic fares, the $1 per ticket raise in 1952, and the enforcement action against North American Airlines.

PUBLIC SUGGESTIONS

During 1945–1958, too, the CAB received many suggestions—both solicited and unsolicited—as to how the air carriers could improve their services, meals and drinks included. Any seasoned air traveler will understand the need for the stewardesses' mint or gum offerings for the takeoff—the better to minimize the pressure of pending variations in altitude for the passengers. However, not all agreed as to the merits of continual consumption of heavy foods. In 1949, board members, though split on the question, suggested that carriers might economize by eliminating meals during flight. Western and Inland both adopted the proposal.[133] Prohibition of alcoholic beverages on airplanes became the object of House action in 1956, though critics decried the move calling it a sop to the dries not unlike the Eighteenth Amendment.[134] Reportedly the carriers set up a code in 1956 suggesting no advertising of liquor and limiting sales to two drinks per person. However, the problem would come up again for argument.

A further accumulation of woes for the CAB accrued from various quarters of the aviation community. The Aviation Securities Committee of the Investment Bankers Association of America called for an overhaul of the CAB's regulatory policies. Specifically, this group claimed that the board allowed overexpansion of competition and frowned on mergers and depreciation policies. The group demanded an increase in fares.[135] The opposite viewpoint constituted the usual mode of attack on the CAB. For example, one critic charged the CAB with promoting the welfare of favored transportation companies rather than workable or desirable competition.[136] Member Hector took this approach in his vigorous dissent of the CAB's denial of TWA's transcontinental Siesta Sleeper service, which had been opposed by United and American.[137]

A case study of the role assumed by the CAB in aviation's labor disputes revealed the record embracing mergers and strikes prior to 1952.[138] The partial merger of UAL and Western (Los Angeles–Denver) brought no compensation to released employees (23 pilots, 14 stewardesses, and 43 ground personnel) despite friendly statements by the CAB which sponsored a mediation conference. The PAA-AOA merger in 1950 brought the CAB in once more as leader of mediatory efforts. Again, the board came only slowly to the realization that if it extended increased mail pay or other boosts to an airline under strike the action might cripple union bargaining. From labor's vantage point the line must incur economic loss. Senator Johnson (Colorado) lamented the board's refusal to allow the merger of Colonial and Eastern in 1954; but it granted the request two years later. Delta and Chicago and Southern were granted a merger, as were Flying Tiger and Slick.[139]

CRASHES AND HINDSIGHT

The crucial impact on the public resulting from a series of tragedies constituted the worst enemy to aeronautical advancement. Crashes during 1946–1947 led to much criticism and soul searching. Delays in introducing GCA (radar) equipment were cited by Congressman Philip J. Philburn of Massachusetts as contributing to accidents: "The wheels of bureaucracy move slowly and painfully even in the face of a great public crisis."[140] Much of this impatience reflected an immature view toward the immediate postwar era encumbered by the painfully slow transition from low to high frequency radio in addition to the lag in wider installation of GCA.

Unfortunately, the politicians blamed the CAA or CAB for almost any crash instead of restricting the criticism to the legitimate instances of governmental neglect. A drove of well-wishers, crackpots, serious inventors—the differences being most difficult to perceive—descended upon the Department of Commerce and CAB with their pet theories. Each promised to prevent further accidents.[141] The crash of a blazing EAL DC–3 in a swamp near Florence, South Carolina, prompted one editor to suggest that perhaps we should return to the practice of avoiding flight when "the birds are walking today. Maybe they know more about flying than we do."[142] More realistically, Secretary of Commerce Harriman noted, "I'm afraid most of us have over-emphasized the equipment's part in producing safety and dependability while giving too little attention to the less tangible human factor."[143] Nevertheless, Administrator T. P. Wright would not discount the need for better aids: "While it is necessary to put many accidents down on the books as caused by pilot error, I am inclined to think that in a good number of these the error would not have occurred if the pilot had had better navigational aids."[144] Granted, the war aids offered no panacea; Wright cited the higher accident rate in the military compared with commercial operations. Obviously, both humans and equipment contributed to the carnage of this era. Joining the CAB in 1946 as Director of Safety was Colonel Wallace S. Dawson, an aeronautical inspector with the old Aeronautics Branch (1928–1929) and later a pilot with EAL for eleven years.

A PAA flying boat crashed at Fort-de-France, Martinique, on August 3, 1945, because the company had not provided approved or adequate letdown procedures nor had the company advised the crew of hazardous weather.[145] The CAA also chided PAA for a crash of another flying boat at Port of Spain, Trinidad, on January 8, 1945. The visibility was unlimited but the first officer, an inexperienced performer, was landing the craft without wearing glasses as required by his certificate. A unique accident—the CAB could find none similar previously—occurred on July 2, 1946, when a TWA liner landed in a field because of fuel starvation. The left engine failed at 600 feet after which the pilot turned left in order to return, only to witness the other engine stopping after 90 degrees of his turn. Miraculously all escaped injury.[146] Twenty-seven people died near Richmond, Virginia, after a pilot shut down the wrong engine when encountering excessive vibration.[147] At Nashville, Tennessee, a pilot mistook the lights of a slow-moving train for runway lights.

Violation of existing air regulations led to the crash at Seattle (January 2, 1949) of a chartered DC–3 operated by Seattle Air Charter, Inc., a one-man organization.[148] One pilot allegedly refused to board the plane, presumably because of excessive ice on the wings. Two CAA men, alerted by a call from this pilot, discussed the situation but were unable to stop the flight which was to bring tragedy to eleven Yale University students and the crew. There were eleven survivors of the crash. Under existing rules, control tower operators could not refuse clearance if the pilot insisted on taking off. One detects the chagrin with which CAA authorities faced criticism of this crash. Liability of the control personnel was out of the question for the pilot knew of the existing weather conditions. Furthermore, the plane had been parked on the field without wing covers during a snowfall of 2 to 3 inches. Snow removal consisted of dragging a rope across the wings. Alcohol was used to loosen the ice on the upperside of the wings but the mechanic failed to clear the underside. The pilot took off overloaded by 1,500 pounds, with the ice and frost on the wings and while the air temperature and dew point were both 29° F.

The crashes of a UAL liner on takeoff, and an EAL liner from 4,000 feet on May 30, 1947, plus the ramming into a mountain by a Pennsylvania Central craft led President Truman to name a President's Special Board of Inquiry on Air Safety. Members were: CAB Chairman Landis; Administrator Wright; M. W. Arnold, ATA; H. P. Cox, ALPA; and Dr. Jerome C. Hunsaker, Chairman of NACA.[149] Meanwhile bizarre causes, indeed, were discovered for these and earlier postwar crack-ups. The CAB blamed the pilot for climbing the wrong direction from Stephenville, Newfoundland, on October 3, 1946—all 39 aboard perished—but hastened to add that the air carrier, American Overseas, should have reminded him of the necessary right turn.[150] The board surmised that the gust lock had been left in the "on" position, thus preventing the UAL plane from rising on takeoff and causing the craft to crash across Grand Central Parkway killing 43 of the 48 aboard (May 29, 1947, at La Guardia Field). As for the Pennsylvania Central Airlines (PCA), later Capital, crash on June 13, 1947, the CAB stated that the pilot accepted faulty clearance from CAA controllers and flew his DC–4 at 1,425 feet over terrain rising between 1,600 and 1,800 feet. All 50 aboard died. Perhaps the most mysterious of all was the crash of the EAL plane—all 53 passengers succumbed—at Bainbridge, Maryland, on May 30, 1947. Ironically, the tragedy was witnessed by two CAB men flying their plane just 3 miles behind the commercial craft.[151] Unsolved, too, was the crash of a PAA Boeing 377 (Stratocruiser) en route to Honolulu from San Francisco on November 8, 1957; no radio warning had been received from the ship carrying 44 persons to death at sea.

The President's Special Board made its final report early in 1948, stressing fires as a major cause of accidents and requesting better salaries for air controllers. Arnold, refusing to sign the report, wrote a dissent which claimed the group should have restricted its activities to the three specific accidents leading to its creation.[152] The freak tragedies continued as all 52 aboard a UAL flight died on October 24, 1947, near Bryce Canyon, Utah, because of fire from combustion of gasoline brought about by an inadvertent overflow of gasoline during fuel transfer out of the No. 4 alternate tank.[153] Meanwhile, the nation's feeder lines experienced no fatalities during 1946–1947. A CAA crew of 3 inspectors checking the new vhf facilities near Ward, Colorado, lost their lives in a crash apparently caused by a sudden downdraft at 14,500 feet on January 21, 1948. The wreckage was not found until May 23, 1948. Quick rescue efforts by the crew of the U.S. Coast Guard *Bibb*, a weather ship, saved all 69 aboard a plane of American International Airways, a nonscheduled craft, on the North Atlantic (October 14, 1947). Here, the CAB ruled excessive gross weight, no cruise control, and the failure to utilize available weather data with reference to speed and navigational fixes.[154] The probable cause of the disaster befalling 43 occupants of a UAL DC–6 near Mount Carmel, Pennsylvania, on June 17, 1948, was carbon dioxide in the cockpit. The crew had discharged the CO_2 bottles because of an activated fire warning when actually no fire existed. The plane continued on for ten minutes of silence after the last report until the crash.[155] Accidentally reloading discharged mail threw off the center of gravity (an excess of 244 pounds) and led to the crack-up of a helicopter, killing the pilot at Los Angeles on January 21, 1949.[156] Another display of faulty maintenance occurred in the crack-up of a plane operated by Strato-Freight, Inc., near San Juan, Puerto Rico, on June 7, 1949. Fifty-three of the 81 aboard died. Investigators found overloading of the craft and use of improper spark plugs—30 of the 36 in the right engine.[157]

Just as the "rash" of crashes occurring in 1947 led to consternation, so did several fateful incidents previously cited at Newark, New Jersey, airport. Three crashes killed 116—in the air and on the ground—affecting the nearby city of Elizabeth during the initial weeks of 1952. Particularly disturbing to congressmen was the crash of a DC–6 two minutes after takeoff with investigators finding the No. 3 engine reverse feathered and No. 4 stopped.[158] Administrator Horne, hoping to prevent further similar tragedy, advised the airlines to separate the wiring for the propeller feathering controls from all other wires in the plane. Then four crashes in the New York City area, covering the first four months of 1952, led to a bad case of jitters for residents and critics. Many blamed—quite unjustly—the CAA and CAB for this tragic turn of events.

COLLISIONS

The accidents in crowded cities included another growing menace—the collision of aircraft—long forecast from the surge of interest in flying and the inauguration of faster planes after World War II. A few examples of the most publicized collisions during 1945–1958 easily reflect human failure, a lack of caution in aircraft design to help alleviate such hazards, and the absence of sufficient governmental precautions instituted against the menace until after the shock of the nation following spectacular collisions. The CAB contended that the failure of a PAA pilot and the pilot of a private plane to observe each other led to a collision over Long Island, New York, on January 30, 1949. Miraculously, the commercial liner was landed safely; the 2 on the private plane perished.[159] The same PAA pilot unfortunately met death with his jet crew and passengers during a thunderstorm in December, 1963. Acrobatics by a navy pilot, according to the CAB, led to the horrendous collision of his plane with a commercial liner of EAL, killing all 15 on the civilian plane and the military flier on July 30, 1949, near Chesterfield, New Jersey.[160] Fate struck quickly again the same year (November 1) when a Bolivian military pilot collided with an EAL plane at Washington, D.C.—all 55 died on the commercial plane. The crash occurred at an altitude of 300 feet and just one-half mile from the end of the runway.[161] The Bolivian, Erick Rios Bridoux, lived to see his pilot certificate revoked and was charged with operating his P–38 "in a careless and reckless manner . . . lack of judgment, caution and disposition to submit to regulation."[162]

For every collision, dozens of "near misses" could be recorded and, indeed, dramatically illustrate the dangers existing on the airways. Congressmen Kennedy and Rooney survived one harrowing "near accident" over Washington, D.C., in 1949. Rooney declared, "It was pretty close if he knew it."[163] Congressman H. G. Haskell of Delaware alleged the receipt of reports of 452 near collisions by the CAB during the first four months of 1956, in addition to 131 midair collisions, of which 17 involved commercial transports, in the past decade. Haskell blamed the CAA for lack of proper separation of aircraft, sometimes allowing two planes to arrive at the same checkpoint simultaneously.

One pilot over the Riverdale checkpoint on April 7, 1956, called the center at Washington, D.C.: "All right, center, let's quit playing around and get some separation and get somebody down out of here."[164] Another airliner took off at Baltimore but had to turn abruptly 1 mile out to avoid a helicopter, then three more helicopters; no one in the tower knew of the helicopters' presence in the area.

The ultimate in misfortune and irony of fate was yet to unfold. On June 30, 1956, a UAL DC–7 and TWA Super Constellation collided in Arizona near the wastelands of the Grand Canyon, killing all 128 aboard. Senator Humphrey voiced the sentiments of his bewildered countrymen when he demanded stricter control of airline operations by the federal authorities.[165] *The Washington Star* recalled the Harding Report (1955) which had said of collisions: "Fortunately, so far, none have been between two of our largest transports when fully loaded."[166] Now such a tragedy was history, and unfortunately, would be repeated a few years later. Editorially, the nation's newspapers demanded action. The *Las Vegas Review Journal* blamed the CAA: "The airlines, of course, will have to assume their portion of the responsibility, but the fundamental error lies with the CAA."[167] The average layman failed to understand that the responsibility in this instance, as in any VFR flying, rested with the TWA pilot who was assigned to fly "1,000 and on top." The CAA, after the crash, quickly established an airway over the Grand Canyon, but once more Americans were numbed. This time (January 31, 1957) at Los Angeles, test planes—a DC–7 and a Northrop F–89 jet fighter—collided at 17,000 feet, the fuselage of the DC–7 falling onto a school yard killing two children. Again, tragedy which should have been anticipated brought action. The CAA would now designate local flying areas for all test flights, "choosing sparsely populated geographical locations in light air-traffic areas."[168] But the military menace scored yet another strike near Las Vegas on April 21, 1958. This time a DC–7 and an F–100 of the Air Force came together as the military craft descended on training orders from 30,000 feet to the airliner traveling at 21,000 feet.[169] The report was unbelievable that the CAA control tower at Las Vegas and the military (6 miles away) at Nellis Air Force Base had no contacts, no coordination of flight data.

The collision at Las Vegas resulted in a bitter argument between the CAA and CAB, the CAB claiming that the CAA did not report the dangerous military penetrations of the airways in the

area until after the crash. Administrator Pyle reported that the
CAB failed to grant the CAA any powers to regulate the military
maneuvers in any different manner and that voluntary agreements were impossible to obtain until after this collision and
one in Maryland.[170] UAL allegedly had lodged complaints to
CAA before the collision without results. Senator Monroney's
conclusion fit the miserable affair well. He called it "almost as
dangerous as a busy intersection at which the red lights were
supervised by one agency and the green lights by another."[171]
But on May 20, the air over Brunswick, Maryland, was the scene
of a collision between a T–33 jet trainer and a Viscount commercial aircraft. The Las Vegas and Maryland crashes together cost
sixty-one lives.

Through the din of outrage from various critics rose the
voice of CAB Chairman Durfee to remind Americans of the
advances in air safety: "Notwithstanding the black banners you
see spread across page one when there is an accident—flying is
safer by far for intercity travel than driving your car. . . . If the
CAB were to insist on positive control today—eighty-five percent
of our air traffic would be grounded."[172] Then, too, the safety
record of the commercial airlines undeniably rated tops. If one
compared this rating with the Military Air Transport Service, he
would find insurance rates approximately ten times higher for
traveling on the military planes.[173]

The whole question of military-civilian collisions again
raised the problem of airspace reservations. Retraction of the
military rights granted during wartime and the emergency in
Korea was, indeed, a painfully slow process for civilian leadership to accomplish. In one case, the CAB ordered the military to
aid by a special regulation allowing civilian aircraft to take off
at Phoenix without interference from military jet traffic.[174] The
CAA had appealed to the CAB for help. Senator Barry Goldwater
lamented the airspace reservations of the military yet clearly
understood the needs of the Air Force which he also served.[175] In
1957, the CAA embarked on a three-stage program to control
flights at various levels, beginning with positive control of all
flights above 24,000 feet. Administrator Pyle, pointing out that
air routes appeared like a crazy quilt, indicated that 2,500
variations in transcontinental flight plans existed for one airline
alone.[176] Another change for the better came with the CAA's
right to reserve airspace, effective April 1, 1958. The Air Coordinating Committee had performed this task since 1947.[177]

Veteran observers hailed the ruling as a victory for the civilian CAA over the military in a last-ditch effort to save valuable airspace.[178] Halford Noggle, with the CAA since 1946, assumed the position as Assistant Administrator of Airspace. Over a year of tug-of-war preceded acceptance by the Department of Defense of the new arrangement. Defense reportedly boycotted the CAB-sponsored discussions of the proposal, but Secretary Donald Quarles relented on February 7, 1958. Defense leaders admitted overcrowding on the airways but contended such control should remain within the jurisdiction of the ACC. A result of the Grand Canyon disaster brought the inaugural of IFR control of all flights above 9,500 feet in the triangle made by New York; Washington, D.C.; and Chicago (The Golden Triangle).[179]

The increasing number of air collisions, especially with such high death tolls brought about by use of larger craft, raised the question of liability. A Supreme Court ruling of 1955 declared the federal government and EAL both liable for claims resulting from the crash of an Eastern DC-4 and a military P-38 (killing fifty-five) in 1949.[180] The government's responsibility was explained by the involvement of CAA control-tower operators. An earlier case had tested the claims of a victim's mother, who asked for $25,000 in a damage suit against the CAA. She alleged negligence on the part of controllers at Washington, D.C., in assigning altitude for the plane which crashed near Leesburg, Virginia, on June 13, 1947.[181] Court instructions defined controllers' advice an "exercise of judgment" and not to be construed as lacking "in due care." Such were the woes confronting the CAB in relation to accidents and the watchdog functions inherent therein. These, in turn, greatly affected the operation of the CAA in its duty to provide measures of safety which should reduce the annual toll of fatalities in aviation.

13

GENERAL QUESADA'S
TEMPESTUOUS REIGN–1959-1961

IN 1959, the reorganized federal entity to be known as the Federal Aviation Agency now existed as a separate unit outside the jurisdiction of Commerce. Simultaneously, the United States joined the parade of nations offering the ultimate in speed and comfort with the inaugural of commercial jet schedules. The keen observer of aviation history might well have thought that progress and economy of operation had reached their zenith with the jet and the new, streamlined, regulatory position of the FAA, along with the long-standing independence of the CAB. True, the air traveler did receive the best transportation facilities in U.S. history as a result of these factors. But the aviation world, particularly in the United States during 1959–1961, witnessed a complexity of events quite demoralizing and damaging to the relationship between the FAA and CAB as well as the aviation industry in general. In retrospect, one might well ascertain that both sides must share the blame for this unhappy state of affairs at a crucial time when foreign competitors eagerly sought to corner portions of the U.S. business and when, technologically speaking, the United States, with its splendidly designed jet aircraft, stood in a position of unquestioned leadership within the world's aviation community.

The center of this gigantic struggle between government and business during the final two years of the Dwight Eisenhower Administration was General E. R. "Pete" Quesada, formerly special assistant to the President for aviation matters and

Chairman of the Airways Modernization Board. Quesada, selected as head of the new FAA, presented a commendable past record of military service.[1] Born in Washington, D.C., he later attended the University of Maryland and Georgetown University before joining the Army in 1924. He entered the air service and was named a second lieutenant in the regular army in 1927. During World War II, Quesada directed operations of the Twelfth Fighter Command, was deputy commander of the Northwest African Coastal Air Force, then led the Ninth Fighter Command before and during the Normandy invasion. A veteran of ninety combat missions, Quesada during 1949–1951, headed Joint Task Force Three—including the Army, Navy, Air Force, and the Atomic Energy Commission—in Operation Greenhouse, resulting in the test detonation of the first hydrogen bomb. Quesada retired with the rank of brigadier general in 1951, after which he took posts as a director and officer of the Olin Industries and Lockheed Aircraft Corporation. Quesada, 54, had married Kate Davis Pulitzer, daughter of the *St. Louis Post-Dispatch*'s publisher, after gracing the social world around the nation's capital as a much sought after bachelor.

James T. Pyle remained with the new FAA as deputy administrator. Quesada's AMB became a part of the new FAA with 351 employees being involved in the transfer. The 27,771 employees of the former CAA, along with 24 workers in the CAB, also moved into the FAA. Among the other early appointments was William B. Davis, Director of the Bureau of Flight Standards, a veteran of twenty years with the CAA, a graduate of Tufts, and a former naval aviator. David D. Thomas became Director of the Bureau of Air Traffic Management. He, too, had recorded twenty years under the CAA, starting as an assistant controller at Pittsburgh, and was a graduate of the University of Tennessee.

Those individuals who lamented the inclusion of former military leaders in key civilian positions observed Quesada's initial actions with extreme caution to detect evidence substantiating their fears. During his first few months in office, Quesada remained calm before the taunts of adversaries both in and out of committee meetings, thus avoiding a show of bad temper predicted by detractors.[2] At the same time, one correspondent noted Quesada's cockiness and quite accurately predicted that "sparks are bound to fly."[3] *Time* reporters, among others, lauded Quesada's early victory in regaining over 50 per cent of the budget requests in the Senate which had been slashed in the House. Furthermore, the former fighter pilot illustrated his desire to promote military-FAA accord by persuading the Air Force to allow the FAA use of additional military radar facilities— many key locations on air "expressways" from California to New York and Florida to Gander, Newfoundland.[4] Quesada further pleased the civilian aviation interests by his determination to release for their use much of the airspace then restricted for the military. Certainly one must conclude that "Ike's" personal pilot on D-Day now had the best interests of the entire U.S. aviation community at heart in his quest for progress in the future. What, then, were the principal factors contributing to the impending feud between a sizable portion of the aviation interests and Quesada? First, his military background—the very manner in which authority is assumed, orders are issued, obedience is demanded, and disobedience harshly punished—brought the well-meaning FAA chieftain into a major conflagration with the ALPA, a segment of his FAA employees, and other individuals in the aviation industry—mechanics, private pilots, aircraft executives, etc. Interestingly enough, the Senate's consideration of Quesada's appointment as FAA head brought rather unusual fears, in addition to the wariness of military control, from the late Senator Clair Engle, Democrat of California. Engle, stating at once that he would not oppose the nomination, nevertheless lamented certain general views attributed earlier to Quesada: "I am informed that General Quesada at one time had the idea that a private airplane had no business going into a major airport such as Washington's National, New York's La Guardia, Los Angeles' International. He denied it later."[5] Engle held fears about Quesada's attitude toward aviation safety and disagreed with his comments to the effect that federal officials should not build further airports.

STRONGER REGULATIONS

Senator Engle's concern regarding Quesada's views on aviation safety proved to be entirely unfounded, for the military leader soon demonstrated an unrelenting zeal in promoting improvement in this sphere. Within less than one year of his appointment, Quesada proved to the experts that he meant business with his "get tough" policies which greatly altered the Civil Air Regulations. For example, copilots faced an intensified training program compared to the past, with flight tests including climbs, turns, slow flight, approach to a stall, takeoff and landing with simulated engine failure, instrument approach, and missed approach.[6] Now an FAA inspector or an FAA-designated company check pilot must conduct the test flight of the copilot once every twelve months instead of allowing the regular flight pilot to perform this task. Written and oral examinations were added to the new standards. Physical standards also drew Quesada's attention, with general tightening of already existing rules. Now license applicants had to obtain physical examinations from designated physicians, not their own doctors. Dr. James Goddard, FAA civil air surgeon, expected few rejections as certificates had already been denied for several diseases, e.g., diabetes mellitus requiring insulin, coronary artery disease, a history of psychosis or certain other mental or nervous disorders, chronic alcoholism, drug addiction, or epilepsy. In 1957, only 0.6 per cent of the 226,390 California applicants for all three classes of certificates were denied for medical reasons; one-half were rejected because of diabetic, cardiovascular, or nervous and mental deficiencies.

Another new rule of a medical nature did bring about considerable debate—the forced retirement of pilots at the age of sixty. Quesada, armed with medical evidence, stressed the fact that sudden incapacitations, due primarily to heart attacks or strokes, occur more frequently in any group after the age of sixty. Furthermore, the FAA assumed the position that medical men cannot predict these attacks. At its inception, the new proposal received the support of the ATA (Air Transport Association) but was bitterly opposed by the ALPA which desired individual testing of pilot fitness.

Further tightening of the CAR's included the requirement that all commercial pilots must complete a minimum of ten hours in instrument flight instruction, part of which entailed the ability to control the aircraft manually, and demonstrate a cross-country, planned flight. Relating to private pilots, the FAA amendments reflected deep concern over the 272 major accidents during 1958, in which 345 pilots and passengers died, and 155 others were seriously injured. Forty-four per cent of these accidents resulted from the inability to cope with emergencies; 46 per cent of the mishaps stemmed from a fundamental weakness in pilot judgment or technique. Consequently, private pilots now must have dual instruction in instruments and simulated loss of visual reference, radio competence, and cross-country training.

Moving from the realm of pilot skill to technical aids, the FAA now declared that airborne radar would become a mandatory feature, with various effective dates according to the type of craft. The aim was to require radar for all IFR flights and night VFR trips when thunderstorms or severe weather were forecast within areas of the flight plan. Opposed at the time by most of the carriers, the use of radar on one airline had aided in achieving a higher percentage of completed trips. The ALPA strongly endorsed Quesada's suggestion. The local air carriers opposed radar for the DC-4 and C-46. The FAA established the final target date of January 1, 1962, for mandatory use of radar on all planes except the C-46. Finally, Quesada moved in on the question of drunkenness aloft by ruling against the consumption of alcoholic beverages aboard an air carrier unless the drink had been served by carrier personnel. The airline could refuse to serve anyone who appeared to be intoxicated. The FAA authorities and previously the CAA claimed no safety hazard from drunks but objected to the nuisance factor.

RESERVATIONS vs. THE MILITARY

Announcement of the changed CAR's, coupled with the FAA's vigorous enforcement of existing rules, led to a lively debate in Congress about the merits of Quesada's initial months at the helm. Senator Engle, echoing his reservations in approving the military man's original appointment, now reviewed his consistent opposition to military generals serving on government boards, agencies, or commissions. Engle considered the administrator as judge, jury, and prosecutor. He berated Quesada's harsh treatment of licensed pilots, the difficulties in getting successful appeal of FAA decisions by the pilots, and the "guilty-till-innocent" approach and offered legislation to allow the CAB review powers over FAA actions.[7] Engle's bills never emerged from committee. Opposing additional military men in civilian positions, Engle, supported by Senator John A. Carroll, Democrat of Colorado, likened the procedure to the "foxes watching the hen houses." Engle continued, "I do not believe that a lifetime of military service qualifies a man to handle these great regulatory agencies. . . . I say that it is time to blow the whistle and to stop it. We shall have a little Pentagon in the civilian regulatory agencies. . . ."[8] Senator Gale W. McGee, Democrat of Wyoming, joined Engle in reminding his colleagues that Quesada had said he would not have military men in the FAA, yet according to McGee, who cited the actual roster of military officials in the FAA, the agency bristled with colonels and brigadier generals—Quesada's old comrades in arms. Senator Carroll lamented, "The time has come now to put the military in its proper place."[9]

One could argue at length over the merits of assigning military brass to civilian posts. But more central to the FAA's existence as a separate agency with Quesada at the helm was the question of his strict enforcement proceedings. Here, the administrator mustered unqualified support from Senator Barry Goldwater, a licensed pilot and military reservist, who added, "I can point out the lackadaisical way our air traffic rules have been enforced."[10] Senator Thomas Kuchel, Republican of California, agreed. Senator Andrew F. Schoeppel, Republican of Kansas, reviewed the arguments against Quesada emanating from sophisticated lobbyists who censured the administrator: "If Administrator Quesada has erred, it is in a public-relations way; he has hurt the feelings of the executives of certain organizations by declining to accept them as exclusive spokesmen for all who fly. . . ."[11] Schoeppel later noted the opposition to his remarks by the Aircraft Owners and Pilots Association (AOPA) but quoted a release from the Air Transport Division—Transport Workers Union (AFL-CIO) representing the airline ground workers—in support of Quesada.

PILOTS AND INSPECTORS

The ground swell mushroomed greatly outside the halls of Congress. One of the most interesting, and probably one of the most childish, arguments encountered arose from the FAA's enforcement of stricter flight testing by placing an inspector on the flight deck of commercial jets. Eastern's pilots dissented by insisting that this third seat be reserved for the third pilot despite the certification of these planes without the extra crew member.[12] The protest enveloped Eastern's operation of twenty-eight flights out of Miami and also affected other points utilizing the same airplanes. The troubles spread quickly to Pan American World Airways, Trans World Airlines, and American Airlines. The ALPA, officially at least, told reporters it had ordered its pilots to fly despite the FAA inspections. However, disruption of service continued for more than a week as pilots from the several lines would suddenly and in large numbers report themselves "sick" and unable to fly. The "strike" had been banned via a temporary injunction ordered by a federal judge on June 14, 1960. In each case, the pilots contended that FAA inspectors should ride in another seat at the rear of the cockpit because the third pilot's seat directly behind the captain was needed by the crew for reasons of safety. The ALPA spokesmen told reporters that only about 2 per cent of all scheduled jet flights were checked by the FAA men. The refusal of two EAL pilots to ride with the inspectors allegedly touched off the undeclared strike.

On June 18, the ALPA called a strike against National Air Lines over disagreements in wages and working conditions. National pilots had been carrying on a battle for several months against the FAA's stricter flight checks, especially after one National captain incurred a $1,000 fine for allegedly not using his check list.[13] Quesada had sent his own FAA pilots through a rigorous checkout of the KC–135 (Boeing 707) and took the course himself. National officials agreed with the FAA and threatened the loss of licenses to all those refusing to fly with the inspectors. National pilots failed to impress Quesada with their plea that the flight tests might be deleterious to the craft's air frame.

In the fight between the pilots and the FAA, Quesada could point to the fatalities occurring in 1959. The highest for any one year, none of these 294 fatalities was attributed to the new jets.[14] Quesada declared the crew at fault in 50 per cent of 136 accidents occurring since the advent of the new FAA.[15] Senate subcommittee members heard of one pilot refusing to admit an FAA inspector to his flight deck and also failing to pay the resulting $1,000 civil penalty. Another captain assumed the posture of sleeping for thirty minutes while being checked by an inspector. An accident fatal to fifteen people involved a pilot who had failed to comply with the required medical test for three and one-half years, was overdue for his proficiency check, and about whom company records were falsified. Another crew failed to utilize the check list during an inspector's check flight. Quesada, certain that he was correct in his war on laxity, challenged the ALPA to set forth specific charges of ill treatment and misconduct by his inspectors.

ALPA DISCONTENT

Clarence Sayen, the ALPA head, appeared before the same Senate committee to assert that Quesada had caused a great amount of resentment among airline pilots through his manner of attacking the whole issue of crew efficiency. The majority of safety problems, according to Sayen, stemmed from terminal area facilities and technological difficulties.[16] Sayen lamented the absence of stringent rules calling for the copilot to be checked out on each plane he flies. The ALPA collected reports of "near misses" because pilots feared FAA incrimination against the pilot who voluntarily reported such occurrences. The ALPA urged compulsory reporting of "near misses" to the FAA (Daily Mechanical Irregularity Reports). Furthermore, the pilots' union berated the FAA for still allowing crews to operate on international runs for an outside limit of fifteen hours in bad weather.

Utilizing the slogan that it is impossible to fly without breaking the CAR's, Sayen told of one captain, with 125 passengers, who continued his takeoff despite an engine failure, later starting the engine in the air. The pilot held that a crash would have occurred had he attempted an abortive takeoff. However, the FAA ordered him removed from the schedule, action which was rescinded only following the vigorous protests of the airline company and the ALPA. The celebrated dive without a crash of a Pan American jet over the Atlantic Ocean in 1959 proved to be one of the most vexing irritants to the FAA. But Sayen reminded his audience that management, not ALPA, crewmen were flying that trip.

Sayen advised Senate leaders that his body condoned the FAA rules requiring airborne radar, a measure long proposed by the ALPA, but hoped for restrictions against the sale of alcoholic beverages, fearing that an accident caused by drinking might be attributed to "crew error." Finally, the ALPA begged for the CAB's review of all FAA rule-making. Meanwhile, the ALPA unsucessfully challenged the sixty-year automatic retirement age ruling in U.S. district court (Southern District of New York). In support of the new FAA sixty-year retirement age one could cite the following limitations imposed by foreign lines for jet operation: KLM, forty-six; Sabena, forty-seven; BOAC and SAS, each fifty-three. In addition, BOAC, KLM, and Iberia retired nonjet pilots at fifty-five; SAS at sixty.[17] It would appear from these examples that the FAA simply attempted to invoke a policy already considered progressive and realistic by foreign governments operating these competing lines.

In May, 1959, Sayen, in letters to Administrator Quesada, charged "Gestapo tactics," especially concerning the cockpit rulings which saw inspectors timing the absences of crewmen from their flight decks. Quesada answered Sayen by claiming most pilots' support of the FAA rulings aimed at avoiding recurrence of shocking midair collisions and other tragedies: "If you will meet us half-way with an attitude of helpfulness rather than harassment I am sure we can work as amicably together in the future as we have in the past."[18] The crusade for safety became intensified when the FAA warned all pilots to abide by the CAR's and the FAA interpretation and implementation of such rules.[19] Suspension would face anyone refusing to allow FAA inspectors to ride in the "jump seat" of the jetliners. Now at every turn one found an impasse between the ALPA and FAA. Medical experts with the FAA desired the opening of pilots' complete past medical records, citing the crash of one pilot (in Piedmont Airlines DC–3 with twenty-six dead) who had been receiving treatments from psychiatrists. The ALPA opposed the release of such records, even though the FAA searchers cited another case of a Midwest dentist with a record of eight light-aircraft accidents in five years.[20] Suspecting drunken flying, the FAA checked with police and discovered fifteen convictions of this person for drunken driving. Obviously, the FAA's request for any and all past information regarding crewmen was reasonable and pertinent.

Despite the warnings and Quesada's militant attack on laxity, the list of fines against the airlines continued. Senator Hubert Humphrey, Democrat of Minnesota, lamented that these fines seemed ineffectual: "I am pleased and aggrieved. . . . A tap on the wrist is not enough when the violation is something that can take human lives and cause severe and heavy property damage."[21] The list of fines appeared like a "Who's Who" of the airline industry—UAL, Pan American, American, Frontier, National, Trans-Texas, Capital, and Wien Air Alaska among those drawing the penalties primarily because of faulty maintenance. Pilots continued to incur FAA reproach. A Delta captain of a DC–8 drew a sixty-day suspension (Delta also previously had invoked the identical penalty) following his ramming a 48-foot tree over 1 mile from the end of the runway at Detroit. The plane landed safely with 107 passengers.[22] Quesada had already retired as administrator when this finding appeared, and he berated the FAA for not being harsher in its judgment because all aids were in order, the weather situation had been announced by radio, and no reason could be given for the maneuver in question. Capital Airlines paid a fine of $1,500 for using 12-ply instead of 16-ply tires on the right main landing gear of a plane; the mechanic and inspector also received $100 fines. TWA paid $15,000 after failing to have seventy flight engineers checked in twelve months.[23]

It would be only fair to General Quesada to outline the major obstacles to his safety campaign accruing from a series of additional horrendous crashes which plagued his leadership and, indeed, continue today to harass the aviation industry, government regulators, and the public. As stated earlier, the initial year of jet operation brought no scheduled-trip fatalities, even though the nonjet fatalities reached an all-time high. In the Senate, Engle in 1961 again voiced his disapproval of Quesada as he reminded his colleagues of his earlier reservations against the general. Engle considered previous observations justified, quoting accident statistics to show how the change in administrators and the change from CAA to FAA had not decreased air tragedies. Engle, a pilot himself, cited the testimony of leaders representing the AOPA, the ALPA, and the National Aviation Trades Association in calling the administrator a dictator.[24] These leaders opposed the sixty-year retirement age, found little statistical evidence offered by the FAA for its new rules, and scorned the elimination of reporting near misses. Senator Goldwater immediately rushed to the defense of the FAA, recalling that he used to call his physician who, without an examination, would send a card over to the FAA for renewal of the pilot license. Under Quesada, the FAA decreed that all private pilots must be examined only by FAA-designated doctors, a practice which had been maintained in the earlier days (pre-1945) of government regulation. Engle objected to the use of special examiners for the simple physical tests which would allow anyone who "can hear the whispered voice at three feet and has 20/30 vision . . ." to obtain the license. Goldwater scoffed at the argument and observed that "a Quesada" was long overdue.

QUESADA ANSWERS

Quesada sought and received a voice in the nation's press to air his policies. In fact, one might conclude that he overextended this privilege when it pertained to commercial accidents, voicing his immediate opinions and observations to newsmen while the CAB labored diligently, if not always successfully, to determine the probable cause. Senator Engle included this type of behavior as a further indictment of Quesada. Near the end of his reign as administrator—he resigned in March, 1961—Quesada summarized his crusade for air safety. Lashing out against the AOPA and the ALPA, Quesada held that these groups, purporting to represent the fliers, labored vociferously to embattle the FAA with charges of militarism and sought to delay its safety measures.[25] Of 38,000 FAA employees, only 130 were military men and just one major division was headed by a military officer. A further embarrassment to Quesada was the ALPA's issuance of a "Do-it-yourself kit" explaining how to write congressmen to oppose the FAA. Strictly negative and fighting all restrictions against pilots, the ALPA and AOPA magazines and confidential newsletters battled Quesada at every turn according to the administrator. Particularly bitter to Quesada was the ALPA charge of faulty FAA maintenance following the breakup in flight of a National plane in January, 1960, only to be followed by the FAA-CAB discovery of a bomb as the cause. Finally, in this and other popularized accounts of his woes, Quesada lamented the aircraft companies' resistance to safety devices—radar and flight recorders—for reasons of costs.

THE ELECTRA

Happily for the historical record, Quesada actually received support from the ALPA for one decision which involved his refusal to order grounded as unsafe the Lockheed Electra after a series of accidents. The FAA, after intensive investigations, ordered the reduction in cruising speed from the original 400 miles per hour to 316, then later to 295 miles per hour. This action allowed the factory to recall individual planes for modifications which might correct a tendency for structural weakness. In an editorial, the *Nation* questioned Quesada's move as "another attempt to substitute publicity for the type of vigorous action that builds public confidence in regulatory agencies."[26] The editors called for temporary grounding, a position they considered even more justifiable when it was learned later that the CAB recommended the grounding in direct contradiction to Quesada's opinion.[27] Quesada told congressmen, after the inspection of fifty-two Electras: "In no case have we identified any condition which would warrant the grounding of the Electra fleet."[28] Aided in the tests by the National Aeronautics and Space Administration (NASA), the FAA leadership considered the 100-knot reduction in speed a safety margin as great as that existing for any plane. Senator Vance Hartke, Democrat of Indiana, pressed the investigation and exposed the difference of opinion between the CAB and FAA. Berating the investigators, Hartke asserted, "We are witnessing government by the grapevine! I cannot get a copy of the CAB report."[29] Senator Stuart Symington, Democrat of Missouri, disagreed: "Whoever is the head person in the CAB, I am not impressed with the attempt to take potshots at the FAA action, because the latter people have made a real effort to ascertain the cause of this problem."[30] Quesada's judicious effort to maintain a neutral but technologically sound position during this controversy was a most laudable and interesting position for the administrator. Near the end of his tenure with the FAA, Quesada concluded, "My most difficult task has been to change the attitude of the people in the FAA from being too sympathetic toward the aviation industry to one that balances public and industry."[31]

MORE ACCIDENTS

A series of accidents jolted Quesada's efforts to achieve near perfection in aviation safety. These began with the dramatic crash of an Electra into the East River at New York City on February 3, 1959. Trouble with the automatic pilot allegedly was involved and American Airlines instigated new rules requiring the continuous use of the automatic position for an entire approach.[32] Ironic indeed was the fact that another liner, a jet belonging to Pan American Airways, encountered automatic pilot difficulties over the Atlantic Ocean on the same date resulting in a terrorizing dive from 29,000 feet to 6,000 feet before recovery was accomplished. In question in both instances was the Bendix PB-20D autopilot. Elsewhere, a Capital Airlines Viscount plummeted to the earth in Virginia on January 19, 1960, killing all fifty aboard.[33] In November, 1959, all the intrigue of a detective thriller enmeshed the horrendous account of a National Airlines crash into the Gulf of Mexico, probers suspecting a bomb as the cause. The madness of these perpetrators could easily be discerned from the fact that since 1938, in three such cases, two persons had been executed and two had died in the ensuing crash.[34] The 1959 mystery crash into the Gulf of Mexico was finally labeled "cause unknown" by the CAB in 1962.[35] Another bomb explosion was allegedly the cause of tragedy in the crash of a National DC–6B over Cape Fear, North Carolina, on January 6, 1960. There were no survivors. The CAB traced the more than $1 million insurance coverage on passenger J. A. Frank, the unusual shredded type of amputation on both his legs, the nitrate on Frank and on the plane, and part of the clock mechanism found in his leg bone located in the hat rack.[36] Murder or suicide were not determined by the CAB, only the probable cause of accidents.

CAB leaders turned evidence of dynamite over to the FBI which had to continue the criminal investigation. Panic reigned among numerous well-wishers who scurried to advise the FAA and CAB about the use of Geiger counters to detect metal in luggage and on the person.[37] Reduction of insurance payments to survivors and stationing of bloodhounds nearby as a "psychological deterrent" were among the other earnest suggestions. Edward E. Slattery, public information officer with the CAB for nineteen years, told aviation authorities attending an international conference in Rome, Italy, in 1961 of the CAB's development of accident investigation, its pioneering in the use of X rays in search of metal fatigue, and other methods producing a record of over 93 per cent in causes found.

Meanwhile, the son and daughter-in-law of Senator Homer E. Capehart, Republican of Indiana, were among those killed in the crash of a Colombian Super Constellation at Montego Bay, Jamaica, on January 21, 1960. Then on March 17, a Northwest Airlines Electra fell apart in the air near Tell City, Indiana, killing all 63 aboard and prompting the raging controversy over grounding as related earlier in this chapter.[38] Included among the investigators of this crash were Philip Goldstein, CAB, and Captain Carl Wilbur, navy medical corps, both of whom had studied the prior Electra crash at Buffalo, Texas (September, 1959).

The aviation world suffered further setback with the crash of a Sikorsky helicopter performing a shuttling service between Midway and O'Hare airports in Chicago; all 13 aboard died. Meanwhile, a ray of brightness emerged when 87 of 88 passengers aboard a Philippine Airlines DC–3 and a Northwest Orient Airlines DC–7C survived separate ditchings of the planes in Philippine waters. Similarly fortunate were 76 who walked away from their burning, overturned American Airlines Electra at La Guardia Airport on September 14, 1960. Not so blessed were the 78 persons killed in the crash of a World Airways DC–6B on takeoff at Agana, Guam (September 20). Sixteen survived.

The gods of fate conjured an additional misery to the turbo-prop Electra on October 4, 1960, at Logan Airport, Boston. Only 11 of 72 aboard survived this Eastern Air Lines crash allegedly brought about by a number of starlings ingested into the jet (prop) engines.[39] FAA air traffic controllers had long known of the danger caused by these birds, especially during spring and autumn migration. The Department of the Interior issued a summary outlining their presence near airports which provided food and roosting. Guns and other "scare" devices should be moved around as the birds apparently grew accustomed to noises.[40] FAA controllers noted the danger at Boston and also in Kansas City. The Boston crash reflected Administrator Quesada's willingness to express his conclusions about the probable cause long before the CAB would be capable of issuing a final report. This type of action undoubtedly evoked chagrin on the part of CAB officials despite the accuracy of Quesada's judgment. Several weeks after the Boston disaster, an Eastern DC–8 screeched to a halt after rolling about 400 feet on takeoff because of sandpipers striking the wings and air intakes. Additional friction emerged over the Boston tragedy via contentions by the Flight Engineers' International Association. One spokesman charged that the flight engineer could help more in case of emergency if the FAA rules allowed such maneuvers.[41] The CAB, investigating until summer, 1962, finally decided that the starlings had caused enough loss of power in the various engines to cause a stall and the crash into Boston Harbor. Doctors at the FAA Civil Aeromedical Research Institute (Norman, Oklahoma) believed the frequency and wave form of sound from the Lockheed Electra to be identical to the noise made by a swarm of crickets, the major source of food for the starlings.

Northwest Airlines lost a DC–4 which crashed into the mountains near Frenchtown, Montana, on October 28, killing all 12 aboard.[42] One day later the nation's air-minded citizens suffered additional revulsion over the needless crash of a chartered C–46 operated by Arctic Pacific, Incorporated. Dead were 22 people, including 18 members of the football team from California State Polytechnic College (San Luis Obispo).[43] Quesada immediately suspended the operating certificate of the airline, and the past irregularities of the dead pilot were revealed to the public. In fact, the pilot, Donald L. J. Chesher, operated the flight only because the FAA order of July 15, 1960, revoking his license had been stayed pending appeal to the CAB. The CAB, in its official report accused the airline and dead pilot of "utter disregard" of air regulations, declaring that the plane was overloaded, the engines were not warmed up sufficiently, and the pilot attempted to take off in a heavy fog.[44] In the interim, survivors of the crash faced the dilemma of legal blind alleys in attempting to obtain compensation. Arctic Pacific had gone out of business; its insurer, Lloyd's of London, refused to pay off because of the company's violation of the contract by causing unsafe conditions.[45]

COLLISION OVER NEW YORK

One of the most agonizing reports of air tragedy ever recorded closed out the fateful year of 1960 with the midair collision (December 16) over New York City involving a United Air Lines DC–8 and a Trans World Airlines Super Constellation. All 128 aboard the planes died, along with 8 persons on the ground. Subsequently a major furor ensued between the FAA and industry, particularly UAL, which blamed FAA controllers for contributing to the alleged "off course" position of its jet.[46] Another note of discord arose between the FAA and CAB, the latter's member G. Joseph Minetti and Chairman Whitney Gillilland disavowing Administrator Quesada's press conference because finding the cause was the legal concern of the CAB.[47] Faulty ground facilities and the general overburden of air traffic control in the New York City area were offered as contributing factors by interested parties. Quesada, from the outset, claimed that all FAA operations were in order. He advised CAB member Minetti of his belief that "UAL . . . is more concerned with financial liability . . . rather than assisting your Board of Inquiry."[48] Quesada reported it was an indelible record that Flight 826 (UAL's jet) was not to proceed past the Preston holding pattern. But it continued 11 miles beyond to the collision at over 400 miles per hour, not the correct 207 miles per hour. Multiple radio aids aboard the DC–8 could have provided further contacts even if the one VOR were inoperative. Other pilots reported difficulty with the VOR following the accident. However, more than 4,000 jet pilots used Preston in ninety days before the accident without reporting irregularities as required under the CAR's. At the instant of the crash, a Pan American pilot was being helped over Idlewild after reporting a faulty VOR. Similar treatment would have been available to the UAL crew.

Minetti, who was to arrange the public inquiry into the accident, resented Quesada's public statements, relevant or not, prior to the hearing.[49] Undoubtedly the CAB had a point of contention here. But an aroused public would support Quesada's relentless search for the truth in connection with this pre-Christmas debacle. Furthermore, the charges of using unrealistic holding patterns and the knowledge that even a passenger's use of a transistor radio might possibly affect the plane's navigational equipment implied additional outmoded practices crying for progressive solution.[50] The most unfortunate circumstance, aside from the loss of lives, was the continuing impasse among the FAA, CAB, ALPA, and industry representatives over the probable cause. Obviously the air traffic control system needed adjustment; just as apparent was the error on the part of the UAL crew for being off course which was the gist of the CAB's eventual probable cause.[51] United Air Lines protested the CAB report, contending the FAA should be held partially responsible for the failure of its controllers to follow the DC–8 at all times.[52] However, litigation over liability was finally decided in 1963, with the government assuming 24 per cent of the damages—despite exoneration of the FAA by the CAB—UAL paying 61 per cent, and TWA the remaining 15 per cent.[53] Attorney General Robert F. Kennedy overruled FAA Administrator Najeeb E. Halaby, Quesada's successor, in supporting the compromise, for the reason that Idlewild controllers had deviated from normal procedures (not necessarily contributing to the accident) which clouded the government's responsibility.

Ironically, two days after the DC–8 brought death to Brooklyn's streets, a U.S. Air Force transport plunged into the streets of Munich, Germany, killing all aboard and at least 35 persons on a two-car streetcar.[54] The year 1961 brought further disaster, though 102 escaped the crash on takeoff of a DC–8, operated by Aeronaves de Mexico, which departed in a blizzard from Idlewild on January 19, 1961.[55] Americans once again became involved in a foreign line's crash. On February 15, 1961, a Sabena Boeing 707 fell at Brussels, Belgium, killing 73 passengers, among whom were 18 of the U.S. figure-skating team.[56] Truly, Quesada's dreams of improved air safety had been momentarily shattered. In 1960, for the second straight year, the accident rate increased (850 fatalities) to 1 per million passenger miles flown, or the highest rate since 1952.[57]

Tension encountered by the FAA following the New York City collision is evident from a petition signed four days later by forty-five controllers at Washington National Airport. Their demand brought about the elimination of one holding point (McLean) for traffic since just 10 nautical miles separated this point from College, another check point. This was too short a distance for swift-moving planes which could easily overshoot the fix.[58] The Air Traffic Control Association, now representing 80 per cent of the control personnel, called for greater reliance on controllers' suggestions before the traffic rules were put into effect. Air controllers, more than once, have been unable to continue in their profession following a collision. The mental anguish has proved too burdensome though personal negligence has not been involved.

A NEW ADMINISTRATOR

Meanwhile, John Fitzgerald Kennedy's dramatic victory at the polls in November, 1960, brought a new administration into the White House and with it a change in FAA leadership. President Kennedy sought to bolster the federal agency's role in aviation safety but also attempted to find an administrator who would be more tactful and thus acceptable to all phases—industry and ALPA—of the aviation world while improving rapport within the FAA and between the CAB and FAA. Najeeb E. Halaby, pilot, lawyer, and financial consultant was selected as administrator on January 19, 1961, and sworn in on March 3, 1961.[59] Born in 1915, Halaby, half Syrian and half Scotch-Irish, earned his student pilot license at seventeen before becoming a commercial pilot instructor for the Army in 1940. Later, he joined Lockheed as a test pilot, then entered the Navy in 1943. After World War II, he served in the State Department as an aviation intelligence officer after which he became foreign affairs adviser to the Department of Defense. He was appointed the first chairman of the North Atlantic Treaty Organization (NATO) military production supply board and joined the Economic Cooperation Administration. He was vice-chairman of the White House Aviation Facilities Study which led to creation of the FAA out of the old CAA. In 1953, Halaby won the U.S. Junior Chamber of Commerce's Arthur Fleming Award as the "outstanding young man in the Federal Service." In addition to having his own law firm in Los Angeles, Halaby was President of the American Technological Corporation, a technical ventures group. Academically, he earned the B.A. at Stanford in 1937 and the LL. B. at Yale three years later. In a gesture of unity and humility, Halaby called a meeting of all former CAA-FAA administrators to advise him on any matters of policy they believed opportune.[60]

The years since General Quesada's retirement as administrator have not witnessed a spectacular breakthrough in technology which has eliminated further human and mechanical error. Many of Quesada's pet beliefs have been incorporated into the everyday policies of the FAA. One might conclude, however, that his successor was capable of serving as administrator without unduly alienating the ALPA, airline officials, personnel of the CAB, or his own governmental servants in the FAA. The difference between Quesada and Halaby lay in the military routine of the former and the predominantly civilian administrative leadership of the latter. As one FAA field official put it: "About eighty percent of the FAA personnel resent the 'by-the-numbers' approach." Other field employees jokingly exclaimed that they had never known what to expect next from "Quesada's Armada."

14

TECHNOLOGICAL VISTAS,
PRESENT AND FUTURE

ADMINISTRATORS E. R. Quesada and Najeeb Halaby remained alert to the tremendous changes desirable in the realm of automation to meet the increased air traffic of the jet age. Introduction of jet airplanes to commercial aviation constituted the greatest single achievement in aviation during 1959–1965. The FAA shared in this development as an overseer, investigator, and regulator. However, the horizons of greater expectations in 1959 had been extended far beyond man's wildest dreams, technologically speaking. Now the experts toyed on the drawing boards with a commercial plane capable of supersonic speeds—exceeding perhaps 2,000 miles per hour. Immediately one detected the existence of another element of concern in the United States over the supersonic aircraft, that is, the political and economic rivalries of the post-1945 era including not only the Soviet-United States debacle but also the ascendancy of our NATO allies who now challenged the United States for the lucrative international air traffic. On the surface, a major economic problem confronted aviation manufacturers and airline executives in the United States, a situation less prevalent in the several European countries where government-owned airlines had little difficulty in wooing appropriations from the national treasuries.

In the United States, aviation had mortgaged its very livelihood to the success of the new jets which scarcely had the opportunity to prove themselves before the question of a supersonic airplane invaded Congress and the aircraft industry. Frankly, if speedy and serious efforts to perfect this "dream craft" were to materialize, the federal authorities must assume a primary role in the design, testing, and in general, the entire development. In 1960, General Quesada spoke to the Investment Bankers of America in terms of an airplane capable of traveling three times the speed of sound and completing the trip from New York to London in two and one-half hours.[1] He further urged cooperation between the FAA and manufacturers of civilian planes with the existing military program for the B–70, also designed to fly upwards of 2,040 miles per hour. Quesada's target date was 1970. Administrator Halaby proceeded with the plans which gained congressional approval—appropriations of $11 million in August, 1961—for a Mach 3 (three times the speed of sound) aircraft. Sponsoring the program, along with the FAA, were NASA and the Department of Defense.[2] Halaby lauded President John F. Kennedy's foresight in lending support to the findings of the President's Project Horizon Task Force which studied the supersonic question and recommended development for civilian use as one of twenty-four national aviation goals for 1961–1970. Project Horizon emanated from the collective know-how of the nation's leading aviation experts assembled by President Kennedy. The report, issued on September 10, 1961, called for a better organized, reoriented government research effort.[3] It further stressed that NASA should concentrate on applied research, leaving the developmental chores to industry. The group urged the possibility of increased exports in an effort to help ease the United States' unfavorable balance of payments.

SUPERSONIC PROBLEMS

The FAA established a unit called the Supersonic Transport Program Management Office to labor with NASA and the Air Force on this supersonic project. Seeking the aid of industry, the FAA secured the services of Frank Kolb, American Airlines, and Russell Rourke, Trans World Airlines, as technical advisors. Technical problems confronting the group included those of aerodynamics with the study of the delta wing and the variable sweep wing. Both governmental and industrial experts began their research favoring steel or titanium alloys as the basic structural material to meet high temperature and long-life requirements without sacrificing speed. Another initial expenditure was used to study the propulsion problems. Finally, noise became a number-one problem: "We are determined to find an engine that will operate at sound levels acceptable to an airport's neighbors . . .," concluded Halaby.[4] Along this line, the sonic boom presented an equally serious operating concern. Conceivably, the pilot would have to climb above 40,000 feet to alleviate the sonic boom's effects on people and buildings along the entire path.

No doubt the joint British-French decision to combine talents in search of a Mach 2 airliner spurred on the American investigators at the end of 1962; additional appropriations of $20 million had been added in the United States to the original research.[5] Meanwhile, reports circulating in this country described Russian interest in the Mach 3, assuming the Russian policy to be one of converting military planes to civilian supersonic use. Because of their increased load capacity—over 150 seats—fewer U.S. supersonic liners would be required than was the case with existing craft. But one Mach 3 liner at approximately $25 million—over four times the cost of a four-engine jet—would strain the financial solvency of the nation's airlines even more than the recent introduction of the Boeing 707 and DC–8. Traffic control would present further need for the extensive refinement of present methods; the pilot who took off from New York would simultaneously gain clearance from London for the landing and fly electronically with a computer to help him make decisions.

Governmental researchers continued their probing to determine whether to sponsor the craft. Industry's committee of experts urged the production of a $20 million aircraft flexible enough for domestic use yet also able to fly at 2,300 miles an hour for international journeys.[6] Meanwhile, European financiers, aircraft manufacturers, and governmental authorities avidly watched the American beginnings of supersonic research. The British enthusiastically heard L. B. Maytag, President of National Airlines, and Robert Six, President of Continental Airlines, praise the Mach 2 airliner and point toward the purchase of the Concord, the craft under joint construction by the British and French.[7] Six reportedly studied the possibility of buying the craft in cooperation with Pan American Airways. He also presented U.S. interests with a "royalty plan" suggesting the payment of an extra sum by each passenger for deposit into the federal treasury to help defray federal support of the supersonic program. Six relayed his views to (then) Vice-President Lyndon B. Johnson, who headed an advisory committee attempting to decide the fate of America's supersonic liner. The Concord might be readied for testing by 1966, entering service two years later.

THE NEW FRONTIER

The FAA's operations and U.S. aviation in general benefited greatly from the hearty concern for aviation held by the late President Kennedy. Much has been said already about his appointment of Halaby and the several special studies instigated in Kennedy's brief tenure of guiding the New Frontier. Early in 1963, the President again reminded federal authorities of the various affected agencies to help the FAA in holding to or bettering the original schedule of 1961 attached to the supersonic air transport.[8] In June, 1963, graduates of the Air Force Academy heard the President once more call for "a supersonic transport superior to that being built in any other country of the world."[9] Kennedy advised congressional leaders that the governmental share in the development in no way would exceed $750 million.[10] Less than four hours before he was assassinated, the President told his breakfast audience in Fort Worth of his pride in that city for its achievements in aviation. The first nonstop world flight took off from Fort Worth, and the controversial TFX military contract was awarded there.[11]

Meanwhile, the airlines, apparently convinced that the United States would produce supersonic craft, deposited funds toward the future delivery of the planes; forty-five orders through 1963 represented Pan American, TWA, American, Alitalia, Japan, El Al, and Northwest.[12] Administrator Halaby noted that 92 per cent of the current air travelers indicated an interest in using the supersonic craft not yet designed. Ironic, indeed, was Halaby's observation that a Washington–Tokyo nonstop flight must await the hypersonic aircraft, the next step beyond the supersonic era. In December, 1963, Halaby wished for testing in 1968 and the initial U.S. supersonic passenger service by 1970.

NOISE OVERHEAD

Within a few weeks world attention focused on Oklahoma City, site of FAA tests on the sonic boom as it related to the supersonic passenger liner. Initially, Halaby expressed reassurance since residents heard only a noise like thunder. However, a plumber filed suit in federal court attempting to halt the experiment. Other complaints followed and Halaby's life was reportedly threatened when he visited the city.[13] The Air Force continued the eight sonic booms daily in spite of a state court's order to suspend the actions; the state's order was dissolved in U.S. district court. The problem of sonic booms, yet unresolved and more serious it would seem than at first glance, constituted just one of the pessimistic conclusions surrounding President Johnson's decision requesting the aircraft people to offer improved plans before the project might be launched. The SST, as the proposed liner came to be known, would now be delayed for months or years, according to the experts.[14] Specifically, Halaby and other federal authorities prevailed as the President approved Lockheed and Boeing to develop the airframe; Pratt and Whitney, along with General Electric, would compete for the design of the jet engines.

The financial question remained a knotty one as industry refused the governmental suggestion that the manufacturers provide 25 per cent of the approximate $1 billion of developmental costs. Industry suggested 10 per cent, while some Republicans in Congress called for 100 per cent payment by the government. FAA leadership, admittedly more hopeful than some quarters, expressed the belief that many of the current roadblocks could be resolved by 1965.[15] Lockheed's original plans called for a liner carrying 218 passengers, while Boeing proposed a version seating between 150 and 225 persons. The Lockheed plane would be similar to the military A–11; the Boeing SST, like the TFX fighter, had folding wings. The FAA now asked for a plane with a range of 4,000 miles and profitable operation at a 60 per cent load factor. Meanwhile, the military rushed for completion of yet another heavier supersonic reconnaissance craft, the RS–71.

In addition to the efforts of the FAA in connection with supersonic aircraft, there continued, at the behest of Project Horizon, cooperation with NASA and the Air Force toward the development of the first intercontinental civilian jet cargo plane (C–141A).[16] Another suggestion by Project Horizon led to the FAA inaugural of Project Little Guy, an attempt to foster general aviation (private flying) by adopting a simplified cockpit for private planes. As before, the FAA continued its research with the help of the military in the hope of finding the most feasible type of craft for the vertical takeoff and landing (V/STOL) program.

Noise abatement for the nonjets, an age-old problem and one described earlier, again brought forth considerable discussion within the FAA which, along with the Federal Housing Administration and the Veterans Administration, adopted the most sensible approach—discouraging home owners from locating near airports.[17] Noise was expensive. In 1961, the airlines expended $2 million per month for sound suppressors, the loss in payload amounting to thirteen coach passengers. Various areas in the country established rules for landing and takeoff by jet planes with the eye to the highest possible reduction of noise.[18] Most acute during 1962 were problems in New Orleans, where property owners petitioned for revisions, and in the Eastern Region, particularly in the New York City area. Americans could view with sympathy the alarm over noise in England where the British Air Line Pilots' Association in 1963 offered a $1,400 prize to anyone who could find a way of reducing the noise of jet engines. An extensive study of the problem was presented to Parliament.[19] Speaking of noise, residents of the Brunswick, Germany, area found that the sound of the French-built Alouette jet helicopters happily led to the death of small rodents by the droves.[20] Japanese citizens complained so bitterly of jet noise that officials banned jet operations at Tokyo International Airport between 11:00 P.M. and 6:00 A.M.[21]

PROJECT BEACON—AIR TRAFFIC

At the outset of his term, President Kennedy ordered another review of aviation needs, instructing Administrator Halaby to prepare a long-range plan to foster safe and efficient control of air traffic.[22] Halaby appointed Richard R. Hough, Vice-President, Operations of the Bell Telephone Company, as chairman of the group which consulted with a scientific body under Dr. Jerrold Zacharias, Massachusetts Institute of Technology. Project Beacon called for positive control of all traffic above 14,500 feet, except in mountainous areas where this control would begin at 24,000 feet. Moreover, on high-use airways, positive control should be maintained as low as 8,000 feet (all altitudes from mean sea level [MSL]). A speed limit should be imposed below 8,000 feet on these high-use airways and serious consideration given to extending the en route airspace up to 3,000 feet above terrain to VFR traffic. Further segregation of controlled and uncontrolled traffic could be imposed around congested terminals. Project Beacon also called for increased attention to helicopter traffic and to unequipped VFR traffic around airports. The system of air traffic control demanded by Beacon also recommended further utilization of the FAA and SAGE (Air Force) radar networks in addition to general-purpose computers for use en route along the airways and around crowded terminals to process flight plans, issue clearances, and perform other routine tasks for the air controllers.[23] Altitude information could be gathered by use of reporting transponders carried on the airplane, thus relieving the pilot of many position reports while in flight. All planes of over 12,500 pounds gross weight should have this instrument.

The FAA swung immediately into action to implement the Beacon findings. The FAA found objections at once to the proposed three-layer structure, amending it with plans to control (positive) the two layers of 0 to 18,000 feet MSL and 18,000 to 45,000 feet above which pilots would operate independently of the lower designations. Much yet remained to be refined before ideal operation. Furthermore, the FAA could not rely solely on SAGE, a military radar designed for peripheral areas of the nation's defenses. Finally, the FAA's opinion held that mandatory requirement of transponders should depend more on the environment of operations than on the weight of the aircraft. Debating the provisions of the Beacon report failed to prevent steps being taken by the FAA to alleviate the airspace problems. General Quesada ordered some 15,000 square miles of space returned to civilian air use in 1960; Administrator Halaby followed a similar approach to the matter.[24] Meanwhile, the program to eliminate low-frequency airways was continued; low- and medium- (radio) frequency routes for jets were entirely abandoned in 1961.

HARASSED CONTROLLERS

It could be safely related that no single plan of air traffic control would be held satisfactory by all of the various users. But progress was necessary when one realized the tremendous increase in IFR operations envisaged by the FAA in 1962 for the next five fiscal years ($6.2 million of operations in fiscal 1961 to $8 million in 1967).[25] The all-important task of controlling the flight of both commercial and military operations evolved by the early sixties into a nightmare of activity at the places of heaviest traffic and, at the least, a headache in other locations. One might safely conclude that the position of air traffic controller, originally resplendent with all the glamour imaginable, had now turned into an exacting, gruelling livelihood, certainly not without its rewards but demanding utter dedication to this unique occupation.

Air Traffic Management comprised over 44 per cent of the FAA's 39,639 personnel in 1961.[26] Foremost in the hierarchy of installations were the air-route traffic control centers (ARTCC), numbering 35 in 1962 but destined for a reduction to approximately 23 such facilities, including 3 military SAGE units. As before, controllers at the ARTCC performed the task of monitoring all IFR flights after originally accepting the flight plans and taking over the control functions from the airport controllers when the flight passed a designated point beyond the airport and until the flight reached another designated point approaching a landing. Next in the chain of command were the airport traffic control towers (ATCT), totaling 192 in 1962. In addition, at 71 other towers, the combined functions of traffic control and flight service station (to be described later) were performed.

Visits to airport control towers confirmed all the literature describing the complicated procedures entailed.[27] A typical center, the one at Olathe, Kansas, has the responsibility of supervising all IFR flights—military and civil—in the area embracing Mason City, Iowa, on the north; Burlington, Iowa, on the east; Ponca City, Oklahoma, on the south; and Hill City, Kansas, on the west.[28] During one day, controllers direct some 2,000 flights in this seventh busiest section in the nation. Air traffic controllers totaled 285 at Olathe, supported by an additional 55 maintenance personnel to keep the center's elaborate electronic equipment in operation.

At Chicago's O'Hare International Airport, the busiest terminal in the world, over 60 controllers man the tower which keeps track of at least 1,200 takeoffs and landings per day.[29] Frightening to the layman is the spectacle of tower personnel watching over 30 planes at one time carrying approximately 4,000 passengers, all within 30 miles of O'Hare. The complete reliance on the latest equipment, including the transponders to aid in the identification of jets, helps relieve the pressure on the controllers. The radar and other communications equipment are in duplicate; even the power supply has alternate sources in case of failure. Other large airports present a similar picture; the New York area faces additional complications because of the close proximity of several airports. At Idlewild, now known as Kennedy International Airport, 37 controllers watch over 1,000 daily operations.

The pressure of near misses or collisions at the busiest towers and centers was not entirely absent from dozens of other locations. Only experience, including painful trial and error, eliminated mistakes one of which found a controller in California giving instructions to a private pilot whose plane the controller thought appeared on the radar screen. Later the controller discovered the plane on radar to be a different one and the private pilot crashed into a mountain, killing all three aboard.[30] Mis-identification could be avoided with accurate transponders on all aircraft. The controller was understandably not blamed for this tragedy. However, the broad range of mishaps emphasizes the fact that controllers do occasionally commit errors, costly as they might be. For example, the CAB officially blamed the FAA controllers, along with the two pilots, for the collision of a Cessna 140 and an Aeronca L–16A on September 30, 1959, at North Philadelphia Airport.[31] FAA controllers occasionally made mistakes which created a potential collision course, one such instance taking place near Salina, Kansas, in 1962 when both American and TWA flights had been assigned the altitude of 33,000 feet.[32] Earlier the same year, Administrator Halaby acknowledged that a harried controller let matters get out of hand by assigning an Eastern Electra and a United Viscount the same altitude of 7,000 feet over Springfield, Virginia. Only a wider circle described by the faster Electra averted disaster here.

The problem of coordination has become tremendous at the centers as well as the busier airport towers. The "handing off" process, transferring the control of a flight from one center to the next, has caused delays of several minutes in departure, e.g., in the Central Region east of Cedar Rapids as one approached the heavy Chicago traffic. A second major factor confronted the FAA in regard to the health and retirement of controllers who contend that early retirement is necessitated by the nature of their regular assignment. In 1965, nothing definite had been achieved pertaining to this dilemma; one might assume that retirement at age fifty-five after twenty years of service might provide a compromise to the demands of the Air Traffic Control Association's (ATCA) plea for recognition of the problem by the Civil Service. And yet, despite its rigors, the position of controller offered a situation akin to the weather forecaster; the work "gets in your blood."[33] The chief controller would prefer being in the tower instead of the office.

Facing the difficulty of recruiting new controllers has been a major hurdle for the FAA; neither college subjects nor other training pointed directly to this unique career. Until 1961, all recruits learned while on the job. Then the FAA instigated a fifteen-week training program at Oklahoma City, followed by an apprenticeship, on-the-job period with experienced controllers.[34] Later it was decided to encourage a number of potential trainees to learn about the controllers' work in the towers, after which the more promising would be assigned to the formal course at Oklahoma City. Controllers faced, in addition to the pressures of the job, the annual physical examination, being held to the identical standards required for a second-class airman's certificate. Controllers asked just what they could do in case they failed to pass the examination sometime prior to their eligibility for retirement. Yet the stability of personnel, particularly at the towers of less than peak traffic, held firm despite the chances offered for transfer to other stations within the same region.

The typical alignment of tasks at any given moment in the airport tower of any size consisted of a ground controller, an approach controller (IFR), a local controller, and the radar controllers. Rotating positions, possibly every hour, lessened the tensions and monotony.[35] There was a high degree of helpful give-and-take and rapport among the controllers on duty. Then, too, controlling with paper and pencil proved different from reliance on the radar approach controller who watched the progress of the flights involved. Standard phraseology stymied the experts seeking the clearest means of communication available. For example, "cleared for touch and go landing" later became "touch and go approved," and yet more recently "cleared for touch and go." However, some argued that "cleared for IFR or VFR" would comprise the most accurate description.[36] The ground controller had to contend with trucks, cars, tractors, and repairmen working near the runways in order to issue the landing or taxiing airman the proper instructions. Only the least busy airport towers allowed the operation of aircraft without two-way radio and resorted in 1964 to the "light gun" with its red, white, and green signals, which could be steady or flashing in nature. Adding further to the controllers' alertness was the fact that all conversations were monitored on tape and retained for thirty days prior to erasure.[37] In the preradar days at Des Moines tower where twenty-three controllers worked, one could sense the anxiety when, even on a clear day, three or more planes maneuvered in the same direction though assigned various positions to avoid collision. Even after radar was installed, the crises still "came in threes," as one controller explained on a hectic day in mid-June, 1962.[38] A United pilot on takeoff declared an emergency and stopped just 3 feet from the end of the runway after all tires blew out; a private pilot and his passenger walked away from their burning craft—a total loss; a third pilot had minor troubles the same day. During this same era, the FAA looked to the day when automation could provide additional support to the harassed controllers. The semiautomatic Data Processing Central (DPC) though gaining attention was still in the area of research.[39]

THE FLIGHT SERVICE STATION

Turning attention to the VFR type of flying, the FAA instigated in October, 1960, the flight service station (FSS), designed primarily to assist the private operations (general aviation).[40] By June, 1962, the FAA operated 337 FSS's and the number grew to almost 600 two years later. However, in August, 1964, plans called for a large reduction of personnel at these service stations through use of manned information and communications facility (MANICOM) and Airport Information Desk (AID) facilities. The MANICOM service would employ two people at a station only during peak activity hours—the station being linked by telephone to the nearest FSS. Under AID, the station would be entirely unmanned with the nearest larger FSS assuming its operations by remote control. To the pilot filing a flight plan, the flight watch communicators (in FSS) issued periodic weather information in addition to monitoring the flight's movement from position to position. Stations notified one another of the late or early arrival of flights, the operators waited one-half hour before thoroughly checking on overdue planes (pilots carried that much extra fuel), and notified "search and rescue" at Dallas, Texas, after one and one-half hours' discrepancy. The Civil Air Patrol would then assist in any search operations. Most pilots would contact FSS for aid if they were located beyond 30 miles from an airport tower. The certified flight briefers manning the FSS must take a course in meteorology and training courses in advanced flight assistance at Oklahoma City. Nine men, two on duty at one time—except during 11:00 P.M. to 7:00 A.M.—manned the FSS at Des Moines. They transmitted on ten frequencies and could receive on eight, issuing the area broadcasts at fifteen minutes past the hour and the airway broadcasts at forty-five minutes after the hour. The briefers periodically encountered chagrin because pilots failed to report their landing or simulated flights were not cancelled properly.[41]

WEATHER ADVICE

The flight-following duties of FSS introduced a major question in the matter of providing up-to-the-minute weather data—especially rapidly changing conditions—to the pilot in flight. Would it not be best to augment the FSS program with a project linking the pilot directly to an experienced Weather Bureau forecaster? The FAA inaugurated this type of service (1961) on an experimental basis at Washington, D.C., and Kansas City.[42] After a slow beginning, the pilot-to-forecaster service became extremely popular, the commercial, military, or private pilots all availing themselves of this information. At Kansas City, calls, about 40 per cent from commercial pilots, averaged fifty a day around the clock. The coverage varied from a 100-mile radius out of Kansas City for planes at 10,000 feet in flight to about 200 miles distance for those at 35,000 feet or higher.[43] An often forgotten ingredient of this cooperative program involved the additional support to the Weather Bureau from these extra sources of data from aloft—the pilots' observations of turbulence or other phenomena. It appeared only logical that in the future the Weather Bureau should be given additional funds to provide further expert advice directly to the pilots instead of having the FSS employees alone perform the task. Subsequently, FAA and Weather Bureau officials planned a Common Aviation Weather System designed to furnish weather data to all aviation users, both civilian and military, and to include rapid cycling equipment for automatic measuring, forecasting, and communicating procedures.[44] The mesonet, an instrument capable of measuring the weather variations that affect airport operations, was tested at the Experimental Center (Atlantic City).

PROJECT FRIENDSHIP

In the realm of military-FAA cooperation, much interest was generated in Project Friendship—the move to have the FAA assume military traffic controllers' duties. Indeed, most of the military controlling has come under FAA. But the military, apparently after second thoughts, believed it wiser to retain its own controllers in the more remote areas of the world. Another concern, the place of the FAA in time of war, originally prompted the attempt to assign controllers to a Federal Aviation Service (FAS) in case of emergency. However, much opposition within the ATCA, whose counsel—former CAB member Oswald Ryan— wisely advised against the action, resulted in a pro-ATCA compromise.[45]

The present status reminds one of the type of military-government control over all U.S. agencies in a given area taken over by the military during World War II. In essence, the FAA would doubtless come under direct jurisdiction of the military (without being in the military), which would have control of communications and other vital services in any future holocaust. The repugnance of FAA controllers and laymen to forced entry into the military might be easily understood in thinking of the great service of the old CAA as a civilian unit during World War II. By the same token, any future war might involve massive bombings of the homeland and with it the disruption of communications so vital to aviation control—in short, a situation never experienced in the United States during World War II. The system of traffic control had evolved into a mutually accepted enterprise, with the FAA training a number of military controllers.[46] Inevitably, differences had arisen; one senior controller (FAA) related that military controllers had to "start from scratch" when later joining the FAA.[47]

In 1962, ninety military officers worked on regular assignment within some phase of the FAA, two-thirds in research and development or air traffic control. Law provided that when the administrator was not a former regular officer of the military, the deputy administrator could be a military man on active duty. In February, 1962, President Kennedy appointed Lieutenant General Harold W. Grant (USAF) as Deputy Administrator. The FAA did take over six military flight centers (500 men).[48] Throughout the period the FAA and the military cooperated in a series of exercises promoting national defense. From the civilian point of view, Operation Sky Shield II was the most noticeable, for in this exercise on October 14, 1961, the FAA cleared the air of all civil operations for twelve hours.[49] Prior to the partial nuclear test ban treaty (1963), the FAA continued its cooperation in tracking the early fallout from nuclear explosions in an effort to warn all air operations of these hazards.

NEW AIRPORTS

The two most dramatic innovations during the first years of the new FAA's control of airports involved the demise of Midway (Chicago) as the world's busiest airport—an honor soon captured by its rival, O'Hare International Airport—and the opening of Dulles International Airport outside Washington, D.C. The arduous bickering of the forties and fifties finally subsided in 1958, when the site near Chantilly, Virginia, 27 miles west of the White House was selected. This "dream" airport, designed by the late Eero Saarinen, was opened for traffic in the autumn of 1962. Dulles Airport stands today as a shining light among the nation's other leading airports which, in fact, appear to one astute traveler as nothing more than a series of "barns" or "sheds" with all their confusion and chaos reflected in the absence of imaginative architecture.[50] The Dulles International Airport incorporated a European innovation by providing the passengers with ease of travel from the terminal to the distant runway approaches where the jet planes are loaded. Specially designed mobile lounges came to be utilized instead of the conventional buses employed in Europe. The Dulles terminal, a combination of functional efficiency and simplicity of beauty, included a glass-walled concourse—luminous with dramatic lighting at night to reveal the tower as if it were erected on a pillar of flame. On the field, the FAA installed another jet-age safety feature— parallel north-south runways 11,500 feet long and 150 feet wide, separated by 6,700 feet. A third runway, west northwest-east southeast in orientation, extends 10,000 feet in length, while space will permit the construction of a fourth runway in the future. Judiciously, the FAA purchased enough adjoining property to retain airport boundaries at a distance from the runways and planted a considerable number of trees to help absorb the noise from jet engines.

The problem of racial segregation at southern airports, discussed under the Eisenhower tenure, continued to plague the Kennedy-Johnson years. Southern congressmen attempted to insert limitations against any executive orders halting the discriminatory practices. Senator Jacob Javits, Republican of New York, charged again that the President could end segregation without the requirement of a special law.[51] In other problem areas, the FAA, as related earlier, testified to the need of eliminating the long delays in travel between city and airport. Furthermore, congestion on the ground caused an average delay of 5.4 minutes in flights during April–May, 1963. Americans were not alone in their woes surrounding airport operation, for Britishers debated a scheme to remove London Airport to Foulness Island, off Southend and link the new site to London via monorail.[52] The nuisance of jet noise would be solved, and the way could be paved for introduction there of the supersonic airliner. In 1964 Tokyo opened its monorail connecting the airport and downtown.

The FAA's supervision of airports continued to be centered in a number of airport district offices. For example, the district office at Chicago held jurisdiction over all of Illinois. The eight airport engineers there felt particularly fortunate in their location because of the widespread support extended to aviation by the State of Illinois. The smaller airports in the state, many with unpaved landing strips, varied greatly in their status; Pekin, Ottawa, and LaSalle were cited as typically active, thriving airports. However, the trend of inflationary costs for small planes worried these FAA spokesmen when considering the future of general aviation.[53]

THE AERONAUTICAL CENTER

In mentioning the numerous technological advances, one must definitely include the modern approach to aviation in the sixties represented by the FAA's Aeronautical Center at Oklahoma City. The facilities were built to be entirely functional and were intended as a training and experimental center benefiting personnel of the FAA in all its regulatory and advisory operations. The $14 million facility was dedicated in 1958.[54] Here the FAA required its inspectors, traffic controllers, and communications personnel to complete initial and refresher courses in air navigation facilities and the flying of various aircraft. Here foreign personnel, brought to the center in cooperation with the State Department or the ICAO, learned to read and understand English. Meanwhile, the FAA transferred its National Aviation Facilities Experimental Center from Indianapolis to Atlantic City. By 1962, to augment the training, the FAA received a DC-7, a Convair 340, and several other planes, some of which had been hired before from outside the agency. The long-range plan called for the development of flight-training simulators suitable for training in the use of piston, subsonic jet, and supersonic transport aircraft.

Along with its stepped-up program of aeronautical training, the FAA participated in extensive aeromedical research aimed at reducing the errors in choosing unsuitable candidates for air traffic control.[55] This unit, the Civil Aeromedical Research Institute (CARI), was located at Oklahoma City. Georgetown Clinical Research Institute in Washington, D.C., conducted an interdisciplinary study of aging pilots. Research bearing on safety included work on air height or 3-D, surveillance radar

(AHSR-1), improved accuracy in altimeters, cockpit voice recordings to aid in accident investigation, and collision-avoidance systems and pilot-warning instruments.

BEACON TRANSPONDERS

The FAA tested 3-D radar on a small plane, a Tri-Pacer, obtaining accuracy within 500 feet at a distance of 20 miles. Researchers used a 100-ton, 165-foot antenna and considered it mandatory to conduct many additional experiments.[56] Findings of Project Beacon stressed the need of beacon transponders in the airplane as necessary to transmit altitude information to the ground radar. Flight testing of the beacon transponders air traffic control radar beacon system (ATCRBS) was begun in fiscal 1963, with a code devised to transmit the data to the ground in 100-foot intervals. Development was also started on a small transponder system, small, light-weight altitude transmission equipment (SLATE), to give altitude data for light aircraft. One collision-avoidance test involved the use of equipment which transmits omnidirectional bursts of pulses at regular intervals, the pulses then being received by other planes in the vicinity— the whole procedure based on range and altitude data. Other experimenters favored a time-reference system with synchronized oscillators. Another phase of research attacked the difficulties inherent in the "handing off" process—one air controller turning over the care of a flight to another controller. The whole process cried for automation. An arresting gear designed to prevent runway overruns by jets was receiving considerable attention. In 1962, an Air France jet crashed at Paris, France, in such an accident.

FLIGHT RECORDERS

The need for improved flight recorders continued to plague the FAA and CAB. The recorder of a UAL Viscount, which crashed near Newport, Tennessee, on July 9, 1964, was found broken, despite efforts to render such devices impactproof.[57] What the FAA desired was a flight recorder capable of analyzing much more data than the airspeed, altitude, heading, vertical acceleration, and time detected by current recorders. Also helpful would be temperature and pressure for each engine, fuel flow, engine vibration, pressure and oxygen operation, radios in use, autopilot operation, ambient air temperature, flap and gear position, and landing gear impact acceleration.[58]

AUTOMATIC LANDINGS

The British figured in experiments of another nature, the search for a completely automatic landing system. Here, again, international prestige loomed at stake, the British, French, and Americans all supporting experimentation in this direction. The French, utilizing the Sud-Lear system—developed by the Sud Aviation company in France and the Lear-Siegler firm in the United States—conducted 250 successful tests over twenty months with the Caravelle. Newsmen accompanied one flight and witnessed the landing with the pilot turning his back to the windshield.[59] The British "autoland" system of three units was being designed for use by 1965. In the United States, the FAA expressed caution over the radar components of its Flarescan system but planned for testing at airports in 1964, no-hands use by 1965, and operation by 1967. Estimating the elimination of 80 per cent of all bad weather trip cancellations, the FAA aimed for accuracy, in the initial stages of development, to permit landings with 100-foot ceilings and one-fourth mile of visibility at major airports. Flarescan would include an imaginary runway projected on the windshield, allowing the pilot to use his judgment as to how accurately the instruments were operating.

MOCK CRASHES

FAA researchers at the Aeronautical Center in Oklahoma City also turned their attention to the possible reduction of the number of fatalities in air crashes. At first, using 4 inches of plastic foam under the seats was considered to provide a tripling of the passengers' tolerance against the vertical impact which had stunned passengers in a crash near Tulsa. After this crash, the stewardesses had had to urge the otherwise uninjured passengers to leave the plane.[60] In April, 1964, the FAA purposely slammed a DC–7A on takeoff against a rocky desert slope in Arizona and tested the reaction in sixteen instrumented dummies and several thousand pounds of engineering equipment aboard. Twelve of the dummies were still strapped in their seats. Admittedly, this was a "marginally survivable" crash, but the experts gained much valuable data to suggest safety measures in plane design, e.g., one model of an air bag inflated in front of a "dummy" passenger successfully cushioned the shock of forward motion upon impact.[61] Theoretically, the NASA experts watching the FAA experiment hoped that a pilot could flick a switch to inflate such rubber or plastic bags. The bags would deflate automatically following the crash so as to free the passengers. Films of the actual crash showed that a dummy with only a seat belt ended up in the next seat forward while one protected by the air bag withstood the impact, recording only a force of eight G's (eight times the pull of gravity) compared to the forty G's with the seat belt. A second planned crash in September, 1964, with a Constellation taking off at 115 miles an hour, brought further gratifying data. Involved also was an attempt to arrest the spraying of fuel on impact through the use of a gelled substance in the fuel tanks.

TURBULENCE

The FAA officials inclined anxiously toward any experiments leading to further knowledge of turbulence. A number of jet crashes, in addition to several dives from which successful recovery had been accomplished—all in 1963–1964—led to a cooperative study of clear air turbulence by United Air Lines, the Air Force, and the Stanford Research Institute.[62] This group examined a theory that clear air turbulence is preceded by or causes a change in the atmospheric field. The researchers now sought a device to alert the pilot of such changes. Similar research had been undertaken in Great Britain.

PILOT TENSION

Additional aeromedical attention came to be focused on the strains jet flying imposed upon the crews. Studies made by spokesmen for the ALPA and the FAA reflected a concern over the exact duties and nervous tensions created by the speedier craft. Results from questionnaires described increased irritability, changed eating and drinking habits, and other complaints. Initially, one suggestion held that in order to combat the lag in crew fitness effectively it might be well to reduce the maximum flight schedule allowed per month on jet aircraft. As a group, the larger number of jet pilots in the country were now over fifty years of age, another factor supporting the proposal of less rigorous schedules.

THE LATEST IN ECONOMIC REGULATION—THE CAB

The FAA leadership pondered its many questions pertaining to commercial aviation. The CAB continued with its monumental task of formulating the most amenable solutions to the broad questions of air routes, foreign competitors to American lines, mergers, and air fares. What appeared to some observers as the perennial delay of action by the CAB in economic matters was described by President Kennedy, New York's Governor Nelson Rockefeller, and leading economists as a broader crisis throughout the nation's entire transportation system which accounted for one-fifth of the country's gross national product.[63] Predicting nationalization of the railroads and airlines unless immediate changes materialized, Rockefeller called for drastic governmental action.

Overcapacity in the airlines has been cited with increasing alarm, particularly now with jet craft and the turboprop planes. A poor year in 1961 reflected a 7.75 per cent increase in capacity yet only 56.2 per cent of the available seats on planes could be sold. The figure for 1960 was 59.47 per cent, while it stood at 67.08 per cent in 1952. Furthermore, only approximately 12 million Americans flew during 1960. Though it might appear as a relatively minor irritation, nevertheless, aircraft manufacturers resented having to pay inflated prices for toilet seats—$123 for one costing $3 to an individual customer—and similarly ridiculous markups for other furnishings in the costly new jets.[64] The CAB was charged by one economist with utilizing persistent efforts to preserve a weak company at all costs.[65] The question of mergers introduced the difficulty of persuading strong airlines to "marry" weak ones, instead of allowing existing giants— American and Eastern toyed with the idea—to join into one still larger successful business. Furthermore, the experts could not agree over the feasibility of establishing another cabinet position, a Department of Transportation.

CONGRESSIONAL IRE

Various experts debated the future of the transportation industry; the CAB continued to face the perennial issues of an economic nature. Congressional ire was expressed against the board in 1959, airing a variety of charges. Diplomacy promoted by the State Department again annoyed several Americans who considered the U.S. government partial to the British airline BOAC.[66] Politics emerged in another case in which Southern Airways won a route over Southeast Airlines by a 3 to 2 vote; Democrats Louis J. Hector and G. Joseph Minetti favored Southeast, while Republicans James R. Durfee, Chan Gurney, and

Harmar D. Denney chose Southern.[67] The *Nashville Tennessean* belittled Durfee for attending none of the earlier sessions but merely voting later with his fellow party members.

In 1960, legislators heard of the lavish parties reportedly extended to CAB officials by airline executives, especially when cases involving the same airlines awaited CAB action.[68] Senator William Proxmire, Democrat of Wisconsin, considered this action a breach of ethics on the board members' part. The Comptroller General rendered the opinion that such activities raised serious doubts as to propriety. TWA sent the Durfees to Rome; Eastern took members to Mexico City. Senator Hubert Humphrey backed Proxmire's assault on Durfee, which included a comparison to the ousted FCC boss John Doerfer whose resignation was accepted for taking favors even without a case pending. The *Nashville Tennessean* berated President Dwight Eisenhower's request to appoint Durfee to the Court of Claims. Senator Alexander Wiley, Republican of Wisconsin, jumped to the support of Durfee following Proxmire's five-hour stand, and contended that Durfee had official business of a sort on all these disputed trips—ceremonial functions and seeking cooperation with the Military Air Transport Service. Wiley noted that Administrator Quesada supported Durfee as did the *Green Bay Press-Gazette* and the *Dallas Morning News*. Durfee won the court nomination by a vote of 69 to 15.

INTERNAL RIFTS

Meanwhile, Minetti and Hector, both noted for their ringing dissents against the Republican majority on the CAB, touched off additional fireworks. Hector quit the CAB in disgust in 1959, declaring that this agency was unsuited for its task.[69] He listed the board's reversal of examiners' decisions in two cases, low morale, frustration in planning, and failure to conclude the General Fare Investigation as major shortcomings against his colleagues. Shortly thereafter Durfee assumed his court post; Denny and Minetti both reportedly wished to resign. Unfortunately, Hector left at a time when his honest leadership had apparently been appreciated and respected by the aviation world. Minetti, the great promoter of overseas charter flights, became a dissenter similar to Harold A. Jones (1948–1951) and Joseph P. Adams (1951–1956), opposing any fare increases and high subsidies in addition to his desire to ferret out any antitrust violations. Meanwhile, several of the air carriers disputed the

CAB's order to furnish coach service over certain routes. Uneasy because of the financial risks of the new jet age, one critic declared it ironic to have the industry controlled by a governmental agency which moved at the pace of a "goose quill pen." The same editors *(Aviation Week)* praised Quesada and the FAA but described the CAB as "the agglomeration of lame duck senators from both parties, faithful political hacks using the board as a rest period on their climb to the federal bench, West Point classmates of the President and Boy Scout leaders will not do the job."[70]

Much was expected from the reorganized board in the summer of 1960. New Chairman Whitney Gillilland, Republican of Iowa, believed that each member should write his own opinions and that the board should be increased to 7 members of two 3-man panels in addition to the chairman.[71] Gurney became vice-chairman of the board at this time. Allan S. Boyd, thirty-seven-year-old Democrat, was named to the board, scorning political considerations injected into route awards. In the CAB, Examiner Paul N. Pfeiffer sought additional judicial action by the board as a means of expediting procedures. In the process, he called for longer board terms, decisions of examiners to be final, consolidation of prehearings, shortened attorneys' statements, and the elimination of much "expert advice."[72] The late James M. Landis, a Kennedy friend, and a former CAB Chairman who perennially suggested changes in operations, now asked for less pressure from the White House, criticized the quality of some CAB appointments, and advised President-elect Kennedy to give increased powers to the examiners.[73] Meanwhile, President Eisenhower had ordered a special study of the CAB resulting in a report—by McKinsey and Company, Inc., and the Budget Bureau—which advised further technical training for the Bureau of Safety, increased tenure for the chairman over the current one-year appointment, and much speedier action in the formal cases now consuming an average of thirty-two months before a decision.[74] Again, politics entered the picture when Senator John Williams, Republican of Delaware, charged improper pressure from Attorney General Robert F. Kennedy in attempting to gain the reversal of a CAB decision causing Northeast Airlines to lose its Florida routes. The CAB declared by the same vote, 3 to 2, that the Justice Department had no right to enter the case at its present stage.[75] Chairman Boyd, and Republicans Gillilland and Gurney comprised the majority.

Strong opposition had been expressed by Eastern and National, among several lines, for over two years against Northeast's application for renewal of its Florida route.

PRESSURE FOR MERGERS

Chairman Boyd, appointed by Kennedy to lead the CAB, impressed airline officials with his businesslike approach to problems and his apparent desire to eliminate as much red tape as possible in CAB operations.[76] He considered the impracticability of extending trunk routes to the major carriers beyond those pending at that moment. Nevertheless, he lamented the necessity of getting into the "arena" with the FAA and State Department over international considerations. While the experts talked of reorganization and battled politicians, the CAB labored also against the many pressures for mergers resulting from apprehension over international rivalries or financial instability. The one merger consummated found United Air Lines combining in 1961 with Capital which had incurred financial ruin in attempting to pay Vickers-Armstrongs, Ltd., of London, for its Viscount turboprop planes, a debt of $34 million.[77] Operating in the red since 1955, Capital—off subsidy since 1951—sought in 1960 to obtain further subsidy of $12,949,000 from the CAB to help counteract foreclosure. Congress refused this request "for failure."[78] The U.S. Court of Appeals subsequently upheld the merger objected to by Eastern, Delta, and Northwest.

Presently, a series of additional requests for consolidation ranged from the stage of rumor all the way to formal application before the CAB. American Airlines, the nation's biggest domestic carrier until United took over Capital, now sought to merge with Eastern, a combine which would carry about 35 per cent of the country's long-distance passengers and save an estimated $50 million per year by eliminating duplication of services.[79] Immediately the Transport Workers Union (TWU) threatened a strike unless all employees would be retained in such a merger, an unlikely possibility. The TWU also threatened against railroad mergers. Presently the CAB, through its examiner, denied the American-Eastern merger for the reason that it would create a monopoly in a number of major areas. The Justice Department had opposed this merger as repugnant to established antitrust measures. Meanwhile, rumors spread about a possible Northeast-TWA combination.

At the close of 1962, officials of the nation's two largest

overseas carriers, Pan American and TWA, applied for merger.[80] Juan Trippe, the Pan Am boss, had asked the government in 1950 for a "chosen instrument" policy, i.e., the choice of one favored American international line to compete with the growing number of government-subsidized foreign carriers. The Pan Am-TWA merger would accomplish this and at the same time give Pan American a chance for new inland (United States) routes. However, internal frictions involving TWA—primarily its fight against Howard Hughes' control—cooled off the merger efforts during 1963. TWA then asked the CAB to end the Pan Am-TWA competition in routes by awarding area franchises.[81] For example, TWA could serve Ireland, France and Spain, the Mediterranean basin, and Africa. Pan Am, according to TWA's offer, would hold exclusively routes to the United Kingdom, Northern and Eastern Europe (including the future potential in Iron Curtain areas). Each would continue its present routes east of Asia Minor and the Middle East. The TWA proposal differed little from a CAB staff report (May, 1962) suggesting the area concept for the lines. The financial struggle within TWA continued to raise the question of Hughes' position bolstered by his ownership of 78.2 per cent of TWA's common stock. But Hughes had lost control of TWA in 1960 when two life insurance companies and a trust company, all of which had loaned money for planes, succeeded in placing his stock in trust. Hughes' stock rested with the Hughes Tool Company which also had interests in Northwest Airlines.[82] Litigation costs proved to be a major burden for TWA. During July, 1964, the CAB allowed Hughes Tool to purchase $92.6 million in TWA notes provided that it divest itself of the interests in Northwest. The CAB, considering requests from American and Northwest for competitive routes with United following the latter's acquisition of Capital, in 1964, awarded the two airlines routes connecting Philadelphia, Cleveland, Detroit, and Chicago.[83]

CHARTERS

Economic control over passenger rates and special flights plagued the CAB as in the years before 1959. The supplemental (nonscheduled) airlines gained a CAB verdict (1959) allowing unlimited planeload charter service and ten flights a month between any individual pair of locations in the country. But the U.S. courts invalidated the ruling in 1960, subsequently causing a new, amended version of the Federal Aviation Act of 1958 to be handed down by Congress.[84] In August, 1964, the CAB voted 3 to 2 in favor of granting all-cargo lines the exclusive right to offer "blocked space" at wholesale rates to high-volume shippers.[85] Republicans Gillilland and Gurney dissented and claimed the decision would force the passenger-cargo lines out of the cargo business. American Airlines immediately obtained from the U.S. district court a temporary restraining order blocking the decision. However, not all supplemental operations carried on during the post-1958 era have been successful. Mention has been made earlier of the Cal Poly charter crash allegedly brought on by sheer negligence of the air carrier. In October, 1961, another charter company, President Airlines, left 103 passengers stranded for several days at Shannon Airport, Ireland, because the DC–7C pilot was not provided with the $6,000 for his gasoline and airport fees.[86] Prior to its flight to Ireland to pick up the passengers, the DC–7C had been detained at New York City five days because of mechanical trouble. President had lost a chartered DC–6B in a crash at Shannon several weeks earlier killing all eighty-three aboard.

AIR FARES

The sticky question of air fares confronted the board time and time again.[87] In 1960, the CAB authorized an increase of 2.5 per cent for twelve trunk lines, plus a $1 charge for each one-way ticket sold. The CAB hoped for a return on investment of 10.5 per cent for the carriers as the result. At the same time, it ruled a 12.75 per cent rate of return for mail subsidy on local service airlines, in no case less than 3 cents a plane mile. A year later, four airlines attempted to promote air travel among people between the ages of twelve through twenty-one with fares of half the first-class charge. The experiment was dropped then because too many people, younger and older, abused the privilege, according to CAB leader Boyd. A revision of the plan was adopted early in 1966. A general increase of 3 per cent was granted all the major lines in December, 1961, many local-service companies following suit. Late in the summer, 1962, the CAB allowed Continental, American, TWA, Braniff, and United to experiment with reductions of 10 to 20 per cent on various jet fares. Later the same year, United put into effect a new, one-class fare costing about 5 per cent above coach prices. United's one-service experiment became a controversial subject, with National favoring the move only if all the other lines agreed.

United's chief competitor, American, flatly opposed the idea and gained support from Continental and TWA.[88] Domestically, the trunk lines gained fare reductions up to 15 per cent on January 15, 1964; the primary cuts affected first-class fares on flights greater than 700 miles.[89] At the same time, family-fare discounts were extended to coach and business classes, as well as the existing first-class trips. Foreign visitors to this country could benefit from the offer by Allegheny and Piedmont Airlines to sell these tourists a $99 ticket allowing unlimited travel over their combined routes for thirty days.[90] Frontier offered U.S. teachers a 60 per cent reduction on first-class fares.

INTERNATIONAL AIR RATES

Reductions in transatlantic fares continued to give the CAB serious headaches and embarrassing diplomatic tangles. First, the CAB, in 1962, allowed the airlines to offer reductions in group excursion fares provided that only bona fide tour groups bought the service.[91] A year later, a most unusual impasse existed between the CAB and foreign airlines within the International Air Transport Association (IATA). The CAB opposed a 5 per cent increase imposed by the foreign companies but relented in the end after the British agitated for the banning of American airlines' service in the United Kingdon. Secretary of State Dean Rusk advised Chairman Boyd to allow Pan Am and TWA to go along with the increase. Though Republicans and some Democrats bemoaned the "retreat" from foreign pressure, it should be understood that all eighty-two airlines, including TWA and Pan Am, had previously voted in favor of the increase.

In a series of tumultuous meetings of the IATA at Salzburg, Austria, in autumn 1963, it was decided to introduce the crazy-quilt, hodgepodge variation of transatlantic fares which became operative in time for the 1964 peak tourist season. The riddle of 1964 transatlantic jet fares placed a premium on the twenty-one-day vacation, but the IATA ignored the most popular ticket— the round-trip economy fare which was lowered by just $1.50 to $484.50.[92] Other prices depended on excursion, off season, peak season, or first-class status of each passenger. The net result, or muddle, found passengers in the position of receiving the same type of service costing anywhere up to $184.50 more for the same flight. Yet one could not underestimate the power of the IATA group. When the CAB had prevented TWA and Pan Am from charging the higher fares in 1963, Scandinavian Airlines System

(SAS) officials secured the differential in fares deposited by the Pan Am passengers before they were allowed to leave the airport in Sweden. Conversely, the IATA once fined SAS $20,000 for unkind remarks concerning the refreshments sold by other lines. Two noticeable, nonmember lines were absent from the discussions in Salzburg and Nassau. The USSR's Aeroflot remained aloof. Icelandic, which had been flying its DC–6B's across the Atlantic since 1952 without a losing year, continued to charge at least $50 less than IATA fares.

THE PERSISTENCE OF THE COLD WAR

Another impasse persisted in 1966 as the long-standing talks between the Soviets and the U.S. officials had not brought into fruition an exchange of routes—New York to Moscow—for Pan American and Aeroflot.[93] General Quesada, after visiting the Russian capital, belittled the Soviets for using what he termed antiquated equipment and unsafe planes incapable of meeting standards at New York, a charge quite difficult to substantiate or refute because of Russian secrecy about its system. Certainly the facilities at Moscow Airport appeared to meet U.S. standards from laymen's casual visits. The Soviets reminded Americans that eight non-Communist countries accepted Aeroflot in their countries for reciprocal arrangements accorded their lines into Moscow. Indeed, it would seem more likely that New York–Moscow traffic has been a "cold-war" victim.

PILOTS, STEWARDESSES, AND ENGINEERS

The new Kennedy team of Halaby (FAA) and Boyd (CAB) met headlong the same agonizing variety of setbacks that confronted their predecessors. One of the most amusing furors, though rife with possible tragedy because of its flagrant abuse of safety regulations, was the disclosure in 1962 that occasionally several pilots had been guilty of improper "shenanigans" in the cockpit, specifically, allowing stewardesses to fly the aircraft and to sit on the pilots' laps. Irate congressmen "thundered and lightened" but the public announcement of such activities crystallized in a very mysterious fashion. Concurrently, the flight engineers, represented by the Flight Engineers International Association, fought valiantly to save their positions against the airlines' move to train copilots in the duties of the flight engineer thus reducing the jet crew by one man.[94] The public forgot about the crewmen's feud but found amusement over "blondes on laps in the cockpit." One former stewardess testified that she was at the controls of an Eastern sixty-passenger flight for thirty-five minutes in 1958.[95] Pan American and TWA stewardesses testified to similar experiences before a House committee hearing conducted by Jack Roberts, Democrat of Texas. Then a TWA flight engineer introduced photographs allegedly depicting stewardesses sitting on pilots' laps in the cockpit. Truly the flight engineers had declared "war" on the pilots in utilizing a trick, infra-red, hidden camera. The ALPA could charge "sensational publicity," but the photographs must not be ignored even though some of the instances reportedly occurred on training flights. Eastern grounded three pilots, and two days later the FAA fined thirteen Eastern pilots for "inattention to flight duty."[96] Meanwhile, newsmen reported that Administrator Halaby was spreading the slogan for all airline crews, "Fly now, play later." A year later, Representative Overton Brooks learned from Halaby that the FAA had inaugurated unscheduled flight inspections in an effort to prevent the recurrence of such laxities.

In the meantime, the Flight Engineers International, the ALPA, TWA, and governmental authorities in the Department of Labor announced an agreement whereby TWA flight engineers presently employed would gain priority for the third-seat duty when the crew was reduced to three men.[97] Labor Secretary Willard Wirtz and President Kennedy hoped other lines would reach similar accord in this labor strife affecting aviation. The summer of 1962 had witnessed a flight engineers' strike on Eastern which, in turn, unsuccessfully requested a "strike subsidy" from the CAB. At the same time Pan American engineers were blocked from striking by a federal court order. President Kennedy invoked emergency provisions of the Railway Labor Act to block a strike for at least sixty days.[98] An uneasy truce had stalled the planned strike against TWA in the middle of June, 1962.

MISFORTUNE STRIKES

Tragedy confronted the FAA and CAB with further headaches; as usual, the violation of CAR's was present in several instances. The crucial role of supplemental airlines again suffered horribly from the absurdities of a few individuals. Graphic in this sense was the slaughter of 74 army recruits in the crash of an Imperial Airlines Constellation near Richmond, Virginia, on November 8, 1961.[99] The surviving pilot and flight engineer, along with the airline, faced a number of charges in the realm of faulty maintenance. In March, 1961, the FAA banned takeoffs for commercial airliners in conditions of less than one-fourth mile of visibility (one mile for VFR flights), a direct offshoot of the supplemental line crash involving the Cal Poly football team the previous autumn.[100]

JET FAILURES

Meanwhile, the new jets, performing with such an amazing degree of safety in the initial months of service, now encountered a series of misfortunes here and abroad. The DC–8 developed a number of malfunctions in the hydraulic system leading to several successful emergency landings, one or two of which were captured for the television audience at New York, plus a lustful crowd bulging around the fences ready to witness a gory ending. The planes were not grounded, though Eastern pilots threatened to strike if the recommended changes were not made.[101]   A United Air Lines DC–8 with leaking hydraulic fluid managed an emergency landing at Denver, Colorado, on July 11, 1961, but veered off the runway, hit an abutment, and burst into flames with 17 killed. A surviving family from Newton, Iowa, charged complete lack of emergency assistance by the airline personnel in their section of the plane, the area where the deaths occurred.[102] Both the FAA and CAB continued to be plagued with the bombing of aircraft. Continental Airlines lost a jet over southern Iowa on May 22, 1962; the probable cause listed an explosion in the tail section as bringing death to 45 aboard.[103] Making a false bomb threat became a most serious offense, punishable by law. But several people, including the divorced wife of Elliott Roosevelt, were apprehended for such a foolish mistake.[104] The FAA and CAB counted on FBI assistance with alleged "crime aboard an aircraft," including the instance of two passengers fighting over leg room on an Air France jet, one sustaining a blow to the head from a wine bottle.[105]

POOR MAINTENANCE

The ugly circumstance of misplaced parts has entered into several crashes in recent years. A Boeing 707 belonging to American Airlines crashed on takeoff into Jamaica Bay (New York City) killing 95 in March, 1962. The CAB blamed the loss on the improper use of tweezers for tying up control wires in the automatic pilot system.[106] In addition, the CAB acknowledged that the FAA's contention that a small bolt had dropped out of the same system might be true. After the Jamaica Bay crash, the FAA ruled that Boeing jet pilots must utilize a "preferred pattern" in operating wing flaps on takeoff. The FAA fixed minimum takeoff speeds and prohibited use of the autopilot on takeoff as long as the craft remained below 1,100 feet. Encountering congestion from private aircraft "sightseeing" near crash scenes, the FAA finally ruled in 1963 against nonessential flying over crash sites.[107] The loss of a 5/16-inch bolt caused the crash of a TWA Constellation near Chicago's Midway Airport on September 1, 1961, killing all 78 aboard according to the final CAB report. The bolt supposedly was missing from the elevator boost mechanism. A Northwest Electra crashed, all 37 perishing, at Chicago's O'Hare Field just sixteen days later. The CAB contended that loosened connectors of the aileron boost assembly had not been retightened during maintenance operations two months prior to this crash.[108] An allegedly faulty rear door aboard an Allegheny Airlines Convair opened in flight causing a stewardess to be pulled out of the craft to her death from an altitude of 4,000 feet.[109]

SWANS, LIGHTNING

At least two whistling swans, each weighing up to 18 pounds, caused the death plunge of a United Viscount near Ellicott City, Maryland, on November 23, 1962; all 17 occupants died.[110] Lightning, always scoffed at before as a factor, was considered to have been a contributing cause of a Pan American's Boeing 707 crash. Eighty-one perished in this crash near Elkton, Maryland, on December 8, 1963. The Elkton crash elicited a proposal by the FAA and CAB that all jetliners be equipped with "wicks" to discharge static electricity. The ill-fated Clipper was not so equipped.[111] Furthermore, the experts studied redesign of fuel tanks and the possibility of using just one type of jet gasoline —the jet-A type provided less "vapor flammability." The Air Force had already banned the use of kerosene in jet fuel. Air France lost two Boeing 707 jets within three weeks in June, 1962. One crashed on takeoff on June 3 at Orly Field, Paris, killing 130 (2 hostesses survived); another fell at Guadeloupe, West Indies, on June 22; all 102 died. In the Orly crash 121 members of the Atlanta, Georgia, Art Association lost their lives.[112] A popular pilot, Edward J. Bechtold, met death in his Eastern Air Lines DC–7B on November 30, 1962, at Idlewild (Kennedy), New York. In the wreck which occurred during poor visibility, 26 survived and 24 died. Bechtold had written an article for later publication criticizing the low margin of safety available on the runway (No. 4) nearest the crash.[113]

MORE CRASHES

Further disasters occurred.[114] Northwest Orient Airlines lost a Boeing 720–B shortly after takeoff from Miami, Florida, in February, 1963. All 43 aboard died. One year later, Eastern Air Lines suffered the loss of a jet following takeoff at New Orleans, with all 58 dead. One month later, a Paradise Airlines scheduled Constellation fell in the Lake Tahoe mountain area in California, losing 81 people. The FAA suspended the operating certificate of Paradise Airlines following the crash at Lake Tahoe.[115] The height of repugnance was generated from the manner in which a demented individual brought death to all 44 aboard a Pacific Air Lines F–27 (a plane without a fatal accident up to that moment) on May 7, 1964, near San Francisco.[116] The pilot was shot, perhaps the copilot, too, according to the CAB. Consequently, the FAA ordered all cockpit doors locked beginning on August 6, 1964.

HIJACKERS AT WORK

Though not proving as fatal as the suicides, shootings, or bombings had been, nevertheless, the hijacking of commercial aircraft became another menace to the airlines and everyone concerned. In March, 1962, some observers questioned the possibility of piracy or sabotage in the sudden disappearance west of Guam of a Flying Tiger Constellation carrying 107 people on a military assignment to South Viet Nam.[117] But no doubt had lingered over an episode where an Eastern Electra was taken over at gunpoint in July, 1961, and the crew forced to fly to Cuba. Less than two weeks later, a crazed father and his boy of sixteen hijacked a Continental Boeing 707 between Phoenix and El Paso. This was the same plane that later crashed over the Iowa-Missouri border from dynamite set off in a washroom. President Kennedy personally ordered the airline not to allow the plane to be taken to Cuba, and the craft was halted by shooting out the tires as it headed for a takeoff at El Paso after the pilot had talked the hijackers into letting him land there for fuel.[118] A French Algerian took it upon himself just a few days later to hijack a Pan American jet over Mexico, forcing the crew to land in Cuba.

DRUNKEN FLYING

The CAB blamed alcohol consumption as a contributing factor in the crash of a light plane (three died) near Spencer, Iowa, on February 13, 1963.[119] Alcohol also figured in the case of a suspended American Airlines' pilot, who, according to Drew Pearson's associates, had been assigned to White House charter flights carrying newsmen. These were not the first cases of "drinking and flying" and the FAA and CAB could realize that even the railroads had in recent years pinpointed drunkenness as the cause of a major accident involving the Northern Pacific Railway near Missoula, Montana, on June 10, 1962.[120]

NEAR CATASTROPHIES

Averted tragedies and valiant emergency landings brightened the picture. At Amarillo, Texas, a Continental Viscount crashed after takeoff, but all aboard walked away from the burning wreckage. A Northwest Airlines DC-7 carrying 102 military personnel and dependents successfully completed a sea ditching off the coast of Sitka, Alaska, an FAA supply boat later taking the entire number aboard to safety.[121] An Eastern DC-8 plummeted 3 miles earthward in 12 seconds, lost 1 engine in the turbulence, but avoided a crash; the plane carried 128 persons.[122] Foreign lines operating into this country counted similar near catastrophies.[123] A Trans Canadian DC-8F plunged beyond the runway at London Airport; all 98 escaped safely. An abortive takeoff because of an engine fire was barely overcome by a spectacular ground loop at the runway's end at Orly (Paris) for an El Al (Israel) Boeing 707 headed for New York. A harrowing experience at sea in September, 1962, involved a Flying Tiger Super Constellation carrying military dependents to Germany. Three engines failed as the plane was ditched 500 miles west of Shannon, Ireland. Miraculously, 48 survived the ordeal though 28 died. A splendid concentration of surface vessels, both military and commercial, as well as air support accomplished the rescue in rough seas. Near O'Hare Airport a chartered DC-3 was unable to maintain altitude and crashed into one end of a nearby house. But 29 of the 30 aboard climbed out safely; no one in the house sustained injury. A private pilot brought his single-engine Cessna down through a power line, along a busy highway, and into a mountain highway tunnel after his engine failed at Idaho Springs, Colorado.

Elsewhere, the fear of lightning and turbulent weather

caused Mrs. Lyndon B. Johnson to return by car from Cleveland to Washington, D.C., following a "jolting discharge of static electricity" from the plane—a United Viscount. Visible later were the effects on the trailing edge of a wing, one propeller, and the radio antennae.[124] A TWA Boeing jet returned to London shortly after takeoff to have its fiber nose cone repaired after lightning tore a 21-inch hole in the nose. Then, too, although "near misses" along the highways occur practically every time a motorist ventures forth, the harrowing experiences along the airways gain the headlines. Military aircraft continued to be a menace to commercial craft, an American Airlines Electra being forced into a sudden dive in order to avert a collision with an Air Force F-101 Voodoo near Syracuse, New York. Five passengers were slightly injured.[125] American and Delta jets took evasive action at the last possible second to avoid collision near Indianapolis, Indiana. At Washington National Airport, a private DC–3 reportedly came in over and dropped in front of a Northwest DC–6 for a landing, causing a heated radio dispute between the two pilots. No accident occurred, but the episode showed possible careless handling of planes by the tower, if not complete disregard for safety on the part of one or both pilots.[126]

FINES AND DECISIONS

Displaying complete impartiality, Administrator Halaby incurred a $50 fine for brushing the wing tip of his FAA craft with an airliner at Washington National Airport in November, 1961. Fines against airline personnel included a civil action of $1,000 against a copilot for feathering the wrong engine on a Western Airlines DC–6B, $2,000 against Pan American plus penalties against the flight engineer and mechanics for faulty maintenance on a Boeing 707, and a similar charge with $250 penalty against TWA.[127] Frontier Airlines, allowed by the CAB to suspend certain local service, faced state of Nebraska fines of $1,000 per day in contempt of the state's order to retain that service.[128] The era since 1959 witnessed an ever-increasing number of legal suits against the U.S. government. The collision over Staten Island, the starlings-caused tragedy at Boston, a governmental chartered plane crash at Guam, and the Cal Poly crash at Toledo were among the top ten cases pending before the courts in 1963. This did not imply FAA responsibility in all these crashes but that the government was a party because of the FAA's role in air traffic control.[129] Airport officials throughout the country winced at the Supreme Court's unanimous verdict in March, 1962, contending that a property owner near an airport is entitled to compensation if the noise and vibration from low-flying planes makes his home unlivable. In another decision, the Court decreed by a 7 to 2 vote that airport operators were liable. Justices Hugo Black and Felix Frankfurter contended that the federal government should pay the damages.[130]

WAR ON THE "NO-SHOW"

In a move calculated to reduce the "no-show" problem, the CAB ruled in 1962 that airlines could assess a penalty of $5 or 50 per cent, whichever was larger, when refunding the unused ticket of a customer who failed to cancel his passage. Likewise, the CAB moved to aid the passenger "bumped" from a plane because of overbooking, allowing the passenger to collect $25 or 50 per cent, whichever was larger, if there were no space on the plane for which he had a reservation.[131] The CAB decreed against three foreign lines—Lufthansa, Sabena, and Air France—for illegally trading transportation for publicity, promotional services, or advertising. Tickets to Europe reportedly had been offered at discounts amounting to 30 per cent.[132] Even the controversial Bobby Baker came to be linked with aviation, but apparently his interests rested mostly with the attempts to get his vending machines installed at Pan American's intercontinental hotels.[133]

The strange type of circumstance that might confront international travelers was illustrated in October, 1963, when a Pan American pilot knew his jet had sustained a blown tire on takeoff at Rome. He decided to complete the flight to New York but could not land because of fog and rain. Proceeding to Windsor Locks, Connecticut, he encountered difficulty from U.S. Customs officials who, despite the emergency, grumbled over handling so many passengers with their limited services. The passengers waited forty-five minutes in the liner after landing.[134]

FLIGHT STANDARDS SERVICE

The vigilance maintained within the FAA's Flight Standard Service has been described at length pertaining to the regulation of commercial operations. For its flight inspection of air navigation facilities, the FAA now owned fifty-five DC–3's, five turbo-prop Convairs, two C–135's (Air Force model of the 707), one B–57, three Lockheed Constellations, and one C–123. Also in

1962, the FAA began trying out semiautomatic flight inspection (SAFI) equipment.[135]

General aviation provided another field in which much attention was needed. For all nonscheduled operations involving aircraft of less than 12,500 pounds, the FAA operated approximately eighty district offices throughout the country with both operations and maintenance inspectors on call at all times. The private (general) pilot most likely came in contact with these officials for the written examinations, flight tests leading to certification, periodic additional spot checks of plane and pilot, and investigation of all accidents, in addition to the determination of any penalty recommended to the FAA's regional counsel.[136]

In February, 1962, the FAA established the position of hearing officer at Los Angeles, Kansas City, and Atlanta for the purpose of making available to any airman facing enforcement action a formal, trial-type hearing.[137] This innovation was one result of Project Tightrope, a study of the FAA's rule-making and enforcement procedures conducted by an advisory group of private attorneys. The rules would subsequently be called Federal Aviation Regulations instead of Civil Air Regulations.

One of the many tasks involved the inspectors' issuance of waivers to allow crop spraying, highway-patrol checking on speeders, photography, and low flights over conservation areas. Most requests could be justified but not the case of a disc jockey who wished to drop marbles from a helicopter.[138] Then, again, the increasing menace to aviation from self-styled scientists launching rockets prompted the assertion from one inspector (officially now called flight service engineers) that nothing could be done unless the rocket struck an aircraft.[139]

The maintenance inspectors of general aviation continued to scrutinize aircraft at the various airports, examining approximately 10 per cent of the planes at each airport in one year. The inspectors must return for periodic refresher courses at the Aeronautical Center, Oklahoma City. The Des Moines office, a typical Flight Standards district installation, covered the western two-thirds of Iowa with a staff of two operations inspectors, two maintenance inspectors, and the general supervising inspector. Two secretaries helped ease the work load by giving the pilot examinations. Often the labor of the Flight Standards personnel has been taken for granted by the public in recent years. Gratifying to the service was the selection of Harold D. Hoekstra, Projects Control Officer of the Engineering and Manufacturing Division of the FAA's Bureau of Flight Standards, as a fellow of Britain's Royal Aeronautical Society.[140]

AN ENCOURAGING OUTLOOK

The wide variety of FAA functions manifested itself in any location with several offices. That cooperation existed among the types of function—air controller, flight watcher, communications maintenance man, flight standards engineer (inspector), and radar specialists—depicted a situation to the credit of the FAA's administration, national, regional, and local. On the other hand, deep-seated rivalries—not particularly dangerous to the smooth operation of the FAA—might be detected at these field offices and appeared to be a most natural phenomenon. For example, a supervisor who might discourage his employees from flying met nothing but scorn from other employees in the same location who toiled outside his jurisdiction.

Then, too, there existed that most common inclination on the part of numerous FAA employees to look with chagrin at the role of politics in the agency and in the appointment of the administrator. Apparently these dedicated officials always strive for the elevation of one from their own ranks who might better understand the pitfalls as well as the merits of the different controls over aviation charged to the FAA.[141] This sentiment differed little from that expressed in other federal agencies working in the realm of scientific and technological matters. For example, the Weather Bureau forecaster looked askance at the colleague engaged in activities not directed at the "heart" of the meteorologists' very existence—actual forecasting.[142]

Interagency cooperation involving the FAA has been cited in numerous instances. However, petty irritations have not entirely disappeared. One Weather Bureau official complained of the FAA's refusal to connect a Weather Bureau perforating machine with Weather Bureau teletype circuits because the latter equipment belonged to the FAA.[143] Weather Bureau field officials have always grumbled about FAA personnel issuing weather advisories to pilots. For the most part, however, one could marvel at the cooperation between the Weather Bureau and the FAA and, indeed, the general support given the FAA by state authorities and other federal agencies as well as the extensive aviation world of airline manufacturing and operation.

The briefest evaluation of aviation's current safety record, the steady increase in passenger miles flown, the utilization largely of comfortable and speedy equipment, and the willingness on the part of industry and the government to pursue research for improvement—all these factors might well lead citizens of the United States in the mid-sixties to anticipate future dramatic successes in the forthcoming supersonic age. Just as has been the case since 1926, the governmental regulators in the FAA and CAB will stand as partners and patrons in this development.

NEW LEADERS

Succeeding Halaby as administrator of the FAA on July 1, 1965, was William F. McKee, formerly with NASA as assistant administrator for management development. McKee, a retired four-star general, left the Air Force in 1964 after completing thirty-five years of military service. He is a graduate of West Point (1929) and began his career in the Coast Artillery Corps before duty as Deputy Assistant Chief of Air Staff for Operations in 1943. He later commanded logistics for the Air Force, gaining his fourth star in 1961. McKee holds three Distinguished Service Medals and other decorations. He won the first annual Distinguished Management Award for outstanding service in air force logistics.[144] President Johnson, in addressing a group at the swearing-in ceremony for McKee, declared that McKee's assignment with the FAA would be to develop a supersonic transport providing safety for passengers, superiority over other commercial aircraft, and yet one which would be economically profitable to build and operate.

David D. Thomas was selected as deputy administrator at the same time. The choice of Thomas brought to this important position two most important qualifications. First, Thomas had been with the FAA for twenty-seven years. Second, he possessed first-hand experience in flying, holding a commercial pilot certificate with multiengine and instrument ratings. Thomas, born in 1913 at New Castle, Texas, worked for American Airlines in Nashville before joining the old CAA as an air traffic controller at Cleveland. Subsequently, he served in various capacities, mostly in air traffic control, including the directing of the FAA's Air Traffic Control Service during 1959–1963.

Named chairman of the CAB on April 28, 1965, was Charles S. Murphy while Chairman Boyd became Undersecretary of Commerce for Transportation. Murphy had served as a law assistant and legal counsel for the Senate during 1934–1946, was an administrative assistant to President Harry S. Truman, and, following several years of private law practice, returned to Washington, D.C., as Undersecretary of Agriculture in 1960. Murphy earned the B.A. and LL.B. degrees from Duke University.

These present leaders of the FAA and CAB were greeted with both heartaches and promising innovations within the ensuing months. On the bright side, medium-range jets, including the Boeing 727 and DC–9, brought improved service even to some feeder routes. These and other smaller jets were also allowed to serve Washington (D.C.) National Airport. President Johnson moved on with a request to gain a department with cabinet rank for all phases of transportation. Though the costs soared, the government proceeded with its plans for the commercial supersonic aircraft, hoping now for flight testing in 1970 and commercial production by 1974. Meanwhile, in 1965, the Boeing 727 jet became involved in crashes killing a total of 131 people—Lake Michigan, August 16; Cincinnati, November 8; and Salt Lake City, November 11. Clarence Sayen, former head of the ALPA, was one of the victims of the Lake Michigan tragedy. Subsequently, the FAA and CAB authorities argued over the safety qualifications of the aircraft. Finally, a crippling strike (July, 1966) involving members of the International Association of Machinists and Aerospace Workers (AFL-CIO) closed operations of five major airlines—Eastern, National, Northwest, Trans World, and United. President Johnson had averted the strike for sixty days by appointing a board to attempt a settlement.

APPENDIX

BUDGET APPROPRIATIONS FOR THE FEDERAL
AVIATION AGENCY AND PREDECESSORS,
FISCAL YEARS 1927–1965*

Fiscal Year		Appropriations
1927	Aeronautics Branch	$ 550,000
1928		3,791,500
1929		4,361,850
1930		6,416,620
1931		9,204,830
1932		10,362,300
1933		9,053,500
1934		7,660,780
1935	Bureau of Air Commerce	5,511,800
1936		5,909,800
1937		6,850,000
1938		10,878,500
1939	Civil Aeronautics Authority	14,351,480
1940		25,768,000
1941	Civil Aeronautics Administration	103,390,537
1942		224,772,687
1943		38,237,775
1944		31,653,000
1945		35,781,478
1946		51,090,000
1947		121,537,720
1948		119,314,334
1949		100,470,000
1950		187,100,000
1951		151,900,000
1952		138,900,000
1953		136,400,000
1954		115,900,000
1955		131,400,000
1956		197,300,000
1957		278,400,000
1958		406,100,000
1959	Federal Aviation Agency	565,000,000
1960		573,500,000
1961		690,400,000
1962		728,900,000
1963		755,000,000
1964		813,400,000
1965		717,400,000

* Data were obtained from the Federal Aviation Agency and from
the *Annual Reports* of predecessor agencies.

PERSONNEL, FEDERAL AVIATION AGENCY AND PREDECESSORS,
SELECTED YEARS, 1928–1965*

Fiscal Year	Total Employment
1928	423
1933	1,478
1934	1,750
1935	1,829
1936	2,044
1937	1,922
1938	2,806
1940	4,841
1945	10,571
1948	15,945
1949	18,423
1950	18,037
1951	18,390
1952	17,066
1953	16,685
1954	15,067
1955	15,554
1956	17,110
1957	21,510
1958	25,805
1959	33,755
1960	38,261
1961	42,958
1962	44,482
1963	46,432
1964	45,473
1965	45,800

* Data were obtained from appropriations hearings and the Federal
Aviation Agency.

PERSONNEL AND APPROPRIATIONS,
THE CIVIL AERONAUTICS BOARD*

Fiscal Year	Total Employed	Appropriations
1942	331	$ 1,179,000
1946	446	1,810,435
1951	577	3,500,000
1957	640	4,607,117
1959	731	6,328,700
1960	755	6,925,500
1961	754	7,853,000
1962	788	8,900,000
1963	836	9,450,000
1964	847	10,240,000

* Data were obtained from appropriations hearings and *Annual Reports* of the Civil Aeronautics Board.

MAJOR FACILITIES OPERATED BY THE
FEDERAL AVIATION AGENCY
(June 30, 1964)*

Facility	Number
Approach light system (ALS)	201
Sequence flash lights (SFL)	200
Airport surveillance radar (ASR)	74
Instrument landing system (ILS)	244
Precision approach radar (PAR)	30
VOR (including TVOR)	489
VORTAC (including one TACAN)†	348
Flight service station (FSS)	335
International flight service station (IFSS)	12
Peripheral communication installation (RCAG)	349
Air route traffic control center (ARTCC)	32
Airport traffic control tower (ATCT)	211
Combined station/tower (CS/T)	66
Long-range radar (LRR; including Norfolk LRR terminal facility)	78
Military radar approach control facility (RAPCON or RATCC; figure includes center approach control)	40
Airport surface detection equipment (ASDE)	11

* Federal Aviation Agency, *Sixth Annual Report, Fiscal Year 1964*, p. 34.

† Includes twenty-one commissioned distance-measuring-equipment portions of TACAN facilities.

NOTES

Chapter 1: AMERICAN AVIATION'S STRUGGLE

1. Jeremiah Milbank, Jr., *The First Century of Flight in America* (Princeton, 1943), p. 183.
2. A.E.M. Geddes, *Meteorology: An Introductory Treatise* (London, 1921), pp. 5–6, 10–12.
3. Milbank, *First Century*, pp. 133–53, 172–78, 183–91.
4. Elsbeth E. Freudenthal, *Flight Into History: The Wright Brothers and the Air Age* (Norman, 1949), pp. 196–201.
5. Freudenthal, *Flight*, pp. 118–24, 188–91, 232–36.
6. Lloyd Morris and Kendall Smith, *Ceiling Unlimited: The Story of American Aviation From Kitty Hawk to Supersonics* (New York, 1953), pp. 48–52.
7. Morris and Smith, *Ceiling*, pp. 66–70.
8. Freudenthal, *Flight*, pp. 235–39.
9. Charles E. Planck, *Women With Wings* (New York, 1942), pp. 14–22.
10. Eugene M. Emme, *Aeronautics and Astronautics: An American Chronology of Science and Technology in the Exploration of Space, 1915–1960* (Washington, D.C., 1961), p. 1.
11. Emme, *Aeronautics*, p. 2.
12. Woodrow Wilson to William C. Redfield, Mar. 9, 1915, General Records of the Department of Commerce, Office of the Secretary, RG 40, National Archives.
13. Emme, *Aeronautics*, pp. 6–9.
14. S. W. Stratton to Secretary Redfield, Jan. 6, 1919, General Records Department of Commerce.
15. Howard Coffin to President Wilson, Feb. 14, 1919, General Records Department of Commerce.
16. Stratton to Redfield, Mar. 15, 1919, General Records Department of Commerce.
17. Newton D. Baker to Stratton, Oct. 10, 1919, General Records Department of Commerce.
18. Stratton to Secretary of Commerce J. W. Alexander, Nov. 22, 1920, General Records Department of Commerce.
19. Elsbeth E. Freudenthal, *The Aviation Business: From Kitty Hawk to Wall Street* (New York, 1940), pp. 62–63.
20. Emme, *Aeronautics*, p. 9.
21. Freudenthal, *Aviation Business*, pp. 64–65; Emme, *Aeronautics*, pp. 13, 18.
22. *New York Times*, Sep. 4, 1925, pp. 1–4, 20; Sep. 5, 1925, pp. 1–5.
23. J. W. Alexander to the Secretary of State, June 3, 1920, General Records Department of Commerce.
24. Freudenthal, *Aviation Business*, pp. 65–68; Henry Ladd Smith, *Airways: The History of Commercial Aviation in the United States* (New York, 1942), pp. 50–59.
25. Smith, *Airways*, pp. 64–65.
26. Freudenthal, *Aviation Business*, pp. 66–67; Smith, *Airways*, pp. 68–72.

27. Smith, *Airways*, pp. 84–93.
28. Matthew Josephson, *Empire of the Air: Juan Trippe and the Struggle for World Airways* (New York, 1943–44), p. 25.
29. Emme, *Aeronautics*, p. 19.
30. 49 *Cong. Rec.*, Part 4 (Feb. 17, 1913), 3276–78.
31. 51 *Cong. Rec.*, Part 1 (Dec. 15, 1913), 929–36; 52 *Cong. Rec.*, Part 3 (Feb. 1, 1915), 2827.
32. 53 *Cong. Rec.*, Part 15 (July 21, 1916), 1530–31.
33. 55 *Cong. Rec.*, Part 1 (Apr. 2, 1917), 189.
34. 58 *Cong. Rec.*, Part 7 (Oct. 8, 1919), 6582; Part 8 (Nov. 5, 1919), 7998.
35. 59 *Cong. Rec.*, Part 1 (Dec. 15, 1919), 611; Part 3 (Jan. 29, 1920), 2189–91, 2228; *New York Times*, Feb. 27, 1919, p. 24.
36. 62 *Cong. Rec.*, Part 2 (Jan. 31, 1922), 1997–2012.
37. Charles E. Hughes to the Postmaster General, June 30, 1921, General Records Department of Commerce.
38. E. H. Shaughnessy to Mr. Hays, Sep. 27, 1921, General Records Department of Commerce.
39. Emme, *Aeronautics*, pp. 9–11.
40. 61 *Cong. Rec.*, Part 8 (Nov. 19, 1921), 7952.
41. *New York Times*, July 7, 1919, p. 14; Dec. 17, 1920, p. 21; Aug. 30, 1921, p. 14.
42. Herbert Hoover to Secretary of the Navy, Apr. 7, 1922, General Records Department of Commerce.
43. Hoover to Edward J. Fertig, Dec. 16, 1922, General Records Department of Commerce.
44. 62 *Cong. Rec.*, Part 2 (Jan. 31, 1922), 1997–2012.
45. Stephan Davis to William B. Robertson, Sep. 8, 1925, General Records Department of Commerce.
46. 61 *Cong. Rec.*, Part 3 (June 17, 1921), 2687.
47. Charles D. Walcott to President Coolidge, Nov. 12, 1925, General Records Department of Commerce.
48. 64 *Cong. Rec.*, Part 2 (Jan. 11, 1923), pp. 1609–11.
49. 65 *Cong. Rec.*, Part 1 (Jan. 8, 1924), 701–5.
50. Godfrey L. Cabot to Hoover, Jan. 2, 1925, General Records Department of Commerce.
51. *New York Times*, Nov. 29, 1924, p. 1; Nov. 30, 1924, p. 2; Jan. 10, 1925, p. 15.
52. 66 *Cong. Rec.*, Part 2 (Jan. 10, 1925), 1589.
53. Freudenthal, *Aviation Business*, p. 75.
54. Smith, *Airways*, p. 92.
55. Freudenthal, *Aviation Business*, pp. 73–74.
56. *New York Times*, Sep. 11, 1925, p. 22.
57. Morris and Smith, *Ceiling*, pp. 251–53; *New York Times*, Nov. 30. 1925, p. 1; Dec. 3, 1925, pp. 1, 12, 24; Dec. 4, 1925, p. 10.
58. "Uncle Sam as Air Boss," *The Nation*, 119, No. 3099 (Nov. 26, 1924), 559.
59. "A New Air Policy for America," *The American Review of Reviews*, 72 (Oct., 1925), 421–22.
60. "Our New Automatic Safety Code," *Scientific American*, 134, No. 4 (Apr., 1926), 269–70.
61. *Ibid.*, p. 269.
62. *Ibid.*, p. 270.
63. John Goldstrom, "Safety in Aviation Improving," *Current History*, 26. No. 1 (Apr.–Sep., 1927), 37.
64. *Ibid.*, p. 39.
65. 67 *Cong. Rec.*, Part 7 (Apr. 12, 1926), 7312.
66. *Ibid.*, 7316–17.
67. Hoover to Cabot, Dec. 11, 1925, General Records Department of Commerce.
68. 67 *Cong. Rec.*, Part 7 (Apr. 12, 1926), 7317–19.

69. *Ibid.*, Part 9 (May 13, 1926), 9351–62, 9386–91.
70. Freudenthal, *Aviation Business*, p. 78.
71. 67 *Cong. Rec.*, Part 9 (May 20, 1926), 9811; *New York Times*, May 22, 1926, p. 18; Aug. 16, 1926, p. 14.
72. Charles C. Rohlfing, *National Regulation of Aeronautics* (Philadelphia, 1931), p. 33.
73. *Ibid.*, p. 35.
74. W. J. Davis, "Clearing the Air for Commerce," *The Annals of the American Academy of Political and Social Science*, 131 (May, 1927), 141–50.

Chapter 2: THE AERONAUTICS BRANCH

1. William A. White, *A Puritan in Babylon: The Story of Calvin Coolidge* (New York, 1938), pp. 290–94, 317–38; Joseph Brandes, *Herbert Hoover and Economic Diplomacy: Department of Commerce Policy, 1921–1928* (Pittsburgh, 1962), pp. 216–20.
2. Recommendations of the Committee on Civil Aviation of the Department of Commerce and American Engineering Council, Oct. 21, 1925, General Records Department of Commerce.
3. Interview between William P. MacCracken, Jr., and Charles E. Planck, on tape owned by Planck, Washington, D.C., obtained in 1962, Federal Aviation Agency.
4. *Ibid.*
5. Charles C. Rohlfing, *National Regulation of Aeronautics* (Philadelphia, 1931) pp. 5, 46–47; *New York Times*, Aug. 10, 1926, p. 21.
6. Jerome Beatty, "He Rules an Empire in the Air," *The American Magazine*, 114 (Sep., 1932), 56–58, 72, 74.
7. William P. MacCracken, Jr., to Arthur S. Bent, Los Angeles Chamber of Commerce, Aug. 30, 1926, General Records Department of Commerce; USDC, *Annual Report of the Director of Aeronautics*, 1927, p. 2.
8. MacCracken to Alva C. Richards, Winchester, Va. Sep. 16, 1926, General Records Department of Commerce.
9. MacCracken to Lt. R. J. Brown, Jr., Sep. 16, 1926, General Records Department of Commerce.
10. MacCracken to Walter H. Beech, Wichita, Kan., General Records Department of Commerce.
11. USDC, *Annual Report*, 1927, p. 3.
12. 68 *Cong. Rec.*, Part 1 (Dec. 17, 1926), 632.
13. Henry Ladd Smith, *Airways: The History of Commercial Aviation in the United States* (New York, 1942), p. 99.
14. Rohlfing, *National Regulation*, p. 65.
15. Charles A. Lindbergh, *The Spirit of St. Louis* (New York, 1953), pp. 3–50; 68 *Cong. Rec.*, Part 1 (Jan. 26, 1927), 2317–21.
16. USDC, *Annual Report*, 1927, pp. 1–2.
17. *Ibid.*, p. 3.
18. MacCracken, interviewed by Planck, 1962.
19. *Ibid.*
20. William P. MacCracken, Jr., "Air Regulation," *The Annals of the American Academy of Political and Social Science*, 131 (May, 1927), 118–23.
21. USDC, *Annual Report*, 1927, p. 3.
22. W. J. Davis, "Clearing the Air," *Annals*, p. 141.
23. Interview with Karl E. Voelter, Federal Aviation Agency, Washington, D.C., Aug. 30, 1961.
24. Katherine M. Miller to Planck, n.d. 1946, file on CAA Organization-History, Office of Public Information, Federal Aviation Agency, Washington, D.C.
25. USDC, *Annual Report*, 1927, p. 5.

26. *Ibid.*, pp. 4–9.
27. Donald R. Whitnah, *A History of the United States Weather Bureau* (Urbana, 1961), pp. 177–83; *Aviation*, 25 (Aug. 11, 1928), 484; U.S. Weather Bureau, *Topics and Personnel*, June, 1926.
28. USDC, *Annual Report*, 1927, pp. 12–17.
29. MacCracken, interviewed by Planck, 1962.
30. USDC, *Annual Report*, 1927, p. 10.
31. *Ibid.*, p. 19.
32. *Ibid.*, pp. 21–23.
33. 68 *Cong. Rec.*, Part 2 (Jan. 26, 1927), 2320.
34. *Hearings Before the House Subcommittee on Appropriations on Department of Commerce Appropriations for Fiscal 1930*, 70th Cong., 2d Sess., 53 (1928).
35. Lloyd Morris and Kendall Smith, *Ceiling Unlimited: The Story of American Aviation From Kitty Hawk to Supersonics* (New York, 1953). p. 252.
36. Matthew Josephson, *Empire of the Air: Juan Trippe and the Struggle for World Airways* (New York, 1943–1944), p. 38.
37. *Ibid.*, pp. 27, 32.
38. William L. Grossman, *Air Passenger Traffic* (New York, 1947), p. 69.
39. USDC, *Annual Report*, 1927, pp. 19–21.
40. *Ibid.*, p. 21.
41. Ernest Jones to Chief, Air Mail, Post Office, Oct. 9, 1926, Civil Aeronautics Administration Central Files, RG 237, National Archives, Washington, D.C.; Lindbergh, *The Spirit*, pp. 5–7.
42. Memorandum, n.d. concerning Cobham's flight, CAA Central Files.
43. Archibald Black, *Transport Aviation*, 2d ed. (New York, 1926–1929), p. 24.
44. Lindbergh, *The Spirit*, p. 64; MacCracken, interviewed by Planck, 1962.
45. Lindbergh, *The Spirit*, pp. 111–15.
46. *Washington Times*, June 6, 1927, copy located in CAA Central Files.
47. Lindbergh, *The Spirit*, pp. 145, 168–69.
48. MacCracken to Karl Betts, Detroit Board of Commerce, May 24, 1927, CAA Central Files.
49. MacCracken to O. A. Montgomery, Detroit Association of Credit Men, June 1, 1927, CAA Central Files.
50. MacCracken to Everett Sanders, secretary to the President, June 7, 1927, CAA Central Files.
51. R. L. Faris to MacCracken, June 23, 1927, and MacCracken to Faris, July 5, 1927, CAA Central Files.
52. John O. LaGorce, National Geographic Society, to MacCracken, Nov. 14, 1927, CAA Central Files.
53. MacCracken to *St. Louis Post Dispatch*, telegram, July 5, 1927, and MacCracken to William B. Robertson, July 6, 1927, CAA Central Files.
54. MacCracken to J. L. Whitney, Oct. 3, 1928, CAA Central Files.
55. C. A. Lindbergh to MacCracken, telegram, June 11, 1928, CAA Central Files.
56. R. A. Vonorsdel, Omaha, to MacCracken, n.d., CAA Central Files.
57. MacCracken to Lindbergh, Mexico City, Dec. 19, 1927, and Dec. 23, 1927, CAA Central Files.
58. Frederic W. Wile, "Washington Observations," n.d., CAA Central Files.
59. MacCracken to W. B. Robertson, Feb. 11, 1928, CAA Central Files.
60. Sen. Robert M. LaFollette, Jr., to MacCracken, Mar. 28, 1928, and MacCracken to LaFollette, Mar. 29, 1928, CAA Central Files.
61. Lindbergh to Congressman Nicholas Longworth, Mar. 15, 1928, CAA Central Files.
62. Lindbergh to Sen. Charles G. Dawes, Mar. 15, 1928, CAA Central Files.
63. MacCracken to N. L. Howard, Chicago, Feb. 2, 1928, CAA Central Files.

64. MacCracken to Congressman George R. Stobbs, n.d., CAA Central Files.
65. MacCracken, interviewed by Planck, 1962.
66. Interview with Charles E. Planck, Federal Aviation Agency, Washington, D.C., April 11, 1962.
67. F. B. Hubachek to George E. Akerson, Department of Commerce, Sep. 29, 1928, CAA Central Files.
68. Hubachek to MacCracken, Sep. 29, 1928, CAA Central Files.
69. MacCracken to Hubachek, Oct. 6, 1928, CAA Central Files.
70. MacCracken, interviewed by Planck, 1962.
71. Richard E. Byrd to MacCracken, Aug. 21, 1928, CAA Central Files.
72. Harry F. Guggenheim to MacCracken, Nov. 9, 1927; and lists of later participants at the conference on civil aviation activities, Dec., 1927, CAA Central Files.
73. MacCracken, interviewed by Planck, 1962.
74. Rohlfing, *National Regulation*, p. 49.
75. Aeronautical Chamber of Commerce of America, "Department of Commerce," *Aircraft Yearbook, 1928*, pp. 145–51, General Records Department of Commerce.

Chapter 3: ORDER THROUGH FURTHER CONTROLS

1. William A. White, *A Puritan in Babylon: The Story of Calvin Coolidge* (New York, 1938), pp. 353, 400.
2. Eugene Lyons, *Our Unknown Ex-President: A Portrait of Herbert Hoover* (New York, 1947–1948), p. 229.
3. USDC, *Annual Report of the Director of Aeronautics*, 1930, p. 1.
4. USDC, Aeronautics Branch, *Air Commerce Bulletin*, 1, No. 11 (Dec. 2, 1929), 8.
5. USDC, *Annual Reports*, 1927–1934.
6. William P. MacCracken, Jr., interviewed by Charles E. Planck, 1962.
7. *House Subcommittee Commerce Appropriations 1931*, 71st Cong., 2d Sess. 52 (1929).
8. *Senate Subcommittee Commerce Appropriations 1934*, 72d Cong., 2d Sess. 118 (1933).
9. 69 *Cong. Rec.*, Part 6 (Apr. 10, 1928), 6145; Part 10 (May 29, 1928), 10657.
10. C. S. Shields, Chief, Mail and Files, to clerks, memorandum of Dec. 15, 1933, CAA Central Files.
11. Administrative Memorandum No. 6, Dec. 22, 1930, CAA Central Files.
12. C. M. Young, Air Regulations Division, to Post Office, Jan. 12, 1927; R. S. Ryan, Post Office, to Young, Jan. 24, 1927, CAA Central Files.
13. J. J. O'Hara, Acting Solicitor, to E. F. Morgan, Acting Secretary of Commerce, Jan. 9, 1929, CAA Central Files.
14. Gilbert G. Budwig, Director of Air Regulations, to Chief, License Division, June 10, 1930, CAA Central Files.
15. MacCracken memorandum of Sep. 1, 1928; MacCracken to the director, May 10, 1929, CAA Central Files.
16. G. Hurst Paul, the *Washington Times*, to Fred Neely, May 20, 1932; John S. Collins, Administrative Division, to Paul, May 26, 1932, CAA Central Files.
17. USDC, *Air Commerce Bulletin*, 1, No. 3 (Aug. 1, 1929), 7.
18. USDC, "Domestic Air News," mimeo., No. 29 (May 30, 1928), 18.
19. USDC, *Air Commerce Bulletin*, 1, No. 5 (Sep. 2, 1929, 11; 2, No. 12 (Dec. 15, 1930), 310–12.
20. USDC, *Air Commerce Bulletin*, 2, No. 22 (May 15, 1931), 581; 3, No. 18 (Mar. 15, 1932), 449; *Annual Report*, 1929, p. 3; 1930, p. 3.
21. *House Subcommittee Commerce Appropriations 1930*, 70th Cong., 2d Sess., 62–71 (1928).

22. *Senate Subcommittee Commerce Appropriations 1933*, 72nd Cong., 1st Sess. 132 (1932); *House Subcommittee Commerce Appropriations 1931*, 43 (1929).
23. Interview with employees of Federal Aviation Agency General Safety District Office, Des Moines, Iowa, Mar. 30, 1961.
24. *House Subcommittee Commerce Appropriations 1930*, 19 (1928); *1931*, 37 (1929); *Senate Subcommittee Commerce Appropriations 1933*, 125–26 (1932).
25. USDC, *Annual Report*, 1928, p. 3; 1929, pp. 5–7; 1931, p. 3; 1932, p. 2.
26. USDC, "Domestic Air News," No. 19 (Dec. 31, 1927), 6–13; No. 32 (July 15, 1928), 25.
27. USDC, *Air Commerce Bulletin*, 1, No. 5 (Sep. 2, 1929), 11; 2, No. 22 (May 15, 1931), 577–80.
28. USDC, *Air Commerce Bulletin*, 2, No. 20 (Apr. 15, 1931), 516–26.
29. USDC, *Air Commerce Bulletin*, 1, No. 15 (Feb. 1, 1930), 7–10; No. 24 (June 15, 1930), 1–3.
30. USDC, *Air Commerce Bulletin*, 1, No. 19 (Apr. 1, 1930), 17.
31. USDC, *Annual Report*, 1928, p. 8; 1929, pp. 11–15; 1930, pp. 4–5; 1931, pp. 4–5; 1932, p. 3.
32. USDC, *Air Commerce Bulletin*, 3, No. 5 (Sep. 1, 1931), 113–17; No. 10 (Nov. 16, 1931), 251–52; *Annual Report*, 1932, pp. 3–4.
33. *Senate Subcommittee Commerce Appropriations 1934*, 121–22 (1933).
34. "Scientific Aids to Aviation," *The Scientific Monthly* 25, No. 1 (July, 1927), 89.
35. USDC, *Annual Report*, 1928, p. 9; 1929, pp. 15–16; 1930, p. 9.
36. Frederick R. Neely to Albert L. Furth, *Time*, Nov. 22, 1930, CAA Central Files.
37. USDC, *Annual Report*, 1933, pp. 8–9.
38. USDC, "Domestic Air News," 31 (June 30, 1928), 20; *Air Commerce Bulletin*, 2, No. 1 (July 1, 1930), 1–10, 24–26.
39. USDC, *Annual Report*, 1928, pp. 7–8; 1931, pp. 8–9.
40. USDC, *Air Commerce Bulletin*, 2, No. 23 (June 1, 1931), 607–12; No. 24 (June 15, 1931), 639–44; 4, No. 3 (Aug. 1, 1932), 65–68.
41. W. Fiske Marshall, Chief, License Division, to John W. Jackson, Pan American Airways, Miami, Mar. 18, 1930, CAA Central Files.
42. *House Subcommittee Commerce Appropriations 1930*, 20–24 (1928); *1934*, 72d Cong., 2d Sess., 70 (1932); USDC, *Air Commerce Bulletin*, 1, No. 17 (Mar. 1, 1930), 1–4.
43. USDC, *Annual Report*, 1930, p. 13; 1931, pp. 10–11; 1932, p. 6.
44. USDC, "Domestic Air News," 19 (Dec. 31, 1927), 16.
45. USDC, "Domestic Air News," 32 (July 15, 1928), 5.
46. 70 *Cong. Rec.*, Part 3 (Feb. 2, 1929), 2658.
47. Clarence M .Young, "What Is Good Flying?" *Scientific American*, 142, No. 5 (May, 1930), 345–48; Gilbert G. Budwig, "Air Regulation," *The Scientific Monthly*, 31 No. 3 (Sep., 1930), 241–44.
48. Clarence M. Young, "Safety Rules for the Airways," *Scientific American*, 146, No. 1 (Jan., 1932), 22–25; USDC, *Air Commerce Bulletin*, 1, No. 16 (Feb. 15, 1930), 6.
49. " 'Lindy' Pleads for Regulation of Stunt Flying," *The Literary Digest*, 99, No. 8 (Nov. 24, 1928), 62–63.
50. USDC, *Air Commerce Bulletin*, 1, No. 19 (Apr. 1, 1930), 4; 2, No. 2 (July 15, 1930), 42; 2, No. 4 (Aug. 15, 1930), 90; George Gardner, acting chief editorial secretary, to Charles H. Gale, May 31, 1932, CAA Central Files.
51. USDC, *Air Commerce Bulletin*, 3, No. 17 (Mar. 1, 1932), 415–17.
52. USDC, *Air Commerce Bulletin*, 1, No. 18 (Mar. 15, 1930), 13.
53. USDC, *Air Commerce Bulletin*, 2, No. 21 (May 1, 1931), 567.
54. Telegram, Aeronautics Branch to Chamber of Commerce, Lakeland, Florida, Apr. 10, 1929, CAA Central Files.

55. USDC, *Air Commerce Bulletin*, 2, No. 1 (July 1, 1930), 15; 3, No. 2 (July 15, 1931), 37.
56. USDC, *Air Commerce Bulletin*, 3, No. 21 (May 2, 1932), 531; 4, No. 17 (Mar. 1, 1933), 428; C. C. Clayton, U. S. Navy, acting hydrographer, order of Feb. 25, 1933, CAA Central Files.
57. Frank J. Carmody, "Aerial Traffic Cops in London and Chicago," *The Literary Digest*, 99, No. 8 (Nov. 24, 1928), 57–58.
58. G. Lloyd Wilson and Leslie A. Bryan, *Air Transportation* (New York, 1949), pp. 129–35.
59. USDC, *Air Commerce Bulletin*, 3, No. 12 (Dec. 15, 1931), 303–6.
60. USDC, "Domestic Air News," 25 (Mar. 31, 1928), 30–32.
61. USDC, "Domestic Air News," 30 (June 15, 1928), 8–9.
62. "Avoidable Causes of Accidents," *Scientific American*, 142, No. 6 (June, 1930), 472.
63. USDC, *Air Commerce Bulletin*, 4, No. 6 (Sep. 15, 1932), 153–56; No. 7 (Oct. 1, 1932), 174–77; No. 13 (Jan. 3, 1933), 309–15.
64. USDC, *Air Commerce Bulletin*, 4, No. 15 (Feb. 1, 1933), 367–69.
65. USDC, *Air Commerce Bulletin*, 1, No. 20 Apr. 15, 1930), 20–21.
66. USDC, *Annual Report*, 1928, p. 10.
67. 71 *Cong. Rec.*, Part 5 (Oct. 31, 1929), 4989–90.
68. 72 *Cong. Rec.*, Part 2 (Jan. 14, 1930), 1562.
69. *Ibid.*, Part 8 (May 16, 1930), 9043–49; USDC, *Air Commerce Bulletin*, 1, No. 18 (Mar. 15, 1930), 1–3.
70. 72 *Cong. Rec.*, Part 7 (Mar. 2, 1931), 6622.
71. *House Subcommittee Commerce Appropriations 1931*, 37 (1929); *1934*, 71–75 (1932); *Senate Subcommittee Commerce Appropriations 1933*, 72d Cong., 1st Sess., 132 (1932).
72. *House Subcommittee Commerce Appropriations 1930*, 43, 70–71 (1928).
73. *House Subcommittee Commerce Appropriations 1932*, 71st Cong., 3d Sess., 48–49 (1930).
74. H. R. Brashear, Los Angeles Chamber of Commerce, to C. M. Young, Feb. 14, 1933; Young to Brashear, Feb. 16, 1933, CAA Central Files.
75. USDC, *Annual Report*, 1930, p. 10.
76. USDC, *Air Commerce Bulletin*, 3, No. 7 (Oct. 1, 1931), 161–65.
77. Jerome Beatty, "He Rules an Empire in the Air," *The American Magazine*, 114 (Sep., 1932) p. 72.
78. *Senate Subcommittee Commerce Appropriations 1933*, 129–30 (1932).
79. *House Subcommittee Commerce Appropriations 1930*, 42–43 (1928).
80. Herbert Hoover, *The Memoirs of Herbert Hoover: The Cabinet and the Presidency*, 2 (New York, 1951–52), p. 135.
81. *Ibid.*, pp. 243–45.
82. William S. Myers and Walter H. Newton, *The Hoover Administration: A Documented Narrative* (New York, 1936), p. 450.

Chapter 4: SERVICES AND PROMOTIONAL ACTIVITIES

1. USDC, *Annual Report*, 1933, p. 11.
2. *Senate Subcommittee Commerce Appropriations 1934*, 72d Cong., 2d Sess., 110–16 (1933).
3. USDC, *Air Commerce Bulletin*, 4, No. 8 (Oct. 15, 1932), 193–200; 4, No. 9 (Nov. 1, 1932), 215–24.
4. USDC, "Domestic Air News," 25 (Mar. 31, 1928), 16–17; No. 31 (June 30, 1928), 3–8.
5. USDC, *Air Commerce Bulletin*, 2, No. 7 (Oct. 1, 1930), 179; *Annual Report*, 1933, p. 11.
6. USDC, *Air Commerce Bulletin*, 4, No. 6 (Sep. 15, 1932), 135–50.
7. USDC, *Air Commerce Bulletin*, 4, No. 15 (Feb. 1, 1933), 361–64.
8. USDC, *Air Commerce Bulletin*, 4, No. 17 (Mar. 1, 1933), 424–26.

9. USDC, *Air Commerce Bulletin,* 1, No. 24 (June 15, 1930), 8–9; 4, No. 1 (July 1, 1932), 13–15.
10. *House Subcommittee Commerce Appropriations 1931,* 71st Cong., 2d Sess., 48 (1929); USDC, *Annual Report,* 1932, p. 10; 1933, p. 10.
11. *Senate Subcommittee Commerce Appropriations 1933,* 72d Cong., 1st Sess., 146, (1932); USDC, *Air Commerce Bulletin,* 4, No. 10 (Nov. 15, 1932), 235–42.
12. USDC, *Air Commerce Bulletin,* 1, No. 3 (Aug. 1, 1929), 7.
13. *House Subcommittee Commerce Appropriations 1931,* 39–40 (1929); *1934,* 72d Cong., 2d Sess., 78–79 (1932); *Senate Subcommittee Commerce Appropriations 1934,* 116–17 (1933).
14. *House Subcommittee Commerce Appropriations 1932,* 71st Cong., 3d Sess., 45 (1930).
15. USDC, *Annual Report,* 1929, p. 37; 1932, p. 19; *Air Commerce Bulletin,* 1, No. 7 (Oct. 1, 1929), 6–10; No. 16 (Feb. 15, 1930), 3–5.
16. *House Subcommittee Commerce Appropriations 1930,* 70th Cong., 2d Sess., 41–43 (1928); USDC, *Air Commerce Bulletin,* 1, No. 2 (July 15, 1929), 29; 4, No. 4 (Aug. 15, 1932), 95.
17. Archibald Black, *Transportation Aviation,* 2d ed. (New York, 1926–1929) p. 206.
18. A. B. Roome to William P. MacCracken, June 19, 1928, CAA Central Files.
19. USDC, "Domestic Air News," 17 (Dec. 1, 1927), 14.
20. USDC, "Domestic Air News," 32 (July 15, 1928), 13–16; 33 (July 31, 1928), 10–15; 35 (Aug. 31, 1928), 6–12; 36 (Sep. 15, 1928), 3–6; 37 (Sep. 30, 1928), 3–5; 53 (May 15, 1929), 9–13.
21. K. Macpherson to John Eckert, East Moriches, N.Y., June 7, 1926, General Records Department of Commerce.
22. *House Subcommittee Commerce Appropriations 1933,* 72d Cong., 1st Sess., 114–15 (1932).
23. 72 *Cong. Rec.,* Part 2 (Jan. 14, 1930), 1562; 75 *Cong. Rec.,* Part 7 (Apr. 8, 1932), 7810.
24. 75 *Cong. Rec.,* Part 8 (Apr. 18, 1932), 8348.
25. C. M. Young to Carl Egge, National Air Pilots' Association, Jan. 7, 1931; Jan. 22, 1931, CAA Central Files.
26. L. H. Brittin, Northwest Airlines, to C. M. Young, May 23, 1931; American Airways to Young, Feb. 27, 1931, CAA Central Files.
27. Ernie Pyle, "Aviation," *Washington Daily News,* Jan. 27, 1932, CAA Central Files.
28. 75 *Cong. Rec.,* Part 8 (Apr. 19, 1932), 8486.
29. *House Subcommittee Commerce Appropriations 1933,* 113 (1932).
30. *House Subcommittee Commerce Appropriations 1934,* 68, 76–77, 84-85 (1932).
31. R. L. Wagner, Boeing Air Transport, to Marshall Boggs, Aeronautics Branch, Nov. 5, 1928; Boggs to Dr. L. J. Briggs, Bureau of Standards, Dec. 17, 1928, CAA Central Files.
32. *House Subcommittee Commerce Appropriations 1933,* 99–100 (1932); USDC, *Air Commerce Bulletin,* 4, No. 12 (Dec. 15, 1932), 277–90.
33. USDC, *Air Commerce Bulletin,* 3, No. 4 (Aug. 15, 1931), 81–87; 4, No. 14 (Jan. 16, 1933), 333–40.
34. USDC, *Air Commerce Bulletin,* 1, No. 4 (Aug. 15, 1929), 21–23; 4, No. 18 (Mar. 15, 1933), 441–445; 4, No. 21 (May 1, 1933), 525–27.
35. C. F. Egge, NAPA, to Marshall S. Boggs, Sep. 18, 1928, CAA Central Files.
36. USDC, *Air Commerce Bulletin,* 2, No. 8 (Oct. 15, 1930), 201–3; 4, No. 5 (Sep. 1, 1932), 121–26.
37. *House Subcommittee Commerce Appropriations 1932,* 56–60 (1930); *1933,* 98 (1932).
38. USDC, *Air Commerce Bulletin,* 4, No. 11 (Dec. 1, 1932), 259–60.
39. C. M. Young to Sen. Gerald P. Nye, Mar. 25, 1930, CAA Central Files.

40. USDC, *Air Commerce Bulletin*, 1, No. 21 (May 1, 1930), 17; Sen. Lynn Frazier to Secretary Robert P. Lamont, Dec. 5, 1929, and Lamont to Frazier, Dec. 5, 1929, CAA Central Files.
41. Harry F. Guggenheim to MacCracken, Sep. 24, 1929, and Lincoln Ellsworth to C. M. Young, Feb. 9, 1931, CAA Central Files.
42. Mr. Akerson, Secretary Hoover's office, to MacCracken, Mar. 15, 1927; MacCracken to W. J. Tate, Apr. 27, 1928, CAA Central Files.
43. Lady Mary Heath to Secretary of Aeronautics, Dec. 16, 1928, and MacCracken to Heath, Dec. 28, 1928, CAA Central Files.
44. C. G. Abbot, Smithsonian Institution, to C. M. Young, Dec. 2, 1930, CAA Central Files.
45. C. M. Young to Amelia Earhart, Jan. 29, 1929, CAA Central Files.
46. Amelia Earhart to Young, Mar. 4, 1929, CAA Central Files.
47. E. P. Howard, Chief, Air Regulations Division, to Earhart, Mar. 27, 1929, CAA Central Files.
48. R. E. Byrd to C. M. Young, Aug. 8, 1930, and Young to Byrd, Aug. 13, 1930, CAA Central Files.
49. MacCracken to Byrd, Apr. 26, 1928, and Byrd to MacCracken, May 7, 1928, CAA Central Files.
50. Koninklijke Luchtvaart Maatschappij voor Nederland en Koloniën to C. M. Young, Mar. 31, 1928, and Young's reply, July 21, 1928, CAA Central Files.
51. Van Lear Black to MacCracken, Jan. 27, 1929; J. Fred Essary, *Baltimore Sun*, to MacCracken, Oct. 3, 1927, CAA Central Files.
52. USDC, *Air Commerce Bulletin*, 1, No. 19 (Apr. 1, 1930), 10–12.
53. USDC, *Air Commerce Bulletin*, 2, No. 22 (May 15, 1931), 583–84; 3, No. 2 (July 15, 1931), 32–34; 3, No. 7 (Oct. 1, 1931), 165; 3, No. 14 (Jan. 15, 1932), 344; 4, No. 10 (Nov. 15, 1932), 242–48; No. 13 (Jan. 3, 1933), 315, 319.
54. 74 *Cong. Rec.*, Part 6 (Feb. 20, 1931), 5514–18; USDC, *Air Commerce Bulletin*, 2, No. 18 (Mar. 16, 1931), 459–64.
55. C. M. Young to Sen. Nye, Mar. 25, 1930, CAA Central Files.
56. G. Lloyd Wilson and Leslie A. Bryan, *Air Transportation* (New York, 1949), p. 617; Kurt Grönfors, *Air Charter and the Warsaw Convention* (Upsala, 1956), pp. 11, 33.
57. USDC, "Domestic Air News," 44 (Jan. 15, 1929), 1, 10–11.
58. *House Subcommittee Commerce Appropriations 1932*, 62–63 (1930).
59. Dudley Cammett Lunt, "The Law of the Air," *The American Mercury*, 17, No. 66 (June, 1929), 198–201.
60. *Senate Subcommittee Commerce Appropriations 1933*, 126 (1932); *1934*, 119–20 (1933).
61. "Our Point of View," *Scientific American*, 142, No. 5 (May, 1930), 349.
62. C. M. Young to Harry G. Slater, Milwaukee, Dec. 9, 1929, CAA Central Files.
63. USDC, *Air Commerce Bulletin*, 2, No. 22 (May 15, 1931), 581–83.
64. *House Subcommittee Commerce Appropriations 1930*, 43 (1928).
65. USDC, *Air Commerce Bulletin*, 2, No. 8 (Oct. 15, 1930), 191; No. 13 (Jan. 2, 1931), 325–34; No. 12 (Dec. 15, 1930), 299–304; No. 24 (June 15, 1931), 644–46.
66. Report of Airways Marking Conference at Wichita, May 10–11, 1928, mimeo., CAA Central Files; USDC, "Domestic Air News," 30 (June 15, 1928), 20; *Air Commerce Bulletin*, 1, No. 2 (July 15, 1929), 20.
67. USDC, *Air Commerce Bulletin*, 1, No. 8 (Oct. 15, 1929), 14.
68. USDC, *Annual Report*, 1931, pp. 20, 29; 1930, pp. 39–40.
69. USDC, *Air Commerce Bulletin*, 1, No. 10 (Nov. 15, 1929), 21; No. 13 (Jan. 2, 1930), 22, 25–26; *Annual Report*, 1930, p. 28.
70. USDC, "Domestic Air News," 29 (May 30, 1928), 5.
71. Voelter interview, Washington, D.C.; USDC, "Domestic Air News," 33 (July 31, 1928), 28.
72. USDC, *Air Commerce Bulletin*, 1, No. 10 (Nov. 15, 1929), 6.

73. *House Subcommittee Commerce Appropriations 1930*, 52 (1928).
74. USDC, *Air Commerce Bulletin*, 1, No. 23 (June 2, 1930), 13.
75. *Washington Post*, Nov. 4, 1928; S. W. Crosthwaite, Chief Administrative Division, to employees, Oct. 1, 1932, CAA Central Files.
76. USDC, *Air Commerce Bulletin*, 4, No. 12 (Dec. 15, 1932), 294–95; No. 16 (Feb. 15, 1933), 386–92.
77. 75 *Cong. Rec.*, Part 2 (Jan. 4, 1932), 1176.
78. James P. Murray to MacCracken, Jan. 15, 1929, CAA Central Files.
79. C. M. Young, memorandum to staff, Jan. 22, 1929, CAA Central Files.

Chapter 5: THE NEW DEAL'S IMPACT

1. Elsbeth E. Freudenthal, *Aviation Business: From Kitty Hawk to Wall Street* (New York, 1940), p. 88.
2. W. B. Courtney, "Wings of the New Deal," *Colliers*, 93, No. 7 (Feb. 17, 1934), 12–13, 48–50.
3. Henry Ladd Smith, *Airways: The History of Commercial Aviation in the United States* (New York, 1942), pp. 216–18.
4. USDC, *Air Commerce Bulletin*, 8, No. 9 (Mar. 15, 1937), 201–2.
5. USDC, *Air Commerce Bulletin*, 9, No. 10 (Apr. 15, 1938), 240.
6. *House Subcommittee Commerce Appropriations 1935*, 73d Cong., 2d Sess., 212–22 (1933).
7. USDC, *Annual Report*, 1934, p. 14; 1938, pp. 16–17.
8. USDC, *Annual Report*, 1933, pp. 10–11.
9. USDC, *Annual Report*, 1934, p. 9; *Air Commerce Bulletin*, 6, No. 1 (July 15, 1934), 3.
10. USDC, *Annual Report*, 1936, p. 9.
11. USDC, *Annual Report*, 1937, p. 7.
12. "Report of Interdepartmental Committee To Consider Flying Pay," Dec. 29, 1934, CAA Central Files.
13. USDC, *Air Commerce Bulletin*, 8, No. 11 (May 15, 1937), 242–43.
14. Charles C. Rohlfing, "Regulation of Aviation: A Case Study in Reorganization," *Annals of the American Academy*, 221 (May, 1942), 56–63.
15. USDC, *Air Commerce Bulletin*, 9, No. 11 (May 15, 1938), 272–73.
16. *House Subcommittee Commerce Appropriations 1935*, 214 (1933).
17. *House Subcommittee Commerce Appropriations 1937*, 74th Cong., 2d Sess., 221–24 (1936).
18. *Senate Subcommittee Commerce Appropriations 1938*, 75th Cong., 1st Sess., 199 (1937).
19. USDC, *Air Commerce Bulletin*, 5, No. 12 (June 15, 1934), 292.
20. USDC, *Air Commerce Bulletin*, 5, No. 3 (Sep. 15, 1933), 79; No. 7 (Jan. 15, 1934), 169.
21. USDC, *Air Commerce Bulletin*, 6, No. 10 (Apr. 15, 1935), 233.
22. USDC, *Air Commerce Bulletin*, 7, No. 4 (Oct. 15, 1935), 91.
23. *House Subcommittee Commerce Appropriations 1936*, 74th Cong., 1st Sess., 28 (1934).
24. David L. Behncke to Major R. W. Schroeder, Bureau of Air Commerce, July 11, 1934, CAA Central Files.
25. USDC, *Air Commerce Bulletin*, 7, No. 6 (Dec. 15, 1935), 145; No. 8 (Feb. 15, 1936), 185–88.
26. Memorandum to Chief Airways Operation Division, June 4, 1937, CAA Central Files.
27. Interview with C. E. Planck, Apr., 1962.
28. Denis Mulligan to Miss M. L. Morse, Lowell, Mass., July 23, 1938, CAA Central Files.
29. USDC, *Air Commerce Bulletin*, 5, No. 10 (Apr. 15, 1935), 258.
30. R. E. Whitehead, M.D., to Col. Cone, Bureau of Air Commerce, Jan. 15, 1937, CAA Central Files.
31. USDC, *Annual Report*, 1936, p. 13; 1938, p. 14; *Air Commerce Bulletin*, 9, No. 10 (Apr. 15, 1938), 248.

32. D. C. Feree and G. Rand, "Pilot Fitness and Airplane Crashes," *Science*, 87, No. 2252 (Feb. 25, 1938), 189–93.
33. USDC, *Annual Report*, 1935, pp. 12–13; 1937, p. 11.
34. *House Subcommittee (Supplemental) Commerce Appropriations 1937*, 74th Cong., 2d Sess., 11 (1936).
35. *House Subcommittee Commerce Appropriations 1938*, 75th Cong., 1st Sess., 222 (1937); USDC, *Air Commerce Bulletin*, 8, No. 2 (Aug. 15, 1936), 32.
36. "New Flying Rules," *Business Week*, No. 427 (Nov. 6, 1937), 32.
37. 78 *Cong. Rec.*, Part 8 (May 10, 1934), 8552.
38. USDC, *Air Commerce Bulletin*, 7, No. 4 (Oct. 15, 1935), 88–90.
39. USDC, *Air Commerce Bulletin*, 5, No. 2 (Aug. 15, 1933), 35–54.
40. USDC, *Air Commerce Bulletin*, 6, No. 6 (Dec. 15, 1934), 144–49; 7, No. 5 (Nov. 15, 1935), 109–11.
41. USDC, *Air Commerce Bulletin*, 6, No. 10 (Apr. 15, 1935), 235.
42. USDC, *Air Commerce Bulletin*, 7, No. 2 (Aug. 15, 1935), 33.
43. USDC, *Air Commerce Bulletin*, 8, No. 11 (May 15, 1937), 231–33.
44. USDC, *Air Commerce Bulletin*, 7, No. 6 (Dec. 15, 1935), 138–40.
45. USDC, *Air Commerce Bulletin*, 9, No. 3 (Sep. 15, 1937), 69.
46. USDC, *Air Commerce Bulletin*, 5, No. 12 (June 15, 1934), 288; 7, No. 12 (June 15, 1936), 287.
47. USDC, *Air Commerce Bulletin*, 7, No. 3 (Sep. 15, 1935), 71.
48. USDC, *Air Commerce Bulletin*, 5, No. 7 (Jan. 15, 1934), 173–74.
49. Kenneth Brown Collings, "Why Not Use Parachutes?" *American Mercury*, 34, No. 136 (Apr., 1935), 444–49; "How To Make Flying Safe," *American Mercury*, 40, No. 158 (Feb. 1937), 151–57.
50. 81 *Cong. Rec.*, Part 3 (Mar. 19, 1937), 2429.
51. USDC, *Air Commerce Bulletin*, 5, No. 4 (Oct. 15, 1933), 118–19.
52. USDC, *Air Commerce Bulletin*, 7, 10 (Apr. 15, 1936), 239–44.
53. USDC, *Annual Report*, 1936, p. 12; 1937, pp. 8–9.
54. H. F. Cole, Air Traffic Control Coordinator, Chicago, Ill., memorandum on the history of air traffic control, Dec. 12, 1940, CAA Central Files.
55. USDC, *Air Commerce Bulletin*, 7, No. 5 (Nov. 15, 1935), 101–4.
56. USDC, *Air Commerce Bulletin*, 7, No. 8 (Feb. 15, 1936), 192–95; 8, No. 2 (Aug. 15, 1936), 32–35.
57. USDC, *Air Commerce Bulletin*, 9, No. 4 (Oct. 15, 1937), 73–77, 97; No. 8 (Feb. 15, 1938), 182; No. 9 (Mar. 15, 1938), 210–13.
58. H. F. Cole, Cleveland Air Traffic Control, to Earl F. Ward, Nov. 13, 1936, with Ward's notation on the letter, CAA Central Files.
59. O. C. Richerson, United Air Lines, to Major L. P. DeArce, Manager, Air Traffic Control, Oakland, Feb. 3, 1938; Ward to Army Air Force, Nov. 30, 1938, CAA Central Files.
60. Bruce E. Braun to B. W. Jacobs, Bureau of Air Commerce, Jan. 26, 1938, CAA Central Files.
61. Braun to Jacobs, Jan. 26, 1938, CAA Central Files.
62. Braun to Chief, Army Air Force, Jan. 4, 1938, CAA Central Files.
63. *House Subcommittee Commerce Appropriations 1938*, 202 (1937).
64. E. C. Davis, Delta Air Lines, to his operations manager, Oct. 27, 1936; T. H. Maxwell, Station Manager, Newark, to Earl Ward, Aug. 22, 1936; John A. Collins, TWA, to Ward, June 30, 1937; TWA report of Nov. 30, 1937, CAA Central Files.
65. Ward to Chief, Airline Inspection Service, Sep. 17, 1936, CAA Central Files.
66. M. F. Davis, Lt. Col., Air Corps, to Bureau of Air Commerce, July 28, 1937, CAA Central Files.
67. Roy Keeley, Senior Airline Inspector, to Bureau of Air Commerce, Feb. 25, 1938; Ward to Air Force, May 11, 1937, CAA Central Files; *House Subcommittee Commerce Appropriations 1938*, 202 (1937).
68. David L. Behncke to Eugene Sibley, Bureau of Air Commerce, Dec. 10, 1937, CAA Central Files.

69. *House Subcommittee (Supplemental) Commerce Appropriations 1937,* 4–12 (1936).
70. *House Subcommittee Commerce Appropriations 1938,* 219–22, 229–34 (1937).
71. USDC, *Annual Report,* 1938, pp. 10–11.
72. Allan F. Bonnalie, "Training the Pilot To Fly the Beam," *Scientific American,* 154, No. 6 (June, 1936), 322–24.
73. *House Subcommittee Commerce Appropriations 1936,* 30 (1934); *1937,* 166–72 (1936).
74. USDC, *Air Commerce Bulletin,* 9, No. 1 (July 15, 1937), 1–3; No. 2 (Aug. 15, 1937), 19–21; 6, No. 1 (July 15, 1934), 17, 20.
75. *House Subcommittee Commerce Appropriations 1937,* 152–56, 216 (1936); USDC, *Air Commerce Bulletin,* 5, No. 1 (July 15, 1933), 16; 7, No. 1 (July 15, 1935), 1–4.
76. USDC, *Air Commerce Bulletin,* 7, No. 3 (Sep. 15, 1935), 73.
77. USDC, *Air Commerce Bulletin,* 7, No. 8 (Feb. 15, 1936), 195; 9, No. 12 (June 15, 1938), 304–6.
78. USDC, *Air Commerce Bulletin,* 6, No. 2 (Aug. 15, 1934), 34–35; *Annual Report,* 1937, p. 8; 1938, pp. 7–11.
79. Eugene Vidal, Director, Bureau of Air Commerce, to the Secretary of Commerce, memorandum, June 12, 1935, CAA Central Files; USDC, *Air Commerce Bulletin,* 6, No. 5 (Nov. 15, 1934), 107–9; No. 8 (Feb. 15, 1935), 179–82; No. 12 (June 15, 1935), 277.
80. "Under the Weather," *Fortune,* 17, No. 6 (June, 1938), 62–63, 104, 106; USDC, *Air Commerce Bulletin,* 8, No. 2 (Aug. 15, 1936), 38–45.
81. USDC, *Annual Report,* 1938, p. 10
82. USDC, *Air Commerce Bulletin,* 6, No. 10 (Apr. 15, 1935), 225–26.
83. Eugene L. Vidal to Amelia Earhart, telegram, May 9, 1935, CAA Central Files.
84. Earhart to Bureau of Air Commerce, Aug. 6, 1935, CAA Central Files.
85. USDC, *Air Commerce Bulletin,* 6, No. 10 (Apr. 15, 1935), 215–16.
86. USDC, *Air Commerce Bulletin,* 5, No. 1 (July 15, 1933), 7; 6, No. 2 (Aug. 15, 1934), 41; No. 7 (Jan. 15, 1935), 159–63.
87. USDC, *Air Commerce Bulletin,* 9, No. 1 (July 15, 1937), 3–5.
88. *House Subcommittee Commerce Appropriations 1938,* 204–7 (1937).
89. "Increased Safety for Aviation," *Science* n.s. *Supplement,* 85, No. 2199 (Feb. 19, 1937), 9.
90. R. C. Copeland, District Manager, Atlanta, to Bureau of Air Commerce, Feb. 26, 1938, CAA Central Files.
91. Brown General Tire to Eugene Sibley, Bureau of Air Commerce, May 5, 1937, CAA Central Files.
92. H. C. Wisehart, Captain, Air Corps, to Rex Martin, Bureau of Air Commerce, Oct. 28, 1936, CAA Central Files.
93. USDC, *Air Commerce Bulletin,* 7, No. 9 (Mar. 15, 1936), 220–30.
94. *House Subcommittee Commerce Appropriations 1936,* 31–35 (1934).
95. USDC, *Annual Report,* 1936, p. 14; 1938, pp. 15–16.
96. 81 *Cong. Rec.,* Part 3 (Mar. 19, 1937), 2428–29.
97. USDC, *Air Commerce Bulletin,* 6, No. 7 (Jan. 15, 1935), 157–58.
98. H. B. Meller and L. B. Sisson, "Smoke and Aviation," for Mellon Institute, Pittsburgh, June 30, 1936, located in CAA Central Files.
99. *Senate Subcommittee Commerce Appropriations 1938,* 256–61 (1937); 81 *Cong. Rec.,* Part 3 (Mar. 19, 1937), 2431; USDC *Air Commerce Bulletin,* 5, No. 9 (Mar. 15, 1934), 225–29; 8, No. 7 (Jan. 15, 1937), 153–57.
100. USDC, *Air Commerce Bulletin,* 7, No. 2 (Aug. 15, 1935), 27–28.
101. C. M. Lample, Superintendent of Airways, to Secretary of Commerce, Oct. 11, 1938, CAA Central Files.
102. Jay A. Mount, to Rex Martin, Jan. 18, 1934, CAA Central Files.
103. Rex Martin, Assistant Director, to acting district manager, Mar. 6, 1935, CAA Central Files.

104. USDC, *Air Commerce Bulletin*, 6, No. 4 (Oct. 15, 1934), 99; No. 11 (Mar. 15, 1935), 272–73.
105. Eugene Vidal, memorandum, Oct. 16, 1933, CAA Central Files.
106. 78 *Cong. Rec.*, Part 11 (June 16, 1934), 12203; *House Subcommittee Commerce Appropriations 1936*, 22–25, 35 (1934).
107. *House Subcommittee (Supplemental) Commerce Appropriations 1937*, 17 (1936); 1938, 188–92 (1937).
108. USDC, *Air Commerce Bulletin*, 6, No. 11 (May 15, 1935), 245–48; 7, No. 3 (Sep. 15, 1935), 59–67; 8, No. 1 (July 15, 1936), 1–11; No. 4 (Oct. 15, 1936), 95–96.
109. John H. Geisse to Col. J. M. Johnson, Sep. 19, 1936, CAA Central Files.
110. "The Private Flying Boom," *Fortune*, 16, No. 2 (Aug., 1937), 53–60.
111. *House Subcommittee Commerce Appropriations 1935*, 216, 219 (1933).
112. *House Subcommittee Commerce Appropriations 1937*, 225 (1936).
113. *House Subcommittee Commerce Appropriations 1938*, 215 (1937); USDC, *Annual Report*, 1936, p. 13; *Air Commerce Bulletin*, 8, No. 5 (Nov. 15, 1936), 139.
114. 81 *Cong. Rec.*, Part 3 (Mar. 19, 1937), 2430.
115. USDC, *Annual Report, 1936*, p. 14; *Air Commerce Bulletin*, 5, No. 8 (Feb. 15, 1934), 189–96; 7, No. 4 (Oct. 15, 1935), 91; 8, No. 2 (Aug. 15, 1936), 71–72.
116. E. Y. Mitchell, Assistant Secretary of Commerce, to Mr. Finger, Industrial Advisory Board, NRA, Aug. 11, 1933; mimeo. reports, hearings of July 10, 1934; endorsement of Independent Aviation Operators; and support of Aeronautical Chamber of Commerce, Dec. 20, 1933, CAA Central Files.
117. W. E. Jackson to superintendent of airways, May 11, 1934, CAA Central Files.
118. Franklin D. Roosevelt to Doctor Wright, Dec. 17, 1936; Roosevelt to Ernest B. Chamberlain, Amelia Earhart Foundation, May 13, 1938, CAA Central Files.
119. Elliott Roosevelt to Vidal, Nov. 7, 1934; Vidal to E. Roosevelt, Nov. 8, 1934; Vidal to Sen. William G. McAdoo, Oct. 17, 1935, CAA Central Files.
120. Secretary of Commerce to Bureau of the Budget, Sep. 15, 1934, CAA Central Files.
121. USDC, *Air Commerce Bulletin*, 5, No. 1 (July 15, 1933), 1; 7, No. 2 (Aug. 15, 1935), 34–35; 9, No. 4 (Oct. 15, 1937), 97–101.
122. USDC, *Air Commerce Bulletin*, 5, No. 6 (Dec. 15, 1933), 156–57; 6, No. 3 (Sep. 15, 1934), 69.
123. William Phillips, Acting Secretary of State, to Secretary of Commerce Daniel L. Roper, Oct. 18, 1934, CAA Central Files.
124. Frederick R. Neely, Bureau of Air Commerce, to Hilaire du Berrier, Paris, Apr. 9, 1937, CAA Central Files.
125. Rex Martin to Major Champsauer, air attaché, French Embassy, Sep. 17, 1935, CAA Central Files.
126. USDC, *Air Commerce Bulletin*, 8, No. 10 (Apr. 15, 1937), 220; 9, No. 1 (July 15, 1937), 10; No. 2 (Aug. 15, 1937), 41.
127. John S. Collins, Chief, Administrative Division, to Assistant Secretary, Dec. 29, 1936, CAA Central Files.
128. J. A. Wilson, Controller of Civil Aviation, Canada, to Howard Rough, July 26, 1938, CAA Central Files.
129. *House Subcommittee Commerce Appropriations 1936*, 35 (1934).
130. Oliver F. Lissitzyn, "The Diplomacy of Air Transport," *Foreign Affairs: An American Quarterly Review*, 19, No. 1 (Oct., 1940), 156–70.
131. USDC, *Air Commerce Bulletin*, 6, No. 11 (May 15, 1935), 269.
132. Lissitzyn, "The Diplomacy," 164.

133. USDC, *Air Commerce Bulletin*, 5, No. 9 (Mar. 15, 1934), 232; No. 10 (Apr. 15, 1934), 261–62; No. 12 (June 15, 1934), 290; 7, No. 6 (Dec. 15, 1935), 151; 8, No. 10 (Apr. 15, 1937), 224.
134. Eugene L. Vidal to Commissioner of Customs, Aug. 6, 1936; Vidal to Secretary of Commerce, May 20, 1936, CAA Central Files.
135. John S. Collins to all district offices, Apr. 1, 1936, CAA Central Files.
136. District Manager, Salt Lake City, telegram to Bureau of Air Commerce, Washington, D.C., Apr. 23, 1936, CAA Central Files.
137. USDC, *Air Commerce Bulletin*, 9, No. 5 (Nov. 15, 1937), 105–11; No. 6 (Dec. 15, 1937), 135–38.
138. 81 *Cong. Rec.*, Part 3 (Mar. 19, 1937), 2428.
139. Henry E. Horner to Vidal, Dec. 7, 1934, and Vidal to Horner, Dec. 13, 1934, CAA Central Files.
140. USDC, *Air Commerce Bulletin*, 9, No. 2 (Aug. 15, 1937), 39.
141. 83 *Cong. Rec.*, Part 5 (Apr. 21, 1938), 5662–63.

Chapter 6: ACCIDENTS, DISMAY, AND REORGANIZATION

1. *House Subcommittee Commerce Appropriations 1936*, 74th Cong., 1st Sess., 38 (1934).
2. USDC, *Air Commerce Bulletin*, 7, No. 1 (July 15, 1935), 12–17.
3. Secretary of Commerce Roper, statement and report of Accident Board on the Cutting accident, June 14, 1935, CAA Central Files.
4. *Ibid.*
5. Eugene L. Vidal to Solicitor, Department of Commerce, Sep. 28, 1935, CAA Central Files.
6. *House Subcommittee Commerce Appropriations 1937*, 74th Cong., 2d Sess., 157 (1936).
7. John H. Wigmore to Col. J. M. Johnson, Department of Commerce, June 23, 1936, CAA Central Files.
8. C. B. Allen, "Why Do Air Liners Crash?" *The New Republic*, 91, No. 1172 (May 19, 1937), 35–37.
9. USDC, *Air Commerce Bulletin*, 7, No. 4 (Oct. 15, 1935), 94.
10. USDC, *Air Commerce Bulletin*, 7, No. 5 (Nov. 15, 1935), 121–22.
11. USDC, *Air Commerce Bulletin*, 7, No. 10 (Apr. 15, 1936), 254–56.
12. Denis Mulligan, Chief, Enforcement Section, to Mr. Martin, Glenn L. Martin Airplane Co., Jan. 17, 1936; Roper to Vidal, report, Mar. 7, 1936, CAA Central Files.
13. W. C. Martin, Donnelsville, Ohio, to Bureau of Air Commerce, Aug. 8, 1938, CAA Central Files.
14. J. M. Johnson to S. Gordon Taylor, Managing Editor, *Radios*, Apr. 9, 1936; Bureau of Air Commerce report, n.d., CAA Central Files; USDC, *Air Commerce Bulletin*, 8, No. 2 (Aug. 15, 1936), 72–79.
15. William P. Lear, Lear Developments, Inc., press release, Apr. 8, 1936; Lear to Vidal, Apr. 8, 1936, CAA Central Files.
16. USDC, *Air Commerce Bulletin*, 8, No. 5 (Nov. 15, 1936), 132.
17. Director F. D. Fagg, Jr., to Assistant Secretary Johnson, Jan. 13, 1938, CAA Central Files.
18. Assistant Director Rex Martin to E. H. Pendleton, New York City, May 7, 1934, CAA Central Files.
19. William Littlewood, American Airlines, to A. P. Kerr, Bureau of Air Commerce, May 4, 1937, CAA Central Files.
20. E. V. Rickenbacker, Eastern Air Lines, to J. M. Johnson, Dec. 28, 1936, and Johnson to Rickenbacker, Dec. 29, 1936; Rickenbacker to Johnson, Jan. 7, and Jan. 13, 1937, CAA Central Files.
21. Memorandum, Bureau of Air Commerce, Apr. 9, 1938, CAA Central Files.
22. Charles M. Bufford, San Francisco, to Bureau of Air Commerce, July 30, 1938; E. L. Yuravich, Chief, Airline Inspection Section, to Chief, Certification and Inspection Division, Feb. 23, 1938, CAA Central Files.

23. David L. Behncke to Vidal, June 4, 1935, CAA Central Files.
24. R. W. DeLany, Airline Inspection Section, to Assistant Director R. W. Schroeder, Apr. 8, 1937, quotes a telegram from Sen. Harry S. Truman, CAA Central Files.
25. Vidal to Mr. Kerlin, Sep. 20, 1933, CAA Central Files.
26. J. M. Johnson to R. H. Sampson, attorney, Los Angeles, May 13, 1937; Johnson to Sen. Royal Copeland, May 5, 1937, CAA Central Files.
27. Vidal to Johnson, Dec. 4, 1935, CAA Central Files.
28. USDC, *Air Commerce Bulletin*, 8, No. 11 (May 15, 1937), 252–55; No. 12 (June 15, 1937), 272; 9, No. 1 (July 15, 1937), 10–12; No. 3 (Sep. 15, 1937), 68–69.
29. J. M. Johnson to J. Ross Gamble, Washington, D.C., Sep. 13, 1937, CAA Central Files.
30. USDC, *Air Commerce Bulletin*, 9, No. 5 (Nov. 15, 1937), 123–36; No. 6 (Dec. 15, 1937), 147–52; No. 8 (Feb. 15, 1938), 188–89; 10, No. 1 (July 15, 1938), 4–7; No. 2 (Aug. 15, 1938), 41–52.
31. "Government Suspension Follows Northwest Airlines' First Crash in Ten Years," *Newsweek*, 11, No. 7 (Feb. 14, 1938), 38–39.
32. Denis Mulligan, Acting Director, memorandum for *Hindenburg* file, Nov. 11, 1937, CAA Central Files.
33. USDC, *Air Commerce Bulletin*, 9, No. 2 (Aug. 15, 1937), 21–38.
34. "The *Hindenburg* Disaster," *The New Republic*, 91, No. 1172 (May 19, 1937), 33.
35. 83 *Cong. Rec.*, Part 7 (May 25, 1938), 7457–58.
36. *Senate Subcommittee Commerce Appropriations 1937*, 74th Cong., 2d Sess., 93 (1936).
37. "They May Have Needed Oxygen," *Fortune*, 16, No. 2 (Aug., 1937), 61, 142, 144, 147–48, 150.
38. Kenneth Brown Collings, "Flying Is Still Dangerous," *American Mercury*, 32, No. 126 (June, 1934), 147–52.
39. Collings, "Blind Flying Is Not Safe," *American Mercury*, 33, No. 129 (Sep., 1934), 90–92.
40. Collings, "How To Make Flying Safe," *American Mercury*, 40, No. 158 (Feb., 1937), 151–57.
41. Collings, "Annual Report on Air Safety," *American Mercury*, 46, No. 181 (Jan., 1939), 22–29.
42. Alexander Klemin, "Airplane Safety," *Scientific American*, 151, No. 5 (Nov., 1934), 259.
43. Robert W. Horton, "Death in the Air," *The Nation*, 144, No. 4 (Jan. 23, 1937), 94–95.
44. Marquis W. Childs, "Is It Safe To Fly?" *Harper's Magazine*, 173 (Oct., 1936), 497–504.
45. *Science News Letter*, 31, No. 827 (Feb. 13, 1937), 102.
46. "The New Aeronautics Authority," *Science*, n.s., Supplement, 88, No. 2276 (Aug. 12, 1938), 7–8.
47. "Safety in the Air," *Popular Science Monthly*, 132, No. 2 (Feb., 1938), 46.
48. "Under the Weather," *Fortune*, 17, No. 6 (June, 1938), 62–63, 104, 106.
49. "The Air Is How Safe?" *Fortune*, 15, No. 4 (Apr., 1937), 75–80, 154, 156, 158, 163–64, 166, 168–70, 173–74.
50. Behncke to J. M. Johnson, Mar. 18, 1936; Schroeder to Col. J. Carroll Cone, Bureau of Air Commerce, Mar. 30, 1936; Johnson to Behncke, Apr. 11, 1936, CAA Central Files.
51. Behncke to Rex Martin, May 5, 1936, CAA Central Files.
52. Cone to Behncke, Oct. 15, 1936, CAA Central Files.
53. Cone and Schroeder, telegrams to ALPA, Oct. 16, 1936, CAA Central Files.
54. Behncke to Vidal, Nov. 12, 1936; Vidal to Behncke, Dec. 1, 1936, CAA Central Files.

55. N. B. Ison, Acting Chief, Airline Inspection Service, to Behncke, Apr. 3, 1937, CAA Central Files.
56. Edgar S. Gorrell, Air Transport Association, to Secretary Roper, May 5, 1936; Gorrell to Vidal, May 5, 1936, CAA Central Files.
57. Cone to Gorrell, Sep. 11, 1936, CAA Central Files.
58. William A. Patterson, United Air Lines, to R. W. Schroeder, Chief, Airline Inspection Service, Mar. 23, 1934, CAA Central Files.
59. Lt. John D. Graves, Air Corps Reserve, to Major Carl Spatz, Army Air Force, June 11, 1935, CAA Central Files.
60. 81 *Cong. Rec.*, Part 8 (Aug. 21, 1937), 9641.
61. A. V. Verville, Aeronautics Development Section, memorandum to Director Vidal, Feb. 5, 1936, CAA Central Files.
62. USDC, *Annual Report*, 1938, pp. 17–18.
63. 80 *Cong. Rec.*, Part 5 (Apr. 1, 1936), 4739–53.
64. USDC, *Air Commerce Bulletin*, 7, No. 9 (Mar. 15, 1936), 220–30.
65. *House Subcommittee Commerce Appropriations 1937*, 166–72 (1936).
66. "Safety Search," *Time*, 27, No. 8 (Feb. 24, 1936), 59–60.
67. 80 *Cong. Rec.*, Part 5 (Apr. 1, 1936), 4746–51.
68. *Senate Subcommittee Commerce Appropriations 1937*, 82–93 (1936).
69. *House Subcommittee Commerce Appropriations 1938*, 168–72 (1937).
70. *Ibid.*, pp. 181–82.
71. *Ibid.*, pp. 177–78.
72. "Vidal Out," *Time*, 29, No. 10 (Mar. 8, 1937), 13–14.
73. 81 *Cong. Rec.*, Part 2 (Mar. 2, 1937), 1717.
74. USDC, *Air Commerce Bulletin*, 8, No. 9 (Mar. 15, 1937), 201–2.
75. "Behind the Airplane Crashes," *Business Week*, No. 386 (Jan. 23, 1937), 16–17; "Dropping the Pilot," *Business Week*, No. 392 (Mar. 6, 1937), 16.
76. *Senate Subcommittee Commerce Appropriations 1938*, 75th Cong., 1st Sess., 195 (1937).
77. 81 *Cong. Rec.*, Part 3 (Mar. 19, 1937), 2419–32.
78. *Senate Subcommittee Commerce Appropriations 1938*, 272 (1937).
79. "Rival Bills for Aviation Control," *Business Week*, No. 410 (July 10, 1937), 43–44.
80. "Fagg's Air Problems," *Business Week*, No. 401 (May 8, 1937), 46.
81. "Behind the Airplane Crashes," 16–17.
82. "Ocean Flying Control," *Business Week*, No. 429 (Nov. 20, 1937), 52; *Newsweek*, 11 (Feb. 14, 1938), 38–39.
83. 81 *Cong. Rec.*, Part 8 (Aug. 16, 1937), 8963, 8968–69; (Aug. 18, 1937), 9202–21.
84. *Washington Herald*, Aug. 20, 1937, quoted in 81 *Cong. Rec.*, Part 10 (Aug. 20, 1937), 2206–7.
85. 83 *Cong. Rec.*, Part 6 (May 11, 1938), 6626–28; "White House Solves Riddle of Federal Air Line Control—Maybe!" *Newsweek* 11, No. 3 (Jan. 17, 1938), 42–43.
86. *Ibid.*, Part 6 (May 7, 1938), 6401–10; (May 9, 1938), 6501–9; (May 11, 1938), 6626–37; (May 12, 1938), 6766–6879.
87. *Ibid.*, Part 6 (May 7, 1938), 6410.
88. *Ibid.*, Part 7 (May 25, 1938), 7457–58; Part 8 (June 11, 1938), 8866; (June 23, 1938), 9616.
89. *Ibid.*, Part 11 (June 15, 1938), 3142–43.

Chapter 7: FIGHTING REORGANIZATION—1938–1941

1. *House Subcommittee Independent Offices Appropriations 1940*, 76th Cong., 1st Sess., 1872–87 (1939); Executive Order 7916, June 24, 1938, CAA Central Files; Executive Order of July 14, 1938, CAA Central Files.
2. B. D. DeWeese to Edward J. Noble, July 22, 1938, and Noble to DeWeese, Aug. 16, 1938, CAA Central Files.
3. U.S. Civil Aeronautics Authority, *Annual Report*, 1940, p. 3.

4. 84 *Cong. Rec.*, Part 2 (Feb. 7, 1939), 1209–10; Part 4 (Apr. 6, 1939), 3876–78; Part 10 (Aug. 1, 1939), 10707; Part 14, Apendix, 3367–68.
5. USDC, *Annual Report*, 1941, p. 151.
6. "Grumble at Air Board," *Business Week*, No. 502 (Apr. 15, 1939), 21.
7. 86 *Cong. Rec.*, Part 5 (May 1, 1940), 5324.
8. *Ibid.*, Part 5 (Apr. 25, 1940), 5025.
9. *Ibid.*, Part 5 (May 7, 1940), 5680–5700.
10. *Ibid.*, Part 6 (May 13, 1940), 5950–67; Part 6 (May 14, 1940), 6027–75; Part 9 (July 25, 1940), 9595–96.
11. USDC, *Civil Aeronautics Journal*, 1, No. 14 (July 15, 1940), 297–98.
12. H. W. Anderson, Chief, Aircraft Inspection Section, to Robert H. Hinckley, Assistant Secretary of Commerce, Dec. 3, 1940, CAA Central Files.
13. U.S. Civil Aeronautics Authority, *Air Commerce Bulletin*, 10, No. 7 (Jan. 15, 1939), 185.
14. J. E. Sommers to Howard F. Rough, Oct. 23, 1939, CAA Central Files.
15. *House Subcommittee Commerce Appropriations 1942*, 77th Cong., 1st Sess., 416 (1941).
16. F. M. Lanter, Acting Chief, General Inspection Section, to Chief, Certification and Inspection Division, June 3, 1939, CAA Central Files.
17. Rough to Harold Neely, Oct. 10, 1939, and Neely to Rough, Oct. 19, 1939, CAA Central Files.
18. L. C. Elliott to Rough, Oct. 27, 1939, CAA Central Files.
19. Elliott to Rough, May 4, 1939, CAA Central Files.
20. Leonard Jurden to Rough, Oct. 14, 1939, CAA Central Files.
21. Rough to the administrator, Oct. 3, 1939, CAA Central Files.
22. R. D. Bedinger to Rough, Oct. 17, 1939, CAA Central Files.
23. S. Griffin to Chicago regional manager, n.d. 1941; D. H. Connolly to Hinckley, Aug. 20, 1941; Rough to the administrator, Aug. 19, 1941; and Neely to Rough, Aug. 9, 1941, CAA Central Files.
24. Sommers to Rough, Mar. 20, 1940, CAA Central Files.
25. USDC, *Civil Aeronautics Journal*, 1, No. 20 (Oct. 15, 1940), 449.
26. U.S. Civil Aeronautics Authority, *Civil Aeronautics Journal*, 1, No. 8 (Apr. 15, 1940), 157; A. S. Koch, Chief, Certification and Inspection Division, to regional manager, Newark, Apr. 25, 1940, CAA Central Files.
27. U.S. Civil Aeronautics Authority, *Civil Aeronautics Journal*, 1, No. 8 (Apr. 15, 1940), 156.
28. *Ibid.*, p. 158.
29. Koch to Sommers, Oct. 16, 1940, Lanter to O. P. Harwood, 1940, CAA Central Files.
30. Sommers to R. S. Boutelle, Director, Bureau of Safety Regulations, May 10, 1940, CAA Central Files.
31. Ellis A. Carson, Sunbeam Electric Co., to Congressman John W. Boehne, Jr., July 24, 1939; Koch to Boehne, July 31, 1939, CAA Central Files.
32. Anderson to Chief, Certification and Inspection Division, June 7, 1940; Anderson to Director, Bureau of Federal Airways, June 8, 1940, CAA Central Files.
33. USDC, *Annual Report*, 1941, p. 158.
34. *House Subcommittee Commerce Appropriations 1942*, 442 (1941).
35. Memorandum, Air-Carrier Inspection Section to Bureau of Safety Regulation, June 17, 1941, CAA Central Files.
36. Administrator C. I. Stanton to Chairman, Coordinating Committee, Oct. 9, 1941, CAA Central Files.
37. A. S. Koch, Director, Safety Regulation, to deputy administrator, May 27, 1941, CAA Central Files.
38. Administrator D. H. Connolly to CAB, Dec. 22, 1941, CAA Central Files.
39. Connolly to Sen. Joseph Ball, Nov. 17, 1941, CAA Central Files.
40. Lanter to manager, Region Two, Oct. 27, 1941, CAA Central Files.

41. Harrington Air Service, Mansfield, Ohio, to Grove Webster, Civil Pilot Training, Dec. 29, 1940; Webster to Certification and Inspection Division, Jan. 6, 1941; Koch to Chicago region Jan. 11, 1941, CAA Central Files.
42. E. J. Weisbruch, Peoria, to Everett M. Dirksen, June 24, 1940, CAA Central Files.
43. Interview with Dr. Louis G. Melaik, Eureka, Ill., Sep. 2, 1961.
44. S. Russell Halley, Rapid City, S.D., to George W. Vest, CAA, Oct. 31, 1938, CAA Central Files.
45. Gordon R. Matthews, Associate Aeronautical Inspector, to regional supervisor, Kansas City, Nov. 23, 1938, CAA Central Files.
46. Ernest J. Camy, Boeing School of Aeronautics, to A. S. Koch, Chief, Certification and Inspection Division, Nov. 6, 1940, CAA Central Files.
47. Chester E. McCarty, attorney, Portland, Oreg., to CAB, Dec. 3, 1940; Lanter, CAA, to McCarty, Dec. 10, 1940, CAA Central Files.
48. Don P. Smith, Interstate Aircraft and Engineering Corporation, to Stewart McDonald, Chairman, Maryland Casualty Co., Dec. 13, 1940, CAA Central Files.
49. Connolly to Harllee Branch, CAB, Aug. 6, 1941, CAA Central Files.
50. Sommers to Boutelle, Bureau of Safety Regulation, Jan. 31, 1940, CAA Central Files.
51. Anderson to Chief, Certification and Inspection Division, Feb. 15, 1940, newsletter, CAA Central Files.
52. Boutelle, TWA (formerly with CAA), to CAA, May 18, 1940, CAA Central Files.
53. E. B. Franklin, Acting Chief, Air-Carrier Division, to Chief, Air-Carrier Maintenance Section (cites Warner's memorandum), July 23, 1941; Koch to assistant administrator, Mar. 28, 1941, CAA Central Files.
54. E. W. Keeler, Senior Air-Carrier Inspector, to Chief, Air-Carrier Maintenance Section, Oct. 7, 1941, CAA Central Files.
55. David L. Behncke, ALPA, to Clinton M. Hester, Administrator, Feb. 2, 1940; E. B. Franklin, Inspection Section, to Assistant Chief, Air-carrier Division, Sep. 25, 1940, CAA Central Files.
56. Stanton to Secretary, FCC, Apr. 24, 1941, CAA Central Files.
57. Lanter, Chief, General Inspection Section, to L. C. Elliott, Regional Manager, Fort Worth, Jan. 30, 1940, CAA Central Files.
58. Edward J. Noble, Chairman, CAA, to Behncke, ALPA, Mar. 1, 1939, CAA Central Files.
59. House Subcommittee Independent Offices Appropriations 1941, 76th Cong., 3d Sess., 850 (1939).
60. Hester to Capt. J. B. Kuhn, EAL, Apr., 1940; Monthly summary of violations against American Airlines, Feb. 18, 1940; Koch to Bureau of Air Regulations, Nov. 23, 1940; Monthly summary of violations, Apr. 6, 1941, CAA Central Files.
61. House Subcommittee Commerce Appropriations 1942, 517 (1941).
62. USDC, Civil Aeronautics Journal, 2, No. 4 (Feb. 15, 1941), 55.
63. U.S. Civil Aeronautics Authority, Air Commerce Bulletin, 11, No. 6 (Dec. 15, 1939), 173.
64. U.S. Civil Aeronautics Authority, Civil Aeronautics Journal, 1, No. 2 (Jan. 15, 1940), 20.
65. U.S. Civil Aeronautics Authority, Civil Aeronautics Journal, 1, No. 12 (June 15, 1940), 507.
66. USDC, Civil Aeronautics Journal, 1, No. 21 (Nov. 1, 1940), 463.
67. John F. Warlick, Acting Chief, Certification and Inspection Division, to Aero Insurance Underwriters, New York City, May 10, 1941, CAA Central Files.
68. USDC, Civil Aeronautics Journal, 2, No. 14 (July 15, 1941), 176.
69. U.S. Civil Aeronautics Board, Annual Report, 1941, pp. 32–33.
70. "Notice to Airmen," No. 1–22, Newark, N.J., Sep. 16, 1940, CAA Central Files.

71. Boutelle, Director, Bureau of Safety Regulation, to L. W. Jurden, Regional Manager, Kansas City, Apr. 13, 1940, CAA Central Files.
72. ALPA, air safety recommendations, Nov. 15, 1939–Dec. 8, 1943, CAA Central Files.
73. Behncke, ALPA, to Hester, CAA, Oct. 24, 1938, CAA Central Files.
74. ALPA to Noble, Jan. 12, 1939, CAA Central Files.
75. Stanton to Fowler W. Barker, Air Transport Association, Apr. 19, 1941, CAA Central Files.
76. J. S. Bartles, TWA, to CAA, Chicago, Dec. 21, 1940, CAA Central Files.
77. U.S. Civil Aeronautics Authority, *Air Commerce Bulletin*, 10, No. 6 (Dec. 15, 1938), 176.
78. USDC, *Civil Aeronautics Journal*, 1, No. 24 (Dec. 15, 1940), 505.
79. "Air Fighters Should Tank Up on Oxygen Before Ascents," *Science News Letter*, 37, No. 1 (Jan. 6, 1940), 12.
80. "Men in White Are Now Serving the Men With Wings," *Science News Letter*, 37, No. 4 (Jan. 27, 1940), 54.
81. "Propose Putting Pilot on Back or Stomach," *Science News Letter*, 37, No. 14 (Apr. 6, 1940), 216.
82. Koch to Hester, Feb. 2, 1940, CAA Central Files.
83. "Two Engines or Four?" *Scientific American*, 159, No. 3 (Sep., 1938), 142.
84. U.S. Civil Aeronautics Authority, *Annual Report*, 1940, pp. 17–18.
85. U.S. Civil Aeronautics Authority, *Air Commerce Bulletin*, 11, No. 1 (July 15, 1939), 4, 24–25.
86. U.S. Civil Aeronautics Authority, *Air Commerce Bulletin*, 10, No. 3 (Sep. 15, 1938), 68, 97–100; No. 11 (May 15, 1939), 297.
87. Koch, Chief, General Inspection Section, to regional managers, July 13, 1938; Lanter to Ernest R. Linebaugh, Aug. 21, 1940, CAA Central Files.
88. A. G. Melvin, Cincinnati, to CAA, June 18, 1941; Lanter to Melvin, July 3, 1941, CAA Central Files.
89. U.S. Civil Aeronautics Authority, *Civil Aeronautics Journal*, 1, No. 9 (May 1, 1940), 206.

Chapter 8: SAFETY, ECONOMIC REGULATION—1938–1951

1. U.S. Civil Aeronautics Authority, *Air Commerce Bulletin*, 10, No. 11 (May 15, 1939), 284–86.
2. *House Subcommittee Independent Offices Appropriations 1940*, 76th Cong., 1st Sess., 1905 (1939); *House Subcommittee Independent Offices Appropriations 1941*, 76th Cong., 3d Sess., 832, 882–90 (1939).
3. H. W. Anderson to Bureau of Safety Regulation, Sep. 6, 1940, CAA Central Files; USDC, *Civil Aeronautics Journal*, 1, No. 23 (Dec. 1, 1940), 493.
4. Report of the CAB, File No. 2951–41, June 29, 1942; File No. 2568–41, June 29, 1942; Report of CAB on EAL crash at Montgomery, Ala., Oct. 18, 1938, CAA Central Files.
5. W. T. Miller, Chief, Air-Carrier Inspection Section, to regional manager, Atlanta, July 7, 1941; Miller to operations unit, Feb. 1, 1941; Miller to Charles Sommers, CAA, Canal Zone, Dec. 10, 1940; Miller to Bureau of Safety Regulation, Dec. 6, 1940; R. E. Franklin, Air-Carrier Division, to regional manager, Atlanta, Aug. 8, 1941, CAA Central Files.
6. U.S. Civil Aeronautics Authority, *Air Commerce Bulletin*, 11, No. 3 (Aug. 15, 1939), 64; No. 6 (Dec. 15, 1939), 160.
7. USDC, *Civil Aeronautics Journal*, 2, No. 9 (May 1, 1941), 106, 116.
8. USDC, *Civil Aeronautics Journal*, 2, No. 11 (June 1, 1941), 134.
9. U.S. Civil Aeronautics Authority, *Annual Report*, 1939, pp. 2, 16–19.
10. *House Subcommittee Independent Offices Appropriations 1940*, 1937–39 (1939); U.S. Civil Aeronautics Authority, *Annual Report*, 1940, p. 4.

11. U.S. Civil Aeronautics Authority, *Air Commerce Bulletin*, 10, No. 6 (Dec. 15, 1938), 169–70; No. 12 (June 15, 1939), 312–13.
12. U.S. Civil Aeronautics Authority, *Annual Report*, 1939, p. 27; 1940, p. 12; memorandum, Accounts Section to Certification, July 5, 1940, CAA Central Files.
13. A. M. Archibald, PAA, to CAA, Nov. 1, 1938, CAA Central Files.
14. USDC, *Civil Aeronautics Journal*, 2, No. 18 (Sep. 15, 1941), 234; 1, No. 11 (June 1, 1940), 230.
15. U.S. Civil Aeronautics Authority, *Annual Report*, 1940, pp. 10–14; U.S. Civil Aeronautics Board, *Annual Report*, 1941, pp. 20–27, 35–37.
16. USDC, *Civil Aeronautics Journal*, 1, No. 14 (July 15, 1940), 300; No. 15 (Aug. 1, 1940), 393; U.S. Civil Aeronautics Board, *Annual Report*, 1941, pp. 18–19; "Air Merger Spiked," *Business Week*, No. 565 (June 29, 1940), 17, 20.
17. Memoranda to Assistant Secretary of Commerce South Trimble, Jr., Dec. 28, 1940; Feb. 6, 1941, CAA Central Files.
18. Charles H. Babb, New York City, to Robert R. Reining, CAA, Oct. 10, 1940; Reining to Babb, Oct. 15, 1940, CAA Central Files.
19. U.S. Civil Aeronautics Authority, *Annual Report*, 1939, p. 26; 1940, p. 8.
20. 84 *Cong. Rec.*, Part 14, Appendix (Aug. 1, 1939), 3710–12; *House Subcommittee Independent Offices Appropriations 1940*, 1937–40 (1939).
21. U.S. Civil Aeronautics Board, *Annual Report*, 1941, pp. 6–7, 20–27.
22. Department of State to Hinckley, Jan. 25, 1940, CAA Central Files.
23. D. H. Connolly, Administrator, to regional manager, Newark, Aug. 16, 1940, CAA Central Files.
24. W. T. Miller to Bureau of Safety Regulation, July 31, 1940; Philip J. Conley, Foreign Research Section, Information and Statistics Service (CAA), to S. E. Gates, International Counsel, CAB, Oct. 27, 1941, CAA Central Files.
25. Edward C. Sweeney, memorandum, Aug. 25, 1939; attaché, Italian Embassy, Washington, D.C., to Hinckley, Dec. 1, 1939; Hinckley's reply, Dec. 9, 1939, CAA Central Files.
26. John Hamilton, "One Reason Why Airplanes Crash," *The New Republic*, 99, No. 1280 (June 14, 1939), 150–53.
27. USDC, *Civil Aeronautics Journal*, 1, No. 22 (Nov. 15, 1940), 473, 479.
28. *House Subcommittee Independent Offices Appropriations 1941*, 801 (1939).
29. Howard K. Morgan, TWA, Kansas City, to Thomas Bourne, Chief Engineer, CAA, Dec. 29, 1939; Bourne to regional managers, Nov. 7, 1939, CAA Central Files.
30. Earl F. Ward, Chief, Airways Operations Division, to Director, Bureau of Federal Airways, Apr. 14, 1939; J. O. Conner, American Airlines, Memphis, to CAA, Atlanta, Dec. 27, 1939, CAA Central Files.
31. R. S. Damon, American Airlines, to Bourne, April 1, 1941, CAA Central Files.
32. USDC, *Civil Aeronautics Journal*, 2, No. 5 (Mar. 1, 1941), 75.
33. *House Subcommittee Commerce Appropriations 1942*, 77th Cong., 1st Sess., 488 (1941); U.S. Civil Aeronautics Authority, *Annual Report*, 1939, pp. 11–12; 1940, pp. 226–27; *Civil Aeronautics Journal*, 1, No. 3 (Feb. 1, 1940), 37–38, 52.
34. D. H. Connolly, "CAA Geared for Military," *Radio News*, 27 (Jan., 1942), 58, 104.
35. H. F. Cole, memorandum on airway traffic control, Dec. 12, 1940; Ward, Chief, Airways Operation Division, to Director, Bureau of Federal Airways, June 7, 1940; Glen A. Gilbert, Acting Chief, Airway Traffic Control, to Chief, Army Air Corps, Oct. 1, 1941, CAA Central Files; USDC, *Annual Report*, 1941, p. 154.
36. Glen Gilbert to Air Corps, Oct. 2, 1941, CAA Central Files.
37. U.S. Civil Aeronautics Board, *Annual Report*, 1941, p. 4.
38. Fred L. Smith, Airport Traffic Control Section, to Chief, Airways Operations Division, Nov. 7, 1940; Harry D. Copland, Detroit, to Chief,

Airport Traffic Control, Jan. 10, 1940; Carl McCluer, Airways Operation, to Copland, Jan. 11, 1940, CAA Central Files.

39. E. Sibley to Director, Bureau of Federal Airways, Oct. 17, 1939, with C. I. Stanton's penciled remarks, CAA Central Files.
40. *House Subcommittee Commerce Appropriations 1942*, 591–628 (1941).
41. *84 Cong. Rec.*, Part 12 (May 5, 1939), 1841–43.
42. U.S. Civil Aeronautics Authority, *Civil Aeronautics Journal*, 1, No. 8 (Apr. 15, 1940), 160.
43. USDC, *Civil Aeronautics Journal*, 1, No. 20 (Oct. 15, 1940), 445–47, 58; *Annual Report*, 1939, pp. 13–16; 1940, p. 30; 1941, p. 165.
44. USDC, *Civil Aeronautics Journal*, 1, No. 22 (Nov. 15, 1940), 482.
45. USDC, *Civil Aeronautics Journal*, 2, No. 14 (July 15, 1941), 175, 182.
46. Bourne to all personnel in Alaska, Dec. 15, 1939, CAA Central Files.
47. *Anchorage Daily Times*, editorial of July 26, 1941; CAA press release of Sep. 22, 1941, CAA Central Files.
48. Howard Rough to the administrator, Aug. 28, 1941, CAA Central Files.
49. Rough to Marshall C. Hoppin, Oct. 13, 1941, CAA Central Files.
50. U.S. Civil Aeronautics Authority, *Air Commerce Bulletin*, 10, No. 3 (Sep. 15, 1938), 70; *Civil Aeronautics Journal*, 1, No. 6 (Mar. 15, 1940), 77.
51. C. M. Lample, memorandum on problems in Alaska, Dec. 1, 1941, CAA Central Files.
52. *House Subcommittee Commerce Appropriations 1942*, 571, 575 (1941).
53. U.S. Civil Aeronautics Authority, *Annual Report*, 1939, pp. 42–44; *Air Commerce Bulletin*, 10, No. 9 (Mar. 15, 1939), 231–32; *House Subcommittee Independent Offices Appropriations 1940*, 1930 (1939).
54. *House Subcommittee Independent Offices Appropriations 1941*, 766–69, 851–79 (1939).
55. *House Subcommittee Commerce Appropriations 1942*, 343 (1941); *Senate Subcommittee on Commerce Appropriations 1942*, 77th Cong., 1st Sess., 141–45 (1941).
56. R. S. Boutelle, Director, Bureau of Safety Regulation, to regional managers, May 15, 1940, CAA Central Files.
57. "CAA Programs and Other Defense Measures in the Higher Institutions," *School and Society*, 52, No. 1352 (Nov. 23, 1940), 518–19.
58. *House Subcommittee Commerce Appropriations 1942*, 668–703 (1941).
59. USDC, *Annual Report*, 1941, pp. 161–62.
60. E. W. Stitt, Bladensburg, Md., to Connolly, June 12, 1941; Connolly to Stitt, July 1, 1941; Daitz Flying Service to CAA, Dec. 16, 1941, CAA Central Files.
61. J. H. Doolittle, Chairman, Collier Trophy Committee, to Clinton Hester, May 4, 1939; Hester's reply, June 1, 1939, CAA Central Files.
62. USDC, *Civil Aeronautics Journal*, 1, No. 17 (Sep. 1, 1940), 409, 413.
63. Bourne to F. W. Reichelderfer, Nov. 14, 1940, CAA Central Files.
64. U.S. Civil Aeronautics Authority, *Annual Report*, 1940, p. 20.
65. *House Subcommittee Independent Offices Appropriations 1941*, 818, 827–32 (1939); *House Subcommittee Commerce Appropriations 1942*, 503 (1941).
66. USDC, *Annual Report*, 1941, pp. 155–56, 162; U.S. Civil Aeronautics Authority, *Civil Aeronautics Journal*, 1, No. 11 (June 1, 1940), 231, 235.
67. *Senate Subcommittee Commerce Appropriations 1942*, 133–35, 493–97 (1941).
68. U.S. Civil Aeronautics Authority, *Air Commerce Bulletin*, 11, No. 2 (Aug. 15, 1939), 31–34.
69. U.S. Civil Aeronautics Authority, *Air Commerce Bulletin*, 11, No. 1 (July 15, 1939), 3.
70. USDC, *Civil Aeronautics Journal*, 1, No. 23 (Dec. 1, 1940), 494.
71. U.S. Civil Aeronautics Authority, *Air Commerce Bulletin*, 11, No. 6 (Dec. 15, 1939), 154.
72. U.S. Civil Aeronautics Authority, *Civil Aeronautics Journal*, 1, No. 9 (May 1, 1940), 198–99, 202–3.

Chapter 9: WORLD WAR II–1941–1945: INTERNAL SECURITY

1. L. C. Elliott to C. I. Stanton, Administrator, July 3, 1943, CAA Central Files.
2. H. A. Hook to Stanton, June 19, 1943, CAA Central Files.
3. Webb Shadle, general council, to the administrator, Mar. 17, 1943, CAA Central Files.
4. R. E. Sturtevant, Air Traffic Control, to Chief, Air Traffic Control, Feb. 10, 1943, CAA Central Files.
5. John Easton, Technical Development Division, to personnel officer, Jan. 14, 1942, CAA Central Files.
6. USDC, *Civil Aeronautics Journal*, 3, No. 16 (Dec. 15, 1942), 197–98, 202.
7. Marshall C. Hoppin to CAA, telegram, Oct. 27, 1942, CAA Central Files.
8. *Senate Subcommittee Commerce Appropriations 1944*, 78th Cong., 1st Sess., II, 253–54, (1943).
9. *House Subcommittee Commerce Appropriations 1944*, 78th Cong., 1st Sess., 106 (1943).
10. Interview with F. W. Reichelderfer, Washington, D.C., Aug., 1961.
11. A. S. Koch, Director of Safety Regulation, to the administrator, Nov. 21, 1941, CAA Central Files.
12. John F. Warlick, Acting Director Safety Regulation, to Region One manager, Aug. 27, 1942, CAA Central Files.
13. Administrator to Secretary of Commerce, memorandum, Jan. 20, 1943, CAA Central Files.
14. Elliott to Stanton, Oct. 14, 1942; Stanton to Elliott, Oct. 21, 1942, CAA Central Files.
15. Stanton to all regional managers, day letter, June 1, 1942, CAA Central Files. See also *House Subcommittee Commerce Appropriations 1945, 78th Cong.*, 2d Sess., 155 (1944).
16. George W. Vest to all regional employees, Dec. 11, 1941, CAA Central Files.
17. E. J. Robins, Facility Security Officer, to the administrator, Oct. 15, 1943, CAA Central Files.
18. USDC, *Civil Aeronautics Journal*, 3, No. 3 (Feb. 1, 1942), 30.
19. Charles E. Planck, *Women With Wings* (New York, 1942), pp. 222–36.
20. "Wartime History of the Civil Aeronautics Administration," MS in Library of Federal Aviation Agency, Washington, D.C., section on training pp. 41–42.
21. Sturtevant, Air Traffic Control, to Chief, Air Traffic Control, Feb. 10, 1943, CAA Central Files. See also *House Subcommittee Commerce Appropriations 1946*, 79th Cong., 1st Sess., 154 (1945).
22. Harold D. Smith, Executive Office of the President (Bureau of the Budget), to CAA, Mar. 10, 1942, CAA Central Files.
23. C. M. Lample, Chief, Airways Engineering Division, memorandum to his staff, Nov. 25, 1942; office notice from the administrator, May 13, 1942, CAA Central Files.
24. *Safeguarding Military Information*, Army Regulations No. 380–5 (Washington, D.C., Sep. 28, 1942), CAA Central Files.
25. Thomas B. Bourne, Director of Federal Airways, to Col. A. W. Marriner, Director of Communications, Army Air Force, July 27, 1942, CAA Central Files.
26. Carl McCluer, Superintendent of Airways, to Chief, Airways Operations Division, Jan. 17, 1941, CAA Central Files.
27. "Wartime History of CAA," p. 3.
28. Robins, Facility Security Officer, to regional manager, New York, May 21, 1943, CAA Central Files.
29. C. M. McNiff (for Robins) to all regional managers, Dec. 28, 1942, CAA Central Files.

30. USDC, *Civil Aeronautics Journal*, 3, No. 12 (Aug. 15, 1942), 153, 156.
31. USDC, *Civil Aeronautics Journal*, 5, No. 6 (June 15, 1944), 67.
32. USDC, *Civil Aeronautics Journal*, 4, No. 12 (Dec. 15, 1943), 164.
33. USDC, *Civil Aeronautics Journal*, 3, No. 7 (Apr. 1, 1942), 88.
34. William Boesch, Airways Maintenance, to P. N. Colliston, Office of Civil Defense, Jan. 8, 1942, CAA Central Files.
35. J. S. Marriott to regional manager-at-large, Washington, D.C., Mar. 27, 1942; minutes of managers' meeting, Jan. 22, 1942, CAA Central Files.
36. R. D. Bedinger, regional manager, Seattle, to all communications stations, Dec. 13, 1941, CAA Central Files.
37. Proclamation on air flights by aliens, Dec. 11, 1941, CAA Central Files.
38. Stanton, memorandum of June 15, 1942, CAA Central Files.
39. Stanton to all regional managers, day letter of June 1, 1942, CAA Central Files.
40. Hoppin to Stanton, Aug. 11, 1942, CAA Central Files.
41. Hoppin to the administrator, Oct. 30, 1943, CAA Central Files.
42. Bourne to acting administrator, Feb. 20, 1942, CAA Central Files.
43. Stanton to Guy J. Swope, Director Division of Territories and Island Possessions, Department of Interior, Aug. 1, 1942; Wayne C. Taylor, Acting Secretary of Commerce, Order No. 242, Aug. 3, 1942, CAA Central Files.
44. Bourne to regional manager, Seattle, Aug. 10, 1942, CAA Central Files.
45. F. M. Lanter, Chief, General Inspection Division, to Region Eight manager, May 25, 1942, CAA Central Files.
46. J. E. Hoover to B. C. Connolly, May 6, 1942; Stanton to Hoover, May 15, 1942, CAA Central Files.
47. Hoover to Stanton, Feb. 17, 1943; Stanton to Hoover, July 21, 1943, CAA Central Files.
48. Robins to regional manager, Alaska, Aug. 25, 1943, CAA Central Files.
49. Hoppin, memorandum of July 4, 1942, CAA Central Files.
50. Stanton to the Secretary of Commerce, July 27, 1943, CAA Central Files.
51. Hook to the administrator, Dec. 29, 1942, CAA Central Files.
52. Ben Stern, Director of Information and Statistical Services, to Charles B. Donaldson, Director of Airports, Nov. 1, 1943, CAA Central Files.
53. Floyd B. Brinkley, publications, to director of information, Oct. 28, 1943, CAA Central Files.
54. Brinkley to Secretary, CAB, Dec. 6, 1941, CAA Central Files.
55. Elliott to CAA, Aug. 9, 1943, CAA Central Files.
56. Bourne, memorandum, May 22, 1943, CAA Central Files.
57. Lample, Chief, Airways Engineering Division, memorandum, Dec. 10, 1942, CAA Central Files.
58. J. E. Sommers to O. P. Harwood, Jan. 7, 1943; Harwood to Sommers, Jan. 15, 1943, CAA Central Files.
59. David M. Giltinan, Secretary, West Virginia Board of Aeronautics, to Sen. H. M. Kilgore, Oct. 30, 1942; Kilgore to Stanton, Nov. 3, 1942, CAA Central Files.
60. Gov. Sam H. Jones (Louisiana) to Stanton, June 10, 1943; Sommers to Jones, Aug. 19, 1943, CAA Central Files.
61. Stanton to regional manager, Atlanta, Oct. 31, 1942; Sommers to the administrator, Dec. 31, 1942, CAA Central Files.
62. Herbert C. Schmidt, Master Builders Association, to all government offices, Nov. 22, 1943, CAA Central Files.
63. Memorandum to Central Depot, Sep. 10, 1942, CAA Central Files.
64. E. J. Gardner, Personnel Officer, to all regions, Oct. 6, 1942, CAA Central Files.

65. USDC, *Civil Aeronautics Journal*, 3, No. 3 (Feb. 1, 1942), 31.
66. *House Subcommittee Commerce Appropriations 1943*, 77th Cong., 2d Sess., 87, 124 (1942).
67. Secretary Jesse H. Jones to the President, Aug. 4, 1942, General Records of the Department of Commerce, General Correspondence.
68. *House Subcommittee Commerce Appropriations 1946*, 74, 80 (1945).
69. 90 *Cong. Rec.*, Part 10 (Aug. 24, 1944), A3720–21.
70. USDC, *Civil Aeronautics Journal*, 5, No. 7 (July 15, 1944), 80; 6, No. 3 (Mar. 15, 1945), 25.
71. USDC, *Civil Aeronautics Journal*, 3, No. 1 (Jan. 1, 1942), 7; 3, No. 2 (Jan. 15, 1942), 18.
72. "Wartime History of CAA," section on CPT and WTS, pp. 1–11.
73. *House Subcommittee Commerce Appropriations 1943*, 123–25 (1942).
74. *Senate Subcommittee Commerce Appropriations 1943*, 77th Cong., 2d Sess., 534 (1942).
75. Fred Hamlin, Acting Director, Information and Statistics Service, to Edward E. Bartholomew, District Flight Superintendent, June 25, 1942, CAA Central Files.
76. Stanton to Sen. Robert A. Taft, Sep. 4, 1942, CAA Central Files.
77. Hamlin to *The Sportsman Pilot*, Jan. 11, 1943, CAA Central Files.
78. 88 *Cong. Rec.*, Part 1 (Feb. 16, 1942), 1281.
79. "Wartime History of CAA" (CPT and WTS), p. 8.
80. *House Subcommittee Commerce Appropriations 1943*, 88–89 (1942).
81. *House Subcommittee Commerce Appropriations 1944*, 108, 165 (1943).
82. *Senate Subcommittee Commerce Appropriations 1945*, 78th Cong., 2d Sess., 178 (1944).
83. Therese Kullman to Mrs. Franklin D. Roosevelt, Feb. 16, 1943, CAA Central Files.
84. *Senate Subcommittee Commerce Appropriations 1944*, I, 9–10 (1943).
85. *Senate Subcommittee Commerce Appropriations 1944*, I, 26–27 (1943).
86. *Senate Subcommittee Commerce Appropriations 1944*, I, 80 (1943).
87. *Senate Subcommittee Commerce Appropriations 1944*, II, 114–16 (1943).
88. *Senate Subcommittee Commerce Appropriations 1945*, 246–47 (1944).
89. 91 *Cong. Rec.*, Part 1 (Feb. 8, 1945), 957.
90. *House Subcommittee Commerce Appropriations 1946*, 104–5 (1945).
91. USDC, *Civil Aeronautics Journal*, 3, No. 11 (July 15, 1942), 141.
92. "Wartime History of CAA," section on airports, pp. 1, 4, 9.
93. *Senate Subcommittee Commerce Appropriations 1943*, 501–6, 519 (1942).
94. *House Subcommittee Commerce Appropriations 1946*, 180–83 (1945).
95. A. J. Strothman to Congressman Clifford R. Hope, Sep. 24, 1943; Stanton to Hope, Nov. 11, 1943, CAA Central Files.
96. *House Subcommittee Commerce Appropriations 1946*, 198 (1945).
97. USDC, *Civil Aeronautics Journal*, 3, No. 11 (July 15, 1942), 145.
98. USDC, *Civil Aeronautics Journal*, 3, No. 3 (Feb. 1, 1942), 32, 37, 41.
99. USDC, *Civil Aeronautics Journal*, 4, No. 9 (Sep. 15, 1943), 114; 4, No. 12 (Dec. 15, 1943), 177.
100. USDC, *Civil Aeronautics Journal*, 5, No. 6 (June 1, 1944), 65; No. 11 (Nov. 1, 1944), 127.
101. "Fields First, Planes Second Is Plan for Aviation Growth," *Newsweek*, 24, No. 6 (Aug. 7, 1944), 58, 60.
102. "New and Improved Airfields," *Science*, 100, No. 2607, Supplement 10 (Dec. 15, 1944), 10.

Chapter 10: WORLD WAR II: FACILITIES, REGULATION

1. "Wartime History of the Civil Aeronautics Administration," MS in Library of Federal Aviation Agency, Washington, D.C., section on federal airways, pp. 3, 13–14.

2. USDC, *Civil Aeronautics Journal*, 6, No. 5 (May 15, 1945), 52.
3. "Wartime History of CAA," section on federal airways, pp. 12–13.
4. USDC, *Civil Aeronautics Journal*, 6, No. 7 (July 15, 1945), 76.
5. Marshall C. Hoppin to C. I. Stanton, June 23, 1943, CAA Central Files.
6. H. A. Hook, to the administrator, Feb. 15, 1943; A. E. Stockburger, Executive Officer (CAA), to W. D. Driscoll, Employees' Compensation Commission, July 9, 1943; F. M. Lanter, Director, Safety Regulations, to contract and service officer, July 21, 1943, CAA Central Files.
7. CAA Roster of May 6, 1943; Stockburger to Driscoll, July 9, 1943, CAA Central Files.
8. W. T. Miller to the administrator, Oct. 29, 1942; Stanton to Col. C. R. Smith, Army Air Force, Air Transport Command, Nov. 2, 1942, CAA Central Files.
9. Houston W. Longine, Jr., Major, Air Corps, to CAA Communications Station, Omaha, July 27, 1943; E. D. Post, Alaska Defense Command, to Gene Marchant, Radio Engineer, CAA, Anchorage, n.d., CAA Central Files.
10. Wilbur B. Peaire, Controller, Washington National Airport, to his manager, Dec. 6, 1943, CAA Central Files.
11. Stanton to Brig. Gen. B. W. Chidlaw, Assistant Chief of Staff, Army Air Force, Jan. 23, 1943, CAA Central Files.
12. Chris Lample, "Rough Draft, " CAA Organization History, MS in Office of Public Affairs, Federal Aviation Agency, Washington, D.C., p. 4.
13. U.S. Civil Aeronautics Administration, *Annual Report*, 1942, p. 41.
14. USDC, *Civil Aeronautics Journal*, 4, No. 5 (May 15, 1943), 64.
15. U.S. Civil Aeronautics Administration, *Annual Report*, 1942, p. 52.
16. "Wartime History of CAA," sections on air-carrier, manufacturing inspection, and flight engineering divisions, pp. 2–5; USDC, *Civil Aeronautics Journal*, 4, No. 4 (Apr. 15, 1943), 45, 47.
17. R. B. Maloy, Safety Regulation, to Chief, Aircraft Engineering Division, Apr. 21, 1943; Lanter, Chief, Safety Regulation, to the deputy administrator, Mar. 19, 1943, CAA Central Files.
18. *House Subcommittee Commerce Appropriations 1944*, 78th Cong., 1st Sess., 166–68 (1943).
19. *Ibid.*, p. 194.
20. *House Subcommittee Commerce Appropriations 1945*, 78th Cong., 2d Sess., 126, 133–39 (1944).
21. U.S. Civil Aeronautics Board, *Annual Report*, 1942, pp. 1–4.
22. "Wartime History of CAA," section on federal airways, p. 33.
23. U.S. Civil Aeronautics Board, *Annual Report*, 1943, p. 3.
24. U.S. Civil Aeronautics Board, *Annual Report*, 1944, pp. 1–4; 1945, pp. 1–4, 19.
25. *House Subcommittee Commerce Appropriations 1946*, 79th Cong., 1st Sess., 86 (1945).
26. *House Subcommittee Commerce Appropriations 1945*, 146–48 (1944); *1946*, 107–11 (1945).
27. USDC, *Civil Aeronautics Journal*, 4, No. 11 (Nov. 15, 1943), 147.
28. "Wartime History of CAA," section on federal airways, p. 17; USDC, *Civil Aeronautics Journal*, 6, No. 9 (Sep. 15, 1945), 97, 108.
29. John L. Huber to management planning officer, n.d., CAA Central Files.
30. Stanton to special aviation assistant to the Secretary, Feb. 15, 1943; Thomas B. Bourne, Director Federal Airways, to special aviation assistant to the Secretary, Feb. 3, 1943, CAA Central Files.
31. USDC, *Civil Aeronautics Journal*, 4, No. 7 (July 15, 1943), 89; No. 9 (Sep. 15, 1943), 115.
32. "Wartime History of CAA," section on federal airways, pp. 25–29.
33. Bourne to the administrator, Feb. 15, 1943, CAA Central Files.
34. *Senate Subcommittee Commerce Appropriations 1943*, 77th Cong., 2d Sess., 239 (1942).

35. *House Subcommittee Commerce Appropriations 1946*, 136–37 (1945); *Senate Subcommittee Commerce Appropriations 1946*, 79th Cong., 1st Sess., 328–31 (1945).
36. *House Subcommittee Commerce Appropriations 1946*, 114–15 (1945).
37. USDC, *Civil Aeronautics Journal*, 6, No. 4 (Apr. 15, 1945), 37, 44.
38. E. Sibley to Chief, Signals Division, Mar. 24, 1943, CAA Central Files.
39. Bourne to Chief, Technical Development Division, Dec. 15, 1943, CAA Central Files.
40. George L. Rand, Chief, Communications Branch, to superintendent of airways, May 31, 1943, CAA Central Files.
41. Stanton to Stanley Hubbard, Minn. Aeronautics Commission, Jan. 18, 1943; E. W. Stanford, Ala. Aviation Commission, to Stanton, Apr. 30, 1943; Lanter, Director of Safety Regulation to Dexter C. Martin, S.C. Aeronautics Commission, Aug. 18, 1943, CAA Central Files.
42. Congressman Jennings Randolph to Stanton, Feb. 15, 1943; Stanton to Randolph, Feb. 15, 1943, CAA Central Files.
43. J. E. Sommers, Deputy Administrator, to director of federal airways, Aug. 30, 1943, CAA Central Files.
44. John F. Warlick, Acting Director, Safety Regulation, to regional manager, Ft. Worth, Mar. 2, 1942, CAA Central Files.
45. Stanton to Bruce E. Braun, Chicago and Southern Air Lines, May 16, 1942, CAA Central Files.
46. R. E. Elwell, General Counsel (CAA), to the administrator, Apr. 17, 1942, CAA Central Files.
47. Lanter to the administrator, Jan. 13, 1943, CAA Central Files.
48. U.S. Civil Aeronautics Board, *Annual Report*, 1942, pp. 12–13, 27; USDC, *Civil Aeronautics Journal*, 3, No. 4 (Feb. 15, 1942), 50–51; No. 8 (Apr. 15, 1942), 105; 4, No. 12 (Dec. 15, 1943), 166.
49. USDC, *Civil Aeronautics Journal*, 4, No. 11 (Nov. 15, 1943), 147, 162.
50. USDC, *Civil Aeronautics Journal*, 4, No. 2 (Feb. 15, 1943), 13.
51. USDC, *Civil Aeronautics Journal*, 4, No. 3 (Mar. 15, 1943), 30; No. 10 (Oct. 15, 1943), 138: *Des Moines Register*, Oct. 26, 1962, p. 2.
52. USDC, *Civil Aeronautics Journal*, 4, No. 9 (Sep. 15, 1943), 126.
53. USDC, *Civil Aeronautics Journal*, 5, No. 6 (June 15, 1944), 68.
54. USDC, *Civil Aeronautics Journal*, 3, No. 8 (Apr. 15, 1942), 106.
55. USDC, *Civil Aeronautics Journal*, 3, No. 13 (Oct. 1, 1942), 167.
56. USDC, *Civil Aeronautics Journal*, 3, No. 6 (Mar. 15, 1942), 78.
57. Glen A. Gilbert, Chief, Air Traffic Control Division, to regional manager, Kansas City, June 12, 1943, CAA Central Files.
58. *House Subcommittee Commerce Appropriations 1944*, 150 (1943).
59. "Safety v. Payload," *Time*, 43, No. 5 (Jan. 31, 1944), 82.
60. "Civilian Pilot Accidents Stress Regulation Need," *Science News Letter*, 46, No. 20 (Nov. 11, 1944), 319.
61. U.S. Civil Aeronautics Board, *Annual Report*, 1946, p. 33.
62. E. R. Scroggie, Chief, General Inspection Division, to W. T. Miller, Chief, Air-Carrier Division, Mar. 11, 1943, CAA Central Files.
63. Memorandum of Feb. 4, 1942, CAA Central Files.
64. CAA Administrator to Civil Aeronautics Board, Dec. 22, 1941, CAA Central Files.
65. Webb Shadle, General Counsel, to the administrator, Apr. 21, 1943, CAA Central Files.
66. *Senate Subcommittee Commerce Appropriations 1944*, 78th Cong., 1st Sess., 213–20 (1943).
67. "Windshields Duck-Proofed," *Science News Letter*, 43, No. 12 (Mar. 20, 1943), 182–83.
68. USDC, *Civil Aeronautics Journal*, 4, No. 3 (Mar. 15, 1943), 29.
69. *House Subcommittee Commerce Appropriations 1945*, 161–63 (1944).
70. U.S. Civil Aeronautics Board, *Annual Report*, 1945, p. 23.
71. *House Subcommittee Commerce Appropriations 1946*, 131–32 (1945).
72. Fowler W. Barker, Air Transport Association, to Stanton, Nov. 6, 1942, CAA Central Files.
73. 91 *Cong. Rec.*, Part 10 (Jan. 25, 1945), A282–83.

74. The Council of State Governments, *Aviation and the States* (Chicago, June, 1944), pp. 4, 6.
75. USDC, *Civil Aeronautics Journal*, 6, No. 8 (Aug. 15, 1945), 86, 93; 5, No. 1 (Jan. 15, 1944), 7; *House Subcommittee Commerce Appropriations 1945*, 180 (1944); "Wartime History of CAA," section on research, pp. 1–11.
76. "Wartime History of CAA," section on federal airways, pp. 52–56.
77. *House Subcommittee Commerce Appropriations 1945*, 157 (1944).
78. *Ibid.*, pp. 159–61.
79. *House Subcommittee Commerce Appropriations 1946*, 163 (1945).
80. USDC, *Civil Aeronautics Journal*, 6, No. 5 (May 15, 1945), 50.
81. USDC, *Civil Aeronautics Journal*, 4, No. 12 (Dec. 15, 1943), 164.
82. USDC, *Civil Aeronautics Journal*, 4, No. 12 (Dec. 15, 1943), 165; "Wartime History of CAA," pp. 1-5; H. F. Rough to George W. Vest, Atlanta, Feb. 16, 1942, CAA Central Files.
83. USDC, *Civil Aeronautics Journal*, 4, No. 12 (Dec. 15, 1943), 163.
84. John F. Simmons, CAA, to the Secretary of State, Apr. 6, 1943, CAA Central Files.
85. "Air Cargo Fight Simmers," *Business Week*, No. 713 (May 1, 1943), 48, 50, 52.
86. John S. Parker, Jr., Technical Assistant to the administrator, to Capt. Charles Marr, Kelly Field, July 29, 1942, CAA Central Files.
87. *Senate Subcommittee Commerce Appropriations 1946*, 293–95 (1945).
88. U.S. Department of State, *Blueprint for World Civil Aviation*, Publ. 2348, Conf. ser. 70 (Washington, D.C., 1945), p. 24; *House Subcommittee Commerce Appropriations 1946*, 75 (1945).
89. Keith Hutchinson, "The Civil Air War," *The Nation*, 158, No. 10 (Mar. 4, 1944), 271–74.
90. USDC, *Civil Aeronautics Journal*, 4, No. 7 (July 15, 1943), 90.
91. 90 *Cong. Rec.*, Part 4 (May 26, 1944), 5070.
92. USDC, *Civil Aeronautics Journal*, 4, No. 12 (Dec. 15, 1943), 166; U.S. Civil Aeronautics Board, *Annual Reports*, 1942–1945.
93. USDC, *Civil Aeronautics Journal*, 6, No. 8 (Aug. 15, 1945), 87.
94. *House Subcommittee Commerce Appropriations 1946*, 75 (1945); *Senate 1946*, 309 (1945).
95. U.S. Civil Aeronautics Board, *Annual Report*, 1945, pp. 8–9.
96. USDC, *Civil Aeronautics Journal*, 4, No. 5 (May 15, 1943), 57, 67; No. 6 (June 15, 1943), 79–80; U.S. Civil Aeronautics Board, *Annual Report*, 1943, pp. 7–14; 1945, pp. 1–3.
97. USDC, *Civil Aeronautics Journal*, 4, No. 4 (Apr. 15, 1943); 44; No. 7 (July 15, 1943), 91; 6, No. 4 (Apr. 15, 1945), 43; U.S. Civil Aeronautics Board, *Annual Report*, 1943, pp. 15–16.
98. U.S. Civil Aeronautics Board, *Annual Report*, 1945, pp. 6–7.
99. *Senate Subcommittee Commerce Appropriations 1943*, 555–58 (1942); *House Subcommittee Commerce Appropriations 1945*, 128 (1944).
100. Matthew Josephson, *Empire of the Air: Juan Trippe and the Struggle for World Airways* (New York, 1943–44), pp. 136, 204.

Chapter 11: POSTWAR EXPANSION—1945–1959

1. T. P. Wright to William Langer, July 12, 1945, "Papers of Harry S. Truman, 1945–1953," MS, Office File 249 (Aviation), OF 3-H, Harry S. Truman Library, Independence, Mo.
2. Wright to President Harry S. Truman, Jan. 11, 1948; Truman to Wright, Jan. 24, 1948, Truman Papers, OF 3-H, Truman Library.
3. *House Subcommittee Commerce Appropriations 1950*, 81st Cong., 1st Sess., 176–77 (1949).
4. USDC, *Civil Aeronautics Journal*, 11, No. 10 (Oct. 15, 1950), 109, 120.
5. USDC, *Civil Aeronautics Journal*, 12, No. 4 (Apr. 15, 1951), 37.
6. *Aviation Week*, 65 (Sep. 10, 1956), 41.

7. *House Subcommittee Commerce Appropriations 1958*, 85th Cong., 1st Sess., 239 (1957).
8. *Senate Subcommittee Commerce Appropriations 1953*, 82d Cong., 2d Sess., 1555–59 (1952).
9. *Ibid.*, pp. 1558–59.
10. Bernard L. Gladieux to the Secretary, memorandum—summary of E. A. Goff case, Jan. 19, 1948, General Records Department of Commerce.
11. *Ibid.*, p. 3.
12. Secretary Averell Harriman to Harry B. Mitchell, Mar. 5, 1948, General Records Department of Commerce.
13. Phillips Moore, Director Office of Airports, to CAA personnel officer, Jan. 11, 1951, Files of Airports Service, Washington, D.C.
14. H. A. Hook to Director, Office of Airports, Dec. 2, 1952. See also E. J. Robins to assistant to deputy administrator, Feb. 15, 1952; and H. E. Dixon to Chief, Procedures and Reports Division, Feb. 4, 1953, Files of Airports Service.
15. "Removal of CAA Administrator Rumored," The Voice of the Pilots and Mechanics of America, Jan., 1949, typed carbon copy, File on CAA Organization History, CAA Office of Public Affairs, Washington, D.C.
16. USDC, *Civil Aeronautics Journal*, 7, No. 1 (Jan. 15, 1946), 1, 3.
17. Lowell H. Swenson, National Aeronautic Association, to Matthew Connelly, Jan. 20, 1948, Truman Papers, OF 249 misc., Truman Library.
18. H. Scherbak to Gen. Harry Vaughan, Feb. 7, 1948, Truman Papers, OF 249 misc., Truman Library.
19. *House Subcommittee Commerce Appropriations 1947*, 79th Cong., 2d Sess., 655–56 (1946).
20. *House Subcommittee Commerce Appropriations 1950*, 92–93 (1949).
21. *Ibid.*, pp. 358–62.
22. U.S. Civil Aeronautics Board, *Annual Report*, 1947, p. 38.
23. *House Subcommittee Commerce Appropriations 1955*, 83d Cong., 2d Sess., 173 (1954).
24. 100 *Cong. Rec.*, Part 1 (Jan. 13, 1954, 200–201).
25. *Senate Subcommittee Commerce Appropriations 1951*, 81st Cong., 2d Sess., Part II, 1300 (1950).
26. "Conflicting Policies Hamper Design Effort," *Aviation Week*, 65 (Oct. 22, 1956), 28–29.
27. Katherine Johnson, "Rizley Backs Subsidy Rights for All Lines," *Aviation Week*, 62 (June 6, 1955), 123–24.
28. L. L. Doty, "Manufacturers Attack CAA Engine Ruling," *Aviation Week*, 69 (Oct. 6, 1958), 36–37.
29. USDC, *Civil Aeronautics Journal*, 7, No. 1 (Jan. 15, 1946), 4; 10, No. 1 (Jan. 15, 1949), 11; *House Subcommittee Commerce Appropriations 1957*, 84th Cong., 2d Sess., 271 (1956).
30. C. F. Horne to Connelly, Feb. 29, 1952, Truman Papers, OF 249, Truman Library.
31. *Aviation Week*, 65 (Dec. 24, 1956), 29.
32. *Senate Subcommittee Commerce Appropriations 1953*, 1585 (1952).
33. 98 *Cong. Rec.*, Part 10 (May 12, 1952), A2995.
34. U.S. Civil Aeronautics Board, *Annual Report*, 1958, p. 25.
35. *Ibid.*, pp. 34–35.
36. USDC, *Civil Aeronautics Journal*, 7, No. 6 (June 15, 1946), 69. 73; No. 11 (Nov. 15, 1946), 143; 8, No. 2 (Feb. 15, 1947), 13–14; No. 3 (Mar. 15, 1947), 26, 37, 44.
37. USDC, *Civil Aeronautics Journal*, 8, No. 11 (Nov. 15, 1947), 125; 9, No. 3 (Mar. 15, 1948), 25.
38. USDC, *Civil Aeronautics Journal*, 13, No. 3 (Mar. 15, 1952), 25; 7, No. 11 (Nov. 15, 1946), 137, 140; U.S. Civil Aeronautics Board, *Annual Report*, 1947, p. 37.

39. 100 *Cong. Rec.*, Part 9 (July 24, 1954), 11865–67.
40. *House Subcommittee Commerce Appropriations 1947*, 927, 929 (1946).
41. 98 *Cong. Rec.*, Part 4 (Apr. 24, 1952), 4333.
42. USDC, *Civil Aeronautics Journal*, 7, No. 3 (Mar. 15, 1946), 27; 10, No. 8 (Aug. 15, 1949), 94.
43. USDC, *Civil Aeronautics Journal*, 9, No. 12 (Dec. 15, 1948), 135–36.
44. USDC, *Civil Aeronautics Journal*, 10, No. 2 (Feb. 15, 1949), 19; No. 11 (Nov. 15, 1949), 121.
45. *Aviation Week*, 63 (Sep. 19, 1955), 139.
46. *Aviation Week*, 66 (Mar. 18, 1957), 30–31.
47. *Aviation Week*, 67 (July 29, 1957), 30–31.
48. Glenn Garrison, "Northeast Check Opens CAA Crackdown," *Aviation Week*, 69 (Oct. 27, 1958), 38–39.
49. *Aviation Week*, 63 (Aug. 22, 1955), 100.
50. *Aviation Week*, 65 (July 23, 1956), 38–39.
51. U.S. Civil Aeronautics Board, *Annual Report*, 1952, p. 33; 1953, p. 23.
52. *Senate Subcommittee Commerce Appropriations 1957*, 84th Cong., 2d Sess., 347–51 (1956).
53. U.S. Civil Aeronautics Board, *Annual Report*, 1957, p. 17.
54. U.S. Civil Aeronautics Board, *Annual Report*, 1949, p. 22.
55. U.S. Civil Aeronautics Board, *Annual Report*, 1955, p. 12.
56. USDC, *Civil Aeronautics Journal*, 8, No. 12 (Dec. 15, 1947), 133, 135.
57. G. Lloyd Wilson and Leslie A. Bryan, *Air Transportation* (New York, 1949), pp. 571–72.
58. D. Philip Locklin, *Economics of Transportation*, 5th ed. (Homewood, Ill., 1960), p. 760.
59. William A. M. Burden to Secretary Henry A. Wallace, Oct. 1, 1945; Wallace to the President, Oct. 2, 1945; President Truman to Wallace, Oct. 4, 1945; and Wallace to Truman, Oct. 10, 1945, Truman Papers, OF 249, Truman Library.
60. Charles L. Dearing and Wilfred Owen, *National Transportation Policy* (Washington, D.C., 1949), pp. 39, 43.
61. *Senate Subcommittee Commerce Appropriations 1950*, 81st Cong., 1st Sess., 336–51 (1949).
62. *House Subcommittee Commerce Appropriations 1952*, 82d Cong., 2d Sess., 120–28 (1951).
63. 95 *Cong. Rec.*, Part 3 (Apr. 7, 1949), 4083–84.
64. C. G. Ross, statement by the President on release of Report of Air Policy Commission, Jan. 13, 1948, Truman Papers, OF 249, Truman Library; "Records of the President's Air Policy Commission, July, 1947–Jan., 1948," RG 220, MS, Harry S. Truman Library.
65. USDC, *Civil Aeronautics Journal*, 10, No. 8 (Aug. 15, 1949), 85, 94; No. 10 (Oct. 15, 1949), 109, 115; No. 11 (Nov. 15, 1949), 124–25; 11, No. 4 (Apr. 15, 1950), 46–47; No. 8 (Aug. 15, 1950), 86.
66. Commissioner F. G. Reinicke to Mayor William O'Dwyer, Sep. 9, 1946; O'Dwyer to President Truman, Sep. 10, 1946; Truman to Secretary of the Navy, Sep. 14, 1946; Truman to O'Dwyer, Sep. 14, 1946; Secretary James Forrestal to the press, Aug. 16, 1946, Truman Papers, OF 249, Truman Library.
67. Hubert H. Humphrey to Matthew Connelly, Apr. 22, 1946; Omar N. Bradley to Connelly, May 2, 1946; Connelly to Humphrey, May 2, 1946; Humphrey to Truman, Nov. 19, 1952; Truman to Humphrey, Nov. 24, 1952; Connelly to Secretary of Air Force, Feb. 16, 1951, Truman Papers, OF 249, Truman Library.
68. C. H. Bloom, Rockford, Ill., to Truman, Feb. 28, 1947; President Truman to Secretary of Agriculture, memorandum of Mar. 16, 1948, Truman Papers, OF 249, Truman Library.
69. *Senate Subcommittee Commerce Appropriations 1949*, 80th Cong., 2d Sess., 354–412 (1948).

70. Claude L. Wilson to President Truman, Jan. 26, 1948; Joe F. Major, War Assets Administration, to H. H. Vaughan, n.d.; Vaughan to Major, Jan. 27, 1948; President Truman to Secretary of the Air Force, memorandum of Aug. 29, 1949; Bryce B. Smith to Truman, Aug. 24, 1949, Truman Papers, OF 249 misc., Truman Library.

71. William Preston Lane to President Truman, June 16, 1949; William D. Hassett, secretary to the President, to Department of Commerce, June 30, 1949; Acting Commerce Secretary C. V. Whitney to Lane, July 19, 1949, General Records Department of Commerce.

72. Governor Lane to President Truman, Nov. 9, 1949; President Truman to Governor Lane, Nov. 10, 1949, Truman Papers, OF 249, Truman Library.

73. R. B. Landry, Air Force, to President Truman, Jan. 10, 1950; Landry to John R. Steelman, Presidential Assistant, Jan. 18, 1950; Stephen I. Spingarn, memorandum for the files, Aug. 11, 1950; President Truman to Congressman Lindley Beckworth, June 21, 1950, Truman Papers, OF 249, Truman Library.

74. Gov. Theodore R. McKeldin to President Truman, Aug. 6, 1951; Truman to McKeldin, Aug. 1, 1951, Truman Papers, OF 249, Truman Library.

75. 98 *Cong. Rec.*, Part 2 (Mar. 5, 1952), 1892.

76. *Senate Subcommittee Commerce Appropriations 1959*, 85th Cong., 2d Sess., 252–53 (1958).

77. *Ibid.*, pp. 289–90.

78. 103 *Cong. Rec.*, Part 11 (Aug. 19, 1957), 15148–61.

79. "The Airport and Its Neighbors," Records of the President's Airport Commission, May 16, 1952, Truman Library.

80. Records of the President's Airport Commission, 1952, Truman Library.

81. Files on cities and airports, Records of the President's Airport Commission, Truman Library.

82. J. C. Hunsaker to S. Paul Johnston, Apr. 18, 1952, Records of the President's Airport Commission, MIT, J. C. Hunsaker folder, Truman Library.

83. "Research and Development To Promote Safety in Aviation," Records of the President's Airport Commission, p. 7, Truman Library.

84. "The Airport and Its Neighbors," pp. 21–27.

85. *House Subcommittee Commerce Appropriations 1954*, 83d Cong., 1st Sess., 188–200 (1953).

86. *Senate Subcommittee Commerce Appropriations 1954*, 83d Cong., 1st Sess., 405 (1953).

87. *Senate Subcommittee Commerce Appropriations 1953*, 1551–59 (1952).

88. *House Subcommittee Commerce Appropriations 1957*, 263–64 (1956).

89. 102 *Cong. Rec.*, Part 3 (Mar. 2, 1956), 3825–29.

90. *Ibid.*, p. 3829.

91. 102 *Cong. Rec.*, Part 3 (Feb. 23, 1956), 3266–80; Part 11 (July 25, 1956), 14398.

92. F. B. Lee to regional administrators, June 29, 1955, Files of Airports Service.

93. C. J. Lowen to Paul H. Sanders, Director, Race Relations, *Law Reporter*, July 2, 1956, Files of Airports Service.

94. Undersecretary of Commerce to administrator, memorandum of Mar. 20, 1956, Hugh H. Cobb, to the files, Apr. 12, 1956, Files of Airports Service.

95. James Pyle to Congressman Overton Brooks, Oct. 10, 1956, Files of Airports Service.

96. Iris Blitch to C. J. Lowen, July 16, 1956; Lowen to Blitch, July 18, 1956, including a copy of Memorandum No. 41, Apr. 4, 1956, Files of Airports Service; 102 *Cong. Rec.*, Part 8 (June 29, 1956), 11460.

97. Pyle to Hon. Charles C. Diggs, Aug. 5, 1958, Files of Airports Service.

98. Deputy Administrator William B. Davis to L. H. Foster, President, Tuskegee Institute, May 15, 1958; Robert P. Boyle, CAA General Counsel, to Foster, June 4, 1958, Files of Airports Service.
99. USDC, *Civil Aeronautics Journal*, 7, No. 8 (Aug. 15, 1946), 101–2; 8, No. 4 (Apr. 15, 1947), 39.
100. 98 *Cong. Rec.*, 82d Cong., 2d Sess., Part 10 (May 12, 1952), A2887 (May 15, 1952), 2984.
101. Telegram, A. J. Bregman to President Truman, June 16, 1952, Truman Papers, OF 249 misc., Truman Library.
102. *Aviation Week*, 63 (July 4, 1955), 85.
103. *House Subcommitttee Commerce Appropriations 1949*, 80th Cong., 2d Sess., 182–85 (1948).
104. *House Subcommittee Commerce Appropriations 1950*, 223, 225, 241, 252, 266, 446.
105. Secretary Sawyer to Ralph S. Damon, Nov. 5, 1948, Damon to Sawyer, Nov. 9, 1948, General Records Department of Commerce.
106. *House Subcommittee Commerce Appropriations 1956*, 84th Cong., 1st Sess., 190–98 (1955); 101 *Cong. Rec.*, 84th Cong., 1st Sess., Part 3 (Apr. 1, 1955), 4262; 102 *Cong. Rec.*, 84th Cong., 2d Sess., Part 11 (July 25, 1956), 14336–37.
107. Executive Order No. 9781 establishing the Air Coordinating Committee, Sep. 19, 1946, "Papers of Edwin A. Locke, Jr., 1945–1952," Harry S. Truman Library.
108. *House Subcommittee Commerce Appropriations 1957*, 230–38 (1956).
109. *House Subcommittee Commerce Appropriations 1958*, 218–36, 259–87 (1957).
110. *Senate Subcommittee Commerce Appropriations 1957*, 194, 203–7 (1956).
111. *House Subcommittee Commerce Appropriations 1958*, 223 (1957).
112. USDC, *Civil Aeronautics Journal*, 9, No. 12 (Dec. 15, 1948), 134; 10, No. 3 (Mar. 15, 1949), 36.
113. USDC, *Civil Aeronautics Journal*, 9, No. 12 (Dec. 15, 1948), 135.
114. *House Subcommittee Commerce Appropriations 1951*, 81st Cong., 2d Sess., 1519, 1517 (1950).
115. USDC, *Civil Aeronautics Journal*, 8, No. 3 (Mar. 15, 1947), 30–31, 33.
116. Edwin P. Curtis, *Aviation Facilities Planning*, final report (Washington, D.C., 1957), pp. 1–38; See also *Aviation Facilities*, the report of the Aviation Facilities Study Group to the director, Bureau of the Budget (Washington, D.C., 1955), p. 1046.
117. 103 *Cong. Rec.*, Part 10 (July 29, 1957), 12938–39.
118. 104 *Cong. Rec.*, Part 8 (June 4, 1958), 10178–79.
119. Lawrence H. Berlin, "Of Space and Time, and Death in the Air," *The Reporter the Magazine of Facts and Ideas*, 15, No. 2 (Aug. 9, 1956), 33.
120. "Congress Should Investigate CAA," *Aviation Week*, 63 (Dec. 26, 1955), 94.
121. L. L. Doty, "CAA Center Tackles Traffic Control," *Aviation Week*, 66 (June 3, 1957), 187, 189, 191, 193.
122. *House Subcommittee Commerce Appropriations 1947*, 659–63 (1946).
123. USDC, *Civil Aeronautics Journal*, 7, No. 11 (Nov. 15, 1946), 139.
124. USDC, *Civil Aeronautics Journal*, 8, No. 1 (Jan. 15, 1947), 12; No. 10 (Oct. 15, 1947), 111; 9, No. 1 (Jan. 15, 1948), 12; No. 10 (Oct. 15, 1948), 113; 10, No. 3 (Mar. 15, 1949), 25; 12, No. 3 (Mar. 15, 1951), 78.
125. C. G. Ross to Gene Dawson, *Indianapolis News*, Feb. 1, 1946, Truman Papers, OF 249, Truman Library.
126. Bernard L. Gladieux, Executive Assistant to the Secretary, to Delos W. Rentzel, Administrator, Mar. 9, 1949, General Records Department of Commerce.
127. Locklin, *Economics*, pp. 769–72; Robert J. Serling, *The Probable Cause* (New York, 1960), pp. 52–85.

128. *Senate Subcommittee Commerce Appropriations 1952,* 82d Cong., 1st Sess., 759 (1951).
129. 100 *Cong. Rec.,* Part 1 (Jan. 11, 1954), 92–93.
130. 102 *Cong. Rec.,* Part 3 (Mar. 2, 1956), 3825–29.
131. *Ibid.,* Part 1 (Jan. 5, 1956), 79.
132. Curtis, *Aviation Facilities Planning.*
133. 103 *Cong. Rec.,* 85th Cong., 1st Sess., Part 10 (Aug. 1, 1957), 13366.
134. 104 *Cong. Rec.,* Part 12 (Aug. 4, 1958), 16087.
135. *Ibid.,* Part 14 (Aug. 18, 1958), 18323.
136. *Ibid.,* p. 18330.
137. Secretary Weeks to General Quesada, Mar. 14, 1958; Administrator Pyle to Quesada, May 15, 1958; Pyle to all CAA heads, Washington, D.C., June 20, 1958, Files of Airports Service.
138. *Senate Subcommittee Commerce* (Airways Modernization Board) *Appropriations 1959,* 583–624 (1958).

Chapter 12: THE CAB—1945–1958

1. *House Subcommittee Commerce Appropriations 1957,* 84th Cong., 2d Sess., 858–59 (1956).
2. 104 *Cong. Rec.,* Part 9 (June 25, 1958), 12197–98; 12202.
3. *Ibid.,* p. 12202.
4. 91 *Cong. Rec.,* Part 13 (Dec. 20, 1945), A5774.
5. Harry Vaughan to E. E. Pershall, May 20, 1945, Truman Papers, OF 249, Harry S. Truman Library, Independence, Mo.
6. Jack Frye, TWA, to Matthew J. Connelly, June 11, 1945, Truman Papers, OF 249, Truman Library.
7. Edward E. Day to John R. Steelman, Feb. 23, 1948, Truman Papers, OF 249, Truman Library.
8. Samuel I. Rosenman to President Truman, memorandum, June 1, 1945, Truman Papers, OF 249, Truman Library.
9. J. Kirk Baldwin, Denver, Colo., to President Truman, n.d., Truman Papers, OF 249, Truman Library.
10. Gov. Sid McMath to President Truman, Oct. 17, 1952, and Truman to McMath, Oct. 30, 1952, Truman Papers, OF 249, Truman Library.
11. Paul E. Fitzpatrick to Matthew Connelly, Oct. 17, 1951; Administrator Nyrop to Fitzpatrick, Nov. 13, 1951, Truman Papers, OF 249, Truman Library.
12. Tom Connally to Matthew Connelly, telephone call, June 23, 1952, Truman Papers, OF 249, Truman Library.
13. John F. Kennedy to President Truman, Nov. 17, 1952, and Langdon P. Marvin, Jr., to Truman, Jan. 15, 1953, Truman Papers, OF 249, Truman Library.
14. Lyndon B. Johnson to William A. Mills, Port Arthur, Tex., Aug. 28, 1950; Mills to Steelman, White House, Jan. 8, 1951, Truman Papers, OF 249 misc., Truman Library.
15. Josephine Alberta, Robinson, Kan., to President Truman, Mar. 12, 1951, Truman Papers, OF 249 misc., Truman Library.
16. Luigi Criscuolo, New York City, to President Truman, Jan. 23, 1952, Truman Papers, OF 249 misc., Truman Library.
17. Albert E. Payne, to President Truman, telegram, Mar. 17, 1946, Truman Papers, OF 249 misc., Truman Library.
18. Hazel Burnelli to Matthew Connelly, Apr. 16, 1946; Connelly to Mrs. Burnelli, Apr. 22, 1946; V. J. Burnelli to Connelly, Apr. 9, 1948, Truman Papers, OF 249 misc., Truman Library.
19. *American Aviation Daily,* July 12, 1946, pp. 56–57.
20. Walter Reuther to President Truman, Mar. 2, 1948; Truman to Reuther, Mar. 6, 1948, Truman Papers, OF 249 misc., Truman Library.
21. J. J. O'Connell, CAB, to Steelman, Oct. 19, 1948; Mrs. J. D. Crane to President Truman, Sept. 29, 1948; C. D. Leffler, Miami (Fla.) Cham-

ber of Commerce, to Truman, telegram, Oct. 4, 1948, Truman Papers, OF 249 misc., Truman Library.

22. David L. Behncke to Steelman, telegram, Dec. 22, 1949, Truman Papers, OF 249 misc., Truman Library.

23. *The Air Line Pilot*, 18, No. 2 (Mar., 1949), p. 1.

24. Lions Club of San Juan, *El Imparcial*, Feb. 28, 1950, p. 17; ALPA brief before CAB, Docket No. 5376, Apr. 3, 1952, p. 3, Truman Papers, OF 249 misc., Truman Library.

25. Earl C. Clements to President Truman, telegram, Dec. 31, 1952, Truman Papers, OF 249 misc., Truman Library.

26. F. J. Lawton, Executive Office of the President, to Mr. Hopkins, memorandum of Dec. 29, 1952; Mary J. Borton, Alexandria, Va., to Truman, n.d., Truman Papers, OF 249, Truman Library.

27. Charles A. Carroll to President Truman, July 16, 1946; J. M. Landis, CAB, to Edwin A. Locke, White House, July 24, 1946; Locke to Carroll, July 25, 1946, Truman Papers, OF 249 misc., Truman Library.

28. File on CAB, Departments of Justice and State study on H. Hughes' hold over TWA, Dec. 3, 1946; Landis to Locke, July 19, 1946, Truman Papers, OF 249 misc., Truman Library.

29. W. J. B. to Steelman, Dec. 30, 1947, Truman Papers, OF 3-I, Truman Library.

30. USDC, *Civil Aeronautics Journal*, 7, No. 7 (July 15, 1946), 91.

31. Edward Warner, CAB, to Truman, Aug. 17, 1945; Truman to Warner, Sept. 13, 1945; L. Welch Pogue to Truman, Mar. 5, 1946; Truman to Pogue, Mar. 11, 1946, Truman Papers, OF 3-I, Truman Library.

32. White House memoranda of Oct. 15, 1947, Oct. 20, 1947, Dec. 31, 1947, Truman Papers, Truman Library; *Washington Post*, Dec. 31, 1947, p. 1.

33. August L. Richards to President Truman, telegram, Jan. 3, 1948, Truman Papers, OF 3-I misc., Truman Library.

34. President Truman to Sen. A. H. Vandenberg and Truman to Congressman Joseph Martin, Jan. 8, 1948, Truman Papers, OF 3-I, Truman Library.

35. Carleton Putnam to President Truman, Jan. 12, 1948, Truman Papers, OF 3-I misc., Truman Library.

36. Statement of J. M. Landis before the House Committee on Interstate and Foreign Commerce, filed on May 10, 1948, Truman Papers, OF 3-I, Truman Library.

37. E. A. Locke, Memorandum for the President, Dec. 30, 1946, Locke Papers, Truman Library.

38. Langdon P. Marvin, Jr., "Sword and Ploughshare," *Air Transportation* (Nov., 1948), 31–32, 43, Truman Papers, OF 249, Truman Library.

39. Sen. Chan Gurney, Committee on Armed Services, to President Truman, Jan. 13, 1948; Truman to Gurney, Jan. 15, 1948; Gurney to Truman, Jan. 16, 1948; Gurney to Truman, Jan. 20, 1948; Truman to Gurney, Jan. 21, 1948; Matthew Connelly, memorandum of Jan. 21, 1948, Truman Papers, OF 3-I, Truman Library.

40. White House Order, Apr. 5, 1948, and news release, Apr. 7, 1948, Truman Papers, OF 3-I, Truman Library.

41. Harllee Branch to President Truman, Jan. 19, 1948; Truman to Branch, Jan. 20, 1948; Oswald Ryan, CAB, to Matthew Connelly, Feb. 19, 1948, Truman Papers, OF 3-I, Truman Library.

42. D. Dawson, File on Russell B. Adams, Truman Papers, OF 3-I, Truman Library.

43. Joseph J. O'Connell to President Truman, June 13, 1950; Truman to O'Connell, July 6, 1950; O. Ryan to Truman, Sep. 22, 1950; Truman to Ryan, Sep. 26, 1950; Delos W. Rentzel to Connelly, Sep. 28, 1950, Truman Papers, OF 3-I, Truman Library.

44. Rentzel to Steelman, Aug. 2, 1948, Truman Papers, OF 3-I, Truman Library.
45. Harry S. Truman to Gurney, Nov. 26, 1952; Gurney to Truman, Nov. 24, 1952; Josh Lee, CAB, to President Truman, Jan. 4, 1950; Guy Harvey, Yankton, S.D., to Truman, Mar. 2, 1951, Truman Papers, OF 3-I, Truman Library.
46. Truman to Josh Lee, Joseph Adams, Chan Gurney, Oswald Ryan, all dated Jan. 16, 1953; Lee to Truman, Jan. 19, 1953, Truman Papers, OF 3-I, Truman Library.
47. 104 *Cong. Rec.*, Part 3 (Feb. 27, 1958), 2975.
48. "Misleading the President," *The New Republic*, 138, No. 11 (Mar. 17, 1958), 5.
49. USDC, *Civil Aeronautics Journal*, 7, No. 11 (Nov. 15, 1946), 148; Harry S. Truman to Sen. Alben Barkley, July 10, 1946, Papers of Edwin A. Locke, Jr., Truman Library.
50. William C. Foster, Undersecretary of Commerce, to Rear Admiral Paul A. Smith, U.S. Representative to the ICAO, May 12, 1948, General Records Department of Commerce.
51. *House Subcommittee Commerce Appropriations 1947*, 79th Cong., 2d Sess., 881–88 (1946).
52. H. A. Wallace, Secretary of Commerce, to the Secretary of State, Sep. 6, 1946, General Records Department of Commerce.
53. Administrator T. P. Wright to Secretary W. A. Harriman, Dec. 26, 1946; Harriman to the Secretary of State, Jan. 6, 1947, General Records Department of Commerce.
54. William A. M. Burden, Assistant Secretary of Commerce, to Livingston T. Merchant, Aviation, Department of State, Jan. 30, 1947; James F. Byrnes to Harriman, Jan. 9, 1947, General Records Department of Commerce.
55. William C. Foster to Secretary of State, Nov. 26, 1947, General Records Department of Commerce.
56. Wallace to Harold D. Smith, Bureau of Budget, Dec. 17, 1945; Executive Order, Dec. 29, 1945; Byrnes to President Truman, Oct. 30, 1946; Executive Order of Nov. 7, 1946, Truman Papers, Truman Library.
57. William D. Hassett, Secretary to the President, to Donald H. Roberts, Tulsa, Aug. 9, 1950, Truman Papers, OF 249, Truman Library.
58. U.S. Civil Aeronautics Board, *Annual Report*, 1946, pp. 5–8.
59. U.S. Civil Aeronautics Board, *Annual Report*, 1947, pp. 30–32; *House Subcommittee Commerce Appropriations 1950*, 81st Cong., 1st Sess., 174 (1949).
60. Ernest Gruening to Secretary Sawyer, Jan. 20, 1950, General Records Department of Commerce; Secretary of Interior Oscar L. Chapman to President Truman, Feb. 28, 1950; Sawyer to Truman, Feb. 17, 1950; Chairman O'Connell to Truman, Feb. 20, 1950; memorandum, David Stowe to President Truman, Stowe Files, "Alaskan Transportation" folder, Truman Library.
61. USDC, *Civil Aeronautics Journal*, 12, No. 2 (Feb. 15, 1951), 23.
62. USDC, *Civil Aeronautics Journal*, 9, No. 10 (Oct. 15, 1948), 119.
63. Harriman to the Secretary of State, Feb. 28, 1947, General Records Department of Commerce.
64. Josh Lee to President Truman, Apr. 30, 1952, Truman Papers (Stowe Files), "Mexican Airline Case" folder, Truman Library; "Truman v. Pan Am.," *Time*, 47, No. 22 (June 3, 1946), 84.
65. *Senate Subcommittee Commerce Appropriations 1955*, 83d Cong., 2d Sess., 2021–28; 2083–2127 (1954).
66. *Ibid.*, p. 2102.
67. *Ibid.*, p. 2119.
68. 99 *Cong. Rec.*, Part 11 (June 26, 1953), A3864.
69. *Ibid.*, Part 12 (July 31, 1953), A4918–19.
70. 100 *Cong. Rec.*, Part 1 (Feb. 2, 1954), 1114–19; 1244.

71. U.S. Civil Aeronautics Board, *Annual Report,* 1957, pp. 1–2, 6; 1958, pp. 7–8; 100 *Cong. Rec.,* Part 2 (Mar. 3, 1954), 2579–80.
72. Frank Shea, Jr., "Supreme Court Jolts CAB Subsidy Policies," *Aviation Week,* 60 (Feb. 8, 1954), 13–14.
73. 100 *Cong. Rec.,* Part 6 (June 11, 1954), 8042 (June 14, 1954), 8140–47.
74. Katherine Johnson, "Delays in CAB Rulings Warrant Court Action, Hoover Group Finds," *Aviation Week,* 62 (Apr. 18, 1955), 126.
75. 101 *Cong. Rec.,* Part 1 (Feb. 4, 1955), 1195–98, 1216–25 (Feb. 7, 1955), 1263–64 (Feb. 8, 1955), 1331–41.
76. "Federal Sanctuary for Lame Ducks," *The New Republic,* 132, No. 8 (Feb. 21, 1955), 5.
77. *Ibid.*
78. *Aviation Week,* 62 (Feb. 14, 1955), 110; 62 (Feb. 28, 1955), 17.
79. *Aviation Week,* 63 (Nov. 21, 1955), 105; 64 (Jan. 23, 1956), 106.
80. *Aviation Week,* 65 (Sep. 17, 1956), 41.
81. 104 *Cong. Rec.,* Part 1 (Jan. 23, 1958), 769; Part 2 (Feb. 3, 1958), 1475–76.
82. *Aviation Week,* 64 (Mar. 19, 1956), 83.
83. *Aviation Week,* 60 (Feb. 8, 1954), 85.
84. U.S. Civil Aeronautics Board, *Annual Report,* 1958, pp. 39–40.
85. U.S. Civil Aeronautics Board, *Annual Report,* 1946, pp. 23–26; 1948, pp. 5–6; 1949, p. 4.
86. U.S. Civil Aeronautics Board, *Annual Report,* 1949, pp. 21, 24.
87. U.S. Civil Aeronautics Board, *Annual Report,* 1952, pp. 7–8.
88. U.S. Civil Aeronautics Board, *Annual Report,* 1950, pp. 27–28.
89. U.S. Civil Aeronautics Board, *Annual Report,* 1958, pp. 16–18.
90. 94 *Cong. Rec.,* Part 4 (Apr. 28, 1948), 5025.
91. Harriman to Landis, Nov. 21, 1947, General Records Department of Commerce.
92. 97 *Cong. Rec.,* Part 7 (July 25, 1951), 8905; Part 8 (Aug. 29, 1951), 10790–91.
93. *Ibid.,* Part 10 (Oct. 11, 1951), 12979.
94. *House Subcommittee Commerce Appropriations 1953,* 82d Cong., 2d Sess., 261–62 (1952).
95. *Senate Subcommittee Commerce Appropriations 1953,* 82d Cong., 2d Sess., 1509–11 (1952).
96. *Aviation Week,* 66 (Apr. 8, 1957), 41.
97. 99 *Cong. Rec.,* Part 7 (July 15, 1953), 8881–82; Part 8 (Aug. 3, 1953), 11004–6.
98. U.S. Civil Aeronautics Board, *Annual Report,* 1946, p. 3.
99. Charles L. Dearing and Wilfred Owen, *National Transportation Policy* (Washington, D.C., 1949), pp. 219, 222; Paul David Zook, "Local and Feeder Airlines and Public Policy," Ph.D. dissertation (Univ. of Ill., 1954), pp. 251–58.
100. D. Philip Locklin, *Economics of Transportation,* 5th ed. (Homewood, Ill., 1960), pp. 802–5.
101. U.S. Civil Aeronautics Board, *Annual Report,* 1950, p. 21; 1958, pp. 11, 13.
102. 99 *Cong. Rec.,* Part 3 (Apr. 30, 1953), 4265–68.
103. U.S. Civil Aeronautics Board, *Annual Report,* 1958, p. 25; Locklin, *Economics of Transportation,* pp. 792–99.
104. U.S. Civil Aeronautics Board, *Annual Report,* 1953, p. 8.
105. Dwight L. Gentry, "The Development of the Air Cargo Transportation and Its Influence on Marketing," Ph.D. dissertation, (Univ. of Ill., 1952), pp. 330–31, 341, 350–52.
106. 101 *Cong. Rec.,* Part 7 (June 17, 1955), 8635.
107. Kurt Grönfors, *Air Charter and the Warsaw Convention: A Study in International Law* (Upsala, 1956), pp. 26, 33, 37, 118–21.
108. 101 *Cong. Rec.,* Part 8 (July 18, 1955), 10860–61 (July 20, 1955), 11096.

109. *Ibid.*, Part 8 (July 20, 1955), 11096; Part 10 (July 30, 1955), 12485, 12511–12.
110. *House Subcommittee Commerce Appropriations 1957*, 723–811 (1956).
111. *Aviation Week*, 68 (Mar. 10, 1958), 32.
112. *House Subcommittee Commerce Appropriations 1957*, 744 (1956).
113. *Senate Subcommittee Commerce Appropriations 1957*, 84th Cong., 2d Sess., 343, 512–13 (1956).
114. *Senate Subcommittee Commerce Appropriations 1951*, 81st Cong., 2d Sess., 1465–1513, 1725–35 (1950).
115. Chairman Nyrop to President Truman, Oct. 1, 1951, Truman Papers, Truman Library.
116. *Senate Subcommittee Commerce Appropriations 1953*, 1501–6 (1952); U.S. Civil Aeronautics Board, *Annual Report*, 1953, pp. 1–2, 14.
117. *House Subcommittee Commerce Appropriations 1955*, 83d Cong., 2d Sess., 566–67, 590–655 (1954).
118. U.S. Civil Aeronautics Board, *Annual Report*, 1954, p. 15.
119. *Aviation Week*, 61 (Nov. 22, 1954), 92.
120. 100 *Cong. Rec.*, Part 1 (Jan. 27, 1954), 920.
121. 97 *Cong. Rec.*, Part 9 (Sep. 18, 1951), 11506–8.
122. *House Subcommittee Commerce Appropriations 1955*, 634–44 (1954); *Senate Subcommittee Commerce Appropriations 1955*, 1713–18, 1992 (1954); *1956*, 84th Cong., 1st Sess., 688–89 (1955).
123. Burton N. Behling and Richard B. Blackwell, *Federal Aids to Domestic Air Transportation* (Washington, D.C., 1956), 1.
124. U.S. Civil Aeronautics Board, *Annual Report*, 1956, p. 15.
125. *Aviation Week*, 60, Part 2 (June 21, 1954), 91–92.
126. 103 *Cong. Rec.*, Part 6 (May 22, 1957), 7444.
127. 104 *Cong. Rec.*, Part 7 (May 22, 1958), 9290–91.
128. 95 *Cong. Rec.*, Part 3 (Apr. 7, 1949), 4102–3.
129. *Senate Subcommittee Commerce Appropriations 1959*, 85th Cong., 2d Sess., 281–83 (1958).
130. 103 *Cong. Rec.*, Part 6 (May 9, 1957), 6660–62 (May 15, 1957), 7040.
131. 102 *Cong. Rec.*, Part 5 (Apr. 10, 1956), 6008 (Apr. 25, 1956), 6908–11.
132. 103 *Cong. Rec.*, Part 6 (May 23, 1957), 7552–53.
133. *Senate Subcommittee Commerce Appropriations 1950*, 81st Cong., 1st Sess., 402 (1949).
134. 102 *Cong. Rec.*, Part 11 (July 25, 1956), 14486–91.
135. *Aviation Week*, 69 (Dec. 1, 1958), 37.
136. Lucile Sheppard Keyes, *Federal Control of Entry Into Air Transportation* (Cambridge, Mass., 1957), 168.
137. *Aviation Week*, 69 (Dec. 1, 1958), 37.
138. Mark L. Kahn, "Regulatory Agencies and Industrial Relations: the Airline Case," *American Economic Review* 42, No. 2 (May, 1952), 686–98.
139. U.S. Civil Aeronautics Board, *Annual Report*, 1954, p. 8; 1956, p. 1.
140. 93 *Cong. Rec.*, Part 1 (Jan. 30, 1947), 705.
141. Michael Sepko, Los Angeles, to Secretary Harriman, June 4, 1947, General Records Department of Commerce. Several other letters are in this same file.
142. Joseph Hanlon, "When the Birds Walk Don't Fly," *Science Digest*, 21, No. 1 (Jan., 1947), 56–57.
143. Harriman to Harvey Conover, New York, Sep. 18, 1947, General Records Department of Commerce.
144. T. P. Wright, "The Air Can Be Safer," *The Atlantic Monthly*, 179, No. 4 (Apr., 1947), 37–41.
145. USDC, *Civil Aeronautics Journal*, 7, No. 4 (Apr. 15, 1946), 46; No. 6 (June 15, 1946), 79; No. 11 (Nov. 15, 1946), 141.
146. USDC, *Civil Aeronautics Journal*, 8, No. 1 (Jan. 15, 1947), 6.
147. USDC, *Civil Aeronautics Journal*, 8, No. 4 (Apr. 15, 1947), 45.

148. Lawrence H. Arnold, Chairman, Seattle First National Bank, to Chairman J. J. O'Connell, CAB, Jan. 6, 1949; O'Connell to Charles S. Murphy, Administrative Assistant to the President, Jan. 28, 1949, Truman Papers, OF 249, Truman Library; USDC, *Civil Aeronautics Journal*, 10, No. 6 (June 15, 1949), 64.
149. USDC, *Civil Aeronautics Journal*, 8, No. 7 (July 15, 1947), 73; No. 8 (Aug. 15, 1947), 85, 91.
150. USDC, *Civil Aeronautics Journal*, 8, No. 10 (Oct. 15, 1947), 102.
151. Robert J. Serling, *The Probable Cause . . . The Truth About Air Travel Today* (New York, 1960), 86–108, 114–19; USDC, *Civil Aeronautics Journal*, 9, No. 1 (Jan. 15, 1948), 6; No. 8 (Aug. 15, 1948), 89.
152. USDC, *Civil Aeronautics Journal*, 9, No. 2 (Feb. 15, 1948), 14.
153. USDC, *Civil Aeronautics Journal*, 9, No. 3 (Mar. 15, 1948), 31.
154. USDC, *Civil Aeronautics Journal*, 10, No. 1 (Jan. 15, 1949), 11.
155. USDC, *Civil Aeronautics Journal*, 10, No. 9 (Sep. 15, 1949), 102; Serling, *The Probable Cause*, pp. 191–92.
156. USDC, *Civil Aeronautics Journal*, 10, No. 10 (Oct. 15, 1949), 117.
157. USDC, *Civil Aeronautics Journal*, 11, No. 4 (Apr. 15, 1950), 41.
158. 98 *Cong. Rec.*, Part 1 (Feb. 14, 1952), 980–82; Part 3 (Apr. 7, 1952), 3656.
159. USDC, *Civil Aeronautics Journal*, 10, No. 11 (Nov. 15, 1949), 138.
160. USDC, *Civil Aeronautics Journal*, 11, No. 1 (Jan. 15, 1950), 11.
161. USDC, *Civil Aeronautics Journal*, 11, No. 11 (Nov. 15, 1950), 131.
162. USDC, *Civil Aeronautics Journal*, 12, No. 3 (Mar. 15, 1951), 35.
163. *House Subcommittee Commerce Appropriations 1951*, 81st Cong., 2d Sess., 1532 (1950).
164. 103 *Cong. Rec.*, Part 5 (May 13, 1957), 6839–42.
165. 102 *Cong. Rec.*, Part 9 (July 3, 1956), 11692–95.
166. *Ibid.*, Part 9 (July 5, 1956), 11897.
167. *Ibid.*, Part 9 (July 3, 1956), 11696 (July 16, 1956), 12785–86.
168. U.S. Civil Aeronautics Board, *Annual Report*, 1957, p. 28; 103 *Cong. Rec.*, 85th Cong., 1st Sess., Part 1 (Feb. 1, 1957), 1393–94.
169. 104 *Cong. Rec.*, Part 6 (May 1, 1958), 7854; U.S. Civil Aeronautics Board, *Annual Report*, 1958, p. 35.
170. *Aviation Week*, 68 (Aug. 25, 1958), 30–31.
171. 104 *Cong. Rec.*, Part 6 (May 1, 1958), 7854.
172. *Ibid.*, Part 8 (June 4, 1958), 10178.
173. *House Subcommittee Commerce Appropriations 1958*, 85th Cong., 1st Sess., 276 (1957).
174. *Aviation Week*, 67 (July 22, 1957), 43.
175. 103 *Cong. Rec.*, Part 2 (Feb. 4, 1957), 1464–69.
176. "CAA to Control Airspace," *Science News Letter*, 71, No. 14 (Apr. 6, 1957), 213.
177. *House Subcommittee Commerce Appropriations 1959*, 85th Cong., 2d Sess., 613–15 (1958).
178. *Aviation Week*, 67 (Nov. 4, 1957), 37–38; 68 (Feb. 24, 1958), 36–37.
179. 103 *Cong. Rec.*, Part 8 (July 1, 1957), 10707–8.
180. *Aviation Week*, 63 (Feb. 26, 1955), 132.
181. USDC, *Civil Aeronautics Journal*, 10, No. 3 (Mar. 15, 1949), 36.

Chapter 13: GENERAL QUESADA'S REIGN—1959–1961

1. U.S. Federal Aviation Agency, *FAA News-Memo*, No. 1 (Washington, D.C.), Jan., 1959).
2. Donald William Dresden, "General Quesada's Toughest Command," *The Reporter*, 20, No. 5 (Mar. 5, 1959), 26–29.
3. Dresden, "General Quesada's," p. 29.
4. "General of the Airways Elwood Richard Quesada," *Time*, 74, No. 1 (July 6, 1959), 66.
5. 105 *Cong. Rec.*, Part 3 (Mar. 11, 1959), 3807–8.
6. 106 *Cong. Rec.*, Part 1 (Jan. 22, 1960), 1083–87.

7. *Ibid.*, Part 8 (May 18, 1960), 10499; Part 9 (June 10, 1960), 12351–55.
8. *Ibid.*, Part 9 (June 10, 1960), 12352.
9. *Ibid.*, p. 123555.
10. *Ibid.*, Part 1 (Jan. 22, 1960), 1087.
11. *Ibid.*, Part 10 (June 15, 1960), 12638.
12. *Des Moines Register*, June 12, 1960, p. 1; June 15, 1960, p. 4; June 19, 1960, section G, p. 10; June 20, 1960, p. 11.
13. "Defiance and Determination," *Time*, 75, No. 3 (Jan. 18, 1960), 19.
14. "Pilots Versus Government—Why the Fight Over Air Safety," *U.S. News & World Report*, 48, No. 4 (Jan. 25, 1960), 47.
15. L. L. Doty, "Quesada Says Laxness Indicated in FAA Aviation Safety Survey," *Aviation Week*, 72 (Jan. 18, 1960), 37–38.
16. L. L. Doty, "Sayen Charges FAA Program Causes Pilot Resentment, Anxiety," *Aviation Week*, 72 (Jan. 25, 1960), 38–39; "Sayen Describes ALPA Safety Stand," *Aviation Week*, 72 (Feb. 8, 1960), 108–11, 113–14, 116–17, 119, 121, 123, 125, 127.
17. R. H. Cook, "FAA Sets Pilot Age Limit, Tightens Rules," *Aviation Week*, 71 (Dec. 7, 1959), 45.
18. "Sayen, Quesada Debate FAA Cockpit Rule," *Aviation Week*, 70 (June 29, 1959), 79–83.
19. "FAA Threatens To Suspend Pilots in Dispute Over Flight Inspectors," *Aviation Week*, 72 (June 13, 1960), 43.
20. "ALPA Opposes FAA on Medical Question," *Aviation Week*, 73 (July 11, 1960), 47.
21. 107 *Cong. Rec.*, Part 10 (July 27, 1961), 13678–79.
22. *Ibid.*, (Aug. 28, 1961), A6741 (unbound).
23. *Des Moines Register*, June 11, 1960, p. 11; Federal Aviation Agency, Office of Public Affairs, *Weekly News Digest*, No. 32 (Washington, D.C., Aug. 8, 1960), pp. 2–3.
24. 107 *Cong. Rec.* Part 1 (Jan. 13, 1961), 714–18.
25. E. R. Quesada, "The Pressures vs. Air Safety," *Harper's*, 222, No. 1328 (Jan., 1961), 58–64.
26. "Symbolic Action," *The Nation*, 190, No. 15 (Apr. 9, 1960), 307.
27. "Question for Quesada," *The Nation*, 190, No. 19 (May 7, 1960), 395.
28. 106 *Cong. Rec.*, Part 6 (Apr. 19, 1960), 8123–24.
29. *Ibid.*, p. 8134.
30. *Ibid.*, p. 8135.
31. U.S. Federal Aviation Agency, Office of Management Services, *Management Services Notes*, 2, No. 1 (Jan., 1961), 1.
32. Robert I. Stanfield, "CAB Opens Hearing on Pan Am 707 Atlantic Dive," *Aviation Week*, 70 (Mar. 23, 1959), 37–38.
33. *Des Moines Register*, Jan. 20, 1960, p. 1.
34. 106 *Cong. Rec.*, Part 1 (Jan. 22, 1960), 1087; *Des Moines Register*, Jan. 17, 1960, p. 1.
35. *Kansas City Star*, June 14, 1962, p. 1.
36. 107 *Cong. Rec.*, (Sep. 20, 1961), A8169 (unbound).
37. *Des Moines Register*, Jan. 25, 1960, p. 1.
38. 106 *Cong. Rec.*, Part 5 (Mar. 21, 1960), 6102–3; *Des Moines Register*, Mar. 18, 1960, p. 1.
39. *Des Moines Register*, Oct. 5, 1960, p. 1; Oct. 6, 1960, p. 1.
40. U.S. Department of Interior, Fish and Wildlife Service, "Bird Hazard to Aircraft," Wildlife Leaflet 429 (Washington, D.C., n.d.), 2–6.
41. *Des Moines Register*, Nov. 16, 1960, p. 4; Aug. 1, 1962, p. 2; May 1, 1962, p. 2.
42. *Des Moines Register*, Oct. 29, 1960, p. 1.
43. *Des Moines Register*, Oct. 31, 1960, pp. 1, 8.
44. *Des Moines Register*, Jan. 23, 1962, p. 4.
45. *Philadelphia Inquirer*, Apr. 15, 1962, p. 1 (sports); 107 *Cong. Rec.*, Part 15 (Sep. 18, 1961), 20106–7.
46. *Des Moines Register*, Dec. 17, 1960, p. 1; Dec. 18, 1960, p. 1; Dec. 19, 1960, p. 1; Dec. 22, 1960, p. 1.

47. "Crash Stirs New York Air Traffic Probe," *Aviation Week*, 73 (Dec. 26, 1960), 27–29.
48. U.S. Federal Aviation Agency, Office of Public Affairs, *FAA News*, #9 (Washington, D.C., Jan. 18, 1961), 3–4.
49. *Des Moines Register*, Dec. 21, 1960, p. 10.
50. *Des Moines Register*, Dec. 25, 1960, p. 1.
51. *Des Moines Register*, June 19, 1962, p. 8.
52. *Des Moines Register*, July 17, 1962, p. 2.
53. "Epilogue to Disaster," *Time*, 82, No. 18 (Nov. 1, 1963), 50.
54. *Waterloo Daily Courier*, Dec. 18, 1960, p. 1.
55. *Des Moines Register*, Jan. 21, 1961, p. 18.
56. *Des Moines Register*, Feb. 16, 1961, p. 1.
57. U.S. Federal Aviation Agency, *FAA News*, #2 (Jan. 9, 1961), 1.
58. David H. Hoffman, "Controllers Want Bigger Voice in FAA," *Aviation Week*, 74 (Feb. 6, 1961), 39.
59. Mark Weaver, ed., Federal Aviation Aeronautical Center, *Beacon* (Oklahoma City, Mar., 1961); Federal Aviation Agency, *Fly By*, Official Employee Publication, 3, No. 2 (Washington, D.C., Feb–Mar., 1961), 2.
60. U.S. Federal Aviation Agency, *FAA News*, #21, Feb. 8, 1961.

Chapter 14: TECHNOLOGICAL VISTAS

1. *Des Moines Register*, Dec. 2, 1960, p. 19.
2. U.S. Federal Aviation Agency, *FAA News* (Apr. 4, 1962), 1–7.
3. White House, Press Releases of Sep. 10, 1961, concerning Project Horizon.
4. U.S. Federal Aviation Agency, *FAA News* (Apr. 4, 1962), 4.
5. *Chicago Daily News*, Dec. 24, 1962, p. 16.
6. *Des Moines Register*, Jan. 16, 1963, p. 2.
7. *Manchester Guardian*, July 11, 1963, p. 7.
8. *Public Papers of the Presidents of the United States: John F. Kennedy*, Jan. 1–Nov. 22, 1963 (Washington, D.C., 1964), p. 56.
9. *Ibid.*, pp. 440–41.
10. *Ibid.*, pp. 475–77.
11. *Ibid.*, p. 888.
12. "Travel at 1,800 Miles an Hour? Why? When?" *U.S. News & World Report*, 55, No. 26 (Dec. 23, 1963), 52–54, 56–58.
13. *Des Moines Register*, Feb. 28, 1964, p. 1; May 13, 1964, p. 7; May 14, 1964, p. 9; Robert Burkhardt, "Sonic Boom Town," *The New Republic*, 151, Nos. 8–9 (Aug. 22, 1964), 5–6.
14. *Des Moines Register*, May 21, 1964, p. 12.
15. *Champaign-Urbana News-Gazette*, July 10, 1964, editorial page; *Des Moines Register*, July 25, 1964, p. 16.
16. U.S. Federal Aviation Agency, *Fourth Annual Report*, 1962 (Washington, D.C., 1963), pp. 58–60.
17. *Ibid.*, pp. 60–62.
18. U.S. Federal Aviation Agency, Aeronautical Center, *Beacon* (Mar., 1961), no pages listed.
19. *London Sunday Times*, July 7, 1963, pp. 12–13.
20. *Waterloo Daily Courier*, June 26, 1962, p. 1.
21. *Des Moines Register*, Dec. 22, 1962, p. 18.
22. U.S. Federal Aviation Agency, *Project Beacon, Report of Task Force on Air Traffic Control, A Study of the Safe and Efficient Utilization of Airspace* (Washington, D.C., Oct., 1961).
23. U.S. Federal Aviation Agency, *Fourth Annual Report*, 1962, pp. 25–29.
24. U.S. Federal Aviation Agency, *FAA News*, #11 (Jan. 19, 1961); *Fourth Annual Report*, 1962, p. 30.
25. U.S. Federal Aviation Agency, *Aviation Forecasts, Fiscal Years 1962–1967* (Washington, D.C., Oct., 1961), p. 31.

26. U.S. Federal Aviation Agency, *FAA News,* #2 (Jan. 9, 1961); *Fourth Annual Report,* 1962, pp. 33–35.
27. Visits and interviews at the airport traffic control towers in Des Moines, Mar. 29, June 14–15, 1961; June 15, 1962; Aug. 22, 1964; and Kansas City, Mo., June 14, 1962.
28. *Des Moines Register,* June 18, 1962, p. 7.
29. *Chicago Daily News,* Aug. 25, 1962, section A, p. 3.
30. *Waterloo Daily Courier,* Aug. 16, 1964, p. 9.
31. U.S. Civil Aeronautics Board, *Aircraft Accident Report,* File No. 2–1408 (Washington, D.C., May 17, 1961).
32. *Des Moines Register,* Aug. 2, 1962, p. 1; Apr. 20, 1962, p. 1.
33. Interview with airport traffic controllers at Des Moines, Mar. 29, 1961.
34. U.S. Federal Aviation Agency, *Weekly News Digest,* No. 43 (Oct. 24, 1960); *FAA News,* #37 (Mar. 10, 1961).
35. U.S. Federal Aviation Agency, Air Traffic Management, Directive No. 50, May 10, 1961.
36. Visit to Des Moines control tower, June 14, 1961.
37. Chief, ATM Field Division 3 to all ATM field facilities (Region 3), June 7, 1961.
38. Visit to Des Moines control tower, June 15, 1962.
39. U.S. Federal Aviation Agency, *Fourth Annual Report,* 1962, p. 39.
40. U.S. Federal Aviation Agency, *Aviation News,* 1, No. 1 (Jan., 1961), 1; *Sixth Annual Report,* 1964 (Washington, D.C., 1965), pp. 34–38; visit to Des Moines control tower, Aug. 22, 1964.
41. Visit to Des Moines FSS, June 15, 1961.
42. U.S. Federal Aviation Agency, *Aviation News,* 1, No. 5 (May, 1961), 4.
43. *Kansas City Star,* June 13, 1962, section D, p. 9.
44. U.S. Federal Aviation Agency, *Fourth Annual Report,* 1962, pp. 23–24.
45. U.S. Federal Aviation Agency, *Weekly News Digest,* No. 39 (Sep. 26, 1960), 4.
46. U.S. Federal Aviation Agency, *Fourth Annual Report,* 1962, pp. 43–45.
47. Visit to Des Moines control tower, Mar. 29, 1961.
48. U.S. Federal Aviation Agency, *Fly By* (Mar., 1962), p. 4; *FAA News,* #20 (Feb. 7, 1961); #37 (Mar. 10, 1961).
49. U.S. Federal Aviation Agency, *Fourth Annual Report,* 1962, pp. 46–47.
50. U.S. Federal Aviation Agency, *Dulles International Airport, Gateway to America* (Washington, D.C., 1960); John Ciardi, "Manner of Speaking," *Saturday Review,* 48, No. 23 (June 6, 1964), 14–15; *Chicago Daily News,* Aug. 25, 1962, section A, pp. 1–16; *Des Moines Register,* Nov. 18, 1962, section G, p. 6; Dec. 9, 1962, section G, p. 17.
51. 107 *Cong. Rec.,* Part 11 (July 31, 1961), 14151–54; Part 13 (Sep. 1, 1961), 17964–68; *Des Moines Register,* Jan. 15, 1964, p. 11.
52. *Des Moines Register,* May 28, 1963, p. 2; Dec. 30, 1963, p. 4; *London Observer,* June 30, 1963, p. 1.
53. Visits to Airports District Office, Chicago, Apr. 10 and Dec. 28, 1962.
54. 104 *Cong. Rec.,* Part 9 (June 26, 1958), 12413; Federal Aviation Agency, *FAA Catalog of Training Courses,* n.d.
55. U.S. Federal Aviation Agency, *Fourth Annual Report,* 1962, pp. 19–20.
56. U.S. Federal Aviation Agency, *FAA News,* #33 (Mar. 2, 1961); *Fourth Annual Report,* 1962, pp. 20–21, 39–40.
57. *Chicago Daily News,* July 11, 1964, p. 3.
58. U.S. Federal Aviation Agency, *FAA News,* #11 (Jan. 19, 1961).
59. "No-Hands Landing," *Newsweek,* 61, No. 11 (Mar. 18, 1963), 94, 97–98.
60. *Waterloo Daily Courier,* Nov. 13, 1960, p. 17.

61. *Des Moines Register*, Apr. 25, 1964, p. 1; May 27, 1964, p. 2; *Waterloo Daily Courier*, Sep. 4, 1964, p. 1.
62. *Louisville Courier-Journal*, Aug. 12, 1964, section 1, p. 7.
63. Edward T. Chase, "The Crisis Behind the Transportation Mergers," *Saturday Review*, 45, No. 15 (Apr. 14, 1962), 19–21, 38.
64. *Mason City* (Iowa) *Globe-Gazette*, Mar. 21, 1961, p. 1.
65. Chase, "The Crisis," 21, 38.
66. 105 *Cong. Rec.*, Part 4 (Mar. 26, 1959), 5366–67.
67. *Ibid.*, Part 14 (Aug. 20, 1959), 16459–60.
68. 106 *Cong. Rec.*, Part 6 (Apr. 19, 1960), 8164–88.
69. L. L. Doty, "Hector Quits, Says CAB Unsuited to Task," *Aviation Week*, 71 (Sep. 21, 1959), 36–37; Doty, "Resignations May Spur CAB Policy Shifts," 71 (Sep. 28, 1959), 40–41, 43; Doty, "Minetti's Dissents Oppose Higher Fares," 70 (June 8, 1959), 41, 43; Doty, "Carriers Dispute Board's Coach Stand," 72 (Mar. 14, 1960), 38–39; R. H. Cook, "Policy Shifts Expected From New CAB," 72 (May 2, 1960), 38–40.
70. Robert Hotz, "Airlines at the Crossroads," *Aviation Week*, 72 (May 2, 1960), 21.
71. R. H. Cook, "Policy Shifts Expected From New CAB," *Aviation Week*, 72 (May 2, 1960), 38–40.
72. R. H. Cook, "Examiners Debate CAB Reorganization," *Aviation Week*, 72 (May 30, 1960), 43, 45.
73. D. H. Hoffman, "Landis Urges Speed-Up of CAB Case Flow," *Aviation Week*, 73 (Nov. 21, 1960), 37; *Des Moines Register*, Dec. 30, 1960, p. 6; Jan. 1, 1961, section G, p. 3.
74. *Des Moines Register*, Nov. 23, 1960, p. 1; Nov. 28, 1960, pp. 21, 38–39.
75. "CAB Merger Policy Clarification Anticipated in N.Y.-Florida Case," *Aviation Week*, 75 (July 10, 1961), 35; *Des Moines Register*, Sep. 20, 1963, p. 2.
76. L. L. Doty, "Boyd Impresses Airlines as CAB Chief," *Aviation Week*, 75 (Aug. 28, 1961), 45.
77. *Des Moines Register*, July 29, 1960, pp. 1, 5; Dec. 31, 1960, p. 11; *Waterloo Daily Courier*, Jan. 25, 1962, p. 24.
78. 106 *Cong. Rec.*, Part 8 (May 17, 1960), 10477.
79. *Des Moines Register*, Jan. 24, 1962, p. 1; Jan. 25, 1962, p. 5; *Waterloo Daily Courier*, Nov. 2, 1962, p. 2.
80. *Chicago Tribune*, Dec. 21, 1962, Part 2, p. 7; *Chicago Daily News*, Dec. 24, 1962, p. 6.
81. *New York Herald Tribune* (Paris edition), July 22, 1963, page no. missing; *Des Moines Register*, Oct. 17, 1963, p. 18.
82. *Des Moines Register*, July 27, 1964, p. 16.
83. *Des Moines Register*, Aug. 5, 1964, p. 16.
84. 107 *Cong. Rec.*, Part 15 (Sep. 18, 1961), 20079–110.
85. *Louisville Courier-Journal*, Aug. 8, 1964, section 2, p. 5.
86. 107 *Cong. Rec.*, Part 15 (Sep. 18, 1961), 20106–7; *Des Moines Register*, Oct. 2, 1961, p. 1; Oct. 3, 1961, p. 6.
87. *Des Moines Register*, June 18, 1960, p. 2; Nov. 26, 1960, p. 11; Oct. 18, 1961, p. 2; Dec. 29, 1961, p. 2; Aug. 17, 1962, p. 17; Nov. 26, 1962, p. 11.
88. "Aviation Class Warfare," *Time*, 82, No. 10 (Sep. 6, 1963), 75–76.
89. *Des Moines Register*, Jan. 13, 1964, p. 4.
90. *Des Moines Register*, Dec. 9, 1962, section G, p. 3; May 8, 1963, p. 6.
91. *Des Moines Register*, Feb. 19, 1962, p. 12; May 14, 1963, p. 2; May 21, 1963, p. 8; *Waterloo Daily Courier*, Oct. 28, 1963, p. 2.
92. Mel Elfin, "The Great Air-Fare Snare," *The Reporter*, 30, No. 6 (Mar. 12, 1964), 36–38.
93. U.S. Federal Aviation Agency, *Weekly News Digest*, No. 42 (Oct. 17, 1960); No. 46 (Nov. 14, 1960); *FAA News*, #2 (Jan. 9, 1961); *Des Moines Register*, Sep. 16, 1962, section G, p. 8; author's visits to Moscow Airport, Aug. 16, 1963 and Aug. 7, 1965.

94. *Des Moines Register*, Aug. 31, 1962, p. 12.
95. *Des Moines Register*, Oct. 2, 1962, p. 7; Oct. 3, 1962, p. 6; Oct. 4, 1962, p. 1; Oct. 6, 1962, p. 5; Nov. 9, 1962, p. 2; Nov. 7, 1962, p. 5.
96. *Des Moines Register*, Nov. 25, 1962, section G, p. 9; Oct. 6, 1963, section G, p. 10.
97. *Des Moines Register*, Nov. 22, 1962, p. 15.
98. *Detroit Free Press*, Aug. 15, 1962, section B, p. 1; *Kansas City Star*, June 13, 1962, section A, pp.1-2; June 14, 1962, section A, p. 1.
99. *Des Moines Register*, Feb. 12, 1962, p. 18; Mar. 21, 1962, p. 10.
100. *Des Moines Register*, Mar. 4, 1961, p. 2.
101. *Des Moines Register*, Oct. 1, 1961, p. 1.
102. *Des Moines Register*, July 13, 1961, p. 1; July 14, 1961, p. 1.
103. *Des Moines Register*, June 3, 1962, p. 1; Aug. 2, 1962, p. 8; Sep. 22, 1962, p. 7.
104. *Des Moines Register*, Jan. 24, 1964, p. 1.
105. *Des Moines Register*, July 31, 1962, p. 1.
106. *Des Moines Register*, Jan. 16, 1963, p. 2; Dec. 18, 1962, p. 7.
107. *Champaign-Urbana News-Gazette*, Dec. 24, 1962, p. 6; *Des Moines Register*, Mar. 7, 1962, p. 18.
108. *Des Moines Register*, Dec. 14, 1962, p. 6; Mar. 23, 1963, p. 2; Jan. 9, 1964, p. 4.
109. *Des Moines Register*, Oct. 21, 1962, pp. 1, 3.
110. *Des Moines Register*, Dec. 14, 1963, p. 2.
111. *Des Moines Register*, Jan. 4, 1964, p. 2.
112. *Des Moines Register*, June 4, 1962, p. 1; June 23, 1962, p. 1.
113. *Des Moines Register*, Dec. 2, 1962, section G, p. 1, 3; Dec. 3, 1962, p. 5; Dec. 4, 1962, p. 4.
114. *Des Moines Register*, Feb. 13, 1964, p. 1; Feb. 26, 1964, p. 1; Mar. 2, 1964, p. 1.
115. *Des Moines Register*, Mar. 5, 1964, p. 1.
116. *Des Moines Register*, June 4, 1964, p. 10; Nov. 3, 1964, p. 1.
117. *Des Moines Register*, Mar. 17, 1962, p. 1.
118. *Des Moines Register*, Aug. 4, 1964, p. 1; Aug. 10, 1961, p. 1.
119. *Des Moines Register*, May 12, 1964, p. 16; *Champaign-Urbana News-Gazette*, Aug. 26, 1962, p. 4.
120. *Des Moines Register*, Sep. 11, 1962, p. 10.
121. *Des Moines Register*, July 9, 1962, p. 9; Oct. 23, 1962, p. 1.
122. *Des Moines Register*, Nov. 11, 1963, p. 1.
123. *Chicago Tribune*, Dec. 21, 1962, Part 2, p. 7; *Des Moines Register*, Sep. 25, 1962, p. 1; Mar. 10, 1964, p. 12; Apr. 12, 1963, p. 7.
124. *Des Moines Register*, Apr. 21, 1964, p. 4; Mar. 30, 1963, p. 1.
125. *Des Moines Register*, Apr. 10, 1963, p. 2; Feb. 23, 1963, p. 1.
126. *Des Moines Register*, Apr. 22, 1962, p. 2-G.
127. U.S. Federal Aviation Agency, *Weekly News Digest*, No. 32 (Aug. 8, 1960), p. 2; *Des Moines Register*, Dec. 20, 1961, p. 2; Dec. 28, 1960, p. 18; Apr. 19, 1960, p. 12; Oct. 1, 1962, p. 13.
128. *Waterloo Daily Courier*, Jan. 3, 1962, p. 21.
129. *Des Moines Register*, Jan. 14, 1963, p. 7.
130. *Des Moines Register*, Mar. 6, 1962, pp. 1, 6.
131. *Des Moines Register*, Jan. 9, 1962, p. 1.
132. *Des Moines Register*, July 30, 1960, p. 7.
133. *Des Moines Register*, Feb. 28, 1964, pp. 1, 7.
134. *Des Moines Register*, Oct. 30, 1963, p. 8.
135. U.S. Federal Aviation Agency, *Fourth Annual Report*, 1962, p. 13.
136. Visits to Flight Standards Office, Des Moines, Mar. 29-30, 1961.
137. U.S. Federal Aviation Agency, *Fourth Annual Report*, 1962, p. 17.
138. U.S. Federal Aviation Agency, *Weekly News Digest*, No. 42 (Oct. 17, 1960), p. 3.
139. Visit to Flight Standards Office, Des Moines, Mar. 30, 1961.
140. U.S. Federal Aviation Agency, *FAA News*, series T#60 (Dec. 8, 1960).

141. Compiled from all visits to FAA facilities cited earlier.
142. Donald R. Whitnah, *A History of the United States Weather Bureau* (Urbana, 1961), 160, 194–95, 236–38.
143. Visit to Weather Bureau, Des Moines, Mar. 29, 1961.
144. U.S. Federal Aviation Agency, *FAA Horizons* (Washington, D.C., July, 1965), 5.

GLOSSARY

AAF—Army Air Force
ACC—Air Coordinating Committee
AEA—American Export Airlines
AID—Airport Information Desk
Airinc—Aeronautical Radio Incorporated
ALPA—Air Line Pilots' Association
AMB—Airways Modernization Board
ANDB—Air Navigation Development Board
AOA—American Overseas Airlines
AOPA—Aircraft Owners and Pilots Association
Apob—airplane observation
APB—Aircraft Production Board
ARTCC—air-route traffic control center
ASID—automatic station identification
ATA—Air Transport Association
ATC—Air Traffic Control
ATCA—Air Traffic Control Association
ATCRBS—air traffic control radar beacon system
ATCT—Airport Traffic Control Tower

BOAC—British Overseas Airways Corporation

CAA—Civil Aeronautics Administration and CAA as the Civil
    Aeronautics Authority during 1938–1940.
CAB—Civil Aeronautics Board
CAF—Civil Service rating, later changed to GS.
CAR—Civil Air Regulations
CARI—Civil Aeromedical Research Institute
CFR—contact flight rule
CPT—Civilian Pilot Training Program
CWA—Civil Works Administration

DCLA—Development of Civil Landing Areas
DME—distance measuring equipment
DPC—Data Processing Central

EAL—Eastern Air Lines

FAA—Federal Aviation Agency
FAS—Federal Aviation Service
FBI—Federal Bureau of Investigation
FCC—Federal Communications Commission
FM—frequency modulation
FSS—flight service station
FTC—Federal Trade Commission
FWA—Federal Works Agency

GCA—(precision beam radar) ground-controlled approach

IATA—International Air Transport Association
IATCB—Interdepartmental Air Traffic Control Board
ICAO—International Civil Aviation Organization
ICC—Interstate Commerce Commission
IFR—instrument flight rules
ILS—Instrument landing system

KLM—Royal Dutch Airlines

MANICOM—manned information and communications facility
MIT—Massachusetts Institute of Technology
MRL—medium-power range loop
MSL—mean sea level

NAA—National Aeronautics Association
NACA—National Advisory Committee for Aeronautics
NASA—National Aeronautics and Space Administration
NATO—North Atlantic Treaty Organization
NOTAMS—Notices to Airmen
NTA—National Transport Association
NYA—National Youth Administration

OMNI, OMNIS—very high frequency omnidirectional range.
    See also VOR.
OPM—Office of Price Management

PAA, Pan Am—Pan American Airways
PICAO—Provisional International Civil Aviation Organization
PWA—Public Works Administration

RFC—Reconstruction Finance Corporation

SAFI—semiautomatic flight inspection
SAGE—semiautomatic ground environment
SAS—Scandinavian Airlines System
SEC—Securities and Exchange Commission
SLATE—small, light-weight altitude transmission equipment

TACAN—(ultrahigh frequency) tactical air navigation aid
TWA—Trans World Airways
TWU—Transport Workers Union

UAL—United Air Lines
UAW—United Auto Workers
uhf—ultrahigh frequency

VA—Veterans Administration
VFR—visual flight rules
vhf—very high frequency
VOR—vhf omni-range
VORTAC—distance and direction system
V/STOL—vertical/short takeoff and landing

WMC—War Manpower Commission
WPA—Works Progress Administration
WTS—War Training Service

BIBLIOGRAPHY

UNPUBLISHED MATERIALS

GENTRY, DWIGHT L. "The Development of the Air Cargo Industry and Its Influence on Marketing." MS, Ph.D. dissertation, University of Illinois, 1952.

Papers of Edwin A. Locke, Jr., 1945–1952. MS, Harry S. Truman Library, Independence, Missouri.

Papers of Harry S. Truman, 1945–1953. Office File 249, MS (Aviation), Harry S. Truman Library, Independence, Missouri.

Records of the President's Air Policy Commission, 1947–1948. RG 220, MS, Harry S. Truman Library, Independence, Missouri.

Records of the President's Airport Commission, 1952. MS, Harry S. Truman Library, Independence, Missouri.

U.S. Civil Aeronautics Administration. Civil Aeronautics Administration Central Files, 1926–1943. RG 237, MS, Labor and Transportation Branch of the Social and Economic Records Branch, the National Archives, Washington, D.C.

U.S. Civil Aeronautics Administration. Files of Airports Service, 1951–1958. MS, Washington, D.C.

U.S. Department of Commerce. General Records of the Department of Commerce, Office of the Secretary, 1915–1926, 1942–1949, RG 40. MS, Business and Economics Branch of the National Archives, Washington, D.C.

U.S. Federal Aviation Agency. "CAA Organization—History." MS, Office of Public Information, Federal Aviation Agency, Washington, D.C.

U.S. Federal Aviation Agency. "Wartime History of the Civil Aeronautics Administration," MS, in the Library of the Federal Aviation Agency, Washington, D.C.

ZOOK, PAUL DAVID. "Local and Feeder Airlines and Public Policy," MS, Ph.D. dissertation, University of Illinois, 1954.

CONGRESSIONAL DEBATES AND HEARINGS

Congressional Record. Washington, D.C.: 1913–1964.

House Subcommittee of Appropriations Committee. *Hearing on Department of Commerce Appropriations for Fiscal Years 1930–1938, 1942–1959.* Washington, D.C., 1928–1958.

House Subcommittee of Appropriations Committee. *Hearings on Independent Offices Appropriations for Fiscal Years 1940–1941.* Washington, D.C., 1939–1940.

Senate Subcommittee of Appropriations Committee. *Hearings on Department of Commerce Appropriations for Fiscal Years 1930–1938, 1942–1959.* Washington, D.C., 1928–1958.

Senate Subcommittee of Appropriations Committee. *Hearings on Independent Offices Appropriations for Fiscal Years 1940–1941.* Washington, D.C., 1939–1940.

LAWS

44 *Statutes at Large* 568 (1926).
52 *Statutes at Large* 1014 (1938).

OFFICIAL REPORTS AND STUDIES

Aviation Facilities Study Group. *Aviation Facilities.* Washington, D.C., 1955.

BEHLING, BURTON N., AND BLACKWELL, RICHARD B. *Federal Aids to Domestic Air Transportation.* Washington, D.C.; American Association of Railroads, 1956.

CURTIS, EDWIN P. *Aviation Facilities Planning,* final report. Washington, D.C., 1957.

EMME, EUGENE M. *Aeronautics and Astronautics in American Chronology of Science and Technology in the Exploration of Space 1915–1960.* Washington, D.C., 1961.

KENNEDY, JOHN F. *Public Papers of the Presidents of the United States: John F. Kennedy, 1963.* Washington, D.C., 1964.

The Council of State Governments. *Aviation and the States.* Chicago, 1944.

U.S. Bureau of Air Commerce. *Annual Report.* Washington, D.C., 1934–1938.

———. *Air Commerce Bulletin.* Washington, D.C., 1938–1940.

U.S. Civil Aeronautics Authority. *Annual Report, 1939–1940.* Washington, D.C., 1940–1941.

U.S. Civil Aeronautics Authority. *Civil Aeronautics Journal,* Jan.–July, 1940. Washington, D.C.

U.S. Civil Aeronautics Board. *Aircraft Accident Reports.* Washington, D.C., 1961.

U.S. Civil Aeronautics Board. *Annual Report, 1941–1958.* Washington, D.C., 1942–1959.

U.S. Department of Commerce. *Air Commerce Bulletin.* Washington, D.C., 1929–1938.

U.S. Department of Commerce. *Annual Report of the Director of Aeronautics.* Washington, D.C., 1927–1934.

U.S. Department of Commerce. *Civil Aeronautics Journal.* Washington, D.C., 1940–1952.

U.S. Department of Commerce. "Domestic Air News," mimeographed. Washington, D.C., 1927–1929.

U.S. Department of Interior, Fish and Wildlife Service. *Bird Hazard to Aircraft,* Wildlife leaflet No. 439. Washington, D.C., n.d.

U.S. Department of State. *Blueprint for World Civil Aviation.* Publ. No. 2348, Conf. Ser. 70. Washington, D.C., 1945.

U.S. Federal Aviation Agency. Aeronautical Center. *Beacon.* Washington, D.C., 1961.

———. *Air Traffic Management.* Director No. 50. Washington, D.C., May 10, 1961.

————. *Annual Reports.* Washington, D.C., 1959–1964.

————. *Aviation Forecasts, Fiscal Years 1962–1967.* Washington, D.C., 1961.

————. *Aviation News.* Washington, D.C., 1961.

————. *Catalog of Training Courses.* Washington, D.C., n.d.

————. Chief, Air Traffic Management, Region 3, to all field facilities. Washington, D.C., June 7, 1961.

————. *Dulles International Airport, Gateway to America.* Washington, D.C., 1960.

————. *FAA Horizons.* Washington, D.C., 1965.

————. *FAA News-Memo.* Washington, D.C., 1959.

————. *Fly By.* Official employee publication. Washington, D.C., 1961–1962.

————. Office of Management Services. *Management Services Notes.* Washington, D.C., 1961.

————. Office of Public Affairs. *FAA News,* two series. Washington, D.C., 1960–1962.

————. Office of Public Affairs. *Weekly News Digest.* Washington, D.C., 1960.

————. *Project Beacon. Report of Task Force on Air Traffic Control: A Study of the Safe and Efficient Utilization of Airspace.* Washington, D.C., 1961.

————. *Project Horizon. Report of the Task Force on National Aviation Goals.* Washington, D.C., 1961.

U.S. Weather Bureau. *Topics and Personnel.* Washington, D.C., 1926.

White House. Press releases on Project Horizon. Washington, D.C., Sept. 10, 1961.

NEWSPAPERS

American Aviation Daily, 1946.

Anchorage Daily Times, 1941.

Champaign-Urbana News Gazette, 1962, 1964.

Chicago Daily News, 1962–1964.

Chicago Tribune, 1962.

Des Moines Register, 1960–1964.

Detroit Free Press, 1962.

Kansas City Star, 1962.

London Observer, 1963.

London Sunday Times, 1963.

Louisville Courier-Journal, 1964.

Manchester Guardian, 1963.

Mason City (Iowa) *Globe-Gazette,* 1961.

New York Herald Tribune (Paris ed.), 1963.

New York Times, 1919–1926.

Philadelphia Inquirer, 1962.

St. Louis Post-Dispatch, 1927.

Washington Daily News, 1932.

Washington Herald, 1937.

Washington Post, 1928, 1947.

Washington Times, 1927.

Waterloo (Iowa) *Daily Courier,* 1960–1964.

UNOFFICIAL STUDIES, BOOKS, AND ARTICLES

Aeronautical Chamber of Commerce of America. "Department of Commerce," *Aircraft Yearbook*, 1928.

"Air Cargo Fight Simmers," *Business Week*, No. 713 (May 1, 1943), 48, 50, 52.

"Air Fighters Should Tank Up on Oxygen Before Ascents," *Science News Letter*, 37, No. 1 (Jan. 6, 1940), 12.

"Air Merger Spiked," *Business Week*, No. 565 (June 29, 1940), 17, 20.

ALLEN, C. B. "Why Do Air Liners Crash?" *The New Republic*, 91, No. 1172 (May 19, 1937), 35–37.

"A New Air Policy for America," *The American Review of Reviews*, 72 (Oct., 1925), 421–22.

Aviation, 25 (Aug. 11, 1928), 484.

"Aviation Class Warfare," *Time*, 82, No. 10 (Sept. 6, 1963), 75–76.

Aviation Week, 1954–1961.

"Avoidable Causes of Accidents," *Scientific American*, 142, No. 6 (June, 1930), 472.

BEATTY, JEROME. "He Rules an Empire in the Air," *The American Magazine*, 114 (Sept., 1932), 56–58, 72, 74.

"Behind the Airplane Crashes," *Business Week*, No. 386 (Jan. 23, 1937), 16–17.

BERLIN, LAWRENCE H. "Of Space and Time, and Death in the Air," *The Reporter, the Magazine of Facts and Ideas*, 15, No. 2 (Aug. 9, 1956), 33.

BLACK, ARCHIBALD. *Transport Aviation*, 2d ed. New York: Simmons-Boardman, 1926–1929.

BONNALIE, ALLAN F. "Training the Pilot To Fly the Beam," *Scientific American*, 154, No. 6 (June, 1936), 322–24.

BRANDES, JOSEPH. *Herbert Hoover and Economic Policy: Department of Commerce Policy, 1921–1928*. Pittsburgh: U. of Pittsburgh, 1962.

BUDWIG, GILBERT G. "Air Regulation," *The Scientific Monthly*, 31, No. 3 (Sept., 1930), 241–44.

BURKHARDT, ROBERT. "Sonic Boom Town," *The New Republic*, 151, Nos. 8–9 (Aug. 22, 1964), 5–6.

"CAA Programs and Other Defense Measures in the Higher Institutions," *School and Society*, 52, No. 1352 (Nov. 23, 1940), 518–19.

"CAA To Control Airspace," *Science News Letter*, 71, No. 14 (Apr. 6, 1957), 213.

CARMODY, FRANK J. "Aerial Traffic Cops in London and Chicago," *The Literary Digest*, 99, No. 8 (Nov. 24, 1928), 57–58.

CHASE, EDWARD T. "The Crisis Behind the Transportation Mergers," *Saturday Review*, 45, No. 15 (Apr. 14, 1962), 19–21, 38.

CHILDS, MARQUIS W. "Is It Safe To Fly?" *Harper's Magazine*, 173 (Oct., 1936), 497–504.

CIARDI, JOHN. "Manner of Speaking," *Saturday Review*, 48, No. 23 (June 6, 1964), 14–15.

"Civilian Pilot Accidents Stress Regulation Need," *Science News Letter*, 46, No. 20 (Nov. 11, 1944), 319.

COLLINGS, KENNETH BROWN. "Annual Report on Air Safety," *American Mercury*, 46, No. 181 (Jan., 1939), 22–29.

———. "Blind Flying Is Not Safe," *American Mercury*, 33, No. 129 (Sept., 1934), 90–92.

————. "Flying Is Still Dangerous," *American Mercury*, 32, No. 126 (June, 1934), 147–52.

————. "How To Make Flying Safe," *American Mercury*, 40, No. 158 (Feb., 1937), 151–57.

————. "Why Not Use Parachutes?" *American Mercury*, 34, No. 136 (Apr., 1935), 444–49.

CONNOLLY, D. H. "CAA Geared for Military," *Radio News*, 27 (Jan., 1942), 58, 104.

COURTNEY, W. B. "Wings of the New Deal," *Colliers*, 93, No. 7 (Feb. 17, 1934), 12–13, 48–50.

DAVIS, W. J. "Clearing the Air for Commerce," *The Annals of the American Academy of Political and Social Science*, 131 (May, 1927), 141–50.

DEARING, CHARLES L., AND OWEN, WILFRED. *National Transportation Policy*, Washington, D.C.: Brookings Institution, 1949.

"Defiance and Determination," *Time*, 75, No. 3 (Jan. 18, 1960), 19.

DRESDEN, DONALD W. "General Quesada's Toughest Command," *The Reporter*, 20, No. 5 (Mar. 5, 1959), 26–29.

"Dropping the Pilot," *Business Week*, No. 392 (Mar. 6, 1937), 16.

ELFIN, MEL. "The Great Aire-Fare Snare," *The Reporter*, 30, No. 6 (Mar. 12, 1964), 36–38.

"Epilogue to Disaster," *Time*, 82, No. 18 (Nov. 1, 1963), 50.

"Fagg's Air Problems," *Business Week*, No. 401 (May 8, 1937), 46.

"Federal Sanctuary for Lame Ducks," *The New Republic*, 132, No. 8 (Feb. 21, 1955), 5.

FEREE, D. C., AND RAND, G. "Pilot Fitness and Airplane Crashes," *Science*, n.s., 87, No. 2252 (Feb. 25, 1938), 189–93.

"Fields First, Planes Second Is Plan for Aviation Growth," *Newsweek*, 24, No. 6 (Aug. 7, 1944), 58, 60.

FREUDENTHAL, ELSBETH E. *Flight Into History: The Wright Brothers and the Air Age*. Norman: U. of Oklahoma, 1949.

————. *The Aviation Business: From Kitty Hawk to Wall Street*. New York: Vanguard, 1940.

GEDDES. A. E. M. *Meteorology: An Introductory Treatise*. London, 1921.

"General of the Airways Elwood Richard Quesada," *Time*, 74, No. 1 (July 6, 1959), 66.

GOLDSTROM, JOHN. "Safety in Aviation Improving," *Current History*, 26, No. 1 (Apr., 1927), 37–40.

"Government Suspension Follows Northwest Airlines' First Crash in Ten Years," *Newsweek*, 11, No. 7 (Feb. 14, 1938), 38–39.

GRONFORS, KURT. *Air Charter and the Warsaw Convention*. Upsala, 1956.

GROSSMAN, WILLIAM L. *Air Passenger Traffic*. New York: Remsen, 1947.

"Grumble at Air Board," *Business Week*, No. 502 (Apr. 15, 1939), 21.

HAMILTON, JOHN. "One Reason Why Airplanes Crash," *The New Republic*, 99, No. 1280 (June 14, 1939), 150–53.

HANLON, JOSEPH. "When the Birds Walk Don't Fly," *Science Digest*, 21, No. 1 (Jan., 1947), 56–57.

HOOVER, HERBERT. *The Memoirs of Herbert Hoover: The Cabinet and the Presidency*. Vol. 2, New York: Macmillan, 1951–52.

HORTON, ROBERT W. "Death in the Air," *The Nation*, 144, No. 4 (Jan. 23, 1937), 94–95.

HUTCHINSON, KEITH. "The Civil Air War," *The Nation*, 158, No. 10 (Mar. 4, 1944), 271–74.

"Increased Safety for Aviation," *Science* n.s. Suppl. 85, No. 2199 (Feb. 19, 1937), 9.

JOSEPHSON, MATTHEW. *Empire of the Air: Juan Trippe and the Struggle for World Airways*. New York: Harcourt, Brace, 1943–1944.

KAHN, MARK L. "Regulatory Agencies and Industrial Relations: The Airline Case," *American Economic Review*, 42, No. 2 (May, 1952), 37.

KEYES, LUCILE SHEPPARD. *Federal Control of Entry Into Air Transportation*. Cambridge: Harvard, 1957.

KLEMIN, ALEXANDER. "Airplane Safety," *Scientific American*, 151, No. 5 (Nov., 1934), 259.

LINDBERGH, CHARLES A. *The Spirit of St. Louis*. New York: Scribner, 1953.

" 'Lindy' Pleads for Regulation of Stunt Flying," *The Literary Digest*, 99, No. 8 (Nov. 24, 1928), 62–63.

LISSITZYN, OLIVER F. "The Diplomacy of Air Transport," *Foreign Affairs: An American Quarterly Review*, 19, No. 1 (Oct., 1940), 156–70.

LOCKLIN, D. PHILIP. *Economics of Transportation*, 5th ed. Homewood, Illinois: Irwin, 1960.

LUNT, DUDLEY CAMMETT. "The Law of the Air," *The American Mercury*, 17, No. 66 (June, 1929), 198–201.

LYONS, EUGENE. *Our Unknown Ex-President: A Portrait of Herbert Hoover*. New York: Doubleday, 1947–1948.

MACCRACKEN, WILLIAM P., JR. "Air Regulation," *The Annals of the American Academy of Political and Social Sciences*, 131 (May, 1927), 118–23.

MARVIN, LANGDON P., JR. "Sword and Ploughshare," *Air Transportation* (Nov., 1948), 31–32, 43.

"Men in White Now Serving Men With Wings," *Science News Letter*, 37, No. 4 (Jan. 27, 1940), 54.

MILBANK, JEREMIAH, JR. *The First Century of Flight in America*. Princeton: Princeton U., 1943.

"Misleading the President," *The New Republic*, 138, No. 11 (Mar. 17, 1958), 5.

MORRIS, LLOYD, AND SMITH, KENDALL. *Ceiling Unlimited: The Story of American Aviation From Kitty Hawk to Supersonics*. New York: Macmillan, 1953.

MYERS, WILLIAM S., AND NEWTON, WALTER H. *The Hoover Administration: A Documented Narrative*. New York: Scribner, 1936.

"New and Improved Airfields," *Science*, 100, No. 2607, Suppl. 10 (Dec. 15, 1944), 10.

"New Flying Rules," *Business Week*, No. 427 (Nov. 6, 1937), 32.

"No-Hands Landing," *Newsweek*, 61, No. 11 (Mar. 18, 1963), 94, 97–98.

"Ocean Flying Control," *Business Week*, No. 429 (Nov. 20, 1937), 52.

"Our New Automatic Safety Code," *Scientific American*, 134, No. 4 (Apr., 1926), 269–70.

"Our Point of View," *Scientific American*, 142, No. 5 (May, 1930), 349.

"Pilots Versus Government—Why the Fight Over Air Safety," *U.S. News and World Report*, 48, No. 4 (Jan. 25, 1960), 47.

PLANCK, CHARLES E. *Women With Wings*. New York: Harper, 1942.

Propose Putting Pilot on Back or Stomach," *Science News Letter*, 37, No. 14 (Apr. 6, 1940), 216.

QUESADA, E. R. "The Pressures Versus Air Safety," *Harper's*, 222, No. 1328 (Jan., 1961), 58–64.

"Question for Quesada," *The Nation*, 190, No. 19 (May 7, 1960), 395.

"Rival Bills for Aviation Control," *Business Week*, No. 410 (July 10, 1937), 43–44.

ROHLFING, CHARLES C. *National Regulation of Aeronautics*. Philadelphia: U. of Pennsylvania, 1931.

————. "Regulation of Aviation: A Case Study in Reorganization," *The Annals of the American Academy of Political and Social Sciences*, 221 (May, 1942), 56–63.

"Safety in the Air," *Popular Science Monthly*, 132, No. 2 (Feb., 1938), 46.

"Safety Search," *Time*, 27, No. 8 (Feb. 24, 1936), 59–60.

"Safety v. Payload," *Time*, 43, No. 5 (Jan. 31, 1944), 82.

Science News Letter, 31, No. 827 (Feb. 13, 1937), 102.

"Scientific Aids to Aviation," *The Scientific Monthly*, 25, No. 1 (July, 1927), 89.

SERLING, ROBERT J. *The Probable Cause*. New York: Doubleday, 1960.

SMITH, HENRY LADD. *Airways: The History of Commercial Aviation in the United States*. New York: Knopf, 1942.

"Symbolic Action," *The Nation*, 190, No. 15 (Apr. 9, 1960), 307.

"The Air Is How Safe?" *Fortune*, 15, No. 4 (Apr., 1937), 75–80, 154, 156, 158, 163–64, 166, 168–70, 173–74.

The Air Line Pilot, 18, No. 2 (Mar., 1949), 1.

"The *Hindenburg* Disaster," *The New Republic*, 91, No. 1172 (May 19, 1937), 33.

"The New Aeronautics Authority," *Science*, n.s. Suppl. 88, No. 2276 (Aug. 12, 1938), 7–8.

"The Private Flying Boom," *Fortune*, 16, No. 2 (Aug.,1937), 53–60.

"They May Have Needed Oxygen," *Fortune*, 16, No. 2 (Aug., 1937), 61, 142, 144, 147–48, 150.

"Travel at 1,800 Miles an Hour? Why? When?" *U.S. News and World Report*, 55, No. 26 (Dec. 23, 1963), 52–54, 56–58.

"Truman v. Pan Am.," *Time*, 47, No. 22 (June 3, 1946), 84.

"Two Engines or Four?" *Scientific American*, 159, No. 3 (Sept., 1938), 142.

"Uncle Sam as Air Boss," *The Nation*, 119, No. 3099 (Nov. 26, 1924), 559.

"Under the Weather," *Fortune*, 17, No. 6 (June, 1938), 62–63, 104, 106.

"Vidal Out," *Time*, 29, No. 10 (Mar. 8, 1937), 13–14.

"White House Finally Solves the Riddle of Federal Air-Line Control—Maybe," *Newsweek*, 11, No. 3 (Jan. 17, 1938)), 42–43.

WHITE, WILLIAM A. *A Puritan in Babylon: The Story of Calvin Coolidge*. New York: Macmillan, 1938.

WHITNAH, DONALD R. *A History of the United States Weather Bureau*. Urbana: U. of Ill., 1961.

WILSON, G. LLOYD, AND BRYAN, LESLIE, A. *Air Transportation*. New York: Prentice-Hall, 1949.

"Windshields Duck-Proofed," *Science News Letter*, 43, No. 12 (Mar. 20, 1943), 182–83.

WRIGHT, T. P. "The Air Can Be Safer," *The Atlantic Monthly*, 179, No. 4 (Apr., 1947), 37–41.

YOUNG, CLARENCE M. "Safety Rules for the Airways," *Scientific American*, 146, No. 1 (Jan., 1932), 22–25.

————. "What Is Good Flying?" *Scientific American*, 142, No. 5 (May, 1930), 345–48.

INDEX